PRAISE FOR BEYOND THE OUTER SHORES

"Eric Enno Tamm ... aims to take Ricketts out from Steinbeck's shadow, to illuminate his association with another major figure in 20th-century letters, the mythologist Joseph Campbell, and to give Ricketts a place of honor in the annals of coastal ecology ... Mr. Tamm's descriptions of Ricketts's trips to Canada offer vivid looks at a landscape remote both in time and place, and a real-life character we know only too well from fiction ... Ricketts the biologist should not be forgotten."
— *New York Times*

"An affecting and mind-expanding group portrait of three creative thinkers, but Ricketts glows the brightest, a friend to bums and geniuses who was happiest knee-deep in a tide pool."
— *Booklist* (starred review)

"An engrossing memoir. Freelance writer Tamm smartly weaves in-depth literary analysis of Steinbeck's fiction into his narrative ... the links drawn among the three friends ... provide a fascinating insight into how art, science and philosophy can nurture, inspire and feed off one another. Tamm writes with impassioned honesty about his subject's many dimensions. Ricketts was ... a true renaissance man, whose avant-garde fusion of life and science inspired the lives he touched."
— *Publishers Weekly*

"Presents Ricketts to the world with thoughtful, carefully paced prose ... [Tamm] has created a work of scholarship — and a wonderfully accessible one, too."
— *Vancouver Sun*

"Clearly, Tamm loves this part of the world, and his book is filled with its history and lore ... [the book] illuminates what has been a shadowy but important part of Ed Ricketts's life, and it leaves us wondering what might have been. I liked this book so much that I read it twice."
— *American Scientist*

"His best ideas about ecology and humanity found voice in the writings of his friends, Steinbeck and Campbell. Now the whole life and work of Ed Ricketts can be found between the covers of *Beyond the Outer Shores* ... Tamm writes with an impassioned but sure hand. His book is meticulously researched and he has a firm grasp of the material ... I read the book when I couldn't sleep for thinking of all the preparations still to be done before our departure to the Sea of Cortez. The thrilling sense of discovery on each page kept me up even longer. I read it again when we returned; it seemed even better the second time around."

— *Nature* magazine

"This is biography at its best. Tamm isn't interested in every small detail ... but instead the whole vast picture: he does a fine job of providing cultural, political, scientific, personal, and literary context for Ed Ricketts and his friends John Steinbeck and Joe Campbell. They come alive with a fullness that is rare in non-fiction."

— *West by North West* magazine

"Just as the tidepools were the starting points for Ricketts' wide-ranging philosophies, so his life is the starting point for Tamm's meditations on the incredibly rich physical and intellectual environment of the West Coast in the 1920s, '30s and '40s. It's an expedition into ideas, influences, littoral landscapes and social surroundings that were the forms and shadows of Ricketts' world. Tamm has preserved and publicized the well-lived life of a man who deserves to be remembered — not just for his friendship with two of the great American writers, but for his own contribution to philosophy, ecology and marine biology, and for his admirable outlook on the world of anemones and men ... Tamm is a fabulous storyteller, and he populates his book with innumerable incidents of anecdote and local lore."

— *Westerly News*

BEYOND
THE
OUTER SHORES

THE UNTOLD STORY OF **ED RICKETTS**,
THE PIONEERING ECOLOGIST WHO INSPIRED
JOHN STEINBECK AND JOSEPH CAMPBELL

ERIC ENNO TAMM

RAINCOAST BOOKS
Vancouver

Raincoast Books acknowledges the ongoing financial support of the Government of Canada through The Canada Council for the Arts and the Book Publishing Industry Development Program (BPIDP); and the Government of British Columbia through the BC Arts Council.

Book design by Sara E. Stemen
Species drawings by Sember Weinman
Maps by Barbara Schramm

NATIONAL LIBRARY OF CANADA CATALOGUING IN PUBLICATION DATA
Tamm, Eric Enno
    Beyond the outer shores : the untold story of Ed Ricketts, the pioneering ecologist
    who inspired John Steinbeck and Joseph Campbell / Eric Enno Tamm.
    Includes bibliographical references and index.
ISBN 1-55192-733-0 (bound) — ISBN 1-55192-853-1 (pbk.)
    1. Ricketts, Edward Flanders, 1897-1948. 2. Steinbeck, John, 1902-1968 — Friends and
    associates. 3. Marine biologists — West (U.S.) —Biography. 1. Title.
QL31.R53T34 2004   578.77'092   C2004-901970-8

Published in Canada by
Raincoast Books
9050 Shaughnessy Street
Vancouver, British Columbia
Canada   V6P 6E5
www.raincoast.com

At Raincoast Books we are committed to protecting the environment and to the responsible use of natural resources. We are acting on this commitment by working with suppliers and printers to phase out our use of paper produced from ancient forest. This book is one step towards that goal. It is printed on 100% ancient-forest-free paper (100% post-consumer recycled), processed chlorine- and acid-free. It is printed with vegetable-based inks. For further information, visit our website at www.raincoast.com. We are working with Markets Initiative (www.oldgrowthfree.com) on this project.

First published in the United States of America in 2004 by
Four Walls Eight Windows

Printed in Canada

10 9 8 7 6 5 4 3 2 1

For Dan Edwards,
who knows why or should

And for my brother Victor,
who helped me realize my dream

CONTENTS

NOTE ON SPECIMEN DRAWINGS

THERE are some marine biologists whose chief interest is in the rarity, the seldom seen and unnamed animal," John Steinbeck once wrote. "These are often wealthy amateurs, some of whom have been suspected of wishing to tack their names on unsuspecting and unresponsive invertebrates. The passion for immortality at the expense of a little beast must be very great."

Ed Ricketts, it must be stated, attained immortality in a different way. Still, in the course of a quarter-century of specimen collecting, Ricketts discovered many new species of marine invertebrates and tidepool fish on the Pacific Coast. It was, however, corollary to his primary scientific work of understanding seashore ecology. Today, some twenty marine organisms bear the species name *rickettsi* or *steinbecki*, in honor of the contributions of both men to marine biology.

At the beginning of each chapter, readers will find small line drawings of many species first discovered by Ed Ricketts and, in some cases, John Steinbeck. The scientific and common names of each species are given, along with the collecting location and date. The original specimens now reside at many prestigious museums in the United States, including the American Museum of Natural History in New York and the Smithsonian Institution in Washington, D.C.

PROLOGUE

*On behalf of the Cannery Row Company, it gives me great pleasure to
welcome visitors from all over the world to our Cannery Row community of merchants and businesses. We all hope you have a memorable
and enjoyable visit!*

—TED J. BALESTRERI, MANAGING GENERAL PARTNER,
Official Cannery Row Visitors Guide

CANNERY Row in Monterey in California is a cliché, a light
breeze, a clanking cash register, a sugary delight, an impulse buy,
a novel, a trinket, a movie, a retailer's dream. Cannery Row is
the tacky and tailored, tinsel and polish and Hollywood, cheap senti-
ment and parking lots and junk food, souvenir galleries of a literary icon,
tank tops, restaurants and discount warehouses and little crowded gift
shops. Its inhabitants are, as the tourist brochure says, "shoppers, newlyweds, tourists and sunbathers on beaches," by which it means Everybody.

That, with sincere apologies to John Steinbeck, is the Cannery Row
of today, more than half a century since he wrote his famous novel by the
same name about the "whores, pimps, gamblers, and sons of bitches"
who inhabited the stink of California's sardine industry.

Much has changed since then. John Steinbeck is dead, and so too,
one could argue, is Cannery Row. In 1957, when it was suggested that the

Row be turned into a tourist attraction, Steinbeck said it should be torn down. "Man's greed killed off the fish. Now they've got to 'kill off' some tourists to make up for it," he said. To Steinbeck, tearing down the old canneries and returning Monterey Bay to its pristine state would have been a fitting and definitive end of an era—the burial of the industrial monsters that had devoured the ocean's bounty and regurgitated it in small tin cans. Cannery Row had killed off the fish and, thus, it too must die.

Cannery Row has lived on though, but in name only. The "Wops and Chinamen and Polaks, men and women in trousers and rubber coats and oilcloth aprons" who breathed life into its environs, and into Steinbeck's novel, are just a memory now. The shells of the old canneries have been converted into pastel-painted malls for jewelers, fashion outlets, art galleries and ubiquitous boutiques. It's a theme park of literary kitsch. And it was all done in the name of celebrating California's greatest writer.

John Steinbeck wrote some thirty books and screenplays that were adapted into as many films and TV series and received twenty-nine Academy Award nominations (including two for Steinbeck himself) and a Pulitzer Prize—and which eventually won the author the Nobel Prize for Literature in 1962. There's a John Steinbeck Society, a Steinbeck Newsletter and Quarterly journal, Steinbeck research centers at two universities and an International Steinbeck Congress—not to mention the doorstop-size biographies and Ph.D. dissertations all dissecting the man and his work. His books continue to sell hundreds of thousands of copies every year, and *East of Eden* even relaunched Oprah's Book Club in 2003. Salinas, Steinbeck's hometown, opened a multimillion-dollar National Steinbeck Center in 1998, dedicated to the man that most citizens of Salinas had actually hated. But the greatest monument to Steinbeck is in Monterey, where a small stretch of Ocean View Avenue called Cannery Row has been converted into a tourist shrine to the novelist and his fictional characters.

* * *

ONE day in May 1999, on my first trip to Monterey, I had a hard time separating the real from the fictional on Cannery Row. There was a Lee Chong market—as in *Cannery Row*—but the owner obviously wasn't named Lee Chong. The store has been renovated into a gift shop, Alicia's Antiques, with a Steinbeck Remembrance Room full of original manuscripts, first editions and memorabilia. Monterey had a legendary madam, too—her name is Dora Flood in the novel. On the site of her former brothel is Mackerel Jack's Trading Co., which seduced me with specials on decorative plates, plastic starfish and painted seashells. I also saw a delivery truck with a "Grapes of Wrath—California Style Catering" logo parked along a side street, although it probably wasn't serving the poor Mexican farm laborers I saw working the dusty fields outside Salinas. And nowadays the heart of Cannery Row is the Steinbeck Plaza, a slick tourist trap, complete with a bronze bust of the Row's great man peering into a sea of shuffling shoppers.

That the central theme of Steinbeck's *Cannery Row* is actually a rejection of this type of mindless materialism, and instead a celebration of the spiritual and the marginal in society, must be one of the most ironic, if not tragic, footnotes in American literary history.

Few today seem aware of the ideas or individual who inspired Steinbeck's novel half a century ago. Steinbeck, for instance, was never the heart of Cannery Row. Even he would have agreed that that person was Ed Ricketts, his best friend, whose old home-office today stands empty and relatively untouched, one of the only buildings on the Row not colonized by kitschy commerce.

More than any place, this two-story building with its sun-blackened, unfinished wood paneling was the spiritual and intellectual heart of Cannery Row. I had traveled thousands of miles from a remote village on Canada's Pacific Coast to pay homage to this place and its legendary proprietor, Ed Ricketts. He was a scientist, a marine biologist to be precise, and more importantly an ecologist at a time when the fledgling field of ecology was nothing more than the esoterica of pedantic scientists tucked away in academia's hallowed halls.

I first stumbled upon Ed Ricketts and a book he had written in my eleventh grade biology class. Alton Crane, our dedicated and well-humored teacher, required that we conduct a much dreaded, much maligned (at least by us students) collecting survey of a local beach in Ucluelet (pronounced *you-CLUE-let*), my hometown and a tiny fishing village located midway up the rugged outer coast of Vancouver Island in British Columbia. The project was called the "Big Beach Transect." Students were supposed to map a cross-section of the craggy beach and its tidal zones. We collected and identified all the marine species there, and then literally drew all of this on a thirty-foot roll of paper illustrating the web of life on the seashore. Although I didn't know it at the time, Ed Ricketts had traveled to Ucluelet and conducted an almost identical survey a half-century before.

I remember his seashore book distinctly. With old black-and-white photos and drawings, *Between Pacific Tides* was no longer the best zoological book for identifying the many different species of crabs, tide pool fish, sea anemones and sea cradles that I collected. There were far better books with spectacularly vivid color photographs for that. But his was thick with information on a species' habitat, food, breeding habits and relationships. It was the only book in our school library that was specifically dedicated to the ecology of the seashore. When it was first published, I have come to learn, it was the only such book in the entire world.

Every year for more than half a century, hundreds of thousands of people around the world read Ricketts' pioneering ecological thinking. They don't actually read his writing per se, although he did coauthor two splendid seashore books, *Between Pacific Tides* and *Sea of Cortez*, which are both relatively well read considering they are scientific tomes. Rather, they hear his voice echo in the novels of John Steinbeck, who fictionalized his best friend in half a dozen novels.

Few people know the true story of Ed Ricketts, whose life-voyage of scientific discovery has been inadvertently obscured and overshadowed by Steinbeck and his mythmaking. Even fewer understand the role Ricketts played in inspiring Steinbeck to underpin his writing with the science of ecology—a fact that is overlooked or grossly understated by many literary critics and scholars even today. And hardly a soul has any idea about Ricketts' enormous influence on Joseph Campbell, the twentieth century's great mythologist.

Ed Ricketts was a lone, largely marginalized scientist—an outcast to academia with no university degrees, no memberships, no honors. His pioneering ideas were at first dismissed by the scientific establishment. He was principally supported—morally, financially and scientifically—in his research endeavors by a ragtag group of bohemian friends, family and, to borrow Steinbeck's words, "no-goods, come-to-bad-ends, blots-on-the-town, thieves, rascals, [and] bums."

Despite his meager means and at times threadbare poverty, Ed Ricketts tried to accomplish what had eluded entire armies of academics, well-funded museums, prestigious university marine stations and international expeditions. He did it not for academic honors (he received none), nor for fame or fortune (he disliked the former and received not the latter). He had a deeply personal thirst for knowledge and discovery, believing he could help humanity take an enlightened leap, as he saw it, into the future.

Yet it is his legend of beer drinking, sexual indulgence and propensity for misadventure, as lionized and fictionalized by John Steinbeck, and not his scientific legacy, that looms larger than life today.

* * *

AT the time of his sudden death, Ed Ricketts was completing, with the help of John Steinbeck, the most ambitious coastal scientific investigation ever attempted. Its geographic scope and zoological breadth were simply unprecedented, and more significantly, the ecological approach employed was visionary, ahead of its time by decades.

Over the past several years, I have ventured humbly in the wake of Ed Ricketts from the Sea of Cortez to Sitka, Alaska—a journey that has ultimately and delightfully led me back to the seashore of my childhood in Ucluelet. What follows, then, is an untold odyssey of sorts. It is pieced together from Ricketts' unpublished research papers, philosophical essays, notebooks, diaries, financial and corporate records, personal correspondence, interviews with family and friends, newspaper clippings, steamship logs and of course the writings of John Steinbeck.

Ed Ricketts was a hero in the Homeric, not Hollywood, tradition. Decades before anyone else, he took up the call of ecology on the seashore and set off on a night-sea journey to an unknown land where he searched the tide pools by day and the stars at night for a boon, a scientific discovery, with which he could redeem a world that seemed, at least to him a half-century ago, to be racing recklessly toward ecological oblivion.

Although this odyssey ends in unspeakable tragedy, the lessons learned as we travel alongside Ed Ricketts are life affirming nonetheless.

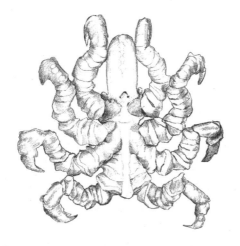

PYCNOGONUM RICKETTSI, SEA SPIDER, NEW SPECIES
COLLECTED BY ED RICKETTS ON MARCH 31, 1925, IN CALIFORNIA.

CHAPTER ONE

OF MYTHS AND MEN

Throughout the inhabited world, in all times and under every circumstance, the myths of man have flourished; and they have been the living inspiration of whatever else may have appeared out of the activities of the human body and mind. It would not be too much to say that myth is the secret opening through which the inexhaustible energies of the cosmos pour into human cultural manifestation. Religions, philosophies, arts, the social forms of primitive and historic man, prime discoveries in science and technology, the very dreams that blister sleep, boil up from the basic, magic ring of myth.

—JOSEPH CAMPBELL, *The Hero with a Thousand Faces*

HE was, as many would later remember, a mysterious fellow—handsome, boyish-looking even, twenty-six years old, slight, not much more than five-foot-seven. He spoke with a plain Midwestern accent. His most extraordinary feature was his eyes—an auburn color that radiated with life and otherworldliness. Women found them irresistible. "One look into his mild but goatish eyes," a woman once noted, made you realize "he loved women in any way, shape or form."

He had recently moved to Pacific Grove, California, from Chicago, a city known in 1923 to be full of gangsters, speakeasies, racketeers, bootleggers and the notorious likes of Al Capone. The citizens of Pacific Grove had good reason to be suspicious of an Easterner, a stranger, no matter how dapper he was, from a veritable city of sin.

He could be seen driving around in a big Mitchell, an old ragtop roadster. The cranky old car would rumble past the town's stately Victorian homes at all hours of the night. He would be coming and going from his place of business on Fountain Avenue between the train station and Holman's Department Store. A sign out front dubiously identified his offices as "biological laboratories." He routinely brought in chemical supplies and cases of empty bottles and gallon jars, and brought out packages that he distributed via the post.

Pacific Grove was founded as a Methodist seaside resort in 1875. Bylaws banned gambling, billiards, dancing, liquor sales (until 1969) and, on Sundays, swimming. Bathing suits were required to have "double crotches or a skirt of ample size to cover the buttocks." Robert Louis Stevenson described the picturesque town in 1879 as "dreamlike . . . a life of teetotalism, religion, and flirtation." But nothing much more, of course. It was probably California's first gated community, surrounded by a fence on three sides and the sea on the fourth. Though the town's padlocked gate and a curfew for juveniles were long gone by 1923, cruising around at ungodly hours was still reproachful behavior indeed.

One night, shortly after midnight, someone saw, or more likely heard, the Mitchell storm down Lighthouse Avenue. Perhaps the person had seen the "laboratories" sign (whatever that meant) and maybe even all the crates of bottles and suspiciously wrapped packages. There was even gossip circulating that the man was a gambler. He certainly liked to drink. Thus, having certain prejudices about those from Chicago, the person immediately suspected the worst—bootlegging—and called the police.

A police officer found the Mitchell parked below the Point Pinos Lighthouse, whose blazing beam caused the frothy combers to catch fire with light before being extinguished on the rocky shore. The officer spotted the handsome young man and an accomplice prowling down in the tide pools and kelp beds with flashlights. They were clearly searching for something. But what? Barrels of Canadian whiskey being floated ashore by rum-running fishing boats from the north?

The policeman approached the two men and asked what in God's name were they doing out on the tip of the Monterey Peninsula so late at night. He was bemused by their answer and decided they were not bootleggers at all, just "very odd" fellows. The officer gave them a warning nonetheless: they had better repair the broken muffler on their jalopy so as not to disturb the peace, a serious offense in Pacific Grove.

* * *

BY January 1930, the laboratories had been moved to a small, two-story waterfront building at 800 Ocean View Avenue in neighboring New Monterey. Half a block up the hill, a railway ran parallel to Ocean View, and it would not have been an overstatement to say that everything below this railway was on the proverbial wrong side of the tracks. It was a rather notorious part of town, and noxious, too: sardine canneries and reduction plants had proliferated along Ocean View in the 1920s, increasing production tenfold. A grotesque stench would waft all the way to the sunbathers at the posh Hotel Del Monte in Old Monterey almost a mile away.

The rancid smell, according to Pacific Grove's blue-blooded churchgoers, was also evidence of the moral decay of New Monterey, an industrial town of Italians, Chinese, Japanese, Slavs, Poles, Mexicans, paisanos and mulattos who worked the canning lines and seine boats. The corner of Ocean View and Irving Avenues, where the laboratories stood, was particularly lecherous. Across the street was an infamous whorehouse. Winos, petty thieves and bums slept in derelict industrial piping on a vacant lot on the other corner. And Won Yee, a shrewd Chinese businessman, ran the Wing Chong Market or "Glorious Prosperous" grocery two doors down. In 1923, police stormed Wing Chong's with a hail of bullets, believing it was a Chinese opium den. One patron was wounded and Yee was charged with possession of narcotics. Two years later he spent thirty days in jail for bootlegging. In this part of town, if your business didn't smell of rotting fish offal, people automatically suspected some other kind of putridity.

So a suspicious eye was probably cast yet again on the owner and operator of the so-called "biological laboratories." He held terribly odd working hours and played Bach, Mozart and Gregorian chants on a custom-built phonograph; the melodies often drifted down to the street below. He was accused of running "a queer and secretive business . . . located in a queer and out of the way place." At first, few understood or were courageous enough to find out what he actually did.

Only two kinds of people were either desperate or daring enough to do so: drunks and children. The local winos quickly realized that the doctor—at least they thought he was a doctor or scientist of some sort—had an endless supply of denatured alcohol, a rare commodity during Prohibition. And so they befriended "Doc," as they liked to call him, to betray him, stealing alcohol at every turn. Mischievous little boys were also drawn to the laboratories. They peered through the garage door and spied shelves upon shelves of dead animals. There were also live rattlesnakes and white rats. The most horrific spectacle they saw was

Pacific Biological Laboratories, 1930s. COURTESY OF ED RICKETTS JR.

museum jars that contained dead babies—sharks, piglets and even a human foetus. The latter had its little legs crossed in a Buddha pose, as if it were praying. "It was rather a startling figure," someone once remarked, "for while it had negroid features, the preservative had turned it to a pale ivory color."

Although it took some time for local denizens to fully appreciate Doc and the goings-on at his lab, the young man from Chicago would over the years attain a legendary status around town and in fact the world, thanks to a most fortuitous meeting later that year.

* * *

ONE day in October 1930, a young struggling writer—his first book had been published the year before and was, he admitted, "an abortion," of which he was "bitterly ashamed"—stepped out of his bungalow onto Eleventh Street in Pacific Grove. The flimsy red house wasn't even his; it was his parents' summer cottage. He lived in it with his new wife. His father helped him with a small monthly allowance. They grew their own vegetables and ate from the sea. They were poor. It was, after all, the beginning of the Great Depression.

It was a wonderful time of year, though. Summer had given way to autumn, and thousands of orange Monarch butterflies fluttered through the sky on their annual pilgrimage from Canada to Pacific Grove's pine forests, their protective winter habitat. The migration was a spectacular phenomenon every October—celebrated today with a "Butterfly Parade"—but it did not enliven the writer's foul mood. He had a nasty toothache and little money to pay a dentist.

A twenty-eight-year-old John Steinbeck sat waiting in Dr. Chas Curry's dentist office, at 582 Lighthouse Avenue in Pacific Grove, not far from his home, when the door to the "slaughterhouse" opened and out came a slight man, whom he had heard about through friends. It was Ed Ricketts. He had a wispy Vandyke beard and was clutching in his hand, according to Steinbeck, "a bloody molar with a surprisingly large piece of jawbone sticking to it." Cursing gently, he held out the tooth for inspection.

"Look at that god-damned thing. That came out of me," Ricketts said, wincing.

"Seems to be more jaw than tooth," Steinbeck replied.

The two men agreed to go for a drink, which spilled over into a friendship between scientist and novelist that would eventually become one of the most famous in American letters. The story of their meeting, as Steinbeck later recounted with considerable burlesque, was a mixture of both fact and fiction, setting a tone that the novelist repeated throughout his life when recounting stories about the man who would become his best friend.

* * *

EDWARD Flanders Robb Ricketts, or Ed to his friends, was born on May 14, 1897, in Chicago to Abbott and Alice Beverly Flanders Ricketts, pillars of the Episcopal Church. He was the oldest of three children and was "from birth, a child of intelligence and rare charm," remembered his younger sister Frances. He was a precocious boy who, although well liked by fellow schoolmates, earned the uncharitable nickname "the walking dictionary."

He took a keen interest in nature very early, as Ricketts himself later recalled. "At the age of six, I was ruined for any ordinary activities when an uncle who should have known better gave me some natural history curios and an old zoological textbook. Here I saw for the first time those magic and incorrect words 'coral insects.'" After graduating from high school, he enrolled at Illinois State Normal University for a year before dropping out to wander New Mexico and Texas, where he worked as a bookkeeper at a country club. He was eventually drafted as a clerk in the Medical Corps for the First World War. Upon discharge in 1919, he went back to his hometown and enrolled at the University of Chicago.

Time and place are vitally important in understanding the education—and ultimately the future endeavors—of Ed Ricketts. Around the time of his birth, Dr. Henry C. Cowles, professor of botany at the University of Chicago, was rambling along the city's southeastern shore of Lake Michigan. From the water's edge, he noticed a pattern of succession, in time and space, from the very water-tolerant plant societies near the shore to dune grasses and finally the mature oak forests well inland, which he described as a "climax" community. In 1899, he published a paper on physiographic ecology and established himself "as the proverbial solitary and self-reliant pathfinder, America's first professional ecologist." Although his scholarly status would diminish over the decades, Dr. Cowles' groundbreaking work placed the University of Chicago at the vanguard of this very new science in North America.

In the early twentieth century, *ecology* was still an obscure word, far outside the popular vernacular. In 1866, Ernst Haeckel, a leading German exponent of Charles Darwin, coined the word *Oekologie*, derived from the same root found in the word *economy*, the Greek *oikos*, meaning *home*. Haeckel defined ecology as "the science of the relations of living organisms to the external world, their habitat, customs, energies, parasites, etc." More simply and etymologically, he called it "the economy of nature." The word didn't show up in its modern English form, *ecology*, until the late 1890s; even so, it would remain an esoteric word throughout the 1920s and 1930s.

At the University of Chicago, Ricketts fell under the influence of a scholastic giant, Dr. Warder Clyde Allee, who was conducting research to apply ecological concepts, long reserved for plant studies, to animal behavior and interdependence. Over the years, Dr. Allee would publish *Animal Aggregations* (1922), a seminal treatise in animal ecology, *Animal Life and Social Growth* (1932), and *The Social Life of Animals* (1938), along with several other important works. He introduced a wholly new concept to a field that for so long had been dominated by that giant of giants, Charles Darwin.

Life wasn't *just* the Darwinian "struggle for existence," the fierce competition for individual survival, Dr. Allee argued. There was also "an underlying pervasive element of unconscious cooperation, or automatic tendency toward mutual aid among animals." Organisms would often instinctively form aggregations to bolster group, and thus individual, survival. Dr. Allee had observed this behavior, for instance, among brittle stars while researching marine life at Woods Hole on Cape Cod, Massachusetts. "[T]he principle of co-operation," Allee wrote in 1932, "should rank as one of the major biological principles comparable with the better recognized Darwinian principle of struggle for existence."

In the fall of 1922, Ricketts took one of the last, yet most influential, courses in his academic career, Allee's "Animal Ecology." He received a B. Allee later remembered Ricketts as "a member of a small group of 'Ishmaelites' who tended sometimes to be disturbing, but were always stimulating." Although Ricketts dropped out of college without graduating after three sporadic years of study, the concepts in Allee's "Animal Ecology" class would stay with him the rest of his life.

That same year he also met Anna Barbara Maker, who came from Johnstown, Pennsylvania. Their short courtship ended with a wedding on August 19, 1922. A year later Ricketts' first and only son, Ed Jr., was born. With his new wife, who went by the name Nan, and infant son he moved to Pacific Grove in 1923. "[I]t was a sunny day when we arrived in California," Nan remembered. "It was all so impossible to realize that it was still winter after going through all that snow. I thought I was in Seventh Heaven." In this land of blue lupines, acacia trees and Monarch butterflies, her husband set up a biological supply business with his college roommate, Albert E. Galigher, whom he bought out after only two years.

By going west, Ed Ricketts would be one of the first scientists, along with Victor E. Shelford, one of Dr. Cowles' graduate students who studied intertidal communities, to bring this young science to the Pacific Coast.

* * *

JOHN Steinbeck found a soul mate in Ed Ricketts, an enigmatic scientist who was a deep thinker and had eclectic interests ranging from Chinese poetry and the ancient scriptures of Lao Tsu to classical music, modern art, Jungian psychology and German literature. He has been called the "renaissance man of Cannery Row," and he certainly was. He lived a life of quiet contemplation and research, and, as legend has it, beer drinking in his lab. "Ed was not a rebel against society," remembers a fellow marine biologist, Dr. Joel W. Hedgpeth. "He simply ignored much of it." Ricketts was a nonconformist for sure. He was also a college dropout, a fact that may have endeared him to Steinbeck, who flouted his parents' expectations and quit Stanford University to become a writer.

They were oddly matched, professionally and also in appearance: Ricketts was small and slight with subtle handsome features; Steinbeck was hulking and awkward-looking with jumbo ears and a pronounced nose. Together, however, they formed a symbiotic relationship from which both would benefit over the years. A friend once said that, as a scientist and a novelist respectively, "Ricketts didn't know how to lie and Steinbeck didn't know how to tell the truth, and they made a great combination together." Steinbeck agreed. "Knowing Ed Ricketts was instant," he later said. "After the first moment I knew him, and for the next eighteen years I knew him better than I knew anyone. . . . "

They would become close friends largely starting in the winter and spring of 1932, with the arrival of yet another Easterner in Pacific Grove. Joe Campbell was a strapping, athletic twenty-seven-year-old—exceedingly handsome. He had been captain of Columbia University's track team and was especially well travelled. He had studied in Paris in 1927, where he held court with modern sculptor Antoine Bourdelle and became friends with Jiddu Krishnamurti, the young messiah of the world Theosophical movement. He was well versed in the classics, reli-

The Ricketts family, mid-1930s. Left to right: Ed Jr., Nan, Nancy Jane, Cornelia (front), Ed Sr. COURTESY OF ED RICKETTS JR.

gion, modern literature, and art; he spoke French and German (he'd studied in Munich for a year); and he'd even earned money playing in a jazz band in New York in the mid-twenties. Upon returning to the United States and completing college, he spent time bumming around his family's cottage in Woodstock, New York. Yet he felt restless, grew tired of his cerebral existence while the country was going through the throes of the Depression. "I have been living aloof, in bookland," he complained to a friend. So he packed up and headed west on the road—a progenitor to the Beat Generation.

Campbell was friends with Idell Henning, the sister of Steinbeck's wife, Carol; Carol was doing secretarial work in the lab for Ed Ricketts at the time. Idell introduced Campbell to the Steinbecks. He soon became part of a circle of friends that included the fledgling writer and artist Ritch Lovejoy, his wife Tal, and Jack Calvin, another writer and acquaintance of Steinbeck's from Stanford. Calvin had married Sasha Kashevaroff, Tal's sister. In February 1932, Campbell moved into a small

ABOVE LEFT: *John Steinbeck, early 1930s.* PHOTO BY SONYA NOSKOWIAK, COURTESY OF ARTHUR F. NOSKOWIAK, SPECIAL COLLECTIONS, STANFORD UNIVERSITY LIBRARIES.

ABOVE RIGHT: *Carol Steinbeck at Los Gatos home, 1941.* COURTESY OF THE NATIONAL STEINBECK CENTER.

RIGHT: *Joseph Campbell, circa 1927.* COURTESY OF THE JOSEPH CAMPBELL & MARIJA GIMBUTAS LIBRARY, SANTA BARBARA, AND JOSEPH CAMPBELL FOUNDATION.

guesthouse, nicknamed Canary Cottage, next door to the Pacific Grove home of Ed Ricketts and his wife Nan and their three small children, Ed Jr., Nancy and Cornelia.

It was a crucial, formative period in everyone's life. The lab on Cannery Row, besides being a rare source of income for everyone during the Depression (they called it the "bank"), became an improbable intellectual and cultural mecca. Artists, writers, painters, musicians, scientists and graduate students from Hopkins Marine Station down the street would frequently drop by. Parties occasionally went on for days. Ricketts, Steinbeck and Campbell would spend hours talking about metaphysics, psychology, art, history and literature, especially Goethe's *Faust*. (Campbell spoke fluent German and Ricketts expanded his scientific German to read the masterpiece in its original language.) Campbell was becoming an authority on mythology and Carl Jung, and talked with Steinbeck about his work in progress, *To a God Unknown,* whose central theme was the power of nature in human mythmaking. "John has a fine, deep, living quality about his work which ought to ring the bell, I think— if his work is ever discovered," Campbell wrote in his diary at the time.

Ricketts and Campbell also discussed at length Oswald Spengler's *Decline of the West,* an unconventional tome chronicling world history and culture from ancient times, combining both the Oriental and the Occidental. Steinbeck, however, detested the book. "[Ed] developed a theory that man's steps forward were not a continuous advance," remembered Carol Steinbeck, "but a series of steps followed by long plateaus in every field. He developed a graph to show the raise in steps and plateaus that ran half way around the office [in the lab]. Every titbit of information went onto it in his very fine, infinitesimal handwriting. It got as far as Spengler."

All three men were searching for the proverbial meaning of life, a paradigm through which they could live meaningful and rich lives, personally and professionally. Ricketts had already started to formulate some seminal ideas, and his friends, particularly Jack Calvin, urged him to write a layman's guide to seashore collecting. Steinbeck struggled to find a voice in his writing, too. "[H]e had no subject of his own, no clearly defined philosophy, only ideas, interests, and attitudes," according to his biographer, Jackson J. Benson. Campbell was also at a personal impasse, in his "own deep swamps" as he recalled. Out of work for five years, he was depressed and confused.

"I've just been saying no to life," Campbell told Ricketts one day.

Well, Ed replied typically, "the best way to start saying yes to life is to get drunk. I'll take some of my laboratory alcohol, [and] we'll make a drink out of it."

They went over to Steinbeck's house and Ricketts made a fruity, fiery concoction in a bowl with plenty of ice and salt around the rim. They started drinking at four o'clock in the afternoon. By two o'clock in the morning Campbell, a novice drinker but a young man in superb physical condition, had drunk them under the table. It must have been a boisterous little party, because before long the police showed up. Steinbeck, who had passed out in bed, got up and answered the door. He explained that they were having a party and invited the officer in for a drink. The policeman took one sip of the watery, salty slop and left. Later everyone drove down to Holman's Department Store where a man was dancing on roller skates atop a platform on a flagpole, trying to break some kind of record.

"That was," Campbell later recalled, "my party to start me out on life."

* * *

CAROL Steinbeck stormed into their house in Pacific Grove one day. She was terribly excited. "Really, I've got the message of 'Roan Stallion,'" she said and began reciting a passage from the poem by California poet Robinson Jeffers:

> *Humanity is the start of the race; I say*
> *Humanity is the mould to break away from...*

She was a beautiful, long-legged redhead and could fill any room with her radiance, intelligence and wit. She was passionate and held her own intellectually and artistically, becoming a crucial influence on and initial editor for Steinbeck. The three men, Campbell, Ricketts and Steinbeck, listened intently to the words spilling from her lips. Her enthusiasm was infectious and each "took something home from Carol's gift of Robinson Jeffers."

The poem captured the zeitgeist for the young men, echoing their thinking about nature, science, humanity and, ultimately, God. Most importantly, Jeffers seemed to point the way forward for them. One phrase in particular—"Humanity is . . . the crust to break through"— became a veritable hallmark for the personal philosophy that was brewing in Ed Ricketts as a result of his voracious reading. Jeffers's central theme of an emergent arising from life's tragedies would also resonate throughout Steinbeck's greatest work. And for Campbell, as his biographer has noted, the poem was "to form a key piece in his own developing life-affirmative philosophy" and would be reflected in his voluminous writings on world mythology and comparative religion decades later.

Carol was unlike any woman Campbell had ever met. "She was resilient and alive, intelligent, bright, sparkling and full of fun," he remembered. He secretly felt a connection to her and soon found his feelings reciprocated during a heady night of drinking. Campbell recorded his "affair" with Carol, which never went beyond a few kisses, in gushing detail in his diary. "She looked particularly sweet there, with her glass in her right hand, sitting and cooing in the oak tree," he wrote of that night. "When she had finished her song she began to talk to me, and I answered her. 'Oh, Joe, you beautiful thing,' she said. 'Oh, Carol,' I said, 'you're wonderful.'"

He felt a "deep mysterious love" for Carol. Their bond was hard to hide from Steinbeck, who grew suspicious and deeply resentful. On May 27, 1932, the situation came to a head. Over coffee at his home on Eleventh Street, Steinbeck asked Campbell if he desired Carol physically.

"No," Campbell said, "that has nothing to do with the situation at all."

"It's worse than I thought," Steinbeck said.

"Yes," Campbell agreed, "it's pretty bad." He added: "There are plenty of beautiful women. It isn't so much the physical beauty that I'm in love with."

Ed Ricketts was relieved to hear about the John-Carol-Joe quagmire. He too was having love problems, but of a far more serious nature. The thirty-four-year-old biologist found himself having a steamy sexual liaison with Xenia, the seventeen-year-old sister of Tal and Sasha, who was going to high school in Monterey. "When I first met him he was engaged in a scholarly and persistent way in the process of deflowering a young girl," Steinbeck later said of his friend, who was "as concupiscent as a bull terrier." Although we must take Steinbeck's words with a grain of salt, if not a pinch more, Ricketts certainly lived freely and held little concern for social or religious orthodoxies.

His marriage to Nan always seemed like a mismatch anyway. "How they stayed together as long as they did I don't know," their oldest daughter, Nancy, later said. "They were so different." Nan wore her hair in a tight bun, and rarely read or drank. She was also a resourceful home-maker. Ricketts was the opposite—a gregarious, beer-loving bohemian who constantly trawled curiosa books for inspiring ideas. Nan grew jealous of the time her husband spent at the lab, where he often drank with Steinbeck. She disapproved of his behavior. "Don't try to change me," Ricketts complained. Nan also suspected her husband of having an affair. For a while, she kept herself preoccupied with sewing clothes and making furniture. But the situation became unbearable. "That was the beginning of the end," Nancy remembered. The family left Pacific Grove in 1932 and moved to Carmel. For the next few years, Ed and Nan would have several short breakups. She would eventually move to Washington state with her two daughters in 1938.

On June 26, 1932, Ed sent a wire to Jack Calvin, who was on his thirty-three-foot boat called the *Grampus*, waiting in Puget Sound to set sail to Juneau, Alaska. Ricketts was planning to travel with Jack and Sasha, ostensibly to collect a little pink jellyfish (*Gonionemus vertens*) and to conduct a survey of the Inside Passage. Depressed and alone, he was also trying to escape his marital woes, for which he was mostly responsible. The wire said he'd be there the next day, and that he was bringing Joe Campbell.

The day before, a Saturday, Ed and Joe were having farewell cocktails at the home of Tal and Ritch Lovejoy. Steinbeck came over around two o'clock. Both John and Joe strained to greet each other amiably. Steinbeck was clearly troubled by Joe's relationship with his wife.

Steinbeck nevertheless said he was glad Joe was going to Alaska, and added that he wished he could go along. They parted, as Joe would write in his diary a few days later aboard the *Grampus*, "with a noble, manly handshake, dramatically wishing each other well." Despite their congenial farewell, they would never become friends—nor would they see each other again for more than thirty years.

The trip to Juneau lasted ten weeks. Shortly thereafter Campbell left California for New York, where he took a teaching position at Sarah Lawrence College. Although the two friends, Ricketts and Campbell, would lose contact over the next seven years, they would later discover, with a certain degree of astonishment, that they had come to separate but almost identical conclusions about the nature of the world and their own life-philosophies. Perhaps this was no surprise, because Ed Ricketts, seven years Campbell's senior, was "not quite a guru, but a special teacher of consciousness as well as natural science" for Campbell. The lessons learned on that summer trip would reverberate throughout Joseph Campbell's lifetime of scholarship.

"I have still a deep nostalgia for those wonderful days," Campbell would tell Ricketts years later, "when everything that has happened since was taking shape. That was, for me at least, the moment of the great death and re-birth that Jung is always talking about, and all of you who were involved in the 'agony' are symbolic dominants of what is left to me of my psyche. Monterey Peninsula is the Earthly Paradise."

* * *

WITH Campbell out of the way, Steinbeck mended his marriage to Carol and befriended Ed. Since his family had left him, Ricketts was spending more and more time at the lab, eventually moving into the small apartment and office upstairs.

The lab and its owner were oddities along the row of canneries, reduction plants and fish packers. It was, in fact, the heart of the industrial strip. The lab became a sort of social club for everyone, with a "coffee-house conviviality" and Ed as its "guru," according to a friend and artist, Bruce Ariss. Hopkins students would also drop in to talk to its offbeat scientist who, unhindered by scholastic pettiness and jealousy, gave freely of his ideas and unpublished research over a cold glass of beer.

On Sunday mornings, Ricketts would sometimes play his phonograph loudly. He noticed that people parked across the street at the whorehouse would have their car doors open so as to hear Beethoven better. "I never heard anything like it and I sat there with tears coming down my face," remembered one of Ricketts' girlfriends, who was serenaded at the lab. "It was so beautiful."

The Depression did little to dampen spirits. Parties would occasionally go all night, if not for days. Up to seventy people—artists, scientists, writers, lawyers, cannery workers, friends, hangers-on, and complete strangers off the street—would drink cheap red wine and Mexican beer in the lab. Steinbeck remembered one of his birthday parties lasting four days. Ricketts placed a quart of beer beside his bed and took a nap on the fourth day. He awoke after twenty minutes or so, groped for the bottle, took a deep drink and then, according to Steinbeck, "smiled sweetly and waved two fingers in the air in a kind of benediction."

"There's nothing like that first taste of beer," said Ed.

Bruce Ariss remembered another party—"the biggest and wildest party of all." As Ariss told it, he and his wife Jean went to a party at the lab that was attended by *another* Bruce with a wife also named Jean. This other Bruce spoke with a British accent and claimed to be a Hollywood screenwriter as well as the British agent who inspired Ian Fleming's James Bond novels. In any case, he turned out to be a nasty drunk and somehow punched both Jeans, knocking them unconscious. An enraged Ariss landed a straight jab on his face and "his nose exploded like an over-ripe tomato thrown against a concrete wall." The spy began throwing wild punches at Ariss while bloody vapor sprayed from his nose. "He was like a harpooned and enraged Moby Dick," Ariss recounted, "bent on blind vengeance." But the Brit, unlike the great white whale, finally went down in defeat. The lab was a catastrophe, looking like a "slaughterhouse" with lights smashed, the door banging in the wind and blood splattered everywhere.

This spy was supposedly Sir Robert Bruce Lockhart. He was a colleague of Sidney Reilly, the real-life British spy who inspired Fleming. Still, Lockhart himself was very much like James Bond. The Scotsman was a womanizer who hobnobbed with European royalty and in 1918 as British vice-consul to Moscow was arrested by the Bolsheviks for conspiring to assassinate Lenin. His personal diaries are today housed in the archives of the House of Lords in London. And so it is to the velvety red chamber of England's aristocracy where one must travel to confirm this outlandish story about the lab. Lockhart was indeed touring the United States in 1934, the same year that his best-selling book, *Memoirs of a British Agent*, came out on film. But according to his detailed diaries, he never traveled west of Chicago. Long afterward, Ariss discovered that this spy-cum-screenwriter was actually an impostor. He had successfully duped the partygoers into thinking he was the famed British spy. Facts notwithstanding, a legend would be born about how Ariss "beat the shit out of 007" at the lab.

Pacific Biological Laboratories certainly didn't fit the profile of a typical New Monterey business. Nan described it as more like a museum than a commercial enterprise. Steinbeck remembered one specimen mounted in a museum jar—the aforementioned human foetus. Ricketts' father, who had retired to Pacific Grove and helped out around the lab, kept it in the basement stockroom. "It was to have been the lone child of a Negress and a Chinese," Steinbeck remembered. "When the mother succumbed to a lover's quarrel and a large dose of arsenic administered by person or persons unknown, the autopsy revealed her secret, and her secret was acquired by Pacific Biological. . . . It was Dad Ricketts' great pride. Children and many adults made pilgrimages to the basement to see it. It became famous in Cannery Row."

For young boys, the lab was also about commerce. Doc, as the kids called Ricketts, because he would often patch up their scratched knees and elbows, sold embalmed cats to medical and veterinarian schools for the study of anatomy. He would drain their blood, strap them to cross-shaped cradles—one friend joked about his system to "crucify" cats—and inject blue, red and yellow dyes into their veins, arteries and nervous systems, respectively. While Ricketts was known to have a special relationship with dogs—many remember him smiling and tipping his hat at them—cats were another matter. Another friend once brought him a mock newspaper headline: INJECT RICKETTS, FURIOUS CATS CRY! Since the SPCA prohibited the raising of kittens for laboratory purposes, Ricketts spread word among the neighborhood boys that he'd pay out twenty-five cents per cat.

"It saddened Ed a little to see how venially warped the cat-loving small boys of Monterey were," Steinbeck would later say. "They sold their own cats, their aunts' cats, their neighbors' cats. For a few days there would be scurrying footsteps and soft thumps as cats in gunny sacks were secretly deposited in the basement. Then guileless and innocent-faced little catacides would collect their quarters and rush for Wing Chong's grocery for pop and cap pistols. No matter what happened, Wing Chong made a small profit."

Once Ricketts' son even found his aunt's cat, Pussy, in one of the gunny sacks. Another time two mischievous boys scammed Ricketts: one boy sold the other's cat for twenty-five cents and then the second boy came in later, crying to get it back. The two boys worked this routine on Ricketts twice before he figured it out. "The people of the Row really loved Ed," Steinbeck went on, "but this affection did not forbid them from subjecting him to any outrageous scheming that occurred to them."

It wasn't that Ed Ricketts was especially gullible; he was just generous to a fault. Ed could often see the swindlers coming a mile away, but he'd play along out of kindness or curiosity. Usually, the bums in threadbare overalls across the street nickel-and-dimed him for liquor money. Even so, he admired these men, a successful and happy breed in their own way.

The most cunning wino was Harold "Gabe" Bicknell, who sometimes collected specimens for the lab. Ricketts would write him very specific orders, instructing Gabe on the number of specimens needed, types of species, sizes, prices and special collecting instructions—"Cats, unlimited number, but don't bring in more than 5 a day until we get more equipment and until sharks are preserved," read one note. The kinds of species varied widely and so did the prices paid, depending on their size:

Nereis marine worms	1–6 cents
Monarch butterflies	1/2 cent
Slime eels	15 cents
Crayfish	1/2–2 1/2 cents
Chitons	1 1/2–5 cents
Slugs	5 cents
Turtles	5 cents
Cats	25 cents
Frogs	2 1/2–12 cents

Centipedes	10 cents
Tarantulas	25 cents
Lamprey fish	5 cents

Gabe's modus operandi was more comical than diabolical. Prior to a collecting trip, he would plead poverty and ask for a cash advance. Ricketts would reluctantly oblige him. Gabe would simultaneously run up a bill at Wing Chong's—on Ricketts' account—probably to buy some cheap intoxicant. Usually with an unwitting accomplice, Gabe would then head to Turlock or Carmel Valley to go "frogging," or along the coast for marine invertebrate collecting. After a few days he'd call or wire—collect of course—for another cash advance. Ricketts would then send a bit more money, say, five dollars. Another desperate wire would follow shortly thereafter. "I don't know what you guys do with all the money," Ricketts once wrote back, knowing Gabe was up to no good. "I can't dig it up as fast as you want it, and you're furthermore getting money faster than the frogs are coming in."

Parcels would eventually arrive at 800 Ocean View Avenue. Ricketts would unpack them to discover that many of the specimens were unwanted, undersized, or even dead and decaying. Gabe would "almost invariably" run up expenses greater than the value of his collecting work. He would then recruit another collecting partner and set up another account with Ricketts—at one point Gabe had three accounts, Bicknell-King, Bicknell-Yantis and Bicknell-Cook, all in deficit—and repeat the lucrative scheme. Each time Ricketts would implore Gabe not to take advantage of his generosity. Once he even pleaded that he was in a "financial jam" himself. But Gabe just couldn't help himself. Ed Ricketts knew this scheming was in his nature and accepted Gabe for who he was.

* * *

JOHN Steinbeck was also an occasional collector for Pacific Biological Laboratories. A mutual love of the sea and science cemented his friendship with the marine biologist. Although a country boy from Salinas, Steinbeck often spent time at his family's seaside cottage in Pacific

Grove, about twenty miles away. In 1923, he also took a summer class at Hopkins Marine Station, a part of Stanford University, where he learned about Dr. William Emerson Ritter.

A major scientist and founding director of Scripps Institution in La Jolla, Ritter saw nature organized as a series of wholes that "are so related to their parts that not only does the existence of the whole depend upon the orderly cooperation and interdependence of its part, but the whole exercises a measure of determinative control over its parts." According to Ritter, individual animals effectively became subjugated to a "superorganism." Steinbeck may have been inspired by these ecological ideas, but they did not show up in his early novels, *Cup of Gold* (1929), *The Pastures of Heaven* (1932), *To a God Unknown* (1933) and *Tortilla Flat* (1935). It would take the friendship and tutelage of Ed Ricketts to bring them to prominence in his work.

After learning about Allee's research from Ricketts, Steinbeck wrote a two-page essay titled "Argument of Phalanx." In it, he applied principles of animal ecology to humans, exploring the relationship between the individual and the group-man, or "phalanx," as he called it. "All life forms from protozoa to antelopes and lions, from crabs to lemmings form and are a part of phalanxes," he wrote, "but the phalanx of which the units are men, are more complex, more variable and powerful than any other." Religion, Steinbeck believed for instance, resulted from a "phalanx emotion." After writing the essay, he discovered that he had unknowingly made four statements of this idea in *To a God Unknown*.

Steinbeck was beginning to find his voice and a philosophy, rooted largely in ecology and nature, which would preoccupy his writing throughout the 1930s and lead to his popular success. "The artist is simply the spokesman of the phalanx. . . . I'm going to write a whole novel with it as a theme," Steinbeck told a friend in 1933. "Ed Rickets," he added, "has dug up all the scientific material and more than I need to establish the physical integrity of the thing. I have written this theme over and over and did not know what I was writing."

In 1936, Steinbeck published *In Dubious Battle*, a brutal novel about striking farm workers. He had already become popular with *Tortilla Flat*, but this novel would bring about critical acclaim. It also prepared him for an epic work that would became a masterpiece of twentieth-century American literature. *In Dubious Battle*'s message is essentially ecological, about group-man as a superorganism. Its tone is of scientific detachment. The author takes no sides, advocates no prescription—scientific, ideological or otherwise—for the social ills vividly portrayed in the novel. All the characters come across as dubious: the labor agitators are manipulative and doctrinaire; the landowners are greedy and cruel; and even the poor striking migrant workers come across as narrow-minded dupes to Party operatives.

Into this fold, Steinbeck weaves a clear-thinking, introspective scientist, Doc Burton, who runs the sanitation system of a migrant camp. Only Doc sees the whole picture and stands apart from the action, like someone peering down watching the critters in a tide pool. Doc is, in fact, modeled directly on Ed Ricketts in demeanor and attitude. And it is through Doc that Steinbeck expresses his ecological philosophy.

"I want to watch these group-men, for they seem to me to be a new individual, not at all like single men," Doc says. "A man in a group isn't himself at all, he's a cell in an organism that isn't like him any more than the cells in your body are like you."

With these words, the first "Doc" character was born in a Steinbeck novel and the writer would begin to transform his best friend, Ed Ricketts, into a legend—both a mythic and real figure in the imagination of America.

PHIALOBA STEINBECKI, SEA ANEMONE, NEW SPECIES COLLECTED BY ED RICKETTS IN MARCH 1940 IN GULF OF CALIFORNIA, MEXICO.

CHAPTER TWO

THE TRILOGY

There is a curious idea among unscientific men that in scientific writing there is a common plateau of perfectionism. Nothing could be more untrue. The reports of biologists are the measure, not of the science, but of the men themselves.

—JOHN STEINBECK & EDWARD F. RICKETTS,
Sea of Cortez: A Leisurely Journal of Travel and Research

ED RICKETTS was not a writer, although he wanted to be one. He thought his friend John was a genius in the way he used the English language. *Of Mice and Men* was one of his favorites. Steinbeck had spent considerable time at the lab while writing the novella, which was published in 1937. Ricketts' son remembered his dad talking about the book a lot. "It was very personal," Ed Jr. said of the book. Perhaps the unflinching friendship of Lennie and George, the book's protagonists, reminded Ricketts of his own symbiotic bond to Steinbeck.

Ricketts began writing widely on ecology, philosophy, literature, politics and even art in the 1930s. He struggled for almost a decade to get published, however. The germ of his first published work actually lay in Pacific Biological Laboratories' original sales catalog of specimens. Ricketts saw a series of catalogs as comprising a sort of textbook of Pacific Coast invertebrates. Friends, especially Jack Calvin, encouraged him to compile his observations from his many collecting trips and scientific essays—one paper on wave shock as a factor in littoral ecology, another on tidal zonation—into a little beachcomber's guidebook.

The project soon snowballed, becoming "a sort of cottage industry" among his friends and the hangers-on who frequented the lab. Calvin became the book's coauthor and worked to spruce up Ricketts' often convoluted prose. Ritch Lovejoy did the drawings. Esteemed scientists from around the world, such as Swedish zoologist Torsten Gislén at Lund University, identified specimens and sent him letters addressed "Dear Dr. Ricketts," although he had no doctoral or even bachelor's degree.

By 1931, a typescript was taking shape, modeled after a seminal 1872 study of the marine fauna of Vineyard Sound and the work of Ricketts' former professor, Dr. Allee. There was only one other book that dealt with the Pacific Coast at the time. Myrtle E. Johnson and Harry J. Snook had published *Seashore Animals of the Pacific Coast* in 1927 and dedicated it to the esteemed Dr. Ritter at Scripps. It was the first comprehensive book on the seashore and was phylogenic in its organization, i.e. one chapter on mollusks, another on starfish and so on. Ricketts, however, had an entirely different idea. His book would be organized according to environmental niches: protected outer coast, open coast, bay and estuary, wharf pilings, etc. It was a novel approach. In fact, his book would be the first to focus on the ecology of the seashore.

"Ed had no talent for systemic zoology in terms of describing new species," remembered Dr. Hedgpeth. "He was more concerned with what was going on in nature, but was rebuffed by the establishment."

Indeed, Dr. W. K. Fisher, a well-respected marine biologist at Hopkins, reviewed Ricketts' manuscript for Stanford University Press (SUP), which had agreed to publish it. He had little good to say. "I am rather averse to setting down on paper my view of 'its quality and the desirability of publishing it,'" he began a stern letter to Professor William Hawley Davie, director of SUP, on December 2, 1931:

> I read the manuscript with somewhat mixed emotions. The facts are authentic so far as I could see and on the whole it was fairly well written, barring a certain vulgarity in places which doubtless can be eliminated by the Editor. The method of taking up the animals from the standpoint of station and exposure on the seashore seems at first sight very logical but from the practical standpoint it seems to me not particularly happy. Both Professor [G. E.] MacGinitie and I were quite frank with Mr. Ricketts on this score.

It was a devastating repudiation from two giants of Pacific Coast biology—Dr. Fisher, director of Stanford's Hopkins Marine Station, and Dr. MacGinitie, director of Caltech's Kerckhoff Marine Laboratory. The broadside stymied the book's publication. Dr. Fisher ended the letter with a gross display of academic chauvinism. "In any event I think the manuscript should be carefully read by a professional zoologist. It must be remembered that neither of the authors can be classified in this category, although Mr. Ricketts is a collector of considerable experience."

Although both scientists would occasionally drink with Ricketts, they apparently held little regard for his ecological ideas. Yet this lowly "collector" was not intimidated by such acerbic criticism. Throughout the Dirty Thirties, with his poverty-stricken friends in tow, Ed Ricketts field-tested and revised the manuscript while keeping true to its original ecological design.

In redrafting the book, Ricketts wanted to travel the "knife edge," as he described it—to write "an account interesting to the layreader, and useful alike to the zoologist." But such a populist approach to science was particularly frowned upon in academia. Dr. Fisher remained unimpressed. "I have found few, very few, who can 'travel the knife edge,'" he wrote in a second prepublication review in 1936. Dr. Fisher dismissed the work as more interesting to laymen than to serious zoologists.

As a concession to Dr. Fisher, Ricketts wrote a five-page "Zoological Introduction" in which he applied Cabrera's Law of ecological incompatibility to the seashore.* This was a "startling perception" on the part of Ricketts, according to Dr. Hedgpeth, since the concept had yet to be applied in marine biology. Because of the continued criticism, Stanford delayed publication yet again. Dr. Fisher's harsh reaction to the "Zoological Introduction" eventually led to its removal from the book as well. The omission of Cabrera's Law, according to Dr. Hedgpeth, "may well have delayed progress in marine ecology of the Pacific Coast for decades."

Stanford did finally approve publication. But Ricketts would have to suffer a series of travails before the book actually rolled off the presses. Late in 1935, Ricketts' father fell ill. "He was a little pixie who

---

* Briefly, Cabrera's Law, which Ricketts quoted from the Biological Abstracts of March 1935, states: "In the same locality... directly related animal forms always occupy different habitats or ecological stations... Related animal forms are ecologically incompatible, and the incompatibility is the more profound the more directly they are related."

Pacific Biological Laboratories burns down during waterfront fire, November 25,
1936. PHOTO ORIGINALLY PUBLISHED IN *MONTEREY PENINSULA HERALD*, COURTESY OF ED
RICKETTS JR.

came bubbling up out of the basement with Alkaseltzer foaming from
his mouth," Carol Steinbeck remembered. "I think Alkaseltzer was the
death of the man." He died early the next year. Ricketts kept busy doing
commercial collecting and working on his manuscript. But still more
tragedy awaited in 1936.

Just after 5:30 in the morning on November 25, Ed awoke for some
unknown reason. He later remembered feeling "impressed with a sense
of stillness but with the notion that something was wrong." He looked
out the front window of the lab and then went to the door. He saw three
men standing in the quiet street, their faces awash in a glow of dancing
light. Flames were leaping out of the windows of the Del Mar Cannery
next door. Ricketts could hear the crackling of the fire.

In a panic, he pulled on a shirt and trousers—no shoes, socks, or
coat—and rushed downstairs to get his car out of the garage. He
reversed the car, stopping at the staircase of the second-story entry. He
jumped out and rushed up the stairs to grab a painting. By the time he

made a second dash inside, the power poles were ablaze and the lights had gone out in the lab. He found a flashlight and searched for two books of records, then quickly left. Within eight to ten minutes the entire lab was a sheet of fire.

It turned out that a workman had thrown an electrical switch to start the daily production line at the Del Mar Cannery. Immediately, the circuit board burst into flames and quickly engulfed the control room. Workers fled and the fire raced through the tin and wood structure. A monstrous cloud of soot slithered up and smeared the sky over Monterey. In three hours, only ash and char and popping sardine cans remained where Ricketts' lab and the cannery once stood. "Everything was destroyed," he told a friend, including his clothing, furniture, family heirlooms, laboratory equipment and his library, which was valued at more than $2,000. He considered it the best scientific book collection outside Stanford University. His entire life's work had literally gone up in smoke. Luckily, only a few months before, he'd sent the original type-script of his book to Stanford University Press. It was the only thing left of fifteen years of research.

Insurance wouldn't cover everything, leaving Ricketts with $13,050 in unrecoverable losses. He sued the electric company, but lost, and therefore was forced to borrow money. He could only afford to rebuild a cheap "shanty," as he called it. At Christmas, friends surprised him with gifts of books (Homer's *Odyssey,* Goethe's *Faust,* the poetry of Blake, Shelley, Keats, Jeffers and Whitman, and Lao Tsu's *Tao Te Ching*) to restock his once vast library. He almost wept from the generosity. By January of 1937, cheap red wine was again flowing at Pacific Biological Laboratories, christening its veritable rebirth. Henceforth, however, Ed would be haunted by nightmares of fire and destruction. He even began scrawling shaky, nearly illegible dream references in his journals.

John Steinbeck witnessed Ricketts endure much toil, heartache and tragedy before his book, titled *Between Pacific Tides*, was published. As a now-famous writer, Steinbeck even wrote the foreword to its revised edition published in 1948:

This is a book for laymen, for beginners, and, as such, its main purpose is to stimulate curiosity, not to answer finally questions which are only temporarily answerable.... This book then says: "There are good things to see in the tide-pools and there are exciting and interesting thoughts to be generated from the seeing. Every new eye applied to the peep hole which looks out at the world may fish in some new beauty and some new pattern, and the world of the human mind must be enriched by such fishing."

The book, like the tide pools it explores, teems with life, with rich, detailed imagery, humor and whimsy, experimentation, mysticism, scientific discovery, cosmic questions. The qualities that make the work truly unique, "the first work of its kind" as one scientist described it, came from the boundless curiosity and, perhaps, the touch of genius within Ed Ricketts.

Animals—some five hundred different species spread over a 1,500-mile coastline from the Mexican to Canadian border regions—are described in a way that anyone can understand: "The pleasant and absurd hermit crabs are the clowns of the tide pools." Ricketts draws his readers in by explaining how lofty lessons can be learned from these little worlds; how, for instance, one discovery in the tide pool "may conceivably make understandable the evolutionary background behind the gregariousness of animals, even human beings."

Ricketts is never too proud to reveal his own limited knowledge of the natural world. After conducting an inconclusive experiment to determine how the moon influences a marine worm's spawning cycle, Ricketts simply admits that modern science is "confronted with a mystery beside which any of Sherlock Holmes' problems seem pale and insipid." But when he does reveal a tide-pool truism—the importance of all creatures, no matter how inconspicuous, to the complex web of life—it's pure poetry:

Great fleas have little fleas
Upon their backs to bite 'em
And little fleas have lesser fleas
And so ad infinitum

These days Between Pacific Tides is considered a definitive sourcebook and a classic in the literature of marine biology. Contrary to Dr.

Fisher, *Between Pacific Tides* did indeed travel the "knife edge." Upon publication, it received fine peer reviews in the magazines *Ecology* and *Nature,* and has become immensely popular over the years. Revised and updated by several scientists and now into its fifth edition, *Between Pacific Tides* is one of the best-selling books ever published by Stanford University Press, selling some 100,000 copies. Over the years it has become a model for innumerable seashore books. *"Between Pacific Tides* was a great departure from the 'dry ball' lists published before its first appearance," explains one contemporary scientist, "and, periodically updated, remains current, if not still ahead of its time, today." That's a heroic accomplishment for a scientific work largely envisioned and written seventy years ago.

April 1939 was a euphoric month for Ed Ricketts, the best of times. After years of nagging criticism, revisions, extensive field-testing and delays, the death of his father, a horrendous fire at the lab (he later referred to it as his "holocaust"), a failed insurance lawsuit and the resulting debt, and separation from his wife, *Between Pacific Tides* was finally— triumphantly—published. One can hardly imagine the sweetness Ricketts must have felt as he held the crisp new book in his hands, all 516 pages of text, drawings and glossy photos still faintly smelling of ink and glue. A party fueled on thirty-nine-cent jugs of wine, beer and a little whiskey no doubt ensued, staggering into the wee, dewy hours of Cannery Row with Ricketts smiling broadly and performing his legendary "tippy-toe mouse dance" to a roar of applause and laughter from congratulatory friends.

* * *

NO doubt, John Steinbeck felt genuine excitement for his friend. The publication of Ricketts' book would even have "some importance for the course of Steinbeck's life." But Steinbeck's joy must have been partially clouded by his own personal despair at the time. That same month Steinbeck published a novel that would become his greatest achievement. Over time the novel would come to be seen as defining an entire generation and the Dust Bowl hardship of the Great Depression in the same way that F. Scott Fitzgerald's *The Great Gatsby* evoked the Roaring

Twenties the generation before, or Jack Kerouac's *On the Road* captured the beatniks the generation after. Steinbeck's was a radical work, because it challenged social orthodoxies and conventional thinking. And although rarely given its proper due today and at the time widely misunderstood, the novel augured a coming epoch, a new "age" as historians like to say, in the latter half of the twentieth century.

Yet in 1939 "radical" also meant communist fiend, Soviet operative, class provocateur, labor agitator, Marxist-Leninist, traitor, all things un-American. The novel's publication thrust Steinbeck, a notoriously private man who shunned the press, into controversy and celebrity that would bedevil him for the rest of his life. Already, even before the book's publication in April, Steinbeck heard that secret agents, purportedly the FBI, were asking questions about him at a Monterey bookshop. He was paranoid about being set up in scandals, especially trumped-up charges of rape or adultery, and perhaps worse, as he explained to a friend:

> They can't shoot me now because it would be too obvious and because I have placed certain informations in the hands of [FBI director] J. Edgar Hoover in case I take a nose dive. So I think I am personally safe enough except for automobile accidents etc. and rape and stuff like that so I am a little careful not to go anywhere alone nor to do anything without witnesses.

(In 1984, a newspaper obtained Steinbeck's eighty-four-page FBI file through the Freedom of Information Act, which confirmed the writer's suspicion that J. Edgar Hoover had started spying on him in 1939.)

The Grapes of Wrath was a ghastly portrait of poverty, filth, human misery, starvation, and injustice. It tells the story of the Joad family, Oklahoma tenant farmers or "Okies," dispossessed from their Dust Bowl homestead by bankers and wealthy landowners. In a jalopy, the Joads go west along Route 66 in search of greener pastures, the proverbial Promised Land, only to confront the scorn of Californians. Steinbeck imbued the novel with an essentially ecological message, about how "machine-man" with his iron tractors loses connection to the land, destroys the land, then consequently destroys his own humanity.

His political observations in the novel, one literary scholar has pointed out, "grew largely from his interest in Ed Ricketts' ideas."

The reaction to *Grapes*—which weighed in at a mammoth 850 pages—shocked even Steinbeck, who thought it wouldn't be a popular book at all and advised his publisher to "print a small edition." After one month, 83,000 copies were in print, a number that would swell to 430,000 by year's end, a staggering success then and now. Since the first edition appeared more than sixty years ago, the novel has never been out of print or sold less than 50,000 copies annually, in English alone.

Ecstatic reviews rolled in from critics at *Atlantic Monthly, Harper's* and *North American Review*. Clifton Fadiman at *The New Yorker* summed up the novel's power: "If only a couple of million overcomfortable people can be brought to read it, John Steinbeck's *The Grapes of Wrath* may actually effect something like a revolution in their minds and hearts." Such praise, however, only fed the hysteria of detractors—namely the Associated Farmers, conservative politicians, the clergy and communist witch-hunters.

Steinbeck wrote the novel in a marathon session—ninety-three working days over five months starting on May 26, 1938. It physically and emotionally crippled him and Carol, who served as his stenographer and initial editor and who came up with its title from a verse in "The Battle Hymn of the Republic." With the manuscript completed in early 1939, they moved into a secluded Spanish-style ranch near Los Gatos, seventy-five miles from Monterey. Medical tests at the time showed that Steinbeck's metabolic rate was "shockingly low" and neuritis left him bedridden for two weeks. The publication of *The Grapes of Wrath* in April of that year thus heralded the worst of times for Steinbeck, "a nightmare all in all."

Hollywood stars quickly came knocking at his door—Burgess Meredith, Charlie Chaplin, Spencer Tracy, Anthony Quinn—the "swimming pool set" as Steinbeck dubbed them. They became occasional visitors around the pool at his Los Gatos home. He was offered $5,000 a week to write screenplays, and the film rights for *Grapes* sold for $75,000, one of the highest prices ever paid for a novel at the time. Director John Ford turned it into an Academy Award–winning blockbuster in 1940, starring a young Henry Fonda as Tom Joad, a character who has been ranked as one of the greatest screen heroes of all time by the American Film Institute.

It was too much for John Steinbeck—the money, adoration, invidious innuendo and threats. "This whole thing is getting me down," he wrote his agent, "and I don't know what to do about it. The telephone never stops ringing, telegrams all the time, fifty to seventy-five letters a day all wanting something. People who won't take no for an answer sending books to be signed. I don't know what to do." By the beginning of July, the *Los Angeles Times* reported that the famous writer had retreated to "a secluded canyon three miles from [Los Gatos], and padlocked himself against the world."

Steinbeck fled to Hollywood that summer to hide out, but also to get away from Carol. Suddenly she seemed to be turning on him too. Her behavior, including bouts of heavy drinking, had become erratic and hateful toward the writer. She had suffered greatly for his career and grew resentful. In Hollywood Steinbeck struck up an affair with actress Gwen (or *Gwyn*, as she later spelled it) Conger, a petite starlet twenty years his junior. When Steinbeck returned to Los Gatos he found Carol hysterical. In late July, while at a party in Beverly Hills, she blew up, screaming viciously at her husband in an embarrassing public feud.

Distraught and bewildered, John Steinbeck needed help. And there was only one place where he could hide out from his estranged wife, snooping FBI agents, newspapermen and scandalmongers. "Once, when I had suffered an overwhelming emotional upset," he later recalled,

> I went to the laboratory to stay with [Ed Ricketts]. I was dull and speechless with shock and pain. He used music on me like medicine. Late in the night when he should have been asleep, he played music for me on his great phonograph—even when I was asleep he played it, knowing that its soothing would get into my dark confusion. He played the curing and reassuring plain songs, remote and cool and separate, and then gradually he played the sure patterns of Bach, until I was ready for more personal thought and feeling again, until I could bear to come back to myself. And when that time came, he gave me Mozart. I think it was as careful and loving medication as has ever been administered.

By autumn, Steinbeck was spending most of his time on Cannery Row, helping Ricketts with work at the lab and reading science books. He had tired of the "swimming pool set," which he felt Carol had fostered. On a number of levels, he sensed he was undergoing some kind of slow death—matrimonially, professionally, creatively, physically. He had barely written a word in 1939, his marriage had effectively collapsed, his health was frail, and war in Europe, which began in September, cast a doomsday spell over his psyche.

"The last two days I have had death premonitions so strong," he scribbled in his journal on October 19, "that I burned all the correspondence of years. I have a horror of people going through it, messing around in my past, such as it is. I burned it all."

But with death came a rebirth too—a rebirth that would confound many who knew him. In a telling letter to Carlton "Dook" Sheffield, his Stanford roommate and lifelong friend, one can peer vividly into the writer's tortured soul and transformation:

Los Gatos
November 13, 1939

Dear Dook:
It's pretty early in the morning. I got up to milk the cow.

I'm finishing off a complete revolution. It's amazing how everyone piled in to regiment me, to make a symbol of me, to regulate my life and work. I've just tossed the whole thing overboard. I never let anyone interfere before and I can't see why I should now. This ultimate freedom receded. I'm keeping more of it than I need or even want, like a reservoir. The two most important [things], I suppose—at least they seem so to me—are freedom from respectability and most important—freedom from the necessity of being consistent. Lack of those two can really tie you down. Of course all this publicity has been bad if I tried to move about but here on the ranch it has no emphasis. People up here—the few we see—don't read much and don't remember what they read, and my projected work is not likely to create any hysteria.

It's funny, Dook. I know what in a vague way this work is about. I mean I know its tone and texture and to an extent its field and I find that I have no education. I have to go back to school in a way. I'm completely without mathematics and I have to learn something about abstract mathematics. I have some biology but must have much more and the twins bio-physics and bio-chemistry are closed to me. So I have to go back and start over. I bought half the stock in Ed's lab which gives me equipment, a teacher, a library to work in.

I'm going on about myself but in a sense it's more than me—it's you and everyone else. The world is sick now. There are things in the tide pools easier to understand than Stalinist, Hitlerite, Democrat, capitalist confusion, and voodoo. So I'm going to those things which are relatively more lasting to find a new basic picture. I have too a conviction that a new world is growing under the old, the way a new finger nail grows under a bruised one. I think all the economists and sociologists will be surprised some day to find that they did not forsee nor understand it. Just as the politicos of Rome could not have forseen that the social-political-ethical world for two thousand years would grow out of the metaphysical gropings of a few quiet poets. I think the same thing is happening now. Communist, Fascist, Democrat may find that the real origin of the future lies on the microscope plates of obscure young men, who, puzzled with order and disorder in quantum and neutron, build gradually a picture which will seep down until it is the fiber of the future.

The point of all this is that I must make a new start. I've worked the novel—I know it as far as I can take it. I never did think much of it—a clumsy vehicle at best. And I don't know the form of the new but I know there is a new which will be adequate and shaped by the new thinking. Anyway, there is a picture of my confusion. How is yours?

There is so much confusion now—emotional hysteria which passes for thought and blind faith which passes for analysis.

I suspect you are ready for a change. How would you escape the general picture? We're catching the waves of nerves from Europe and making a few of our own.

Write when you can.
John

The "new thinking" was the study of science. It became "a sort of sea anchor with which he tried to ride out the storm." Steinbeck completely abandoned fiction writing and, oddly, wanted to produce a high-school-level textbook on the marine biology of San Francisco Bay under Ricketts' tutelage. Why, at the height of his literary career, with cash and kudos flooding in, would America's best-selling author abandon the very craft he seemed to have mastered? The answer eluded many literary critics.

One of the greatest American men of letters in the twentieth century, Edmund Wilson, set the tone—and one can arguably say the misunderstanding—for a generation of critics who excoriated Steinbeck, notwithstanding his popular appeal. "Mr. Steinbeck almost always in his fiction is dealing either with the lower animals or with human beings so rudimentary that they are almost on the animal level...," wrote Wilson in an influential review of *The Grapes of Wrath*. "This animalizing tendency of Mr. Steinbeck's is, I believe, at the bottom of his relative unsuccess at representing human beings." Steinbeck's fiction was weak, flawed, belittling, Wilson argued, because his characters were simply not human, or not human enough. But Wilson completely missed the philosophical and scientific import of what Steinbeck was actually saying.

Anthropocentricism—the placing of human beings at the center of the universe—has been the very foundation of Western thinking, from ancient times through the Age of Reason into modernity. In eras bubbling with religious and imperial zeal, society saw nature as a gift from God, and its exploitation as a divine right. "The world is made for man," Sir Francis Bacon wrote, "not man for the world." The Enlightenment harkened a new world in which science would give mankind absolute dominion, in a biblical sense, over nature. With the new inventions of the Industrial Revolution, humans polluted and plundered the planet's bounty: the soil, oceans, forests, lakes and rivers, and their myriad creatures.

Singularly, however, one event effected a sea-change in this man-centered worldview in North America. In the 1930s, huge dust storms blew over the Great Plains, transforming the sun into a lusterless ball in a gray sky. The Dust Bowl, vividly described in the opening chapter of *The Grapes of Wrath*, is arguably the worst environmental catastrophe of the twentieth century. It destroyed entire harvests, displaced some 300,000 farmers and precipitated violent social unrest and even starvation. A group of pioneering Midwestern plant ecologists concluded, however, that the Dust Bowl was a wholly *man-made* disaster; misguided farming practices had destroyed the native sod which was a vital buffer against wind and drought.

It's a conclusion that resonates throughout Steinbeck's epic novel—"The land bore under iron, and under iron gradually died," he wrote—and made John Steinbeck, argues his biographer, "the only major literary figure of his time to embrace and bring to his writing one of the most—if not *the* most—important concepts of the twentieth century, a concept that has changed radically the way man views himself and his relationship to his environment."

As Galileo rankled the Vatican for confirming that the earth was not the center of the universe, so too was Steinbeck attacked for trying to show that the earth itself was not a man-centered world. Humans were biological beings, Steinbeck suggested, and were thus united by the same natural laws that shape the rest of the animal kingdom. He was not denying the uniqueness of the human species—its distinct cognitive, linguistic and emotive powers—as Wilson contended, but rather recognizing that humans were *one* with nature.

The fate of civilization, in effect, rests perhaps less on how man treats his fellow man than on how man treats the environment. That humanity's survival depended on the health of the global commons—a fact that sounds trite today in light of global warming, species extinction and habitat destruction—was a prophetic statement half a century ago. And while literary scholars criticized Steinbeck for animalism and gross sentimentalism, it has been the scientific community who has largely vindicated the writer, proclaiming Steinbeck a conservationist, an ecological prophet and the first American writer to herald the Age of Ecology.

John Steinbeck knew, as Ricketts had once written, that "the study of animal communities has this advantage: they are merely what they are, for anyone to see who will and can look clearly; they cannot complicate the picture by worded idealisms, by saying one thing and being another: here the struggle is unmasked and the beauty is unmasked."

In *The Grapes of Wrath,* John Steinbeck unmasked the human struggle and was persecuted with "worded idealisms" for doing so. By turning to marine biology and the tide pools, he hoped to apply his own eye to this "peep hole," and to fish for the same beauty and struggles among animal communities that he had unmasked among human society. "Our fingers turned over the stones," Steinbeck said of seashore collecting, "and we saw life that was like our life."

* * *

IN December of 1939, Ed and John bought a truck and rigged it with a tiny pump, refrigeration plant, small aquarium, microscope and bookcase for collecting expeditions. On the side of the truck, an eager Steinbeck painted an insignia, $^\pi\sqrt{-(R+S)^2}$, which was supposedly a mathematical theorem representing his friendship with Ricketts. "I can't tell you what all this means to me, in happiness and energy," he wrote his literary agent, Elizabeth Otis, on December 15. "I was washed up and now I'm alive again, with work to be done and worth doing." They spent Christmas Day at Tomales Point, north of San Francisco, where Steinbeck collected, among other species, a tiny sea spider, *Pycnogonum rickettsi.* (Ricketts first collected this species on March 31, 1925, and shipped the specimens to Dr. Waldo Schmitt at the Smithsonian, who identified it and named it in honor of its discoverer.)

By this time, the San Francisco Bay textbook had been placed on the back burner. Steinbeck was spearheading a much bigger, more adventuresome project, an expedition down the Baja Peninsula. Ricketts had always wanted to collect in this remote corner of the world, but didn't have the financial resources to do so. Now Steinbeck agreed to finance the trip. Steinbeck also obtained the proper travel permits from the Mexican embassy, chartered a new fishing boat for transportation and approached his agent to find a publisher for the travel log of the voyage. Book royalties would eventually pay for the cost of the expedition.

On the morning of March 11, 1940, a bon-voyage party was held aboard the *Western Flyer,* a seventy-six-foot sardine purse seiner moored in Monterey Bay. The entire town was caught up in the excitement, offering "advice enough to move the navies of the world" to the crew of the *Western Flyer.* The trip would be a six-week expedition to the Gulf of California, or, as it's more romantically known, the Sea of Cortez. Fifty to sixty people crowded the *Western Flyer*'s deck and galley, swilling beer,

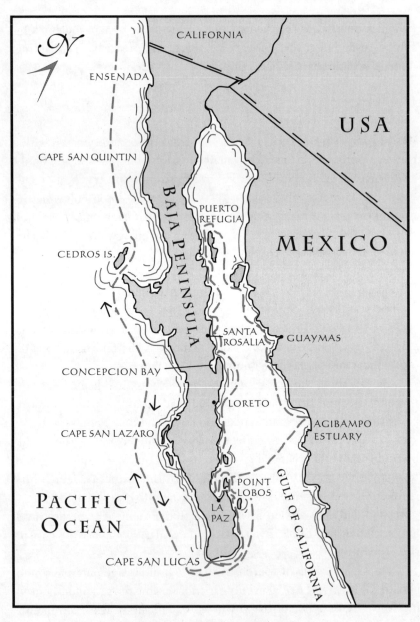

SEA OF CORTEZ
1940 Voyage of the *Western Flyer*

storytelling and saluting the crew—"perhaps the strangest crew ever signed aboard a local work boat," in the words of a reporter from the *Monterey Peninsula Herald.*

There was Captain Tony Berry, a serious young man with dark, brooding eyes; Hal "Tex" Travis, the engineer; Horace "Sparky" Enea, a short Italian seaman and cook; Ratzi "Tiny" Colletto, a suave ex-boxer who was the ship's Don Juan and deckhand; an aloof Steinbeck; his wife, Carol, sporting a yachtsman's cap and binoculars; and the Row's ever enigmatic Ricketts, whose neatly trimmed beard and "twinkling eyes," as the reporter described them, made him the most distinguished looking of the unlikely gang of explorers.

As the newspaperman was about to snap a photograph, Steinbeck slipped conspicuously behind everyone, hiding his face behind Carol's head. Later he explained to Sparky that he did not want his face known any more than necessary. Indeed, the crew shouldn't *ever* photograph him during the trip. A published picture, he uttered conspiratorially, could be used as a way of identifying him for the purpose of blackmail.

The expedition was, in fact, an escape. Steinbeck wanted to get away from the controversy surrounding *The Grapes of Wrath.* He also planned to coauthor with Ricketts a "leisurely journal of travel and research" in the spirit of Darwin's *Voyage of the Beagle.* It was an unusual turn for America's most celebrated and vilified novelist of 1939. The collaborative writing venture with Ricketts—the first and only for John Steinbeck—would be the author's salvation from the world.

Just past noon, empty whiskey bottles clinking on deck, the *Western Flyer* set off toward the southern tip of Monterey Bay, where a white, frothy line demarcated the open ocean, and marked, symbolically, a threshold of sorts for John Steinbeck. A strong north wind blew and Steinbeck heard the whistling buoy roar "like a perplexed and mournful bull." He hoped the intimacy of a voyage at sea would mend his frayed marriage to Carol and carry him away, at least temporarily, from worldly and professional woes. The scientific expedition would be about relearning a fundamental biological truth: "the first rule of life is living."

The crew's hard work—scouring sun-baked beaches, collecting thousands of specimens and packing them in the boat's fish hold each

TOP: *Some of the crew pose on the* Western Flyer's *bridge for a newspaper photo. Back row, left to right: Engineer Hal Travis, Captain Tony Berry, John Steinbeck (hiding conspicuously behind his wife Carol), Ratzi Colletto. Front row, left to right: "Sparky" Enea, Mrs. Tony Berry (who stayed behind) and Carol Steinbeck.*
COURTESY OF THE NATIONAL STEINBECK CENTER AND THE *MONTEREY PENINSULA HERALD.*

BOTTOM: *The* Western Flyer. COURTESY OF ED RICKETTS JR.

Left to right: Two Mexican hunting guides, John Steinbeck and Ed Ricketts in Puerto Escondido during the Gulf expedition, 1940. This is the only known photograph of Ricketts and Steinbeck together. COURTESY OF TONI VOLCANI.

day—was only eclipsed by their hard drinking and philosophizing. Both Steinbeck and Ricketts wanted to be lost in time, and the Gulf provided just such a refuge.

Reading *Sea of Cortez*, one can readily visualize Ricketts and Steinbeck reclined on the *Western Flyer*'s deck with bottles of cold Carta Blanca, floating under a starry night. They would often play a game they called "speculative metaphysics," in which their thoughts would meander and branch out "like a tree growing tall and bushy." Finally, they came to agree that the unifying idea of ecology should emerge as the central theme of their coauthored book, which would consist of a long narrative and an appendix of species collected.

After more than five weeks of exploration, the *Western Flyer* turned toward home on April 13. As it rounded Cape San Lucas into the open ocean, the sky grew threatening and the wind increased. Suddenly, a great clap of thunder exploded overhead and everyone braced himself as the seine boat plunged into the huge, rolling swells of the Pacific. For three days they battled foul weather. When they reached San Diego, they turned on the radio to learn of the Nazi invasion of Norway.

By this point Ricketts was terribly seasick, and he eagerly jumped ship in San Diego. In the last entry of his log, he wrote: "I had kept up in good spirits throughout but feel depressed and lonely now. Part probably hangover, part let-down from the last few days which were fairly happy, but most probably due to seeing how, when people come back from a trip, everyone has some one person who sidetracks everything else just for him. . . . [I]t's nice to be loved best and only, and who hasn't that lacks an important part of life."

Beyond lay a tempestuous world. For Ricketts, whose wife and two daughters had moved to Vancouver, Washington, in 1938, a longing for love and companionship would almost approach panic in the days and months to come. And like the thrashing vessel, heaving and pitching in the heavy seas, Steinbeck knew that he, too, faced a rising storm.

Barely a month after returning, *The Grapes of Wrath* won the Pulitzer Prize. Even though it had been in print over a year, *Grapes* was still receiving fiery, if by this time perfunctory, denunciations. Detractors accused its author of being a liar, and spread rumors that Steinbeck was a pervert, a drunkard, a dope fiend and that even impoverished, landless farm workers — the novel's heroic protagonists — wanted to kill him. Others attacked Steinbeck as a Jew and *The Grapes of Wrath* as, incredibly, a Zionist conspiracy. "The painting Steinbeck made in this book is a lie, a black, infernal creation of a twisted, distorted mind," railed one California congressman. It had been banned by school boards and even burned. While Steinbeck was away in the Sea of Cortez, First Lady Eleanor Roosevelt felt compelled to come to the writer's defense. "I have never believed that *The Grapes of Wrath* was exaggerated," she said after touring camps for migrant farm workers in California.

* * *

UPON returning to Monterey, John and Carol immediately departed for Mexico City (another escape), where Steinbeck would write and scout locations for a film. They returned to California a few months later, but

Steinbeck didn't begin to write *Sea of Cortez* until January 1941, a year in which he separated from Carol, sold the Los Gatos ranch and shacked up with Gwyn, the Hollywood actress and now his girlfriend, in a Pacific Grove bungalow.

Ricketts, who had tired of his lonely, bachelor lifestyle, was on the mend himself that year. He had met Toni Jackson, a young writer and mother who was going through a divorce in San Francisco. She was attractive and sprightly, and also a thoroughly modern woman: smart, opinionated and independent. They began a romantic correspondence and Ricketts grew close to her five-year-old daughter, Kay. By June, Ed and Toni were living together at the lab, while Kay stayed with relatives, since Cannery Row was no place to raise an impressionable young girl. Their relationship was unconventional for the times. Toni even took Ed's last name, on occasion, so as not to raise suspicion among Kay's schoolteachers.

It seems true, as Steinbeck once said, that "Ed did not like his sex uncomplicated," but the writer went too far when he suggested that if Ed "could have found a woman who was not only married, but a mother, in prison, and one of Siamese twins, he would have been delighted." Sex certainly fascinated and preoccupied Ricketts. He once wrote "an outline for the study of sex," in which he wanted to dissect sexuality from biological, ethnological and psychological perspectives. He talked openly about sex, and his scientific notebooks, as Steinbeck correctly claimed, do contain amusing asides on his own sexual relations. "This morning when I awakened Toni early," reads one such comment in a notebook, "I thought that men are justified in offering women any amount—a sack of gold, jewels, a mink coat, a car and an apartment—for sexual intercourse."

So one can imagine the excitement Ricketts must have felt when in June of 1941 Henry Miller, one of the most scandalous authors of his generation, walked into the lab. The expatriate writer was living in Paris, in part because his books were banned in the United States for being pornographic. He was touring his home country and had earlier in the year sent a letter to the lab looking for John Steinbeck, a fellow scandal-ridden writer. Toni, who was typing up the *Sea of Cortez* manuscript, recognized his name and dispatched an enthusiastic invitation.

Ricketts was enthralled, feeling an immediate connection to Miller. Later, in his "New Tidepool Book," after eighty-five pages of notes on marine invertebrates Ricketts made some tantalizing observations on the reproductive habits of Henry Miller: "He's hated or idealized — rarely rated fairly and for only a small part of his work, the so-called pornographic aspects. Miller had an active sexual drive, so active that he must have utilized it or else go crazy."

Ricketts gave the writer a copy of *Between Pacific Tides,* which Miller relished, and Steinbeck read him bits of *Sea of Cortez*, which he and Ricketts were finishing that month. Steinbeck liked Miller too, or at least that's what Ricketts told Miller. Actually, the two writers never became friends or corresponded. Ricketts, however, impressed Miller. "I saw Ed real and whole the moment he stepped over the threshold of the lab," Miller later recalled. The writer thought the biologist was "one of the rare souls on this earth." He sent Toni a copy of *Tropic of Cancer* and Ed a manuscript copy of *The World of Sex.* (Both books were prohibited entry into the United States at the time.) Although Miller felt his American visit was futile — "The country is vast and empty," he told Ricketts. "The most depressing country I know of. I loathe it" — he said their meeting had made his entire trip worthwhile. He liked the Pacific Coast so much that upon his return to the United States in 1944 he moved to Big Sur, just down the road.

Toni finished typing the manuscript of *Sea of Cortez* the next month (and actually wrote its short glossary). Steinbeck wrote the book largely from a log kept by Ricketts (the writer didn't keep a log himself), some of the biologist's scientific writings and one of Ricketts' philosophical essays. The draft was then passed back and forth for corrections and comments. Ricketts was immensely satisfied with the result. They had collected more than six hundred species, sixty of which were unknown to science at the time. "It would be an understatement for me to say that this little trip of ours is growing to be an important expedition," he told Steinbeck, "and that out of it are coming some fairly significant contributions to invertebrate zoology, to marine sociology and even — I wouldn't be surprised — to human thought."

Pat Covici, Steinbeck's editor at Viking, had recommended that the book's authorship be broken up, with Steinbeck taking credit for the

270-page narrative and Ricketts for the 328-page phyletic catalog of collected species. "I find your suggestion outrageous," Steinbeck shot back. "This book is the product of the work and thinking of both of us, and the setting down of the words is of no importance. I not only disapprove of your plan but forbid it." The writer and biologist were emotionally and intellectually entwined in the book. "We worked together, and so closely," Steinbeck later admitted, "that I do not know in some cases who started which line of speculation since the end thought was the product of both minds. I do not know whose thought it was."

* * *

SEA *of Cortez: A Leisurely Journal of Travel and Research* was really part of a larger undertaking, first conceptualized by Ricketts, but then taken up enthusiastically by Steinbeck. Perhaps as early as 1932, upon returning from his expedition to Alaska with Jack Calvin and Joseph Campbell, Ricketts conceived of producing a manual of invertebrates for the entire Pacific Coast of North America. He had wanted *Between Pacific Tides* to cover the coast from Mexico to Alaska, but he had to concede that central California had received "undue attention," largely because of expediency; traveling to coastal hinterlands, south to the Baja and north to the Aleutians, was logistically difficult, time consuming and prohibitively expensive.

With book royalties flooding in at a level unimaginable only a few years before, Steinbeck bought half the stock in Pacific Biological Laboratories in 1939. The bank loan to rebuild the lab after the catastrophic fire was, Steinbeck knew, "bleeding the laboratory like a cat in the basement." Ricketts' livelihood and the lab's very existence — never mind the prospects of faraway scientific adventures — were in peril. So Steinbeck saved the "improbable business" and his friend from bankruptcy.

Even after *Sea of Cortez* was finished, there was still a glaring hole in the Steinbeck-Ricketts collaboration: the stormy waters of the extreme North Pacific. The crew of the *Western Flyer* kicked around the idea of a "northern sequel" to *Sea of Cortez* upon their return. On February 11, 1942, Ricketts laid out his aspirations in a letter to Stanford University Press:

"My study of the marine invertebrates has divided itself geographically into three divisions. The first, on the animals of the US and Canada, appeared in [*Between Pacific Tides*]. A second, the appendix to 'Sea of Cortez,' extended the range to the south. . . . The third part . . . will deal with the Aleutians, Gulf of Alaska, Bering Sea, etc."

Yet the northern sequel, the final book in an ecological trilogy of the Pacific, would have to wait.

* * *

STANLEY Edgar Hyman, writing in *The New Republic,* was one of the few critics who understood the significance of *Sea of Cortez.* Although Hyman egregiously failed to even mention Ed Ricketts in his review, he saw the book as a "valuable key" to Steinbeck's beliefs and ideas:

> Not only is "Sea of Cortez" the record of an ecological study of marine fauna, but all Steinbeck's books are now revealed as ecological studies. "The Grapes of Wrath" was a textbook in ecology, from the dust storms that forced the Okies off their land (unscientific farming and inadequate conservation were a crime against ecology, and dust and drought were the punishment) to the crimes against social ecology that the Associated Farmers sprang on the Joads in California.

This "valuable key," however, sank into oblivion almost immediately upon release, leaving Edmund Wilson's misguided critique to color a generation of literary scholars. Two days after its publication on December 5, 1941, the Japanese attacked Pearl Harbor. As hysteria swept the country, America largely forgot the book; its sales were meager and it soon went out of print.

Everyone redirected himself for the war effort. Steinbeck moved to the East Coast with Gwyn, whom he later married. He lived primarily in New York and volunteered for a variety of wartime agencies. He wrote the propagandist novel *The Moon Is Down* (which included a "Doc" character) about resistance to Nazi occupation for the agency that eventually became the CIA, and he wrote *Bombs Away* for the U.S. Air Force. He also went to Europe and North Africa as a war correspondent in 1943. Still, his thoughts never strayed far from the Pacific Coast, as he wrote a friend while waiting to go overseas: "all last week I had a strong nostalgia for the Peninsula. Got to dreaming about it. I wish I could go back. . . . I hope when [the war] is over that I'll have a little money left so I can go back to the Grove and spend a couple years on a book I want to write."

Ed Ricketts also enthusiastically volunteered his unique skills for the war effort. He met with U.S. Navy intelligence officers in San Francisco to offer his scientific services. He was doing extensive research on the Japanese Pacific Islands, gathering copious information on their geology, biology and oceanography. Ricketts planned to write a book about the so-called Mandated Islands. He figured, rather naïvely as it turned out, that the navy would appreciate his specialized knowledge when planning beach invasions and high-seas warfare amid these little-known islands. Steinbeck even wrote a letter to the Secretary of the Navy on his behalf, but the offer was ignored. Ricketts remained in Monterey throughout the war, serving as a U.S. Army medical technician at the local barracks, the Presidio.

Ricketts was uninspired by his duties and soon grew bored and, apparently, mischievous. At one point he combined grenadine, alcohol and codeine from the medical dispensary to make a fiery cocktail dubbed "Ricketts' Folly." Steinbeck later heard "that the commanding officer of the unit, and he a major at that, after two drinks of it had marched smartly and with no hint of stagger right into a wall, and that he had made a short heroic speech as he slid to the ground." After his release from the army in July of 1943—Ricketts joked that he was discharged on account of "physical decrepitude, extreme age, [and] bad moral effect on the younger men (they say I drink, and not alone)"—the biologist took a job as a chemist for the California Packing Corporation, or Cal Pack. He also began planning an expedition to complete the "northern sequel."

Longing for his old friends and native country, Steinbeck moved back to Pacific Grove in October 1944 with Gwyn and their newborn son. Ricketts was bolstered by his friend's return. He wrote to Dr. L. R. Blinks, the new director of Hopkins Marine Station, on November 11, describing how he and Steinbeck were going to finish their trilogy of the

BERING
SEA

ALEUTIAN ISLANDS

GULF OF ALASKA

CANADA

QUEEN CHARLOTTE
ISLANDS

Pacific Biological Station,
Nanaimo (1908)

VANCOUVER
ISLAND

Minnesota Seaside Station,
Botanical Beach (1901-06)

Friday Harbor Laboratories,
San Juan Islands (1904)

Oregon Institute of Marine Biology,
Coos Bay (1931)

USA

Hopkins Marine Station,
Pacific Grove (1891)

Kerckhoff Marine Laboratory,
New Port Bay (1928)

Scripps Institution, La Jolla (1903)

MEXICO

PACIFIC
OCEAN

GULF OF
CALIFORNIA

PACIFIC COAST
OF NORTH AMERICA

Pacific. "The plan," he wrote, "is to complete this by an investigation and report on the extreme North Pacific, then to build up a working collection of specimens and the necessary library, and finally to work up a fairly comprehensive manual of the marine invertebrates . . . from the Bering Sea to Panama."

Yet as Ricketts' enthusiasm grew, Steinbeck's romanticism for the Pacific Coast quickly faded. He complained about "the feeling of persecution." In Monterey, businesspeople refused to rent office space to him, the gas board cut his wartime rations and a permit to renovate his house was refused. Many people still considered the writer a radical and a traitor for vilifying California's landowners in his novels. Some locals would cross the street rather than pass him on the sidewalk. Steinbeck thought the townspeople had become "pure poison." Friends even came to resent his money and celebrity. "The old easy relation isn't there," Dook told him. "I find that I'm afraid of you—or what you've become." Steinbeck felt betrayed.

"You remember how happy I was to come back here," he wrote Pascal Covici in the spring of 1945. "It really was a home coming. Well, there is no home coming nor any welcome. What there is is jealousy and hatred and the knife in the back. I'm beginning to think I made a mistake."

A mere five months after his return, Steinbeck left for Mexico to do more filmmaking. He went with great bitterness, unsure if he would ever return to California. "This isn't my country anymore," he mourned. "And it won't be until I am dead. It makes me very sad." It was a prophetic statement, considering that today the area is known around the world as "Steinbeck Country."

However, there was one person who would eventually draw him back to California. "Our old friends won't have us back," he told Covici, "—always except for Ed. . . . There's no one to talk to except Ed."

In April 1945, as Steinbeck left Monterey, Ricketts started preparing for his first expedition to the wilderness coast of Vancouver Island in British Columbia. He would leave the next month, accompanied by Toni. The voyage would be the first in a series exploring the "outer shores," as Ricketts called the North Pacific region, which included the West Coast of Vancouver Island, the remote Queen Charlotte archipelago, the outer islands of southeast Alaska and the 1,200-mile string of islands known as the Aleutians. Steinbeck would join him on the final trip and coauthor the third book in the trilogy, *The Outer Shores.·*

* * *

RICKETTS' and Steinbeck's trilogy of the Pacific—an ecological treatise whose zoological and geographic scope was staggering, encompassing some two thousand marine species and stretching more than four thousand miles, as the seagull flies, from the Baja to the Bering Sea—would be a spectacular feat. It would be the most comprehensive inventory of the Pacific Coast's fauna ever written. It would also be one of the greatest surveys of seashore ecology ever attempted.

But more than that—more than anything else—the trilogy would be the measure of a profound relationship between Ed Ricketts and John Steinbeck, which was "closer than most friends and closer, without any sexual implications, than most husbands and wives."

HYPSOBLENNIOPS RICKETTSI, BLENNY, NEW SPECIES
COLLECTED BY ED RICKETTS ON MARCH 28, 1940,
IN CONCEPCION BAY, BAJA CALIFORNIA, MEXICO.

CHAPTER THREE

TERRA INCOGNITA

The hero adventures out of the land we know into darkness…

—JOSEPH CAMPBELL, *The Hero with a Thousand Faces*

ON the night of Saturday, June 2, 1945, the hefty cast-iron hands on the clock tower of Victoria's city hall stopped ticking at 10:30 P.M. So loud was the ring of the tower's 2,170-pound bell, and so quiet was this quaint capital of British Columbia, that city officials turned off the clock so as not to disturb their tired citizens. After six of the grimmest, bloodiest years of the twentieth century, spring had not only brought fine weather and new blossoms, but also peace in Europe on the eighth of May. Headlines in the city's *Daily Colonist* spoke of more good news to come: GREATEST RAID YET ON TOKYO'S PLANTS! JAPS LOSE HEAVILY IN OKINAWA ATTACK! JAPS FLEE AS CHINESE DRIVE ON! Victorians slept sounder that spring night than they had in years.

At around eleven o'clock, though, a short blast of a steam whistle pierced the city's quietude. Down on the Belleville Street dock, the S.S. *Princess Norah* was about to set sail.

Ed and Toni had arrived in Victoria's inner harbor early that morning. Laden with twelve heavy trunks, they'd left Monterey on May 31 aboard the 8:05 A.M. Del Monte Express for San Francisco, where they transferred to train No. 24 for a twenty-six-hour ride to the King Street Station in Seattle. They then boarded a ferry that sailed on an overnight voyage up Puget Sound, zigzagged through the verdant San Juan Islands and then crossed the international borderline into Victoria, nestled on the southern tip of Vancouver Island. Ricketts had been to Victoria several times before, in the 1920s and '30s, to collect in the region. He enjoyed its colonial charms immensely.

The *Princess Norah* would take them from Victoria to the island's outer shores. The ship, boasted a tourist pamphlet, was a "new and luxuriously appointed steamer" that was temporarily replacing her older, smaller and less comfortable sister ship, the *Princess Maquinna*, during the busy summertime schedule. "The *Maquinna* is an ugly ship," remembered one passenger. "With her thin, elongated funnel and her ill-proportioned bow, she is ugly from any direction in which you look at her. But like the Ugly Princess of the fairy tale she has stolen the hearts of the people, and I doubt if any vessel afloat could be more beloved." She also stole the affections of Ed Ricketts, who sailed aboard her when she returned to regular service later that month. He took special note of the *Maquinna*'s specifications in his travel log, but barely mentioned the *Norah*.

About fifteen minutes past eleven o'clock, the *Norah* left the terminal. With war still raging in the Pacific, the steamship was completely blacked out. It ploughed its way out of the harbor into Juan de Fuca Strait and then out along the island's southwest coast. The region's windswept, unsheltered headlands and wicked seas have claimed so many ships—more than 150 in as many years—that mariners call it the "Graveyard of the Pacific."

The search for the elusive Northwest Passage had brought Captain James Cook here in 1778, but he saw little in the sorrowful weather. "It is in this very latitude where we now are," Cook confided to his log book, "that geographers have placed the pretended Straits of Juan de Fuca. But we saw nothing, nor is there the slightest probability that any such ever existed."

Ricketts had read those very words in Cook's published journals while conducting research on the region in the library at the University of California, Berkeley. He was well aware of the travails of early explorers. "One of the charms of these outer shores is that the methods of transportation are two generations back," he noted. Sounding, for instance, was done with a handheld rope and weight. In fog or darkness, the captain would simply sound the ship's whistle and listen for its returning echo to gauge the distance from shore. This type of dead reckoning was risky and often led to tragic consequences.

In 1906 the American passenger ship *Valencia* had left San Francisco with 154 people aboard. Blindfolded by fog and swept north by currents, it finally grounded at Pachena Point on Vancouver Island. Although they were a mere twenty yards from shore, most of the crew and passengers were unable to get to safety up the coast's steep cliffs. For two days, a ferocious sea pounded the vessel until it broke in two, sending 117 people to their deaths. Only the sinking of the *Titanic* six years later could outdo the horror and magnitude of the disaster.

The coast had earned its deadly "Graveyard" moniker. Indeed, the sea has been a source of fear throughout the ages. It has come to symbolize the unknown, the unconscious, the infinite and the primal abyss. In ancient Greece, the god Oceanus reigned over the sea and later the word *oceanus* came to mean those waters which lay far outside the sight of land. Christianity did not demystify the pagan sea gods, but demonized them instead. What began in the mythical age evolved and twisted into a modern maritime cult of superstitions, taboos, tall tales and sea serpents. "An ocean without its unnamed monsters," Steinbeck and Ricketts wrote in *Sea of Cortez*, "would be like a completely dreamless sleep." As far back as the Bible, the sea had represented the omnipotence, and vengeance, of God:

> *They that go down to the sea in ships, that do business in great waters;*
> *These see the works of the LORD, and his wonders in the deep.*

Yet those who did venture along Vancouver Island's outer coast weren't in God's hands alone, but also in those of Captain Martin MacKinnon. In 1916, the young seaman joined the *Maquinna* and served fourteen years as its third, second and first officer. He then captained another steamer for nine years before returning to the *Maquinna* as master in 1939. He spent more than half of his career sailing the same ship along the same route. Once a passenger asked MacKinnon how he knew where the myriad rocks were. "I have no idea where all the rocks are," he replied, "but I know where they aren't."

Ricketts and the captain felt an immediate affinity for one another. Toni thought they acted like long-lost brothers. And like his friendship with Steinbeck, it started with a drink. "Capt. MacKinnon, scotch as the country he came from," Ricketts later told Steinbeck, "was a very friendly and a very inquisitive and . . . a very drunken man." Every time the steamer called into the port where Ricketts stayed that summer, the captain would "light on down the path and come up to my place for a little talk and, he'd hope (and was generally right), a drop of whiskey."

Every ten days, MacKinnon would take passengers on a night-sea journey from picturesque Victoria to a dark wilderness coast. Little news came from the outer shores; even the "Mail & Ships" column in the *Daily Colonist* made no mention of the West Coast route. Most stories were of pioneer hardship or harrowing shipwrecks: sometimes several vessels would be lost in a single squall. Headline writers, hardly dipping their pen nibs into the inkwell of hyperbole, would describe the route as the "Worst Run in the World."

"It's amazing how few people even in Victoria have been on the West Coast," Ricketts confided to his journal, "it's far more a *terra incognita* to them than here it was to us. . . . They regard it as an almost hopeless wilderness of rain and storm."

*   *   *

TERRA *incognita* the outer shores certainly were. Vancouver Island was one of the world's last great islands, about 12,400 square miles, to be discovered and mapped by European explorers.

The Pacific, some seventy million square miles blanketing a third of the earth's surface and more than twice the size of the Atlantic, leapt belatedly into the world's consciousness. In the sixteenth century, Portuguese discoverer Ferdinand Magellan named it *Mar Pacifica*. Spanish explorer Balboa traversed the Isthmus of Panama in search of gold and first stepped foot on the Pacific Coast in 1513. Spanish ships slowly inched their way north, arriving in San Francisco Bay by the 1540s.

Maps showing Spanish exploration at the time depicted a coastline that simply disappeared above Baja California. The immense Pacific was nothing more than a "South Sea," as it was popularly known. Its northern hemisphere was a mysterious void, a cartographic question mark. Over the next two hundred years, the north Pacific would be depicted with imaginary continents, fictitious inland seas and lost islands. In 1650, Joannes Jansson's map of the South Sea showed a vast *Terra*

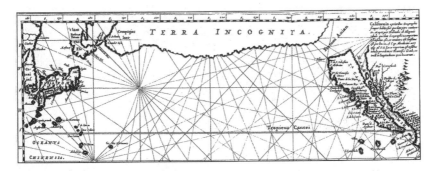

"South Sea" map by Joannes Jansson, 1650, shows terra incognita *where the North Pacific actually lies.*

Incognita continent stretching to Asia, where the North Pacific actually lay. It also depicted the Baja Peninsula as an island, a common misapprehension at the time.

An actual coastline—a vague contour that was nothing more than a dotted line for thousands of miles—started to appear on world maps by 1784. Russian fur traders and explorers (the most famous being Vitus Bering) island hopped along the Aleutian chain southward, while the Spanish sailed northward from their new settlement at Monterey, established in 1770. From there, Juan Perez set sail in the *Santiago* in 1774 to Vancouver Island and the Queen Charlotte Islands; Cook came next in 1778 on his final round-the-world voyage; and then French explorer La Pérouse arrived a decade later to chart the area and improve Cook's initial maps.

Yet Vancouver Island would not become an *island*—at least not on maps—until its namesake, Captain George Vancouver, conducted a detailed survey and circumnavigation from 1792 to 1794. So by the time Captain MacKinnon was plying the West Coast route more than a century later, these were certainly well charted waters—at least hydrographically speaking. Yet there was still much to be discovered about Vancouver Island's stormy coast in 1945.

* * *

BRITISH COLUMBIA
CANADA

Quatsino Sound

PORT ALICE

CAPE COOK

Kyuquot

Kyuquot Sound

Ceepeecee

VANCOUVER ISLAND

Nootka Sound

Hesquiat

ESTEVAN POINT

Ahousat

Clayoquot Sound

TOFINO/CLAYOQUOT

Kildonan

PORT ALBERNI

UCLUELET

VANCOUVER

Barkley Sound

BAMFIELD

Clo-oose

JUAN DE FUCA STRAIT

PORT RENFREW

N

Canada/USA Border

VICTORIA

CAPE FLATTERY

PACIFIC OCEAN

USA

- - - - -

Ricketts' Route

SEATTLE

THE OUTER SHORES
1945 Voyage to Vancouver Island

THE *Norah's* first stop was at Port Renfrew, several hours' journey from Victoria. The ship then continued on to the village of Clo-oose, home of the Ditidaht tribe, arriving around five o'clock the next morning. Captain MacKinnon, who was "still slightly swacked (but a better seaman than his sober young mate)," tried to find a mooring buoy off Clo-oose, whose location on the unprotected coast prohibited the construction of a landing wharf.

Clo-oose had attracted dozens of émigré families who came because of promises of a road, railway and a three-hundred-room tourist resort—none of which ever materialized. The poor settlers struggled. Family heirlooms and livestock were lost coming ashore at Clo-oose, whose name, ironically, means "safe landing" in the local native dialect. Often winter weather was too brutal for ships to deliver supplies and food. For weeks at a time, settlers ate little more than seashore fauna. "When the tide was out, the table was set," a missionary's wife recalled, "and when the tide came in, the dishes were washed."

On that dreary early morning of Ricketts' arrival, only a few families remained. They waited on the shore for hours in a bone-chilling fog. MacKinnon sounded the ship's horn, hoping that the native boatmen and settlers could hear the whistle—the familiar *long-short-long-short* blast—three or four miles from shore.

"Doc, this is the shit of a life," MacKinnon complained to Ricketts in his Scottish brogue.

By the time the *Norah's* anchor was dropped and engine turned off, the silhouette of a canoe appeared out of the fog. With great agility, the natives paddled over the rolling surf. "They are like the Gulf [of California] Indians," Ricketts wrote, "they're born in their dugouts." From the top deck, Ricketts watched as the Clo-oose natives slid alongside the iron hull in their red-cedar canoes. It was almost twenty feet from the *Norah's* top deck to the dugout bobbing in the waves below. The native boatmen and the *Norah's* crew passed five or six children back and forth when the canoe rose on the crest of a wave. "The kids are perfectly quiet," Ricketts observed, "they make no sound or motion, I suppose [they are] scared but you can't tell it from their action." One piece of freight slipped from a crewman's hands and plunged into the frigid water, but it was instantly recovered.

Many of the Ditidahts came aboard the steamer just to buy newspapers and magazines or to eat a "swank" meal in the dining room. "It must be quite wonderful for them to come aboard from their wilderness and not very good houses, onto a warm, dry, brilliantly lighted steamer with all the trappings of the civilization that's so far away from them...," Ricketts wrote. "For 10 cents they can buy the wonderful and illustrated adventures of Superman."

As the steamship continued up the coast, briefly stopping to supply several lighthouses, Ricketts would occasionally retire to his stateroom to read, or spend time on deck breathing in the salt air. "I would read and eat and sleep and watch those Indians, a wonderful restful time," Ricketts wrote in his log. "And go out in the rain and wind and see that fantastic coastline go by. I get a curious feeling that's a combination of fear of the sea and of seasickness, and cold, and liking of the sea and its animals and loving that lovely difficult west coast; it's very exhilarating."

Around noon the next day, some twelve hours since their departure, Captain MacKinnon navigated the ship into Bamfield, located in the sheltered waters of Barkley Sound. The small hamlet was home to the terminus of the transpacific cable to Australia and also the Shipwreck Mariners' Trail, which ran through the dense rainforest to Port Renfrew.

Ricketts assembled his supplies and equipment for an exploration of the local tide pools during the *Norah*'s lackadaisical stopover here. He carried a small rucksack of supplies and various instruments: raincoats, a roll of local charts, flashlight, tide table, jars of alcohol to preserve specimens, a first-aid kit and, of course, "a little whiskey, never forget the whiskey."

Ed and Toni found a trail to the seashore. "That first sight of the rocks in a new region is certainly marvelous," Ricketts wrote. They perused the shore and gathered a few specimens of red-spine sea urchins, purple-ringed top snails, tubeworms with tangerine tentacles, anemones that looked like giant white powder puffs, marine moss, sponges and scores of snapping crabs. All in all, some forty to fifty species were collected in that one brief stop.

The steamer left Bamfield and headed back out into the sound and through the Broken Group Islands. It steamed inland and up a twenty-five-mile-long inlet that led to Port Alberni. Along the way, the *Norah* stopped first at Kildonan, a cannery town elevated on pilings at the base of a steep fjord, and then carried on to several logging camps. At Franklin River, with racing tides and howling winds, Captain MacKinnon experienced grave difficulty bringing the *Norah* into dock. "Takes a nice skill and judgment in handling," Ricketts observed. MacKinnon attempted a landing three times, wasting almost an hour, before securing the ship to the dock. "It's like MacKinnon says, a shit of a life," Ricketts recalled. "No wonder he drinks."

After an overnight stop in Port Alberni—"The metropolis of the west coast," according to Ricketts, because of its railway, cinema, restaurants, liquor store, fine hotel, and plywood mill—the steamer headed back down the inlet to the western entrance of Barkley Sound and a small native and fishing village called Ucluelet. Pronounced *you-CLUE-let*, the name means "people with the safe landing place" in the native language. Ricketts thought it was one of the best names on the coast, sounding "like the song of a thrush." The steamer left Ucluelet in the early afternoon, passing a rocky headland on which squatted the Amphitrite Point Lighthouse, which looked like a tiny Aztec temple. The *Princess Norah* then traveled west for some thirty miles, to another lighthouse on Lennard Island. The steamer slipped behind the island and into a vast inland sound.

Stubbs Island is a tiny pearl of an island nestled protectively in an immense oyster of natural beauty known as Clayoquot (pronounced *CLAH-quat*) Sound. Barely half a mile wide, the island, thick with evergreens, is capped on its north shore with golden sand dunes that sweep out to two points in the water. As the *Princess Norah* plied through Clayoquot Sound's strong tidal currents on the dreary evening of June 4, 1945, the island's beaches seemed to sparkle, however faintly, in this dark, brooding land. Ed and Toni disembarked at a small settlement on the island in the heart of the archipelago.

* * *

WHAT was once *terra incognita* is no longer. "One day," wrote a Clayoquot pioneer in 1945, "when the war is over all the West Coast territory will be opened up. There is so much yet unknown, so much beauty unimagined, so much unexplored, a wealth of mines and riches, and one day it will be the greatest playground of the Pacific. People will swarm in and the silence will be broken."

And she was right. In the 1990s, Clayoquot Sound and its ancient cedars, hemlocks and Sitka spruce became, in the words of environmental lawyer Robert F. Kennedy Jr., "the flashpoint in one of the defining environmental battles of our time." The fight between logging companies, the local Clayoquot tribes and conservationists took on global proportions. Hollywood director Oliver Stone even spearheaded a group of glitterati—including Tom Cruise, Barbra Streisand and Robert Redford—who denounced clear-cut logging in Clayoquot Sound as a "chainsaw massacre" in a full-page ad in the *New York Times*. The conflict eventually culminated in the largest mass arrest (more than 850 people) in the history of Canada.

In 2000, the United Nations declared Clayoquot Sound a UNESCO Biosphere Reserve because of its pristine temperate rainforest—a relatively untouched trove of biodiversity. Today one million visitors swarm to the region each year—tourists, environmental protesters, sport fishermen, surfers, students, newlyweds, the rich and famous, retirees and armies of academics, researchers and scientists. It is arguably one of the most studied ecosystems in North America, if not the world.

Yet in 1945, the West Coast of Vancouver Island was a veritable unknown to scientists. Although Ricketts was on a trek well traveled by Enlightenment explorers, in those days naturalists spent most of their time exploring the coast's lush rainforests. After weathering thousands of miles of ocean, the officers and seamen, malnourished and suffering scurvy, only turned to the sea for food. They discovered from the Nuu-chah-nulth native people, whom Cook mistakenly called Nookta, a cornucopia in the brine: salmon, mussels, clams, halibut, rockfish, lingcod.

Captain Cook may not have found the Northwest Passage, the coveted trade route to China from Europe, but the newfound waters and their creatures would come to serve imperial purposes nonetheless; sealing, whaling and fishing provided food and materials for an industrializing Europe. So in 1857, when the Lords of the Admiralty dispatched H.M.S. *Plumper* to survey the Pacific Coast's fish populations, it was to inventory the natural riches for the plucking of empire. By the beginning of the twentieth century, the British Society for the Advancement of Science had declared the Pacific Coast "the great resource of the food supply of the Empire."

The eager Americans dispatched their own research vessels here too, the *Hassler* in 1881 and the *Albatross* in 1888. They also established the coast's first biological station, the University of Minnesota Seaside Station, in 1901, at Botanical Beach near Port Renfrew. So extensive was American exploration in the area that by 1961, when *Fishes of the Pacific Coast of Canada* was published, almost two-thirds of the species had been collected and described by American scientists.

The science of ecology came to this coast rather late, however. Marine ecology was born in 1832 with the publication of French zoologists J. V. Audouin and Henri Milne-Edwards's scheme of intertidal zonation. Soon all of Europe seemed to be scouring beaches, clutching in their hands recent copies of Edward Forbe's *A Natural History of European Seas* or Philip Henry Gosse's superbly illustrated *A Naturalist's Rambles on the Devonshire Coast*. "[T]he fever of seashore study reached strange heights in Victorian England," Dr. Joel Hedgpeth wrote in *Treatise on Marine Ecology and Paleoecology,* "when a well-ordered holiday was incomplete without exercises in the identification of seaweeds and zoophytes."

This zeal swept across the Atlantic and around the world thanks to the *Challenger* Expedition in 1872, which heralded the beginning of oceanography as a science. The next year, the United States Fish Commission published its first report, which included A. E. Verrill and S. I. Smith's classic "Report upon the invertebrate animals of Vineyard Sound." In 1888, the Woods Hole Marine Biological Laboratory at Cape Cod was established, and Pacific outposts soon followed: Hopkins Marine Station in Pacific Grove (1891), Minnesota Seaside Station near Port Renfrew (1901), Friday Harbor Laboratory in Puget Sound (1903), Scripps Institution in La Jolla (1903), and Pacific Biological Station on Vancouver Island's East Coast (1908).

By the 1920s and '30s, a flood of tidal and oceanic research was being conducted around the world: Charles William Beebe—the Jacque Cousteau of his day—published *Galapagos, World's End* in 1924 (Ricketts owned a copy); Johnson and Snook's *Seashore Animals of the Pacific Coast* came out a few years later; researchers began the Great Barrier Reef Expedition in 1928; and T. A. and Anne Stephenson conducted a ten-year survey of the South African coast in the 1930s. Ricketts had read these books and many earlier works: *The Naturalist in Australia* (1897), *The Depths of the Sea* (1874), *Three Cruises of the United States Coast and Geodetic Survey Steamer "Blake"* (1888), and *A Naturalist in Indian Seas* (1902).

Yet in searching scholarly journals and bibliographies at Berkeley, Ricketts came up with but a trifle of studies about Vancouver Island's outer coast. What research had been done was zoological in nature and, as was in vogue among scientists, terribly specialized: research on a new species of this or that, bacteriology or, for example, an examination of the nervous system of barnacles. There was little in the way of ecological work. The aforementioned Victor E. Shelford, a pioneer ecologist, spent some time at Botanical Beach and Friday Harbor doing ecological surveys, but admittedly never really followed up on his marine work.

Compared with much of the world, the seashore of Vancouver Island—especially its rugged West Coast—was relatively unmapped, scientifically anyway. At the time of Ricketts' journey, there had been no major ecological surveys. "The cataloguing of what we've got and how and where it occurs is the first step in any inquiry," Ricketts wrote in his log. "Until we have that we can't start. And on the Pacific coast of North America, more than perhaps anywhere else in the world except the equivalent coasts of South America and Africa, we haven't that."

So that day in Bamfield, with Ricketts dipping his surgeon-like hands into the tide pools, marks a milestone in the region's rather short history of scientific discovery. It was a mere 167 years since Cook's naturalist, William Anderson, had first set foot on the coast. Yet Ed Ricketts had a plan that was radically different from the eighteenth- and nineteenth-century naturalists and modern marine biologists who came before him. "The average expedition," he wrote to Steinbeck about their modus operandi in the Gulf, "takes material indiscriminately by dredging, seining, tow-netting both in deep water and on the surface and usually far from land, and pays special attention to rare or unknown forms. We operated on the opposite plan: the commoner the animal, the more attention we devoted to it, since it, more than the total of all rare forms, was important in the biological economy."

Ed Ricketts wanted to systematically collect, catalog, identify and describe all the seashore species along with their habitats, and breeding and feeding patterns. It was the interplay of all these factors that fascinated him. He wanted to map the "biological economy" of Clayoquot Sound. Thus it was Ed Ricketts, first and foremost, who would bring the science of ecology to bear on the tide pools of this wicked wilderness coast.

BRANCHELLION LOBATA, MARINE LEECH, NEW SPECIES
COLLECTED BY ED RICKETTS IN FEBRUARY 1928 IN CALIFORNIA.

CHAPTER FOUR

CLAYOQUOT, STUBBS ISLAND

[I]t's certainly a lovely place of green gold hummingbirds, I never saw so many in my life before, and thrushes always singing, and rhododendrons in bloom until you can't see over them, and white sea gulls flying by the black mountains. I can't think of a better or a prettier place to come for work and rest, if you could get that pub to close down. Drink 'em out of beer is what I say.

—EDWARD F. RICKETTS,
Transcript of the Outer Shores Journal, 1945

IT was a welcoming, enchanting, even intoxicating place. Seafarers had been calling into Stubbs Island to get drunk ever since the local Clayoquot Trading Post started selling beer and hard liquor to sealing schooners in the 1890s. The lack of alcohol had always been one of the coast's great "hardships," as Ricketts lamented in his journal, making Stubbs a prized port of call for sailors and fishermen throughout the region's history.

"The liquor situation is pretty serious," Ricketts noted woefully. "On the whole west coast of Vancouver Island, an air line of perhaps 300 miles and a shore line of at least a thousand, there are only 2 government liquor stores, and 3 pubs."

On Saturday nights, pioneers living in the village of Tofino just a half-mile across the water, or even in homesteads dotting remote inlets thirty miles away, would travel by boat to the Clayoquot Hotel for a night of beer drinking. The hotel had a famous pub that was well known up and down the Pacific Coast. Ricketts had heard of it from Italian fishermen in California, who'd stop at the island on their annual pilgrimage to Alaska's salmon fishing grounds. Having the only pub on the outer coast, Clayoquot was paradise for Ricketts, who loved beer, a staple he rarely did without.

The original Clayoquot Hotel was built in the early 1890s, during the sealing industry's peak. It would burn down twice before the third and final hotel was raised in the early 1920s. Around the turn of the century, Stubbs was sold to local entrepreneurs Thomas Stockman and

TOP: *Clayoquot settlement on Stubbs Island with wharf trestle in the foreground and Lone Cone on Meares Island in the distance.* COURTESY OF THE HAMILTON FAMILY, KEN GIBSON COLLECTION.

BOTTOM: *Betty Farmer in front of Clayoquot Hotel, circa 1942.* COURTESY OF RUTH WHITE.

Walter Dawley. The latter then bequeathed it to Pierre Malon, his son-in-law, as part of a dowry. Bill White, a young crewman aboard the coast's hydrographical survey vessel, helped Malon at the hotel during the ship's off-season. A comedian, prankster and the life of any party, Bill was a natural slinging beers in the saloon. When the hotel's Chinese cook quit in 1939, Bill asked his sister Betty Farmer to come to Clayoquot to work. Betty's husband had died suddenly only a year or so before and she enthusiastically took up her brother's offer. She immediately fell in love with Stubbs Island and convinced Bill to be her business partner. Together, they purchased the entire island in 1941.

Short, slight and bespectacled, Betty's diminutive stature belied her larger-than-life persona and fierce determination. She got along well with everyone and had a special affection for the local Nuu-chah-nulth people. She always kept a watchful eye over patrons during bad drinking spells, too. She was a fantastic cook who ran a clean and respectable hotel. She was the island's matriarch, warm and affectionate, but not a woman you'd want to cross.

Immediately after the *Norah* docked, passengers scampered down a long, curved wooden pier to the Clayoquot Hotel, a two-story building clad in dark cedar shingles and white-trimmed windows. It housed some nine guestrooms, a kitchen, dining hall, ballroom and the pub. Upon arrival, Ricketts saw "people rushing ashore to get cases of beer." There was always great frenzy, and even greater thirst, at Clayoquot on "boat days."

The *Norah*'s crew unloaded their suitcases, collecting equipment, traveling bookcase and microscope case onto the wharf. Betty, Bill and his pregnant wife Ruth greeted Ed and Toni. Ruth remembered one thing—more than anything else—about that first meeting with Ed Ricketts. "He had very penetrating, bright brown eyes," she recalled. "They seemed to sparkle a lot."

The pioneer settlement included some tumbledown buildings by the wharf, a blacksmith's shop, a power station, hotel, schoolhouse, unused jail (it was originally built as a "drunk tank"), trading store and several cottages. The wooden buildings stood along a sheltered half-moon bay. There was also a "Japtown" of jerry-built homes back in the forest. It had been forcibly abandoned in 1942 when its residents,

Japanese-Canadian squatters, were declared "enemy aliens" and carted off to wartime internment camps. Ricketts made special note of the Japanese in his journal. "In 1945," he wrote, "there was a fine political fight going on up there, and [one] candidacy was announced on the bald platform 'We don't want the Japs in here—ever.'"

Ed and Toni were politically involved in this same struggle—the internment and subsequent release of Japanese-Americans during the Second World War—in Monterey. An impassioned Toni went on the stump, making speeches, organizing meetings and collecting names on a petition defending the rights of the Japanese to return to their homes unmolested. On May 11, 1945, the petition was published on a full page of the *Monterey Peninsula Herald.* The bold headline declared: THE DEMO-CRATIC WAY OF LIFE FOR ALL. John Steinbeck, by this time a famous writer, lent his name to the cause.

Ricketts, too, put pen to paper, feeling compelled "to blaze the trail of mutual understanding and respect." Besides signing the petition, on April 26, about a month before leaving for Clayoquot, he sent a blistering letter to the editor of the *Herald.* It began:

> The anonymous ad in Monday's *Herald* entitled "Organization to Discourage Returns of Japanese to the Pacific Coast" re-emphasizes to me Hitler's essential success as a teacher. We think of this former German leader, with his theory of racial superiority, as a complete failure.... But in this asylum of the oppressed, his seed bears fruit. It is ironical that only here his ideas live on, in a country built on a theory he shunned—the theory that all men, created equal, must be allowed equal opportunities in life, liberty and the pursuit of happiness, regardless of race or creed.

At risk of being targeted by vigilantes, Ricketts condemned the racist "hoodlums" who perpetrated drive-by shoots on Japanese-American homes and torched their property. Who would be next, he wondered, the Filipinos, Negroes, Jews, Chinese, Germans, Poles? "And so Hitler, suffering in his own land a death perhaps neglected and dishonored, richly succeeds here in America," Ricketts ended the letter. "Truly a prophet hath no honor in his own country."

Alas, such tolerance toward the Japanese was lacking in Clayoquot Sound after the war. The local town council passed a resolution that "all Orientals be excluded completely from this Municipality, and shall be prevented from owning property or carrying on business directly or indirectly within the Municipality." The Japanese-Canadians—stripped of their property, their livelihoods, their liberty and dignity—would never return to Stubbs Island. Today, a few old wine bottles, a rusted teakettle and bitter memories are all that remain of Japtown.

It had only been abandoned for three years, but by 1945 Ricketts found the island's "lush and tropical" vegetation overrunning the Japanese shantytown. "[I]t takes over very quickly an unused shack just as the jungle would," Ricketts noted. The tangle of devil's club, berry bushes, rhododendrons, salal, ferns and thick peat moss were a product of the heavy rains. Stubbs Island was within twenty miles of the wettest place in North America, Henderson Lake, which averaged some 170 inches of rainfall per year. The local weather observer recounted that the authorities in Victoria once asked him to recheck the incredible level of precipitation. "They didn't think that much rain possibly could have fallen in the past 24 hours," he told Ricketts. Yet when he went back to check the gauge, he found it overflowing. "[A]ctually he'd reported too little!" Ricketts noted.

Yet in this harsh land, Stubbs Island provided amenities aplenty. Situated midway up Vancouver Island, it was a perfect staging point for expeditions to adjacent fjords: Barkley Sound to the east and Nootka, Kyuquot and Quatsino Sounds to the west. "This whole island is very surprising to me," wrote Ricketts. "I had told Toni she must expect the very most rigorous in living conditions, dirt, discomfort, inconvenience and probably millions of fleas." Upon arrival, they were led through a chicken yard and cow pasture (Betty's cow, Dixie, was the island's milk supplier), up some "rickety" stairs to an apartment over the "junky" trading store.

"I almost fell down from surprise," Ricketts later recalled, upon entering his new summertime abode. "Hardwood floors, a bathroom that usually worked, running water that usually ran, electric lights during most of the night. Fantastic." Betty had adorned the "comfortable . . . even luxurious" apartment with a portrait of a stunning Burmese princess and a huge jolly Buddha. (Her husband had been a British colonial magistrate in Burma, now Myanmar.) Its "fantastic" library included titles on communism, socialism, labor unions and Russian literature, reflecting Betty's politics. (Some locals jokingly referred to Clayoquot as the "Little Kremlin.") Ricketts also found a fine natural history book, *Common Life of the Sea Shore*, and one of his favorites, mystic Jacob Boehme's *Signature of All Things*. He had only come across Boehme's book two other times in his life and was elated to thumb through the precious title.

* * *

RICKETTS was enamored with Clayoquot's majestic landscape and storied past. He had borrowed from the Victoria public library a copy of *British Columbia Coast Names: Their Origin and History 1592–1906,* by John T. Walbran, captain of the Canadian government steamship *Quadra.* The book was (and remains) an indispensable travel reference, giving local histories and descriptions of the coast. Many geographic names in the region simply reflected explorers' first impressions: Dark Island, Deception Channel, Surprise Reef, Obstruction Island, Disappointment Inlet. British merchant captain Napolean Fitz Stubbs arrived here in 1860 and, it seems, did nothing exceptional to earn the namesake of such a wonderful island. Besides early explorers, traders, missionaries and settlers, many place-names were of ancient origins from the local indigenous peoples.

"The name Clayoquot," Ricketts read in *Coast Names*, "is derived from [the aboriginal words] 'Tla-o' or 'Cla-o,' meaning another, or different. 'aht' means people or village, hence 'Cla-o-quaht' means people different from what they used to be. There is a tradition to the effect that the inhabitants here were originally quiet and peaceful, later they became quarrelsome and treacherous; hence they were called by their neighbours 'Cla-o-quaht.'"

Later, the name became associated with the first permanent white settlement on the West Coast of Vancouver Island. In 1874, Frederick Christian Thornberg, a stoic Danish seafarer, took charge of Stubbs Island. He bought furs, seals and dogfish oil from natives through a small hole in the side of a trading post. He married Lucy, the daughter of a local chief, and had six children. Only one survived to adulthood, Freddie Jr., who worked as Betty's handyman for many years.

Shortly after arriving, Thornberg found bleached human skulls on the sand spit and near his store. He buried them under some willows. He heard a story about a fierce local chief who had made a stealthy night raid on the hated tribe of Kyuquot up the coast. (Apparently, this would be the last great tribal war on the coast.) The victorious warriors brought back eighteen captives. They steered their three large dugout canoes onto Stubbs' north shore, across the water from their home village of Opitsat on Meares Island. One by one, the captives were dragged from the canoes and thrown to the sand. As legend has it, the chief decapitated each and stuck their severed heads on poles out on the sand spit.

Years later, Thornberg heard the story from the chief himself. To his astonishment, the murder weapon was neither axe nor knife, but *Mytilus californianus*, a California surf mussel. "Giants of the tribe," as Ricketts described them, the blackish-blue bivalves can grow up to ten inches long. On the island's exposed rocky headland, Ricketts found the surf mussel "of good size and in great clusters." Sharpening the shells on rocks, natives used them for harpoons and spearheads. "I put my knee in his back and grabbed the long hair on the back of his head," the chief said of his technique to execute the first captive. He wrenched back the man's head, exposing a taut throat, and started sawing with the razor-like mollusk shell. Blood spewed out of the doomed man's jugular. The chief sliced through to the spine, which he snapped by twisting the head, and then cut the neck clean through. "Quite easy," he told Thornberg. By the last victim, the spit was awash in a sea of blood.

It has been said that the coming of Catholic missionaries in the 1870s had a "civilizing" effect on the Nuu-chah-nulth, but this probably had more to do with British gunboat diplomacy and a series of epidemics—smallpox, measles, consumption, among others—that killed much of the native population. The coming of the white man, and his laws, guns, alcohol and diseases, marked the end of the powerful chiefdoms of the Nuu-chah-nulth tribes. The Nuu-chah-nulth people were once, Ricketts wrote, "a fierce and warlike tribe whose worst exploits now are beer stealing (about which they're very clever) and an occasional drunken murder." Yet Ricketts' understanding of the local native people

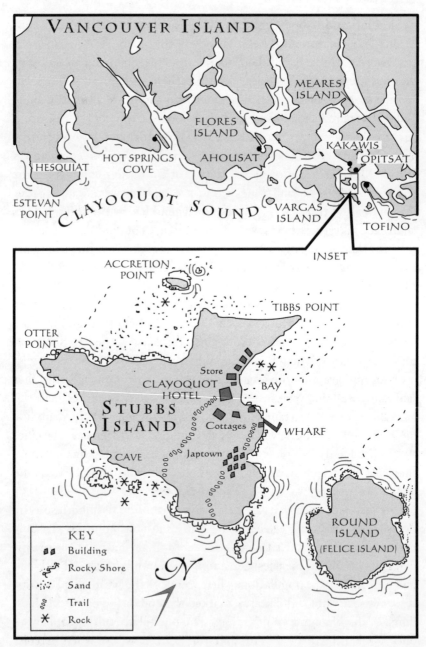

VANCOUVER ISLAND

MEARES ISLAND

FLORES ISLAND

KAKAWIS

OPITSAT

HESQUIAT

HOT SPRINGS COVE

AHOUSAT

ESTEVAN POINT

CLAYOQUOT SOUND

VARGAS ISLAND

TOFINO

INSET

ACCRETION POINT

TIBBS POINT

OTTER POINT

Store

CLAYOQUOT HOTEL

BAY

STUBBS ISLAND

Cottages

WHARF

CAVE

Japtown

ROUND ISLAND
(FELICE ISLAND)

KEY
Building
Rocky Shore
Sand
Trail
Rock

N

STUBBS ISLAND, CLAYOQUOT SOUND

went well beyond the stereotype of the "drunken Indian." He did note that alcohol was a scourge to these people—one night a group from Opitsat woke him while they were stealing cases of beer from a shed next to his apartment—but the biologist would severely question just how "civilized" Western civilization was in its treatment of indigenous peoples and their ancient culture.

The settlement of Clayoquot Sound mirrors the history of Ricketts' hometown of Monterey in a number of interesting ways. Fur traders, missionaries and settlers followed Spanish and British explorers. Many Chinese immigrants, who originally came to the Pacific Coast in search of gold in the 1850s and '60s, ended up constructing railways, the Canadian Pacific in British Columbia and Southern Pacific in California. Once the railroads were completed, the Chinese then went to work in canneries, in Clayoquot Sound and on Cannery Row. Japanese fishermen started arriving in Monterey in the early 1890s and on Stubbs Island in the 1920s.

The denizen that changed Monterey and that started showing up in large numbers in Clayoquot Sound in the 1920s was *Sardinops sagax*, the sardine, or more properly the Pacific pilchard. The silvery little fish turned the small stretch of Ocean View Avenue in Monterey into Cannery Row. Production exploded in the 1920s, peaking in the 1941–42 season at 250,000 tons. By 1946, "the sardine capital of the world" consisted of twenty-four canneries, reduction plants and fish packers. Although the sardine had always frequented the adjacent waters of Vancouver Island, huge schools suddenly appeared in 1925. In that year alone, production skyrocketed more than tenfold. By 1927, twenty-six reduction plants were spewing out oil, fish meal and fertilizer on Vancouver Island's West Coast, including two in Clayoquot Sound.

Industrialists in both British Columbia and California thought it an inexhaustible resource, but Ricketts knew otherwise. He would spend much of the next few years studying the fluctuating sardine stocks and arguing against the folly of unhindered plunder. He began compiling three decades' worth of British Columbian sardine statistics and became increasingly worried and vocal about conservation in the fishery. The sardine was grossly underresearched and Ricketts thought that if he could obtain consistent catch data from Monterey and Vancouver Island canneries, he could make fish stock "predictions of some value" for the entire Pacific Coast. He would be one of the first to understand fisheries in ecological terms, linking sea temperatures, ocean upwellings and plankton levels to fish stock populations. His analysis and dire warnings, however, would go catastrophically unheeded.

* * *

WHEN one wife of a local pioneer arrived in Clayoquot Sound in 1919, she felt that she "had reached the very back of beyond." One day, she wandered into a grove of hemlocks that grew to enormous heights. "It was like a vast cathedral," she remembered, "where the silence was intense."

Clayoquot Sound has indeed become a cathedral, a place of worship and rest. Today, it is a mecca for millions of city dwellers in search of communion with nature. Tens of thousands flock to the area's many luxurious resorts and spas for "Sacred Sea" hydrotherapies, full-body seaweed wraps and Dead Sea salt remedies. In the winter, visitors also come to experience, as one local hotelier described, "Old Testament weather," with thirty-foot seas, hurricane-force winds and deluges of biblical proportions. Seeking solace in nature has become a New Age religion, a fanciful fusion of spirituality, science and sea.

Ed Ricketts would likewise spend much time tangled in seaweed and caked in sea salt. His entire first week was spent exploring the intertidal habitat of the tiny island. The seashore was, he later described to a local missionary, like heaven on earth. He fell in love with this rugged place, which seemed to be full of surprises at every turn. No sooner had Ricketts settled into his apartment than he heard a startling humming sound from the store downstairs. He recognized the melody as a Gregorian chant. He ran downstairs in a hurry and spotted "a nice young Indian woman who helped Betty about the hotel."

"Was that you singing?" Ricketts asked incredulously.

"Yes," she replied, "the priests taught us."

Looking over shelves of canned goods and dried foodstuffs, the woman finished her shopping and set off home in her red-cedar canoe. Ricketts watched her dugout slip quietly across the mighty sound with the silhouette of Lone Cone, a large conical-shaped mountain on Meares Island, in the distance.

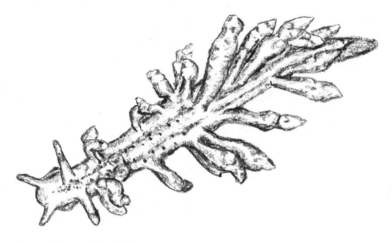

EUBRANCHUS STEINBECKI, SEA SLUG, NEW SPECIES NAMED AFTER
JOHN STEINBECK AND IDENTIFIED BY DAVID W. BEHRENS IN 1987.

CHAPTER FIVE

THE GREAT TIDE POOL

*[A] man looking at reality brings his own limitations to the world. If
he has strength and energy of mind the tide pool stretches both ways,
digs back to electrons and leaps space into the universe and fights out of
the moment into non-conceptual time.*

—JOHN STEINBECK & EDWARD F. RICKETTS,
Sea of Cortez: A Leisurely Journal of Travel and Research

WAY out on the tip of the Monterey Peninsula, at the water's edge, is a magical, marginal world. Ed Ricketts knew it better than anywhere on earth. It was for him the great Source; the ocean was not only the begetter of life, but the biologist's bread and butter, too. For it was here that he collected the thousands of little "beasts" that he sold through his lab to earn a meager living—a subsistence for the Pacific Coast's queerest hunter-gatherer.

Steinbeck, who visited the area countless times, described it like this:

It is a fabulous place: when the tide is in, a wave-churned basin, creamy with foam, whipped by the combers that roll in from the whistling buoy on the reef. But when the tide goes out the little water world becomes quiet and lovely. The sea is very clear and the bottom becomes fantastic with hurrying, fighting, feeding, breeding animals. Crabs rush from frond to frond of the waving algae. Starfish squat over mussels and limpets, attach their million little suckers and then slowly lift with incredible power until the prey is broken from the rock. And then the starfish stomach comes out and envelops its food. Orange and speckled and fluted nudibranchs slide gracefully over the rocks, their skirts waving like the dresses of Spanish dancers. And black eels poke their heads out of crevices and wait for prey. The snapping shrimps with their trigger claws pop loudly. The lovely, colored world is glassed over. Hermit crabs like frantic children scamper on the bottom sand.

And now one, finding an empty snail shell he likes better than his own, creeps out, exposing his soft body to the enemy for a moment, and then pops into the new shell. A wave breaks over the barrier, and churns the glassy water for a moment and mixes bubbles into the pool, and then it clears and is tranquil and lovely and murderous again.

The Great Tide Pool, as the area is popularly known, was more than a physical locale. It was both metaphor and microcosm, for writer and scientist respectively. To Steinbeck it was the refuge he returned to after the war, in order to write a novel (from which the above quote is drawn); for Ricketts it was a point of reference — "the fusion point of faunas from the North and South" — to which he could compare unexplored tidal regions. More profoundly, however, the Great Tide Pool was a microcosm, "a world under a rock" as Steinbeck and Ricketts wrote in *Sea of Cortez*. Here the marine biologist would try to discover, as he stated at the beginning of his outer shores notebook, "an unknown and probably unknowable matrix underlying the nature of things."

Everywhere there was color, life and movement. Ricketts described the seashore as "possibly the most prolific zone in the world—a belt so thickly populated that often not only is every square inch of the area utilized by some plant or animal but the competition for attachment sites is so keen that animals settle upon each other—plants grow upon animals, and animals upon plants."

∗   ∗   ∗

AND so it was on the seashore of Stubbs Island. On his first day of collecting, Ricketts described it as "a very rich region perhaps not ever before collected over."

On the damp morning of June 5, Ed and Toni rose out of bed late. Their forty-eight-hour high-seas journey had been tiring; Ricketts was also recovering from seasickness and a cold. They spent the early afternoon getting acquainted with their "luxurious" new apartment. They unpacked their supplies—flashlights, rolls of charts, jars and vials, porcelain trays, containers of chemicals (Formalin, Epsom salts, menthol, novocaine, chromic acid), forceps, a coffee strainer (for catching tide pool fish), glass slides, scissors, scalpels, razors, rubber gloves, lab coats, talcum powder and a medical kit. He arranged his indispensable books—*Coast Pilot, West Coast Shells, Marine Decapod Crustacea of California, Hydroids, Between Pacific Tides* and *Sea of Cortez*—for easy reference. He also unpacked a microscope, a typewriter and his son's portable phonograph. The apartment soon took on the look, and sound, of a rudimentary lab with perhaps Bach's *The Art of the Fugue* or Mozart's *Don Giovanni* filling the air.

Ed and Toni assembled what they needed for collecting and bundled themselves for the weather; Ricketts donned his heavy army pants, rain hat and sheepskin-lined coat. To the pocket of his wool shirt he pinned a twenty-power Bausch & Lomb magnifying glass on a little roller chain. "He used the glass constantly," Steinbeck remembered. "It was a very close part of him—one of his techniques of seeing." Between two and four o'clock, Ed and Toni collected on a 3.6-foot tide.

Ed Ricketts may have spent half his life in gumboots, a sou'wester and soggy sleeves, but he was in a new region and he delved into his work with rigor and enthusiasm. To the untrained eye, this beach would have looked like any other along the Pacific Coast, but to Ricketts it was a world of subtlety and beauty.

People who went collecting with him were invariably awed. "Ed Ricketts had the best eyes I have ever seen at work," a journalist once recalled. "He would sneak up on a tide pool which I swore was absolutely empty of life and point out dozens of nearly invisible transparent creatures." He seemed able to clear his mind, like a Zen master in meditation, to perceive the imperceptible, to find the hidden creatures, and hidden meaning, in the tide pools. "He would see things in tide pools where I would see nothing," Ruth White remembered. "One time he found these little transparent fish and all you could see were two little black dots for the eyes. The tide pools would be teeming with life where the regular person would only see the big things."

Ed Ricketts approached the seashore methodically that first day in Clayoquot Sound. Using a sharp, flat instrument and with considerable effort, he pried a chiton (*Katherina tunicata*) from a rock's underside. He quickly tied it to a glass slide before the mollusk could curl up protectively like a pill bug, and then dropped it in a jar of Formalin, a preserving solution of water and formaldehyde. The crab life was plentiful, too. He turned over a large boulder and spied a flurry of porcelain crabs (*Petrolisthes cinctipes*). Their flat carapaces allowed them to scurry into nearby crevices. With the choice of fight or flight, this cowardly crustacean would rather cast off a claw or leg than be captured. It was *Hemigrapsus nudus*, the purple shore crab, that stood its ground. According to Ricketts, it could "back up its nasty disposition with a pair of nutcracker claws." The biologist adeptly plucked and then dropped several specimens into a jar of fresh water, a lethal environment for any marine species. Within two hours on "this one bad tide," Ricketts and Jackson had collected a hundred specimens, including starfish, sea sponges, beach bugs, sea anemones, sea cucumbers, hermit crabs, sea slugs, tide pool fish, and many marine worms.

Back at his makeshift lab in the apartment, he went about the delicate task of preserving the specimens. Ideally, such specimens should look like they are still living—not discolored, shriveled, dismembered or decayed. "The almost universal cry of specialists engaged in species determination is that specimens arrive in such bad condition that their work is made doubly difficult," Ricketts wrote in "A Note on Preparing Specimens" in *Sea of Cortez*. "Only extreme care can rectify this."

If handled incorrectly, the sea anemone, for instance, would crumple up like the withered buttercup after which it is misleadingly named (since it is an animal and not, as its common moniker suggests, a plant). That day Ricketts collected four species. Voracious feeders, anemones simply wait for curious or careless passersby to fall for their inviting bed of petals, which are actually tentacles armed with nettle cells to sting and capture prey. Even a hardy and belligerent crab can be paralyzed and then sucked into its gullet, where it is dissolved by digestive juices. Hypersensitive to chemical and physical stimuli, the tentacles of the sea anemone retract if suddenly shocked. A simple touch will produce such an effect. Through trial and error, Ricketts devised an ingenious process to preserve them:

A fairly good method is gradually to introduce a saturated solution of Epsom salts into the pan where the animals are expanded, using a drip-string. This is followed later with Novocain, or best of all, but usually unavailable, with cocaine, which is put into the water directly over the animal. Finally, Formalin is introduced with a drip-string. Any shock, either chemical or physical, will cause immediate retraction of the tentacles.

Flatworms presented an entirely different problem. "They are so delicate that the bodies are easily injured in picking them up," Ricketts explained. "When they are crawling on a rock it is satisfactory to place a thin-bladed knife in their path; when the flatworm oozes onto the knife-blade he can be lifted into a container."

Once Ricketts had brought back to the apartment the hundred specimens from his first collecting trip, there was much painstaking, time-consuming work to be done. "Sorting, laying out, preserving, labeling and noting these took all the rest of the day," he wrote, "what with investigating the local beer situation which was one of the reasons I chose this place as headquarters."

*　*　*

TO the layman, the seashore of Stubbs Island is a mind-boggling place. Animals such as sea anemones, sponges and hydroids are easily confused with plants. A labyrinth of social organization exists among the animals. Their habitats vary from calm mud flats and sloughs to surf-battered offshore reefs. How does one bring order—and hence understanding—to this briny, chaotic kingdom? Could there truly be a matrix, as Ricketts wondered, underlying the nature of things on the seashore?

There certainly could be. Systematics—the study of the kinds and diversity of organisms and of the relationships between them—is an ancient scientific pursuit. Two thousand years ago, Aristotle developed his own rudimentary classification of animals: those with blood (*Enaima*) and those without (*Anaima*). He began what was—and remains—a fundamentally inward-looking approach to ordering the natural world: plants and animals were grouped together based on their anatomical characteristics, their inner structure.

Swedish botanist and the father of modern classification Carl von Linné believed that by understanding the integrated structure of the natural world he could illuminate the Creator's divine design for the entire universe. He wanted to see the hand of God in nature. Linné's *Systema Naturae*, published in 1735, is the basis for modern classification and nomenclature, which assigns species binominal Latin names. Organisms are categorized into hierarchical groups (taxa) with the species being the basic unit.

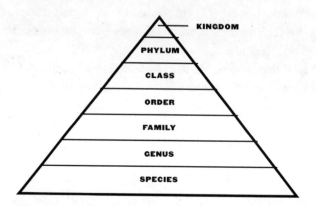

Fully conceived, the Linnean system views nature as a monumental pyramid with simple one-celled organisms and plants at or near the base and more anatomically complex species higher up. At the peak stands man himself, looking heavenward—"the crowning work of God on earth," according to Louis Agassiz, the celebrated Swiss-American zoologist who inaugurated the first seaside collecting trips on the Atlantic Coast in 1873.

What's more, there was a divine purpose underpinning Linnean systematics and, by extension, the very foundation of the natural sciences. God, as a matter of scientific fact, had built this grandiose structure for a reason. "All these treasures of nature," Linné wrote, "so artfully contrived, so wonderfully propagated, so providentially supported throughout her three kingdoms, seem intended by the Creator for the sake of man. Everything may be made subservient to his use."

That dreary Tuesday afternoon, Ricketts approached the shore of Stubbs Island from a wholly different perspective. The Rickettsian system was predicated on "non-teleological thinking," which rejected the very notion, dating back to Aristotle, that nature reflected the purpose of an almighty Creator. Furthermore, Ricketts classified an organism not based on its inner structure, but rather on its relations to the outer world, its biotic and physical environment, on its *ecology*. In effect, he turned on its head the idea of a taxonomic pyramid built on the species-unit with *Homo sapiens* at its glorious pinnacle.

"[I]t seems apparent," reads a defining passage in *Sea of Cortez,* "that species are only commas in a sentence, that each species is at once the point and the base of a pyramid, that all life is relational to the point where an Einsteinian relativity seems to emerge."

There was order on the seashore of Stubbs Island, to be sure. If species were the commas, then their ecological relationships were the words that Ricketts would read to understand the natural world. He had devised a clever "ecological arrangement," which has since been copied by numerous marine biology textbooks and seashore guides. It was a view of nature that looked far less like a hierarchical pyramid of species, and far more like an interconnected web of life.

Ricketts' was a schematic simple enough for anyone to understand and use. Instead of grouping animals into taxa, he grouped them into ecological niches. In *Between Pacific Tides,* his veritable *tableau vivant,* he described how "three co-ordinate and interlocking factors" largely determine the distribution of marine invertebrates. These were the degree of wave shock (protected outer coast, open coast, bay, estuary, and wharf), the type of bottom (rock, sand, mud, or some combination of these), and the tidal exposure (uppermost beach, high-tide region, mid-tide region and low-tide region). Each habitat of the Pacific Coast could easily be categorized according to these environmental conditions. Over the years, Ricketts had assembled detailed profiles of the kinds of species living in each niche.

While even the most intelligent layman or amateur collector may not know to which phylum, class, order or genus an unknown animal belongs, he or she will be able to easily identify its habitat. After that is accomplished, the collector then refers to the profile of species commonly found in that habitat and matches the newfound specimen with one of those species. It was a novel design that opened the world of the seashore to anyone who was willing to explore it.

Dr. Fisher was rather scathing about such populist science. But Ricketts was unfazed. He and Steinbeck even wrote a stinging rebuttal to "dry-ball" academics in *Sea of Cortez*. "[S]uch men are not really biologists," they wrote. "They are the embalmers of the field, the picklers who see only the preserved form of life without any of its principle. Out of their own crusted minds they create a world wrinkled with formaldehyde."

They were determined to keep their "vulgar sense of wonder" and not be wavered by Dr. Fisher or other "little stuffy men [who] object to what is called 'popularization.'" Indeed, Ricketts said he designed *Sea of Cortez* "so that it can be used by the sea coast wanderer who finds interest in the little bugs and would like to know what they are and how they live. Its treatment will revolt against the theory that only the dull is accurate and only the tiresome, valuable." And that, perhaps, was the most radical idea of all underpinning Ricketts' trilogy of the Pacific—the idea of creating a modern ecological treatise for the masses.

There were limitations to Ricketts' model, however. "Ecological arrangements cannot yet, possibly cannot ever, achieve the finality so characteristic of the taxonomic order [in which] an animal belongs irrevocably in the one place finally assigned to it...," Ricketts admitted. "Any ecological classification will be inexact, suggestive rather than definitive; a given animal may occur in several environments, and even its primary assignment to one may not be certain until documented by quantitative methods."

Ecology was to science what Impressionism was to art. Impressionism was an artistic movement made manifest by relationships, of primary and complementary color, of light and dark, to vividly record visual reality, especially in nature. "Art," Cézanne once said, "is a harmony parallel to nature." Ricketts was a great connoisseur of modern art and once wrote a review of local artist Elwood Graham for the *Monterey Peninsula Herald*, comparing an abstract painting to an abstract in scientific writing. "[T]he abstractor is concerned with conveying the meaning, the inner essentiality of the work," he wrote. "In much this same way the modern painter approaches his subject." After his lab burned down, Ricketts ordered new reproductions of paintings by Cézanne, Manet, Degas, Rembrandt, Monet and Renoir from museums in New York.

In Renoir's *By the Seashore*, of which Ricketts ordered a color post-card from the Metropolitan Museum of Art, there are no definitive lines or solid shapes in the common-day scene of a woman sitting, as the painting's title offers, by the seashore. Individually, the short brush strokes of opalescent paint are incoherent, meaningless. But taken *in toto* the dabs emerge as a lush portrait of shimmering daylight, giving a lively, meaningful and more realistic impression, as it were, of the natural world.

Ecology wasn't focused on the particular, either. It wasn't definitive or as analytical as taxonomy. It was, according to Ricketts, "suggestive," or to use a fitting synonym, "impressionistic." Through an understanding of relationships, the new science tried to paint a holistic picture, which was perhaps a bit blurry, like Renoir's paintings, but nevertheless a more illuminating and accurate reflection of nature.

When out collecting, Ricketts would often come across a new species or a species he had never before seen in a particular habitat. He would make note of when and where it was found. Each specimen was like a single brush stroke on a canvas that stretched thousands of miles along North America's Pacific Coast. After twenty-five years of research, Ricketts had painted tens of thousands of such brush strokes, creating a detailed ecological portrait of the coast from Cape San Lucas on the Baja Peninsula to Cape Flattery on the Olympic Peninsula.

Both Impressionism and ecology were part of the late nineteenth century's Modern movement and created radically new pictures of the world—pictures that were at first rejected by the artistic and scientific establishments. According to one scientist, Ricketts' ecological approach was "a radical departure from the traditional and contrary to that practiced by the reigning priesthood of biology." Like the Impressionists, Ricketts was in the avant-garde of his field.

Ecology was revolutionary in that it toppled the pyramid. Man—God's "crowning work"—lost his throne. Ecologists would supplant the zealous belief in our dominion over nature with the more humble principle of interdependence; what we do to nature we effectively do to ourselves. It was a paradigm shift in Western thinking that became bitterly and tragically realized, on a monumental scale, in the 1930s.

The Dust Bowl was a grassroots revolt: the Great Plains essentially rose up in fiery dust storms against the sodbusters and a system of agriculture that had destroyed the natural ecosystem of the prairie grass-lands. It was man, not the Lord, as Steinbeck declared with his epic novel, who had trampled over nature "where the grapes of wrath are stored." This environmental crisis represented the first time that ecologists served as land-use advisors to the nation. In a 1936 report, President Roosevelt's Great Plains Committee came to its epochal conclusion:

> It is an inherent characteristic of pioneering settlement to assume that Nature is something of which to take advantage and to exploit; that Nature can be shaped at will to man's convenience. In a superficial sense this is true; felling of trees will clear land for cultivation, planting of seed will yield crops, and applications of water where natural precipitation is low will increase yields. However, in a deeper sense modern science has disclosed that fundamentally Nature is inflexible and demands conformity.

Alas, the horrific lesson of the Great Plains—that humans would have to change their ways to create harmony with nature—had yet to be learned in the great tide pools of the Pacific in the 1940s. The ocean seemed inexhaustible. The massive industrial canneries dotting the coastline from Cannery Row to Clayoquot Sound spoke of mankind's mighty dominion. This seascape was about to change, however.

* * *

THE primal chaos before Creation. The Source. The Sea. The story of life on the planet is, Ricketts knew, essentially a story of life at sea. To understand the ecology of the seashore is to understand, in effect, the evolution of life from dim geologic times.

Some four billion years ago, the earth was but water—a vast primordial ocean that had been squeezed out from the molten mantle below the earth's surface. Volcanoes percolated, spewing life-generating compounds into the atmosphere. From modern lab experimentation, scientists believe that ultraviolet sunlight and lightning crackling in an atmosphere of hydrogen gas, carbon dioxide, methane, ammonia and water vapor created a photosynthetic reaction that produced earth's first organic compounds, the harbingers of life. As the planet cooled and the murky clouds condensed, a deluge of rain came down into vast basins within the planet's crust. It was pretty much like the Old Testament describes: "darkness was upon the face of the deep." The earth consisted of a warm, slimy brown sea beneath an ominous, volatile sky.

Somehow—and this remains a mystery to modern scientists—the complex organic compounds eventually evolved into the first single-celled organisms. They sought out light and food, and reproduced. Some 2.5 billion years later, after the seafloor had buckled and tectonic uplift formed rudimentary continents, a great evolutionary leap occurred. One day a tiny sea creature, perhaps a tetrapod, emerged and scurried curiously onto *terra firma*—beginning an evolutionary crusade that still continues 360 million years later.

In surveying the seashore of Stubbs Island, Ricketts saw this evolutionary progression from sea to land. As he wrote in an unpublished tidal paper in 1932, "with the littoral associations we are dealing with marine animals pushing up toward land, rather than with land animals colonizing downward." On his third day of collecting on Stubbs Island, Ricketts explored the high-tide and spray zones on the north end of the island. The tide was so high, 10.1 feet above the mean level, that at one point he found himself crawling through the underbrush to get around a cleft on the shore. In this fringe region, where the shore was only wetted occasionally by ocean spray at high tides, he noted very few animals.

He did identify two species of *Littorina* ("shore dweller" in Latin), which are popularly known as periwinkles. These marine snails only stay close enough to shore to wet their gills, and in experiments, some have been kept dry for six weeks without dying. Out of curiosity, Ricketts once fed a periwinkle to a sea anemone, expecting its powerful digestive juices to dissolve the snail and spit out an empty shell. "But it was an intact and healthy *Littorina* that emerged, like Jonah," Ricketts observed. These animals had adapted themselves to extraordinarily un-marine conditions. Indeed, Ricketts figured "some species of *Littorina* are well along in the process of changing from sea-dwellers to land-dwellers."

Another species he collected that day, and which also showed great evolutionary adaptation, was *Acmea pelta*, a limpet. These mollusks look like tiny Chinese hats encrusted on rocks. "The higher up these beasts

Ed and Toni collect on mussel-barnacle bed in Clayoquot Sound, circa 1945–46.
COURTESY OF ED RICKETTS JR.

occur," Ricketts recorded, "the higher must the peak of the shell be in order for the beasts to store enough moisture to see them through the long tidal emergence."

The struggle for existence had created—through the process of natural selection over thousands of years—a highly specialized fauna in the high-tide zone. Animals had to adapt to freezing temperatures in the winter and hot, sun-baked days in the summer. Few species could survive here. Those that did thrived, creating large colonies. It was a pattern the biologist saw in other habitats on Stubbs Island, too.

On the island's outer coast, huge green combers rolled in from the high seas and smashed down on the rocky headland with terrific force. Animals had to have "phenomenal staying powers," as Ricketts described, to survive this wave shock. Tough skins, thick shells and strong attachment mechanisms, like the tube feet of starfish or the horny hairs of mussels, were necessary to withstand the thousands of tons of water during vicious winter storms. Animals needed to be so specialized that wherever a stretch of exposed rocks occurred, Ricketts would find three animals—the purple starfish (*Pisaster ochraceus*), the California mussel (*Mytilus californianus*) and the goose barnacle (*Mitella polymerus*, now called *Pollicipes polymerus*). Ricketts called these "horizon makers," because they invariably marked the mid-tide line on exposed rocks between Baja California and the Bering Sea. The surf mussels colonized every rock and crevice so that the entire zone, from a distance, looked as though it were paved in blackish-blue asphalt.

Yet life, even in the most forbidding environment, wasn't just about competition for survival. The thick bed of midnight-blue mussels and goose barnacles provided a habitat for other animals—minute crabs, isopods, flatworms—that could not normally survive here. The mussels and barnacles helped to trap plankton and detritus for food for these commensal species. One modern ecological survey found 142 different species thriving among the mussel-barnacle beds on the West Coast of Vancouver Island. The animals were engaged in what Dr. Allee called "unconscious cooperation."

So when a Clayoquot chief stripped away a swath of large surf mussels to use their razor-sharp shells to behead his captives, the bare rock soon grew a film of algae. Limpets would then come grazing on this plant food, followed by barnacles, then mussels, starfish and many other animals that formed a robust community. An orderly ecological succession, the replacement of one species by another, occurred as the first group made living conditions suitable for the next, and so on, until a stable or "climax community" of starfish, mussels and barnacles was born.

It was a precarious climax, however. The seashore environment was so harsh, Ricketts wrote in his Stubbs Island notes, that "animals manage to survive in the tide pools, but just barely so, and that the added hand of man is more than they can stand." He noticed in southern California, for instance, that the region was being progressively invaded by northern species, which forced the rare indigenous species to make a "last stand" in the warm bays and estuaries. Yet in these places, such as San Diego and Los Angeles harbors, they were being further wiped out by industrial pollution. The few remaining endangered species would hang on until, as Ricketts lamented, "the collector plucks them, and that's the end of them." Since he had been in Monterey, some rare brittle stars had already disappeared from the Great Tide Pool; he figured his "slight bit of collecting" probably helped to exterminate the species.

Ed Ricketts knew that even as a lone collector his ecological impact could be great. He was always careful to replace overturned rocks and generally to disturb a habitat as little as possible. And because he was exploring a region that had never been collected over before, he kept very accurate records for Clayoquot Sound. He listed species taken in his notebook, which were then cross-referenced with numbers on specimen labels. His notes were rigorous, including collecting dates, times, tides and geographic descriptions of the region and, of course, the scientific names and quantities of species. It was a time-consuming process, but it ensured the accuracy of his inventory. He wanted his research to form a biodiversity baseline for future investigators.

Stubbs Island provided Ricketts with a diverse array of collecting environments. Its northern shore was a golden sand spit, and its southern headland stuck out like a chiseled jaw and took severe beatings during winter squalls. There was also a protected bay, a mud flat, wharf pilings, tide pools and an eelgrass habitat. Considerable collecting needed to be done in each spot, and there was little time to do it. Ricketts worked rain or shine, but mostly rain, as he recorded in his travelogue:

> Weather so far cold, cloudy, usually slightly windy. Often there is misty rain early in the morning at which time the water surface is at its quietest. At no time yet have I seen the surface with that oily look. And usually there are wind riffles and the waves are lapping the shore. Twice during the late afternoon there have been glimpses of the sun and yesterday you could even see the sunset. But I haven't yet seen the tops of the mountains, clouds cut them off cleanly about half way up.

The day after this entry, Friday the eighth of June, he started out early to collect on an extremely low tide. The weather was predictably cold and steely. Ricketts was nevertheless pleased with collecting thirty-nine different species in a mere two hours that morning. The lowest tidal zone had a greater number of species than the other three zones combined. "Triton is a fruitful deity," Ricketts once wrote, "and here if anywhere is his shrine." Because littoral organisms are essentially aquatic animals that must adapt themselves to terrestrial conditions on the seashore, they tend to gravitate toward low-tide zones where they have the whole ocean to draw from. This became even more apparent two days later, when a new moon with its "spectacular" low tide allowed Ricketts to increase his take to fifty species on a single morning collecting trip.

After ten days, with only one short jaunt to nearby Echachis Island, Ricketts had collected 178 different species from a dozen collecting trips. It was a fantastic haul considering how small the intertidal zone actually was: just over ten feet in height and covering a distance of two and a half miles around Stubbs Island. The seashore is one of the most densely populated, biologically rich habitats on earth.

> *Species collected on Stubbs Island, June 5–14, 1945*
> Sea Sponges—3 species
> Hydroids—7 species
> Sea Anemones—4 species
> Polyclads (flatworms)—3 species
> Nemertean (ribbon worms)—5 species
> Bryozoa (marine mosses)—7 species
> Echinoderms (starfish, brittle stars, sea urchins, sea cucumbers)—15 species
> Polychaeta (bristle worms)—24 species
> Sipunculids and Echiurids (worms)—2 species
> Cirripeds (barnacles)—6 species
> Decapods (shrimps, hermit crabs, crabs)—17 species
> Small Decapods, Isopods, Amphipods (sea spiders, beach hoppers, pill bugs)—19 species
> Chitons (sea cradles)—8 species
> Pulmonata (snails)—1 species
> Nudibranchs (sea slugs)—5 species
> Tectibranch—1 species
> Limpets—8 species
> Bivalves (clams, cockles, scallops, mussels, oysters)—13 species
> Shelled snails—11 species

Tunicates (sea squirts)—10 species
Tide pool fish—9 species
TOTAL—178 species

* * *

THERE was something peculiar about how Ed Ricketts described "the good, kind, sane little animals" of the tide pools in his field notebooks, essays and books. Hermit crabs were "the clowns of the tide pools." A sea sponge was "famous and cosmopolitan." An ill-tempered crab acted like a "Tartar," while another species strode around the seafloor like a "Great Mogul." At night, beach hoppers lived a "bohemian life" holding "high carnival—leaping about with vast enthusiasm." A giant worm, whose burrow in the sand provided lodging and food for a reddish scale worm, pea crab and a little goby fish, was a "fat innkeeper...the portly chief of as motley a crew of guests as one could hope to find."

Surely if Edmund Wilson could lambaste John Steinbeck for an "animalizing tendency" in his fiction, then the reverse could be said of Ed Ricketts: there was a definite anthropomorphic flair in his scientific descriptions of marine invertebrates. His specimens sounded like colorful characters in a Shakespearean play.

In his classic history of ecology, *Nature's Economy,* Donald Worster points out that anthropomorphism has been an undercurrent in scientific writing throughout the ages. "Every generation...writes its own description of the natural order, which generally reveals as much about human society and its changing concerns as it does about nature."

In the eighteenth century, for instance, the animal world eerily reflected the human one. Linné's taxonomic system was basically feudalism for animals. It was a social hierarchy in which each higher species ruled those below it—man, of course, ruled over all of them. By the end of the Industrial Revolution in the mid-nineteenth century, however, this old social order began to change drastically, as did our view of nature.

Europe became imbued with a laissez-faire ethic, class struggle and competition for scarce resources. It was survival of the fittest—a Dickensian worldview that Charles Darwin would also perceive in nature. During its seminal years (1850–1900), ecology was considered, even more than economics, the "dismal science," focused on the struggle for existence. The economy of nature was, as Ricketts once wrote, truly "Victorian."

The turn of the century marked yet another era for ecology, one that spawned modern conservation in North America. The Progressive movement heralded a new spirit and gave rise to new ideas that were necessary to understanding, and reforming, the functioning of a complex industrial society. Ideas such as holism, cooperation, integration and interdependence became the bedrock of both the Progressive movement and the first American ecologists. Later, the ecologists would go so far as to transform their own model of nature, as Worster explains, "into a reflection of the modern corporate, industrial system." By mid-century, the science had become bio-economic, using metaphors of producers (plants) and consumers (animals) to describe processes in nature.

Another major shift in ecological thinking occurred by the Second World War. With the collapse of the laissez-faire economic order in the 1930s, the rise of fascist and communist regimes and industrialized warfare, ecologists began turning to nature for moral guidance—so disillusioned were they with humanity. They began to explore the idea of using models of nature, of animal behavior, for instance, to understand humanity. As Darwin had applied evolutionary biology to mankind, so too did ecologists apply their new science to human beings.

In his 1938 treatise, *The Social Life of Animals*, Dr. Allee transferred his ecological discoveries to modern society. He concluded prophetically (since a world war had not yet broken out) that "the present system of international relations is biologically unsound." Noting that "group struggles to the death between members of the same species, such as occur in human warfare, can hardly be found among non-human animals," Allee proposed the creation of an international body to regulate competition and cooperation among nation-states, among human societies.

Perhaps inspired by Allee and writing a year later, Ricketts saw a growing rift in the human world that was also mirrored among animal communities. Ideological conflict, which the marine biologist observed with the rising tide of totalitarianism, had an elemental parallel in the tide pool:

Even the two chief philosophies of human society are paralleled on the shore: those dedicated to the principle that the individual serves the state, chiefly as a unit or cog in that supra-personal social organization that is the colony; and those based on the democratic principle that the state serves the all-important individual. The latter are exemplified by the octopus and by other actively predacious animals which, by their individual skill through intelligence and sensory ability, function as free entities.

Can we truly see our own reflection on the glassy surface of the Great Tide Pool? The hardship and misery of the Great Depression and the unfathomable brutality of the First and Second World Wars indelibly etched themselves on Ed Ricketts. In 1942, he had even written an article entitled "One Man's Approach to the Problems of International Understanding." He sent it to *Harper's, Atlantic Monthly, Cosmopolitan* and *Reader's Digest,* arguing unsuccessfully, since the essay was never published, that "a field biologist's slant on this war will have a quality of novelty."

In the tide pools of the outer shores, with war in the Pacific nearing a cataclysmic end, Ricketts became intent on searching for not just a greater understanding of animal life, but also an ecological basis for human ethics. He grew convinced that his discoveries in the tide pools could help restore the balance in a shattered world.

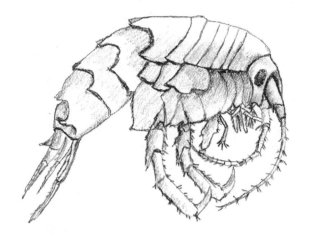

PANOPLOEA RICKETTSI, SAND FLEA, NEW SPECIES COLLECTED
BY ED RICKETTS CIRCA 1930 IN MONTEREY BAY, CALIFORNIA.

CHAPTER SIX

BREAKING THROUGH

I suspect now that the pattern is universal, we fail to see the transcending simplicity of it only because of obstacles on our inward horizons.

—EDWARD F. RICKETTS,
"The Philosophy of Breaking Through"

EVEN her most smitten admirers admitted that she was an ugly ship. She had been painted battleship gray for the war and had one outstanding feature, setting her apart from the Canadian Pacific Railway Company's other coastal liners: iron bulwarks enclosed her upper decks to protect passengers from the ravages of Vancouver Island's stormy waters. When she was built in 1913, the Victoria *Colonist* declared her "a marvel of skilled workmanship that could not be excelled in any other shipyard in any part of the world." The newspaper claimed she was handsomely designed, but most people knew otherwise.

Still, she was the S.S. *Princess Maquinna* and she was a legend. "[A] boat, above all other inanimate things, is personified in man's mind," Steinbeck once wrote. This could certainly be said of the *Maquinna*. From 1913 until 1952 when she was decommissioned, she ran the outer shores route so loyally that people called her "Old Faithful." Every ten days, the steamer would make the 848-mile round-trip journey from Victoria to Port Alice in the island's northern-most fjord, servicing some thirty isolated fishing settlements, cannery towns and native villages. By the time Ed and Toni stepped aboard on the afternoon of Thursday, June 14, she had already traveled this coastline the equivalent of circling the globe more than twenty times.

Captain MacKinnon throttled the engine as the *Maquinna* approached Clayoquot's wharf. He then ordered reverse full-steam, and the ship's single funnel spewed out black soot that stained the overcast sky.

S.S. Princess Maquinna *painted battleship gray for the war, summer 1945.*

MAURICE CHANDLER PHOTO, ROBERT D. TURNER COLLECTION.

Ricketts had made reservations to sail to Port Alice to complete his survey of Vancouver Island's outer coast. The two-day journey zigzagged in and out of channels, sounds, bays and inlets. The *Maquinna* only ventured out to the high seas to get around Estevan Point and Cape Cook, the two most dangerous juts of land to mariners. Most of the trip meandered through inland waterways, where the gravest hazards to navigation were fog, rocks, reefs and racing tides.

It was a lackadaisical trip. The steamer would stop here and there to deliver a mailbag or food or to pick up a passenger or lumber. There was afternoon tea and a midnight supper. Captain MacKinnon and his officers dined and socialized with passengers. Stewards pointed out landmarks and gave oral histories at various points of interest. Otherwise, there really wasn't much to do aboard. Regular passengers played bridge and parties would occasionally erupt in the aft lounge with boisterous piano playing and dancing. Drinking was a common pastime, too. "It was at Tofino," a passenger once remembered, "that we realized to our absolute horror that we were running out of scotch." Having heard these woeful stories, Ricketts had taken action by "self-consciously" carting a couple cases of beer up the *Maquinna*'s gangway.

Captain MacKinnon steered the ship from Stubbs Island around hidden sandbars and shoals into Father Charles Channel, which lead, as one would expect, to a Catholic mission on Meares Island. MacKinnon blew the ship's whistle, alerting missionaries of the steamer's arrival, and anchored in St. Mary's Bay, an elbow in the channel. Ricketts could see the white chapel and schoolhouse at the base of Lone Cone, an adjacent mountain. A small outboard brought to the steamer some mail and a Catholic priest who was, Ricketts recalled, a "very alert pleasant young fellow addicted to cigars."

The *Maquinna* then continued through the inland channel, sailing below Cat Face Mountain to the native village of Ahousat. The steamer's arrival was a grand affair for the Nuu-chah-nulth. "When the *Princess Maquinna* was approaching Ahousat, when it was still on the other side of Cat Face Mountain, you could feel it," an Ahousaht chief once recalled. "You could hear it. This was back when there were no sounds from machinery; when a man could go to the top of the hill and call people to a feast in the traditional way.... A huge machine like that, ploughing the waves, disturbs the environment, sets your heart a-pumping."

Ahousat was tucked in the end of an inlet on Flores Island. "This is one of the sad and dirty Indian villages," Ricketts described. "The Catholics have no hold here." Indeed, Ahousat had no missionaries of any kind in 1945. The dock was full of natives waiting to travel on the *Maquinna* to canneries up the coast. There was, at this time, a color divide aboard ship; Asian and aboriginal people traveled in second class or on the freight deck.

Ed and Toni disembarked here to do a quick spell of collecting. While walking along the dock, Ricketts "saw one of those things that moves me so much." There was a young Ahousaht woman who was ill with tuberculosis and had an abscessed eye. She was carrying a baby. "It was the old business of people in trouble and taking it and being wonderful...," Ricketts wrote in his log. "I smiled at the woman and really meant it and she smiled back in that wonderful way that Indians do; I haven't ever seen such illumination in a white; just gives you that marvelous sense of contact that transcends language and custom."

Later, aboard the steamer and underway, the Catholic priest came over to Ricketts and introduced himself. Father J. T. O'Brien, according to Ricketts, was a "good man who combined qualities of earnestness and humor." O'Brien came from Eastern Canada and had studied philosophy in the seminary—a detail that immediately caught the attention of Ed Ricketts.

Throughout the late 1930s, Ricketts worked on a series of three philosophical essays which, he told Joseph Campbell, "pretty well sum up the world outlook, or rather inlook" that had been developing in him for years. He worked arduously on the essays, revising and editing them continuously. At every opportunity, he encouraged friends to read them and to provide feedback. Ricketts even shared them with Henry Miller during his visit in 1941. "I think that in the [essays] you succeeded in putting most clearly things which other men write huge tomes about and fail to make clear," said Miller. Yet, he thought Ricketts' life-philosophy was "too radical for immediate acceptance" by society. Indeed, Ricketts had sent the essays to magazines everywhere, and although Steinbeck once personally intervened to convince *Harper's* of their worth, they would remain unpublished.

The essays are actually introspective musings, like someone thinking out loud. Ricketts titled his first essay "Non-teleological Thinking." He defined "non-teleological thinking" as an antidote to the predominate Western thinking first taught by Aristotle, that knowledge of a thing, beyond its classification and description, requires an explanation of causality, or why it exists. Everything has an ultimate purpose. "Non-teleological thinking," on the other hand, Ricketts wrote, "concerns itself not primarily with what should be or could be or might be, but, rather, with what actually 'is,' attempting at most to answer the questions what or how, instead of why." He argued that teleological thought, especially of a religious variety, divided the world into good and bad, right and wrong. It was a terribly moralizing, didactic way of understanding the world. Non-teleological thinking, however, allowed the dualities of the world to dissolve into oneness, revealing hidden truths with great clarity. It was about acceptance and understanding. Ricketts wrote:

The whole is necessarily everything, the whole world of fact and fancy, body and psyche, physical fact and spiritual truth, individual and collective, life and death, macrocosm and microcosm . . . conscious and unconscious, subject and object. The whole picture is portrayed by *is*, the deepest word of deep ultimate reality, not shallow or partial as reasons are, but deeper and participating, possibly encompassing the Oriental concept of "being."

Ricketts was a great admirer of Oriental philosophy. The Taoist notion of "quietism," or what Zen Buddhists call "radical empiricism," particularly influenced his thinking. He cherished his copies of Lao Tsu's *Tao Te Ching*, the ancient Chinese text of philosophy and mysticism, and D. T. Suzuki's *Essays in Zen Buddhism*. The latter was translated in 1926 and was one of the first texts to introduce Buddhism to the West. A Zen master, Suzuki explained in his book that Buddha "took life and the world as they were and did not try to read them according to his own interpretation." This way of thinking, from which Ricketts so obviously drew inspiration, led to *satori*, or enlightenment. According to Suzuki:

> Satori may be defined as an intuitive looking into the nature of things in contradiction to the analytical or logical understanding of it. Practically, it means the unfolding of a new world hitherto unperceived in the confusion of a dualistically-trained mind. . . . All its opposites and contradictions are united and harmonized into a consistent organic whole. . . . With the removal of the obstruction, a new vista opens before one, boundless in expanse and reaching the end of time.

Ricketts called this moment of reaching enlightenment "breaking through." It was the subject of his second essay, "The Philosophy of 'Breaking Through.'" The ability to "break through" came only through intense struggle, and few people, Ricketts reckoned, "glimpse the 'white fire' through and beyond the tragedy with which they are chiefly engrossed." In essence, non-teleological thinking combined with great hardship—suffering a tragedy, perhaps—causes an epiphany that allows a person to intuitively and lucidly see the interconnectedness of all things and, in turn, to feel more "deeply and wildly" connected to the world than ever before. "The greater the struggle, the greater the possible breaking through," Ricketts wrote, echoing a passage from Suzuki: "For the more you suffer the deeper grows your character, and with the deepening of your character you read the more penetrating into the secrets of life."

Ricketts' philosophy of life came very close to paralleling Zen's struggle to reach Nirvana. The marine biologist was trying to open a "third eye," as Suzuki wrote, "to the hitherto undreamed-of region shut away from us through our own ignorance. When the cloud of ignorance disappears, the infinity of the heavens is manifested, where we see for the first time into the nature of our own being." In the same vein, Ricketts wrote: "The deep thing is almost completely hidden away from us; in order to see it even partially we have to spend our life tearing down, removing the barriers: of custom and protection and tradition that the race has built up. Because only when these are down . . . can we appreciate the really deep thing."

Ricketts found symbols of "breaking through" everywhere. He saw it in the science of Darwin; in the psychology of Jung; in the literature of Goethe; in the philosophy of Emerson's transcendentalism, Hegel's dialectic, and Nietzsche's "superman"; in the music of Bach; and especially in the poetry of Robinson Jeffers.

His third essay, "The Spiritual Morphology of Poetry," was a search for "breaking through" in the world's great poets. He called them the "mellow" poets, such as Chinese poet Li Po, John Keats, Walt Whitman and William Blake. Ricketts took the phrase "breaking through" from "Roan Stallion," the poem by Jeffers that Carol Steinbeck had read aloud on that memorable day in 1932. Both Ricketts and Campbell would return to one stanza in the epic poem, quoting it repeatedly throughout their lives:

> *Humanity is the start*
> *of the race; I say*
> *Humanity is the mould to break away from, the crust to break through, the*
> *coal to break into fire,*
> *The atom to be split*

Tragedy that breaks man's face and a white fire flies
out of it; vision that fools him
Out of his limits, desire that fools him out of his limits, unnatural crime,
inhuman science,
Slit eyes in the mask; wild loves that leap over the walls of nature, the wild
fence-vaulter science,
Useless intelligence of far stars, dim knowledge of the spinning demons
that make an atom,
These break, these pierce, these deify, praising their God shrilly with fierce
voices: not in a man's shape
He approves the praise, he that walks lightning-naked on the Pacific, that
laces the suns with planets,
The heart of the atom with electrons: what is humanity in this cosmos? For
him, the last
Least taint of a trace in the dregs of the solution; for itself, the mould to
break away from, the coal
To break into fire, the atom to be split.

These three philosophical essays were the cornerstones of Ed Ricketts' worldview, rooted in mysticism, ecology, intuitive thinking, Jungian psychology and Oriental philosophy. To experience the "deep thing," Ricketts believed, to see the oneness of the universe, was to go beyond mere intellect, to go beyond even the "wild fence-vaulter science."

Although the essay had been written six years earlier, Ricketts brought along a copy of "The Philosophy of 'Breaking Through'" to Vancouver Island. He wanted to revise it, yet again, for publication. Steinbeck had lifted almost verbatim the "Non-teleological Thinking" essay and made it chapter 14 of *Sea of Cortez*. It has become known as the Easter Sunday "sermon" in the narrative. Perhaps Ricketts hoped the writer would now incorporate "breaking through" into *The Outer Shores*. It would have been a logical outgrowth; the "northern sequel" would be a philosophical sequel as well.

Aboard the *Maquinna*, Ricketts chatted with Father O'Brien about *Sea of Cortez* and promised to send him a signed copy. He may have even mentioned his own non-teleological "sermon" in the book, but ultimately he knew the "church couldn't stomach" such thinking. Still,

Ricketts admired the priest's "great youthful exuberance." He was surprised that Father O'Brien was not only interested in the ideas, art and culture of the Nuu-chah-nulth, but actually respected them, too. He even overheard the Father talking in the local dialect. "Other missionaries think the Indian ways have to be stamped out," Ricketts wrote, "or at best they're not interested and certainly don't respect them."

"You must have been with Indians a great deal [yourself]?" Father O'Brien asked Ricketts. No, Ricketts replied, except once when he spent a week or so with a Makah Indian and his wife while collecting at Cape Flattery on the Olympic Peninsula. Well, Father O'Brien went on, "that Indian woman you saw told me that you knew Indian people. She said you must have spent quite a lot of time with them."

Ricketts felt very affected by this comment. He had seen the same "deep smile" of the Ahousaht woman in the faces of the indigenous people while in the Gulf of California with Steinbeck. He respected their ancient ways immensely and worried that the encroachment of modernity would lead to their cultural annihilation. In *Sea of Cortez*, Ricketts and Steinbeck poignantly described their first meeting with some wary natives:

> They sat in the canoe holding to the side of the *Western Flyer*, and they held their greasy blankets carefully over their noses and mouths to protect themselves from us. So much evil the white man had brought to their ancestors: his breath was poisonous with the lung disease; to sleep with him was to poison the generations. Where he set down his colonies the indigenous people withered and died. He brought industry and trade but no prosperity, riches but no ease.

Yet soon after returning from the Baja Peninsula, Ricketts and Steinbeck had their gravest philosophical falling-out over this very topic—the conflict between modernity and the ancient aboriginal ways.

* * *

BACK in June of 1940, about a month after returning from the Gulf, Steinbeck had gone to Mexico City to write and direct a film, *The Forgotten Village*. Ricketts had joined John and Carol, but he'd felt a certain "feeling of coldness" from the Steinbecks. He was rarely invited over to their villa for dinner and preferred not to be around the feuding couple anyway. "A new experience for me," he wrote in a letter home, "being the poor cousin." For the first time, their friendship became strained, perhaps in part because Ricketts had strongly objected to the central thesis of the film. "I don't think it's much good," he had told Toni. He disagreed with it so strongly that he even wrote an "anti-script" with a "motif diametrically opposite to that of John's 'Forgotten Village.'"

Steinbeck's dramatized documentary is a propaganda piece exalting the importance of science in the betterment of humanity. Yet the story is also about modern science undermining traditional knowledge in a Mexican native pueblo. With their children sick and dying from contaminated water, the native people turn to their *curandera* (medicine woman) for a cure. Portrayed as naïve, intolerant and backward, the villagers reject the modern medicine being advocated by a young native boy. Juan Diego, according to Ricketts, "becomes so imbued with the spirit of modern medical progress that he leaves the traditional way of his people to associate himself with the new thing." The defiant boy sneaks medicine into the pueblo and saves the dying children. But the village exiles him for his heresy. Juan leaves the village and enrolls in a state-run modern school in the city. The film ends with Steinbeck proclaiming that change is coming: Juan Diego, and all the boys like him, will eventually return to help their pueblos in their "long climb out of darkness."

At this time, Steinbeck was so disillusioned by his experience surrounding *The Grapes of Wrath* that he lost faith in humanity. He spent eight months studying marine biology under Ricketts' tutelage and had come to the conclusion that "the only heroes left are the scientists and the poor." He looked to the cool, hard rationalism of science as a panacea to the ills of the world. He became, in effect, an overzealous student and Ricketts his disapproving teacher.

There is great irony and unrealism in *The Forgotten Village*. Illness and death from contaminated water cannot be blamed on the failure of aboriginal remedies (many of which have been scientifically proven today). It was industrial pollution, habitat destruction and urban squalor—very modern phenomena—that probably caused the water to become deadly in the first place. Numerous new diseases—smallpox, measles, whooping cough and tuberculosis—that were unknown to North America's indigenous peoples before European contact also caused widespread death.

These diseases effectively undermined aboriginal belief systems by rendering the shaman's traditional medicines useless. In Clayoquot Sound, for instance, a sect of evangelical Christian missionaries called Shantymen exploited this spiritual chink by setting up a hospital in Tofino. It wasn't the natives who were closed-minded and hostile, as in Steinbeck's film, but rather these medical missionaries. Ricketts heard many stories about "their intolerance and unrealism." He was particularly appalled at how the Shantymen "try to bludgeon some of their intolerant and revealed-religion ideas into the natives along with very good medicine."

All around him, Ricketts saw the symbols of modernity—automobiles, cinemas, steamships, telegraph wires, modern schools—overwhelming indigenous peoples. He fretted that "the spread of this [modern] spirit is so rapid and devastating that it upsets the age-old relation between man and the land, and between man and man." This hadn't happened yet, not completely anyway, in the Clayoquot Sound of the 1940s. However, Ricketts figured their "deep smile" would be lost as "American culture with its dearth of inner values" spread and obliterated traditional ways of life.

Ricketts felt that Steinbeck's film should be instead about a "wise old man" who "appropriately might point out the evils of the encroaching mechanistic civilization to a young person." Ricketts cautioned that society should restrain its insatiable drive for material gain. Other values were as important, if not more so, for human happiness. Although materially poor, Ricketts pointed out, the native people were spiritually rich. Their "curiously illuminating smiles" came about despite the "almost unbelievable rigors of poverty and disease." Ricketts argued that society must travel a knife edge, avoiding the extremes of both material and spiritual deprivation. "An American," Ricketts wrote, "would do well to trade his material possessions and his health for such transcendent joy."

In 2000, Yale professor Robert E. Lane published *The Loss of Happiness in Market Democracies*. In it he illuminated a disturbing trend that Ricketts had warned about half a century ago. According to Lane, "as our material prosperity increases, the gap between income and satisfaction with life seems to be widening." Drawing on extensive research in economics, sociology, psychology, and biology, Lane found that once a person has achieved a minimal standard of living, material wealth has almost nothing to do with happiness. "Close relationships, rather than money, are the key to happiness," he wrote, echoing the same conclusion Ricketts had reached. The need for relationships is biologically ingrained in humans, Lane explained, so much so that "the number of one's personal friends is a much better indicator of overall satisfaction with life than is personal wealth. . . . By ignoring our biologically programmed need for each other, we risk physical and mental distress." In short, the roots of happiness are ecological—not material.

Society's material pursuit has obviously come at considerable distress to the environment as well. The very things that were once hailed as improving quality of life—such as widespread car ownership, suburban housing, electricity and cheap disposable consumer products—are now threatening the environment and ultimately human welfare. Particulates in automobile exhaust cause respiratory illness and even death. Urban sprawl eats up farmland and forests. Landfills contaminate groundwater. The burning of fossil fuels warms the atmosphere. Modern society has gone askew, threatening both human happiness and health.

In Clayoquot Sound today, a renaissance of sorts is underway to strike a new balance. Old aboriginal customs are being brought back in an attempt to rekindle mankind's relationship with nature. Many native leaders—and a growing chorus of environmentalists and community activists—talk about managing the area's biosphere, its natural wealth of fish and forests, according to the ancient principles of *Hishukish Ts'awalk* and *Isaak*. The Nuu-chah-nulth phrase *Hishukish Ts'awalk* (pronounced *he-SHOOK-ish TSA-walk*) means "everything is one" and *Isaak* (pronounced *E-sock*) means "respect."

In 1945, however, understanding the value of aboriginal ways and warning about the perilous excesses of modernity made Ed Ricketts a proverbial lone voice in the wilderness of Clayoquot Sound.

* * *

THE *Maquinna* left Ahousat in the twilight and steamed to Hesquiat, another native village and the final port-call in Clayoquot Sound. It was nightfall by the time the ship left the sheltered Hesquiat Harbor for the high seas around Estevan Point, home to the tallest lighthouse on the coast. At 150 feet with massive concrete flying buttresses, it looked like a candlestick from afar. But not on this night. Its light had been extinguished since June of 1942, when a Japanese submarine surfaced and fired its guns at the light.

Estevan Point was certainly a storied locale. In fact, it was the point where modern history began on Vancouver Island. One day in June of 1774 the Hesquiaht people saw something they thought was an immense bird on the ocean off Estevan Point. As it came into shore, however, they saw that it was actually a large canoe and figured it was coming "back from the land of the dead with their bygone chiefs." As the canoe neared the village, they realized it was full of men, strange in color and appearance—white men in fanciful regalia. The ship was the *Santiago,* which had sailed from Monterey under the command of Spanish explorer Juan Perez. The viceroy of Mexico had given Perez instructions to "examine the coast as far north as 60 North latitude; to take possession of the lands for Spain and to plant bottles containing the evidence." The Spanish laid claim to the territory, although the British held an entirely different view of its history.

Just beyond Estevan Point, the *Maquinna* crept toward shore, passing its namesake Maquinna Point at the entrance of Nootka Sound. It was here, the British argued, that modern history truly began. The gateway to the sound is named Cook Channel, after Captain James Cook. To the east of the channel is Bligh Island, named after William Bligh, who was infamously mutinied on the *Bounty* and was the master of H.M.S. *Resolution* on Cook's voyage to the North Pacific in 1778. The *Maquinna* veered to port, steering clear of Bligh Island and the cluster of islets known as the Spanish Pilot Group, and arrived at a cannery on Nootka Island around four o'clock in the morning the next day. Toni was awake and went into the cannery's cookhouse where a Chinese cook gave her hot cakes, bacon and coffee galore.

The Nootka Cannery was located in Boca del Infierno Bay—the cannery's boilers were certainly the "mouth of the inferno" to the fish. It was also the spot where a great dispute had once brought the world to the brink of war. Toni became enamored by the area's epic history and later wrote a story for a local Monterey magazine, *What's Doing*. Titled "Forgotten Nootka," the story began:

> A monument, a table, an old Spanish cannon "somewhere back in the brush" on the wild west coast of Vancouver Island. These are all that remain to mark one of the most historic spots on the Pacific Coast.... Once a word to conjure with in London, in Madrid, in Calcutta, China and Boston, the name "Nootka" today means nothing, and the quarrel over the two silver spoons and the log hut which electrified Europe and changed the course of history is forgotten.

Captain James Cook first landed at Nootka Island on March 29, 1778. There he met the legendary Chief Maquinna. Cook declared sovereignty over the territory in the name of the king of England, though the Spanish would later argue that two silver spoons discovered in the native village at the time of Cook's arrival were evidence that Juan Perez had traded with the Nuu-chah-nulth in 1774. The Spanish seized the trading post in 1789, naming it Santa Cruz de Nutka. Under threat of war from the bellicose King George III (who later went insane), the Spanish relinquished it the following year as part of the Nootka Convention. The North Pacific was now open to unfettered British settlement.

Toni would also discover a fascinating connection between this bygone outpost and Monterey. "[T]he threads connecting Monterey and Nootka are actual as well as historical," she ended her tale, "for the Spanish friars, leaving Nootka, took with them twenty Nootka Indians who settled at Soledad and Monterey. When they left, the little village of Nootka had seen its great days; in another ten years it would revert to its pristine quiet, broken only by the rasp of paddles against gunwale as a lone dug-out crept along the shore."

After the stop at the Nootka Cannery, the *Maquinna* steamed out into Cook Channel and down the narrow Tahsis Inlet eight miles to Ceepeecee, named after the acronym for the Canadian Packing Corporation. It had built a cannery town here in 1926. The little settlement was, according to Ricketts, "clean and well ordered [with] Chinese cooks preparing wonderful meals; dormitories, cottages, dining halls, recreation rooms, and the inevitable Indian shacks." The steamer stopped here at eleven o'clock in the morning to unload supplies, drop off workers and take on cases of canned salmon. One passenger remembered that the *Maquinna*'s winch would "shake the fillings out of your teeth" when loading cargo. They stayed long enough for Ricketts to collect ten to fifteen different species along the shore.

In Nootka Sound, the *Maquinna* made a couple more stops and then set off for the small settlement of Kyuqout (pronounced *ky-YOU-cut*) in the adjacent sound. They arrived around one o'clock the following afternoon and then left for Port Alice in Quatsino Sound. After a high-seas journey around Cape Cook, the *Maquinna* made its way down the thirty-kilometer-long sound, which almost pinches off the top of Vancouver Island. The steamer called first at Coal Harbor, the most inland port in Quatsino Sound and the Pacific Coast's last whaling station (it closed in 1967). In 1945, however, it was used largely as a wartime seaplane base. From here, the steamer ploughed back through a tight narrows and then twenty kilometers south down Neroutsos Inlet to Port Alice. They arrived at 7:41 P.M., according to the *Maquinna*'s log.

Port Alice was a company town. In 1917, the Whalen Pulp and Paper Company had built a sixty-acre town with some fifty homes, a hotel, store, rooming houses and a mill. Mr. Whalen named the town after his wife, Alice, and a nearby lake after his daughter, Victoria. The town's 1,500 residents lived right next to the mill's belching smokestacks and toxic outfall. Although Port Alice wasn't very pretty, its natural setting certainly was; the town was situated on a deep blue inlet below a canopy of forested mountains.

Ed and Toni had been aboard the *Maquinna* for almost forty-eight hours. In the evening twilight, they walked halfway up the waterworks road through the wet woods to Victoria Lake. They could hear the thrushes singing. Ricketts found a new slug that he sketched in the fading light. Then they returned to the steamer. Being a Saturday night, there was a dance and a social ashore. On the *Maquinna* ladies were pretting themselves for a night on the town. The merrymaking, however, fell far short of the expectations of Ed Ricketts. "A sad sad dance, not at all like the peppy and drunken country dances at Tofino," he recalled. "These aren't, however, wilderness people, or fishermen or farmers. They're townspeople brought up here for a contract; they hate it and maybe they don't even try very hard to have fun."

As if this wasn't disappointing enough, the next day the biologist went looking for marine life on the floats and pilings. "Nothing," he noted:

> Not even any barnacles. So then on the rocks. Nothing also, or almost nothing. Chemical contamination is the answer, wastes from the pulp mill now working as a rayon war plant. The rocks, gravel, pilings, floats in this chemically laden water are covered with guck, with slimy muck. It festoons on the timbers of the floats. . . . I turn over a lot of rocks in a thorough investigation, because everything else here was right for a good fauna. Almost completely and utterly sterile.

Ricketts did find some minute and attenuated worms wriggling under the rocks. He thought it was a "curious fauna" and wondered how they lived in the toxic waters. He noticed that freshwater animals started to colonize the area once the marine conditions became so unfavorable that all the marine fauna died off or moved away. (In 1965, the entire town decided to move away too, four miles down the inlet to Rumble Beach, where British Columbia's first "instant municipality" was born.)

Life wasn't very lively in Port Alice *or* its tide pools. So Ricketts spent the rest of the day climbing back up the waterworks trail over the high ridge to Victoria Lake. All the while, he listened to the songs of the thrushes. From the mountainside he could see the tiny steamer, which looked "like a toy far below and off in the distance." By late afternoon he hurried back, worrying that at any moment the ship's whistle would sound and the *Maquinna* would depart without him.

The ship set sail at 5:27 P.M., as Captain MacKinnon noted precisely in the *Maquinna*'s log, and stopped briefly up the inlet. A motorboat brought out two young pioneers who were "working at liquor bottles." The *Maquinna* then continued through the sheltered sound. Passengers lounged around the grand piano. Stewards were likely entertaining other passengers with seafaring tales. Tea was being served on the CPR's fine china. The two drunks kept swilling their whiskey. It was, at least for an hour or so, a quiet Sunday evening. The mood was languid until they reached the open ocean.

A grim feeling immediately flooded the ship, a wave of seasickness. Many passengers became ghostly white. There was little appetite for dinner. "Outside it got rough," Ricketts wrote, "we stood up forward as long as we could against the wind and spray, [and] then she started to take an occasional dash of water aboard." He and the chief engineer tried to estimate the sweep of the mast. Ricketts figured it was fifteen, while the engineer thought twenty degrees. They were rounding Cape Cook, the eastern extremity on Brooks Peninsula and one of the most ruthless spots on the coast. The *Maquinna* squeaked and groaned in every joint as she rounded the stormy cape.

The ship's purser, Charles W. Young, told Ricketts about his own "harrowing trip" one winter. It was so rough, Young recalled, that the crew tied the typewriters to the floor, fastened everything in cabinets and drawers, closed the purser's office and braced themselves in their bunks. A sudden lurch threw him against a fixture. He soon started feeling pain and nausea, and he urinated blood. "Then he got scared," Ricketts recalled, "[he] knew he was hurt but there wasn't a thing anyone could do about it." It took four days of "howling weather" to get to a hospital in Victoria. All the while, the purser was "sick and in pain and scared."

The horrific stories and heavy seas were too much for Toni. She took some Nembutal (a seasickness barbiturate) and scopolamine (a sleeping pill) and went to bed. A sleepless Ricketts stayed on deck. For a while, he was alone staring at "wicked" Cape Cook and the gloomy gray combers crashing over the bow. One of the drunken men who had come aboard earlier appeared "staggering and beastly." A wave flung him across the deck and nearly overboard, as the ship pitched wildly. "How are drunken people so saved?" Ricketts wondered. "I guess he handled himself drunk better than I ever do sober." Rounding the cape, the ocean quieted on the leeward side of the peninsula and Ricketts slipped below deck to get some rest as Captain MacKinnon steered the passage home.

It was a fruitful, though harrowing, trip. It became apparent to Ricketts that the balance, the connection, between man and nature had been terribly poisoned by that wartime rayon mill in Port Alice. He saw it as much on the faces of the mill workers as in the marine life. This contrasted sharply with the illuminating smile of the Ahousaht woman. In a profound way, Ed Ricketts was beginning to understand that the town's "sad sad dance" and those lifeless tide pools were inextricably connected.

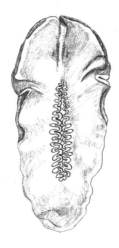

LONGIPROSTATUM RICKETTSI, MARINE FLATWORM, NEW SPECIES
COLLECTED BY ED RICKETTS IN APRIL 1940 IN GULF OF CALIFORNIA, MEXICO.

CHAPTER SEVEN

STORIES TO TELL

When you collect marine animals there are certain flat worms so delicate that they are almost impossible to capture whole, for they break and tatter under the touch. You must let them ooze and crawl of their own will onto a knife blade and then lift them gently into your bottle of sea water. And perhaps that might be the way to write this book—to open the page and to let the stories crawl in by themselves.

—JOHN STEINBECK, *Cannery Row*

T was a miserable day—rain and lots of it. Ed and Toni had arrived back at Clayoquot from Port Alice the day before, after two stormy days huddled below the *Maquinna*'s iron deck. Ed woke around 9:45 A.M., still feeling the fatigue and queasiness of days on a rolling sea. He quietly read a scientific paper on Vancouver Island decapods (crabs, shrimp and other ten-legged animals), which had been forwarded to him from Monterey. He also went for a long walk that afternoon, in spite of the foul weather.

The rain came down in sheets, making everything appear dull and forlorn. The forest's green sheen turned battleship gray. Storm clouds, rolling in off the Pacific at terrific speeds, were as dark and thunderous as cannonballs. And the local mountains, Lone Cone and Cat Face, were beclouded, their peaks veiled like mournful widows. "They look black," Ricketts observed, "and the sea gulls flying past them make a wonderful white pattern."

Ricketts cowered beneath his oilskin sou'wester and raincoat. He walked along the half-moon bay, collecting huge clamshells as he went. The sea anemones, he noticed, cowered too; they curled against the deluge in their beautiful protective petals. Rainwater, however fresh and pure, is poison to the salt-loving creatures of the deep.

On the mud flats behind the Clayoquot settlement, Ricketts spotted several oystercatchers. With their pointed red beaks, they were prying limpets from the rocks for food. Ricketts approached cautiously but the deeply suspicious birds flushed in fright. "When oystercatchers fly,"

Ricketts wrote, "they have that most wonderfully nostalgic plaintive note." The scene reminded him of Walt Whitman's poem "Out of the Cradle Endlessly Rocking," in which the poet translated the song of a mockingbird into human words, "notes of yearning and love."

Much work waited back at his makeshift lab in the apartment. Ricketts spent most of the next day identifying and sorting the specimens from the Port Alice trip. He also wrote a list of standard equipment for future trips, packed fish specimens in bottles of alcohol and dispatched them to Dr. Loren Woods at the Field Museum of Natural History in Chicago, and studied some scientific papers—in particular an as-yet-unpublished English translation of Sven Ekman's *Tiergeographie des Meeres* (1935), or *Zoogeography of the Sea*. He also ordered more liquor at the trading store.

The *Princess Maquinna* came in only once every ten days. Pioneers would be forced to stretch their wartime rations. "[It's] a mystery to me how we make out so well," Ricketts wrote. Supplies of fresh meat and vegetables, cigarettes, newspapers, magazines, "His Majesty's Mails" and cases of beer and whiskey would come in on the steamer. Having had their supplies just replenished, Bill and Ruth decided to throw a party in their cottage that evening.

Their home was set back from the beach behind the trading store and near the forest and Betty's rhododendron garden. Everyone crowded into the cosy living room with its small brick fireplace and hardwood floors. Ed, Toni, Bill, Betty, Ruth and several other islanders gathered for drinks, songs and stories. There was one story, in particular, that the island homesteaders wanted to hear from their American visitor. Was the story that John Steinbeck had written true? The pioneers wanted to know about Cannery Row—about Steinbeck's novel *Cannery Row*, that is.

The novel had been published six months earlier and almost instantaneously turned eight blocks of Ocean View Avenue into one of the most famous streets in America. It also thrust Ed Ricketts into the limelight. "Cannery Row in Monterey in California is a poem, a stink, a grating noise, a quality of light, a tone, a habit, a nostalgia, a dream." It certainly was all those things, as Steinbeck wrote in the novel's opening passage. It was also more than mere fiction. "The book is only fiction in form and style," Steinbeck admitted.

The previous summer Steinbeck had taken the manuscript down to Ricketts at the lab. The biologist read the book and found it to be "very funny, exceedingly funny." He also immediately recognized the novel's enigmatic hero named Doc. "It's mostly about me..., " Ricketts wrote to his son, still serving overseas. "Because I occurred in it so obviously and so frequently, [Steinbeck] wanted me to OK it, and though it makes me out to be a very romantic figure, and I'll practically have to leave town after publication until things quiet down, still it's a fine job and I approved thoroughly."

It was, according to Steinbeck, "a crazy kind of a book about Cannery Row and the lab, etc. All fiction of course but born out of homesickness. And there are some true incidents in it." Indeed, as one literary scholar has explained, "Almost every detail about Doc has its parallel in the actual life and personality of Ed Ricketts." It is nearly impossible to separate the man from the myth, Ed Ricketts from Doc, in *Cannery Row*. "Through the magic of Steinbeck's pen," it has been said, "Ed became the first and only marine biologist to become heroic in American fiction." The author actually said as much and wrote a terse, though telling, dedication in the novel:

For
ED RICKETTS
who knows why or should

Even before its publication, *Life* magazine wanted to come down to Cannery Row to photograph the novel's real-life characters, to unmask Steinbeck's fiction. Both the writer and Ricketts refused to cooperate with *Life*. Ricketts fretted about his loss of privacy. "I dislike the publicity," he complained to his son. By January 1945, there was even talk of a Hollywood movie and Ricketts figured he'd have to move on account of the unwelcome attention. "I imagine Cannery Row will outsell *The Grapes of Wrath*," he told his son just before leaving for Vancouver Island. "[John] will make a fortune out of it."

It did, in fact, become a best-seller, and Ricketts' worst fear came true: even 1,500 miles from Cannery Row, fame followed Ed Ricketts. The Clayoquot pioneers and Captain MacKinnon somehow caught wind that he was the famous Doc of *Cannery Row*. The biologist even became known locally in Clayoquot Sound as "Doc" Ricketts.

Ricketts has been called Steinbeck's alter ego, his persona in art, his fictional voice. However lionized, exaggerated or sentimentalized Ricketts may be in *Cannery Row*'s Doc, there is no doubt that the character contains all the energy, spirit and philosophy of the friend whom Steinbeck loved. Taken as a whole, the novel is fiction, but many passages and details contain a ring of truth. One anecdote from *Cannery Row*, for instance, is taken directly from Ricketts' life:

> Once when Doc was at the University of Chicago he had love trouble and he had worked too hard. He thought it would be nice to take a very long walk. He put on a little knapsack and he walked through Indiana and Kentucky and North Carolina and Georgia clear to Florida. He walked among farmers and mountain people, among the swamp people and fishermen. And everywhere people asked him why he was walking through the country.
>
> Because he loved true things he tried to explain. He said he was nervous and besides he wanted to see the country, smell the ground and look at grass and birds and trees, to savor the country, and there was no other way to do it save on foot. And people didn't like him for telling the truth. They scowled, or shook and tapped their heads, they laughed as though they knew it was a lie and they appreciated a liar. And some, afraid for their daughters or their pigs, told him to move on, to get going, just not to stop near their place if he knew what was good for him.
>
> And so he stopped trying to tell the truth. He said he was doing it on a bet—that he stood to win a hundred dollars. Everyone liked him then and believed him. They asked him in to dinner and gave him a bed and they put lunches up for him and wished him good luck and thought he was a hell of a fine fellow. Doc still loved true things but he knew it was not a general love and it could be a very dangerous mistress.

However strange, the facts of this account are essentially true. Ricketts was a student at the University of Chicago and did go on such a walk. He even wrote about the experience in an article titled "Vagabonding Through Dixie" for the June 1925 issue of *Travel* magazine.

Ruth White thought Ricketts was a great storyteller. One tale, in particular, stood out in her memory. It was his story about "the lady with snake eyes." This was also the first Ed Ricketts story that John Steinbeck had borrowed for use in his own writing. Back in 1938, Steinbeck published a short story called "The Snake" in his book *The Long Valley*. Later, Steinbeck explained that the episode at the lab unfolded exactly as he had written it:

> Very briefly, this is the incident. A woman came in one night wanting to buy a male rattlesnake. It happened that we had one and knew it was a male because it had recently copulated with another snake in the cage. The woman paid for the snake and then insisted that it be fed. She paid for a white rat to be given it. Ed put the rat in the cage. The snake struck and killed it and then unhinged its jaws preparatory to swallowing it. The frightening thing was that the woman, who had watched the process closely, moved her jaws and stretched her mouth just as the snake was doing. After the rat was swallowed, she paid for a year's supply of rats and said she would come back. But she never did come back. What happened or why I have no idea. Whether the woman was driven by a sexual, a religious, a zoophilic, or a gustatory impulse we never could figure. When I wrote the story just as it happened there were curious reactions. One librarian wrote that it was not only a bad story but the worst story she had ever read. A number of orders came in for snakes. I was denounced by a religious group for having a perverted imagination, and one man found symbolism of Moses smiting the rock in the account.

Roars of laughter burst forth from the islanders upon hearing this surreal tale. "He seemed to like that story," Ruth recalled. "It really startled him." It was a wild yarn, which only fed everyone's curiosity about the stories in *Cannery Row*. That night and during other evenings in which they would gather around a bonfire on the beach, Ricketts recounted the true stories of Cannery Row.

Yes, Ricketts explained, across the street from his lab, just as in the novel, stood, as Steinbeck described, "Monterey's largest, most genteel and respected whorehouse." Its proprietor, Flora Woods, was a legendary madam whose dark hair was usually hidden under a beautifully coiffed "flaming orange" wig and whose neck and hands were stunningly bejeweled. She was of such enormity—some three hundred pounds—that her gowns had to be custom made. She opened the Lone Star Cafe in 1923 and named it after her first husband's home state of Texas, although everyone simply called it Flora's. She was by most accounts a law-abiding woman, notwithstanding prostitution laws of course. She became an upstanding pillar of charity in the community. She paid the grocery bills of Cannery Row's working poor during the Depression, helped the widows and orphans of policemen and firemen and always donated ten times more to civic organizations than "respectable" businesses did. On Christmas Day, more than fifty destitute families would find food baskets overflowing on their steps. "What a wonderful woman to work for," recalled one of Flora's girls, "she just was so kind-hearted. Everybody in town knew her, they all loved her, so did we girls who worked for her."

There was affection and friendship between Ed and Flora. The biologist would help counsel hysterical girls, talking them through their troubles, nodding understandingly in his non-moralizing, non-teleological way. He would also patch up the cut faces and torn ears that came about when booze and boys collided on Saturday nights. In return, a paper bag containing six ice-cold bottles of beer would occasionally appear on his doorstep. "She's one hell of a woman," Ricketts said of Flora. "I wish good people could be as good." Steinbeck fictionalized her as Dora Flood in his novel and the brothel as the Bear Flag Restaurant. "Dora is a great woman," Steinbeck wrote, "a great big woman with flaming orange hair and a taste for Nile green evening dresses."

Across the street also stood the aforementioned Wing Chong Market, which stocked food and catered to cannery workers. Won Yee opened the store in 1918, and in 1934 it was taken over by his son and a partner. Yee had a rough start on the Row with police raids and harassment, but the store prospered nonetheless. In *Cannery Row*, Steinbeck immortalized Won Yee as Lee Chong. "Lee Chong is more than a Chinese grocer," Steinbeck wrote. "He must be. Perhaps he is evil balanced and held suspended by good—an Asiatic planet held to its orbit by the pull of Lao Tze and held away from Lao Tze by the centrifugality of

Gabe Bicknell on cover of Penguin Classics edition of Cannery Row. *Cover photo by* Life *magazine photographer Peter Stackpole.* PHOTO BY AUTHOR.

abacus and cash register—Lee Chong suspended, spinning, whirling among groceries and ghosts. A hard man with a can of beans—a soft man with the bones of his grandfather."

Drunks and bums would stagger in and out of the store, in the novel and in real life, too, to buy bottles of cheap liquor. They slept across the street from the lab in the old industrial pipes of a vacant lot. Ricketts told the island pioneers how some would occasionally earn a few dollars collecting for him. Gabe was even looking after the lab while Ed and Toni were away that summer.

Before Ricketts had left for Vancouver Island, *Life* magazine sent photographer Peter Stackpole to Monterey "to get anything on Steinbeck and Cannery Row." He found Gabe and photographed him for the magazine. This hilarious portrait, complete with Gabe's toothless grin, now appears on the cover of the Penguin Twentieth-Century Classic edition of *Cannery Row*. Gabe, of course, was Steinbeck's prototype for Mack, the crafty leader of the bums in the novel. Shortly after the book's publication, Gabe came to the writer quite drunk and complained that a lot of feelings had been hurt down on the Row because of the novel. "The ones you left out," said Gabe.

The novel not only confused the real and fictional, but confounded critics too. Its episodic structure meandered. The characters were comical, though forlorn and tragic and even suicidal. Nothing actually happens in the novel—nothing but a brawling drunken party at the lab, that is. What was John Steinbeck trying to say? This couldn't be the same crusading polemist of *The Grapes of Wrath*. Critics were merciless: the *Times of London* called the novel a "straggling and arbitrary sequence of trivial events." Another said *Cannery Row* wasn't just "a trivial and seemingly meaningless and purposeless novel," but "a sentimental glorification of weakness of mind and degeneration of character."

Cannery Row is arguably the most misunderstood, and maligned, novel in the Steinbeck canon. He professed to have written it on four levels and complained at the time that no critic had yet stumbled on the design of the book. Just before leaving for Clayoquot, Ricketts too wrote a friend telling him that few readers had penetrated "the superficialities (however charming) of *Cannery Row*." Toni agreed, writing an insightful insider's review in Monterey's *What's Doing*:

> The reviewers chortled over the humor, quaintness, and charm of *Cannery Row*, while the critics, who must take things seriously, handed Steinbeck everything from a slap on the wrist for sentimentalizing bums and loafers, to a poke in the nose for abdicating his role as reformer (like in *The Grapes of Wrath*) and pretending that life isn't terribly, terribly earnest. A single critic, Malcom Cowley, puzzled by an underlying sense of violence in the book, read it again more carefully and concluded that if *Cannery Row* was a cream-puff, it was a "very poisoned cream-puff." If Cowley had read it yet again, said Steinbeck, he would have found how very poisoned it was.

Scholars have called *Cannery Row* Steinbeck's *Odyssey,* a satire-par-ody, an ecological parable, a fictional manifestation of the Ricketts-Steinbeck philosophy expressed in *Sea of Cortez. Cannery Row* is indeed the clearest expression of "non-teleological thinking" and "breaking through" in Steinbeck's work. And at the heart of the story is the metaphor of the Great Tide Pool: "Cannery Row after hours..., " writes one literary scholar, "is a tide pool teeming with life after the ocean of commerce recedes." Its underlying theme is ecological.

The bums—Mac and the boys—are the parasitic pea crabs living off other creatures' refuse. An impoverished couple, Mr. and Mrs. Sam Malloy, make a home for themselves in an old, unused cannery boiler, like hermit crabs living in an abandoned snail shell. Dora's girls are Cannery Row's sea anemones—"soft and brilliant flowers, inviting any tired and perplexed animal to lie for a moment in their arms." When Steinbeck says that in the Great Tide Pool the "smells of life and rich-ness, of death and digestion, of decay and birth, burden the air," he could just as easily be describing Cannery Row—or the entire world for that matter.

Cannery Row is also considered Steinbeck's war novel, though admittedly "it never mentions the war—not once." Steinbeck would later say that it was "a nostalgic thing, written for a group of soldiers who had said to me, 'Write something funny that isn't about the war. Write something for us to read—we're sick of the war.'" It was, in fact, an anti-dote to the war. *Cannery Row* describes a morally hypocritical world "where men hungering for love destroy everything lovable about them."

Echoing a passage from *Sea of Cortez,* in which Steinbeck and Ricketts describe "a strange duality in the human which makes for an ethical paradox," Doc says in the novel: "It has always seemed strange to me. The things we admire in men, kindness and generosity, openness, honesty, understanding and feeling are the concomitants of failure in our system. And those traits we detest, sharpness, greed, acquisitiveness, meanness, egotism and self-interest are the traits of success. And while men admire the quality of the first they love the produce of the second."

The world outside Cannery Row is a Faustian one. As Doc says, "The sale of the souls to gain the whole world is completely voluntary and almost unanimous—but not quite." Here one is most surely hearing the voice of Ed Ricketts, who was so enamored by Johann Wolfgang von Goethe's telling of the tale of the old scholar who makes a pact with Mephistopheles that, according to Steinbeck, he "enlarged his scientific German so that he could read Faust and hear the sounds of the words as they were written and taste their meanings." Ricketts thought Goethe's *Faust* was "the peak of an age" and a manifestation of "breaking through." He was also the only one to recognize *Cannery Row*'s Faustian design.

Cannery Row is ultimately an idyll, a "dream" as Steinbeck wrote, that does not and could never exist. It's an imaginary respite in a world at war. In 1945, it was pure escapism that a weary public was desperate to read. The mystical milieu of Doc's lab, Cannery Row's bums and the unworldly tide pools seemed so far away from the realities of Europe's fire-bombed cities, the maimed young men returning home and the horrors of the Holocaust, which were just starting to appear in newspapers. The Clayoquot settlers listened to "Doc" with rapture.

* * *

IN the following two weeks, Ricketts conducted fourteen more collecting trips, continuing to explore Stubbs Island and rowing to Round Island, just several hundred yards away, and to Deadman Islet, "about 45 minutes hard pull against the tide." He also kept busy identifying specimens, a task made difficult by the dark, dank weather. He wired an extra light to his desk, which was jammed up against the window. The lightbulb pulsated noticeably while he worked in the evening. "The lights are queer," he described:

> You never turn them on or off. They go on when Bill starts the light plant, they stay on until the . . . diesel oil he put in it is used up, then they flicker and die out over a period of oh say 60 seconds and that's all you can do about it. If you're in the midst of work that's just your hard luck. But fortunately they run until 1 or 2 A.M. sometimes later, and I get up early, so I'm usually pooped out enough to welcome the interruption.

More parties also interrupted his scientific work. On the first of July, everyone ventured to neighboring Vargas Island for a picnic to celebrate Dominion Day, Canada's national holiday. The next night they all went to a swinging dance, complete with brass band, at the Royal Canadian Air Force base, which was cut into a large swath of boggy rainforest near Long Beach, between Ucluelet and Tofino. Ricketts, who never liked to dance, snuck out at 10 P.M. to capture "a few of the giant hordes of beach hoppers" on Long Beach. On the Fourth of July, Ed and Toni hitched a ride in the Jeep of Captain Peter Ackley, an American in the Canadian army. They drove along Long Beach and did some specimen collecting on the way to Ucluelet, where an impromptu Independence Day celebration ensued at the seaplane base there. "I don't know where the army gets all its liquor under rationing," wrote Ricketts.

The marine biologist spent his last few days in Clayoquot Sound collecting, sorting and dispatching bundles of fish, sea cucumbers, sea spiders and shrimp to specialists abroad. After five weeks his first "outer shores" expedition was complete. The summer of revelry and research was at its end.

Yet there was much more to discover on the coast. Ricketts mentioned to the Clayoquot pioneers that he hoped Steinbeck would join him on his next trip. A month before Ricketts' own departure, the writer had left for Mexico to produce a film based on *The Pearl*. Steinbeck wrote the novella from Mexican folklore that he and Ricketts had heard on their Baja expedition, and which was originally recounted in *Sea of Cortez*. Ricketts figured that Clayoquot Sound would be fertile ground for Steinbeck, whom he thought was somewhat unhappy in New York. Steinbeck could probably spin a wonderful yarn from the local lore.

The writer almost certainly would have been inspired by the outlandish tale of Fred Tibbs, a chivalric Clayoquot pioneer with a disfigured face and enormous dimples who built his own Camelot on a nearby island. He constructed a four-story wooden castle complete with medieval-style battlements and a tower where he placed a portrait of a beautiful princess. Tibbs called it "Dream Isle." As a young boy, Steinbeck loved Sir Thomas Malory's *Morte d'Arthur*, and he even underpinned *Tortilla Flat* with Arthurian themes. His last major work, posthumously published in 1976, was a modern retelling of medieval legends, *The Acts of King Arthur and His Noble Knights*.

On Monday, July 9, 1945, Toni and Ed bade farewell to a party that was only getting started on Stubbs Island. They climbed up the gangway onto the *Maquinna,* waved good-bye and sailed away into the evening. "The aftermath of your departure was something long to be remembered," Bill later wrote in a letter addressed to "Doc & Toni." "We all got gloriously drunk on the other three bottles. Betty went up to milk the cow and passed out, hanging onto its tail."

* * *

THE war weighed heavily on Ed Ricketts—weighed heavily on his psyche, his finances and his scientific research. With his son still fighting in the Pacific, his thoughts never ventured far from the war and its implications. He had watched for the second time in his life the planet plunge into the horrors of mass mechanized warfare. Civilization had simply gone mad, he figured. Countries should junk their military budgets, he wrote at the beginning of his Vancouver Island journal, and "devote that money and thought and energy to the common enemy—degenerative diseases, public health, psychiatry and human relations . . . what a difference that would make in our human misery and our bad dreams and our unexplained personal depressions." It certainly would have made a difference to Ed Ricketts. He was terribly troubled by what he saw in the world, describing it as "prejudice blown into intolerances and served up as fascist empires by little men with big power drives."

Sailing down the coast back to Victoria, he reflected on his maiden voyage to *terra incognita* with one eye on events across the Pacific.

I got to thinking about the ecological method, the value of building, of trying to build, whole pictures. No one can controvert it. An ecologist has to consider the parts each in its place and as related to rather than as subsidiary to the whole. It would undoubtedly be good if political leaders, if there [were] such, would get to know that method. If they could realize no man is an island to himself, anymore than the animals are that make up a community, that make up a region, that make up a coastline, he'd be careful to look at more than his own narrow segment.

Ricketts' allusion to John Donne's "For Whom the Bell Tolls" was prophetic. Dr. Fisher at Hopkins Marine Station had once told John Steinbeck that you could find any scientific discovery in the poetry of the preceding generation. Within a week of Ricketts' arrival home in Monterey, it must have become dreadfully apparent what Robinson Jeffers had meant, writing two decades earlier, by "unnatural crime, inhuman science." On July 16, 1945, scientists unleashed upon the world, to borrow a prescient phrase from Jeffers' poetry, "the spinning demons that make an atom."

Science took a macabre turn with the detonation of the first atom bomb. Ed Ricketts saw suicidal faults in modern society and fretted that an international "race riot" in the era of the atom bomb could lead to total annihilation of the human species. "We are an engineering world," he once wrote, "overbalanced on the mechanical side, and the very mathematics that could help us, goes instead into computing statistics, and atom smashers, and production for victory."

No single event is more responsible for the beginning of wide-spread ecological concern around the globe than the explosion of the first atom bomb. History would record that the "Age of Ecology began on the desert outside Alamogordo, New Mexico, on July 16, 1945, with a dazzling fireball of light and a swelling mushroom cloud of radioactive gases." The mass destruction of two cities, radioactive dust and genetic damage, the poisoning of the atmosphere with strontium-90 and the obliteration of Bikini Atoll by nuclear testing, all awoke the global public to the technological madness of modern man.

The outer shores of the North Pacific would come to play a pivotal role in the growing antinuclear and environmental movements. In 1971, twelve activists set sail in an old fishing boat, the *Phyllis Cormack*, from Vancouver, B.C., to Amchitka, a tiny island in the Western Aleutian Islands. They wanted to bear witness to the detonation of the largest underground nuclear bomb in history by the U.S. government. The world cried out against this "insane ecological vandalism," as one crew-man described the test. This became the founding protest of Green-peace. Humanity had finally come to realize that no island, Amchitka or any other, was an island unto itself in the nuclear age.

In his quest to understand the relationships of seashore animals, Ed Ricketts would grow increasingly interested, over the coming months and years, in trying to shed light on the ecology of human relations. The scientist began some rudimentary speculations about the biological basis of xenophobia, since fear of strangers seemed as evident in animal communities as in human communities. It was a point he noted that rainy morning in Clayoquot Sound when he scared off the oystercatchers: "fear and hatred of strangers work just as potently with animals as with men."

Ed Ricketts carried this knowledge with him and worried that he hadn't, alas, done enough to illuminate the world in this time of darkness. Having returned to his modest lab on Cannery Row, he somberly ruminated about what seemed to be, at least at the time and in the face of such gruesome world events, the utter insignificance of his research. "In the remote field of marine biology," he wrote, "I have been distressed at being able to contribute so very little to a world structure that obviously needs so much."

ISOMETRIDIUM RICKETTSI, SEA ANEMONE, NEW SPECIES COLLECTED BY ED
RICKETTS ON APRIL 9, 1940, AT GUAYMAS IN GULF OF CALIFORNIA, MEXICO.

CHAPTER EIGHT

THE LAB

*This little house was called Pacific Biological Laboratories, Inc., as
strange an operation as ever outraged the corporate laws of California.*

—JOHN STEINBECK,
"About Ed Ricketts," *The Log from the Sea of Cortez*

CANNERY Row would never be the same after the war. Actually, the world would never be the same either—after that otherwise warm and gentle morning of August 6, 1945, in Hiroshima.

The proverbial winds of change had started blowing as early as September 1939. Everyone in Monterey could smell it, the rancid odor of fish offal from the sardine reduction plants. "[T]he canneries started up as soon as war was declared," Ricketts wrote a friend, "the first of the profiteers."

The Row roared to life, along with Hitler's blitzkrieg into Poland that month. Ricketts' lab would actually shake from the machinery clanking, stamping, pressing, boiling, bubbling, banging, and screeching next door. Even when the canneries were closed for the season, other activities would pick up steam. "Flora is staging grander and grander openings and I imagine you know just exactly what I mean, so things aren't too quiet around here," Ricketts told another friend. At times, Flora's patrons were too intoxicated to fight even each other, let alone the Nazis. Drunkards and bums would chase each other up and down the Row. Sitting on a cabinet near the lab's front window, Ricketts' teenage son would toot on his trumpet (which Steinbeck had bought him), looking out at the inebriated frolic. Like the rest of the United States, the war started to pull Cannery Row out of the doldrums of the Great Depression.

The respite of indulgence and wanton abandon wouldn't last, of course. Everything suddenly changed—and not for the better—on

December 7, 1941: The Japanese torpedoed Cannery Row's boisterous revelry, along with the bulk of the U.S. Navy's Pacific fleet moored in Pearl Harbor.

Unlike the canneries, the war was anything but profitable for Ed Ricketts. Sales of *Sea of Cortez*, which had just been published, collapsed and Ricketts ended up owing Steinbeck "a small fortune" for financing their trip. The war also gave Stanford University Press an excuse to delay the second printing of *Between Pacific Tides,* denying Ricketts another source of income.

By this time, however, Carol and John Steinbeck had become astronomically wealthy, or at least it seemed out-of-this-world to the couple who had lived in poverty for most of the thirties. Book and film royalties were rolling in. One day Carol showed Ed a check for a mind-boggling sixty thousand dollars, a fantastic sum since the biologist's own annual income was barely one thousand dollars. "The money's coming in so fast I don't know what we'll do with it," she complained to Ricketts.

But by the outbreak of the war their marriage had descended into bitter acrimony. They got divorced and Steinbeck moved to New York with his new girlfriend, Gwyn. His connection to the Monterey Peninsula would never be the same. Others left too: Ritch and Tal Lovejoy moved away and Ed Jr. went to the Bay Area to work at a cannery until he was drafted overseas; he ended up as a clerk in the Allied headquarters of General Douglas MacArthur in Brisbane, Australia.

"Monterey is changing very much," Ricketts wrote his youngest daughter, Cornelia, on June 20, 1942. "About the only activities are in connection with the Presidio and [Fort] Ord [the local army bases]. The summer tourist business apparently is pretty well shot. . . . Most people that we know have gone away."

Ed Ricketts faced tough times. By the spring of 1942, he was ill with a "bum" stomach. "Sometimes even I can't drink as much beer as I want," he joked to Cornelia, "which, as you know, is a serious catastrophe with me." He was flat broke; he had scarcely bought any new clothes in five years. "You'll be ashamed to go around with me," he told her. He hadn't seen his two daughters in five years and struggled with alimony payments. "There were times when we were hungry, not starving, but hungry," remembered Nancy, his eldest daughter. Despite his age, poor health, heavily indebted business and three dependencies, Ricketts was drafted into the army. Steinbeck thought this was "spiteful on the part of the draft board." The biologist closed the commercial lab, though expenses kept piling up.

Authoritarianism crept into people's once lackadaisical lives. The army started giving Flora trouble, too. She tried to be more inconspicuous in her business affairs — "affairs" being a double-entendre considering the number of married men in her clientele. She started advertising room and board. But the ploy was obvious to everyone. "I suspect somehow that it puts out room and board with added attractions!" Ricketts joked. By the end of the summer of 1942, "the lovely nice sporting house," as he called Flora's, had become "a war casualty." The authorities shut it down. They pulled out all the beds — "and boy were there a lot of them!" Ricketts observed — tore down the building and then erected a concrete warehouse to store fish meal. With her business disbanded, poor Flora Woods, once a madam of great charity, would soon be receiving handouts herself; many of Monterey's solid citizens took up a collection for her.

Everyone could sense the easy, carefree days were over. A few months after Pearl Harbor, the *Monterey Peninsula Herald* asked Ricketts, a self-proclaimed "old-timer," to write a retrospective that appeared in the newspaper's annual Sardine Edition under the headline ED RICKETTS COVERS THE WATERFRONT FOR 20 YEARS. The decades had passed "kaleidoscopically," he told readers in his touching collection of anecdotes. He strained not to end the article on an ominous note, however. "In any case," he concluded rather lamely, "we can be sure that 1941–42 marks, for better or worse, the start of a new period." Yet he knew, everyone knew, what war meant: the worst of times were about to befall Cannery Row.

So when Ed and Toni arrived back from Clayoquot Sound with the war almost over, they returned to a Cannery Row that was more serious, perhaps a bit somber, and even — and this was most incredible of all — somewhat sober.

Once, in the early thirties, when Ed went on an inland frog collecting expedition, Gabe and some of the other bums broke into the lab, swilled all the denatured alcohol and busted up the place in the process.

(Steinbeck comically recounts the incident in *Cannery Row*.) "Ed was fuming as was his habit when irritated," remembered his wife Nan, "and forbid them ever to come near the lab. Of course, they stayed away for awhile and of course they came back, with frogs and promises to not repeat the incident."

While Ed and Toni were away on Vancouver Island for almost seven weeks, Gabe found the lab's garage door partly open and, in an unusually responsible act, wired it shut. He then called up the local newspaper to stop their subscription and burned the papers that had piled up. Ricketts returned to find the lab in perfect order, his laboratory alcohol unmolested, and Gabe "sober for a change." Times had certainly changed on Cannery Row.

* * *

AS a commercial enterprise, preserving and selling specimens, Pacific Biological Laboratories Inc. essentially became defunct because of the war. Its corporate records are today housed in the California History Room of the Monterey Public Library. The minutes of the board of directors' meeting on July 29, 1939, are particularly noteworthy: John Steinbeck was elected vice president, having loaned the corporation six thousand dollars at 3 percent interest per annum payable at thirty dollars plus unpaid interest per month. (There's no record that any payments were ever made.) "The fact that the institution survived at all is a matter that must be put down to magic," its illustrious vice president magnanimously proclaimed, since he had, in fact, saved the lab from bankruptcy. "A board of directors' meeting," he added, elucidating on its corporate governance, "differed from any other party only in that there was more beer."

Pacific Biological Laboratories (PBL) did exist in a legal or technical sense during the war (it remained incorporated), but that was the extent of it. There was little demand for specimens and Ricketts spent most of his time in the army at the Presidio anyway. "So, PBL is going to pieces in its own amiable way," Ricketts wrote Jack Calvin in 1943. After being honorably discharged, he became a part-time chemist for Cal Pack, since there was little work in the lab. Orders came infrequently and he only

sporadically attempted to fill them, with help from the "hopeless and undependable" Gabe.

Still, the lab was very much his home and from 1945 onward a rather busy marine research head-quarters, albeit with no govern-ment-funded support, no official accreditation or affiliations, no staff (other than family, friends and a few drunkards-cum-collectors) and no philanthropic endowment (other than occasional cash infusions from the vice president). It became arguably one of the most outlandish entities in California corporate history, investing tens of thousands of dollars over the years in research and development without any hope, or apparently even any desire, of a return on investment. By the summer of 1945, Ricketts had started to dedicate an enormous amount of time and money in completing the "northern sequel."

When Ed and Toni returned home from Clayoquot Sound, they faced a daunting task—identifying, preserving, sorting and cataloging the thousands of specimens they had collected on Vancouver Island. It would take literally months of painstaking work to document it all. He unpacked the specimens, re-sorted them and prepared letters and pack-ages to send, at great cost, to specialists around the world for identifica-tion. Often he'd ship a hundred or more specimens to a museum expert thousands of miles across the country.

Today, there are hundreds and thousands of specimens collected by Ricketts at the most prestigious museums in the United States: 1,313 in the invertebrate and fish collections at the Field Museum in Chicago, 420 at the Smithsonian Institution in Washington, D.C., an estimated 300 to 500 specimens at the California Academy of Sciences in San Francisco, and many more in uncounted collections at the American Museum of Natural History in New York, the Museum of Comparative Zoology at Harvard University and even the Museum of Zoology at Lund University in Sweden.

Ricketts started building his own comprehensive database of species as well, using index cards that would be cross-referenced with the actual specimens, his notebooks, typed collecting reports and various bibliographies. It was a tremendously time-consuming endeavor, and a largely selfless one. As he explained to his son:

> I am devising some printed forms for uniform records so that 80 to 100 years from now my work can be checked if desirable. Trouble with so many pioneer workers in biology is that they keep things pretty much in their own minds, and later on, when methods become more precise and delicate, more detailed workers can't check the earlier results because there's no documentation. I'd like to see all my work backed up by the specimens themselves. If that can't be, because of limitations of suitable space, I want the records and the literature to be there.

Upon their return to Monterey, he also prepared a long-term program of Pacific Coast exploration to be carried out over the next several years: a trip to Ecuador in 1946 "if finances permit it," an expedition to Anchorage via car to explore the Gulf of Alaska in the summer of 1947, and then a final voyage, perhaps by chartered vessel as they had done on the *Western Flyer*, to the Bering Sea, Aleutian Islands and Kamchatka in 1948. He also thought about several shorter trips in the meantime: to San Felipe Bay, Guaymas, San Ignacio Lagoon and Cedros Island on the Baja Peninsula; to Acapulco in Mexico; to the Pearl Islands in Panama; to Humboldt Bay in northern California; to Coos Bay in Oregon; and possibly a six-week trip to the Queen Charlotte Islands on British Columbia's remote north coast. He also quickly realized that his collecting work hadn't been completed to his satisfaction in Clayoquot Sound and resolved to return the following summer of 1946. Besides, he loved the area and it would be wonderful to see Betty, Bill and Ruth again.

There was so much exploration that needed to be conducted and so many more books that could be researched and written on Pacific Coast ecology that John Steinbeck had actually proposed, back in the summer of 1944, that Pacific Biological Laboratories undergo an unlikely corporate expansion, notwithstanding its precarious balance sheet and dismal prospects for commercial revenue generation.

Sandwiched between the Del Vista Packing Company and the Del Mar Canning Company at 800 Ocean View Avenue, the lab was a jerry-built, two-story structure that was twenty-five feet wide and about thirty-five feet long. It was made out of rough-hewn posts and beams, and shack-like board. The entire building, raised like a phoenix from the ashes of the 1936 fire, cost Ricketts $981 to build, plus another $175 for plumbing and pipes, although he saved a bit of money by salvaging the old galvanized fittings and conduit. Architecturally, it was a glorified shanty, but a structurally sound one; the building stood for sixty years before it underwent a restoration and seismic retrofit in the 1990s, which won the California Governor's Award for Historic Preservation.

Like so much of what we know of Ed Ricketts, the best description of his home—his lab—comes from John Steinbeck, who fictionalized it as "Western Biological" in *Cannery Row*. His vivid sketch is most likely a composite of the pre- and post-fire labs, although the second Cannery Row lab was modeled largely after the first, so happy was Ed Ricketts with its functionality and comfort.

It is a low building facing the street. The basement is the storeroom with shelves, shelves clear to the ceiling loaded with jars of preserved animals. And in the basement is a sink and instruments for embalming and for injecting. Then you go through the backyard to a covered shed on piles over the ocean and here are the tanks for the larger animals, the sharks and rays and octopi, each in their concrete tanks. There is a stairway up the front of the building and a door that opens into an office where there is a desk piled high with unopened mail, filing cabinets, and a safe with the door propped open. Once the safe got locked by mistake and no one knew the combination. And in the safe was an open can of sardines and a piece of Roquefort cheese. Before the combination could be sent by the maker of the lock, there was trouble in the safe. It was then that Doc devised a method for getting revenge on a bank if anyone should ever want to. "Rent a safety deposit box," he said, "then deposit in it one whole fresh salmon and go away for six months." After the trouble with the safe, it was not permitted to keep food there any more. It is kept in the filing cabinets. Behind the office is a room where in aquaria are many living animals; there also are the microscopes and the slides and the drug cabinets, the cases of laboratory glass, the work benches and little motors, the chemicals. From this room come smells—formaline, and dry starfish, and sea water and

TOP: *Upstairs living quarters in the lab, circa 1947–48.* COURTESY OF ED RICKETTS JR.

BOTTOM: *Downstairs work area in the lab, circa 1947–48.* COURTESY OF ED RICKETTS JR.

menthol, carbolic acid and acetic acid, smell of brown wrapping paper and straw and rope, smell of chloroform and ether, smell of ozone from the motors, smell of fine steel and thin lubricant from the microscopes, smell of banana oil and rubber tubing, smell of drying wool socks and boots, sharp pungent smell of rattlesnakes, and musty frightening smell of rats. And through the back door comes the smell of kelp and barnacles when the tide is out and the smell of salt and spray when the tide is in.

To the left the office opens into a library. The walls are bookcases to the ceiling, boxes of pamphlets and separates, books of all kinds, dictionaries, encyclopedias, poetry, plays. A great phonograph stands against the wall with hundreds of records lined up beside it. Under the window is a redwood bed and on the walls and to the bookcases are pinned reproductions of Daumiers, and Graham, Titian, and Leonardo and Picasso, Dali and George Grosz, pinned here and there at eye level so that you can look at them if you want to. There are chairs and benches in this little room and of course the bed. As many as forty people have been here at one time.

Behind this library or music room, or whatever you want to call it, is the kitchen, a narrow chamber with a gas stove, a water heater, and a sink. But whereas some food is kept in the filing cabinets in the office, dishes and cooking fat and vegetables are kept in glass-fronted sectional bookcases in the kitchen. No whimsy dictated this. It just happened. From the ceiling of the kitchen hang pieces of bacon, and salami, and black bêche-demer. Behind the kitchen is a toilet and a shower. The toilet leaked for five years until a clever and handsome guest fixed it with a piece of chewing gum.

John Steinbeck suggested they sell the lab, because it was getting too valuable for Ricketts to live in. The cannery industry was booming (albeit unsustainably) along the Row and properties were fetching tempting prices. Steinbeck thought the now valuable lab could be sold at a tidy profit and a cheaper waterfront lot purchased where they could construct "a good residence and lab which shall be headquarters for our future work."

It sounded financially feasible—at least after several beers during a board of directors' "meeting." So on November 11, 1944, taking his vice president's advice, Ricketts wrote the new director of the Hopkins Marine Station, Dr. L. R. Blinks. Ricketts proposed that Stanford University provide him and John Steinbeck a dollar-a-year lease for unused property at the marine station. A new and improved lab would be built there, which would be bequeathed to the university upon their deaths. The letter read in part:

> We have in mind a combination establishment, research, residence, biological supply house, which shall serve as headquarters for our exploration and investigations into the fauna of the Pacific during the next twenty years or so (I am 47, John a few years younger). Of the three part faunistic study projected some years back, two parts have been completed and published [*Between Pacific Tides* and *Sea of Cortez*]. The plan is to complete this by an investigation and report on the extreme North Pacific [*The Outer Shores*], then to build up a working collection of specimens and the necessary library, and finally to work up a fairly comprehensive manual of marine invertebrates . . . restricted to Pacific coast species from the Bering Sea to Panama, and from shore to 25 or 50 fathoms.

Ricketts envisioned a two-and-a-half-story building, fifty feet by sixty feet, comprising a library, laboratories, museum, offices and living quarters. Stanford University agreed to the plan, and Ricketts worked studiously on an extensive, itemized proposal for the building in April of 1945, just before departing for Clayoquot. He drew up numerous floor plans and blueprints, sketched the building's façade and typed a meticulously detailed description covering fixtures, furniture, doors (French, Dutch and regular), louver ventilators, cement work, electrical wiring, scientific equipment, heating, even doorknobs. The proposal must have taken weeks to write.

By the third week of May, Ricketts was told that the university's business office and Hopkins Marine Station would recommend a lease to Stanford University's Board of Trustees. The new building would be financed in part by the sale of the lab; a local cannery offered them up to $18,000. Steinbeck also agreed to contribute a few thousand dollars, in exchange for, as Ricketts described in a letter to Dr. Blinks, "a fairly detached office which can serve as permanent headquarters for him during our lifetime." The new facility would be Ricketts' fourth and probably final lab — and effectively a seaside retirement home for the biologist and writer.

*   *   *

SHORTLY after arriving back from Vancouver Island, a crisis occurred that threatened to imperil everything. Kay, Toni's ten-year-old daughter who stayed with relatives while they were away, had been suffering from headaches. Toni also noticed that one of her daughter's eyes was wandering. She took her to a neurological specialist at Stanford University Hospital in San Francisco. The diagnosis shocked Toni and Ed: Kay had a malignant tumor, cancer of the brain. "There was no hope extended that she could be cured," Ricketts wrote his son, "but that she would live happily for perhaps a couple more years and that the end then would be swift and not bad."

The doctor immediately recommended a delicate operation to prevent blindness and to reduce the pressure in her head, which was causing pain and adverse symptoms, including double vision. But only days before the brain surgery, Toni thought she saw signs of improvement. The remission was medically unexplainable. "A modern miracle," Ricketts called it. Kay was soon discharged and went to Portland to visit her father, while Toni and Ed recovered from the "shock and confusion."

In December of 1945, Ed Jr. came back from serving in Southeast Asia, bringing some joviality to the lab with his swinging jazz and trumpet playing. Kay, although not yet back in school, was steadily improving. But Ricketts, according to his personal journals, felt as if he and his girlfriend of five years were drifting apart. The incident with Kay obviously shook the couple terribly, and her future was still uncertain. It was the beginning of very trying times for their relationship.

There were parties galore in the New Year, but even these gleeful occasions strained the couple's relationship. Although Ed was gregarious, Toni was far more sociable, a "party gal." Occasionally the biologist would slip downstairs to get some work done while a party continued upstairs in the lab. At a friend's party one night in February, Ricketts left at 1 A.M., feeling Toni had given him the cold shoulder. He returned to

Toni Jackson, Kay Jackson and Ed Ricketts, circa 1947–48.
COURTESY OF ED RICKETTS JR.

the lab and, as was his habit, picked up his large black notebook and pen.

He was depressed. He felt that as a "self-reliant gal, perhaps primarily a career gal," Toni wasn't particularly interested in his "neurosis." In shaky handwriting, he scribbled some notes: "She isn't terribly interested in me. . . . I won't get any help from her. I'm entirely on my own. We are separate people leading our own lives." Then, his hand steadied. "I feel angry. Feel like telling her we might as well have things out, that a separation seems to me inevitable since I can't go along with her social needs and she can't go along with my affectional and sexual needs."

The New Year brought more bad news, too: the deal to construct the new research headquarters, which Ricketts worked on so tirelessly the year before, fell apart. The deal was contingent on selling the lab, but the local sardine industry's catch that season had plummeted by almost 40 percent from the previous year; the boom was about to go bust. The cannery pulled out of the deal to buy the lab.

Ed and Toni never appeared to work through their problems, to bridge the growing gap in their relationship. On March 16, 1946, Ricketts wrote a "progress" report in his notebook, resolving "to allow for Toni, but not to depend on her in any way," to not have sexual intercourse more than twice a week, to keep up a "large work plan" and to have "not more than one or two drinks in an afternoon or during an evening." Although he led an unscheduled existence, or rather, one that was governed by the ebb and flow of the tide, it became apparent that he needed to be much more regimented in his daily life. Times were tough, personally and financially.

He was only on retainer for sixteen hours a week at Cal Pack (because of the lack of sardine landings), so he tried to rebuild his biological supply business. He hired Gabe to go on several collecting trips from March 23 to 27. He also agreed to revise *Between Pacific Tides* yet again for Stanford University Press, which kept delaying its second edition. There was also a considerable amount of scientific correspondence to be written for *The Outer Shores*, and he started organizing his second summer trip to Vancouver Island.

In April, he wrote to Joseph Campbell, telling him enthusiastically about his plan, his dream, to get to the Aleutians, Bering Sea and Kamchatka, and to create a manual of invertebrates from Panama to Asia. He would turn forty-nine years old on May 14, and he figured he would have another twenty years of good health to "lay a good foundation for the next guy." No matter his psychological, romantic, or financial travails, Ed Ricketts pressed ahead to complete the trilogy.

*　*　*

WHEN John Steinbeck finished *Cannery Row*'s typescript, he had taken it to Ed for his blessing. Ricketts read it through carefully, cracking a knowing smile here, wincing at some outrageousness there. When he was done, he told Steinbeck: "Let it go that way. It is written in kindness. Such a thing can't be bad."

"But it was bad in several ways neither of us foresaw," Steinbeck later lamented. "As the book began to be read, tourists began coming to the laboratory, first a few and then in droves. People stopped their cars and stared at Ed with that glassy look that is used on movie stars.

Children looking into lab on Cannery Row, 1945. PHOTO BY PETER STACKPOLE.

Hundreds of people came into the lab to ask questions and peer around." The lab became a fishbowl and Ed Ricketts its exotic inhabitant. It went on for months, people peeping in and wanting to talk to "Doc." On April 9, 1946, Ricketts wrote Steinbeck to complain:

> We had last Sunday the only really bad Cannery Row experience to date. It was pleasant noon, I was sitting barefoot and with nothing on otherwise but shirt, drinking coffee, reading. Toni just got up and was reaching for her dressing gown. Kay going out had left the door unlocked, which we're careful not to do Saturday or Sunday; there are tourists. So this god damn fellow came in saying not a word, started to walk in our bedroom. I said "how do you do," blocking the way, asked him if he was looking for someone. Toni got behind the door. Said he wanted to see Doc, that his wife dared him to come in. With some actual pushing I headed him out into the office, closed our door and he

THE LAB ‖ 155

still had the nerve—though I told him now this was pretty much a private dwelling—to say he'd like to bring his wife in. At which here she was coming up the stairs. Ended up that I actually pushed him out the door against his wife, shut and locked it in his face with as much non-violence as I could. Well I didn't get angry, never did feel even actually unkind. But it proves something or other alright. His last words were "wait a minute, want you to tell me what you did with all those frogs, those tom cats; bothered by a lot of people coming in you ought to charge admission." The others have been good people—very much moved by their inward most kind projections onto what they think I am. And they certainly merit gentleness. But this guy was what you call unsavory at least.

Despite these frequent interruptions, Ricketts kept busy preparing for his second collecting trip to Vancouver Island and farther north to the Queen Charlotte Islands in British Columbia. He, Toni and his twenty-year-old son, Ed Jr., planned to leave Cannery Row a week after his birthday, in late May.

But even thousands of miles from Monterey in a tiny village on the remote Queen Charlotte Islands, Ricketts couldn't escape his celebrity status. "It's rumored up here already that I'm the Doc of *Cannery Row*," he later told Steinbeck. "How do rumors get around so quickly? And already I've autographed a copy of the book."

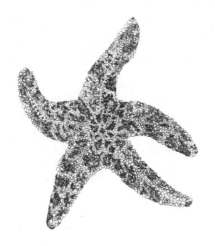

PISASTER OCHRACEUS SEGNIS, PURPLE STARFISH, NEW SUBSPECIES
COLLECTED BY ED RICKETTS ON MAY 13, 1925, IN BAJA CALIFORNIA, MEXICO.

CHAPTER NINE

THE JESUS WALK

And the sea arose by reason of a great wind that blew. So when they had rowed about five and twenty or thirty furlongs, they see Jesus walking on the sea, and drawing nigh unto the ship: and they were afraid. But he saith unto them, It is I; be not afraid.

—King James Bible, John 6:18–20

IT was a cool Wednesday morning, the air moist from a breeze coming in off Monterey Bay. Ed, Toni and Ed Jr. stood waiting for the regular 8:30 A.M. Del Monte Express at the train station in Pacific Grove. Beside them sat a mountain of luggage.

The date was May 22, 1946, and if all went according to schedule they would be in Seattle the following day making their way back to Clayoquot Sound. After a short delay in Seattle, thanks to a railway strike and the late arrival of their mountain of luggage at King Street Station, the trio climbed aboard the S.S. *Iroquois* at midnight on Thursday to set sail from Seattle to Victoria.

They arrived in the provincial capital the next morning and ate breakfast aboard the steamer before going through customs, where they filled in forms for importing their camera, microscope and other scientific paraphernalia. They checked into the Empress Hotel. It was Empire Day and the flagship hotel was thronged with people celebrating Queen Victoria's birthday in the city that bore her name. The regal fête did not impress Ed Ricketts, nor did Victoria's pompously attired celebrants. "I never saw so many unappetizing women," he groaned in his journal.

They stayed only one night in the jubilant capital, enough time for Ricketts to obtain government liquor permits in order to purchase two quarts of Canadian Club whiskey and to conduct a bit of research at the Victoria Public Library. They also visited Jo Brydges, Betty Farmer's sister, who was also a widow and would move to Clayoquot in 1948 to run the hotel with Betty.

As usual, Captain Martin MacKinnon greeted them like old friends aboard the *Princess Norah* on Saturday night. (The *Maquinna* was laid up for painting.) It was, Ricketts wrote in his log, a "very quiet night." The steamer set sail at midnight on her regular night-sea journey, first calling into Port Renfrew, then the "boat landing" at lonely Clo-oose, Bamfield before noon the next day, several short stops in Barkley Sound including the canneries at Kildonan, an overnight stop in Port Alberni, back down the inlet to Ucluelet the next morning, then Tofino and finally Clayoquot by early afternoon on May 27. By all accounts, it was an uneventful two-day sailing.

The island settlers heard the *Norah*'s familiar whistle blast as she ploughed into Clayoquot Sound. They had received a telegram from Ricketts about his arrival and now gathered on the wharf as the *Norah* neared. Later that night they celebrated with a salmon feast. Toni caught her first fish ever, from the wharf in a drizzling rain. "[S]he was a thrilled gal," Ricketts recalled. They cooked the largest one, about five pounds, although "Doc," as Ricketts was now famously called in Clayoquot Sound, wasn't particularly fond of the catch *du jour*. "The flesh of these young salmon is poor," he complained, "looks wonderful, vivid red, but no taste, just like eating watery and tasteless meat."

Work commenced immediately the next morning. Ricketts set off to the other side of the island to do specimen "prospecting." In the afternoon, he poisoned a tide pool with a one-ounce jar of powdered derris root (a tropical climbing plant whose active agent is rotenone, a commercial insecticide). "After half hour or so," he observed, "the fish [came] wiggling up to the surface. Actually [seemed] to be trying to crawl out of the pool."

Ricketts made few outright expressions of joy or pleasure at being back in Clayoquot Sound. His travelogue is impersonal, distinctly matter-of-fact. Yet feelings of exuberance, wonderment and happiness seep into his scientific observations. An animal he spied swimming just beyond the dock was "fabulous" and "beautiful." Racing out after it in the kicker, he discovered it to be a big pelagic worm of the syllid family, *Autolytus magnus*. At night, while focusing the beam of a flashlight into a swift tidal current to watch aquatic animals swirl by, he wondered why a certain sea worm was so attracted to the spot of light. There were also

Ed Ricketts and Toni Jackson walking on wharf at Kildonan, Vancouver Island, 1946. COURTESY OF ED RICKETTS JR.

great "oooh's" and "aaah's" one early morning when Betty and Toni captured a stunning crab, *Phyllolithodes papillosus*, which had a smooth ivory carapace and big claws in "vivid burnt orange." More thrills erupted when they trapped a great octopus. Later that same day, they collected many ruby red sea anemones.

Ricketts sent some of these anemone specimens to Dr. Oskar Carlgren at Lund University's Department of Zoology in Sweden. Dr. Carlgren had named three new sea anemone species collected in the Sea of Cortez after their collectors: *Palythoa rickettsi, Isometridium rickettsi* and *Phialoba steinbecki.* He agreed to identify all the sea anemone specimens for their "northern sequel" as well. Upon close inspection of these B.C. specimens, the esteemed zoologist concluded that Ricketts had discovered another new species.

* * *

ON their fourth day of collecting, Ed Ricketts and his son took the kicker over to neighboring Round Island. (Officially, it's named Felice

Island.) They pushed its bow up onto the beach and lashed a rope to the shore so it wouldn't float away on the incoming tide. They wanted to collect on a unique habitat that extended out from Round Island.

Clayoquot Sound is a vast labyrinth of deep bays, channels and inlets, whose immense waters must pour through tight passages and narrows, no more than several hundred yards wide at places, to the open ocean. The half-mile entrance between the peninsula where Tofino is situated and Stubbs Island is one of these bottlenecks, with Round Island plugged in between like a cork. When the tide ebbs, seawater heaped up in a deep fifteen-mile-long inlet bursts from Clayoquot Sound through this entrance like champagne from a bottle, so great is the pressure as the sea recedes. The tide spews out on each side of Round Island, through Van Nevel Channel to the west and Duffin Passage to the east. As a result of these racing tides and their tremendous influence over the centuries, a sandbar has formed between the two waterways.

Streaming out three-quarters of a mile from Round Island, the sandbar is rich with clams. Ricketts collected four of the most common species here. At low tide, flocks of seagulls descended on the clam beds to snatch up the tasty siphons of the butter clams (*Saxidomus giganteus*), geoducks (*Panope generosa*), horse clams (*Schizothaerus nuttallii*) and bent-nosed clams (*Macoma nasuta*). The cornucopia was irresistible, deliciously so.

It was too tempting for Ed Ricketts and his son. They began an almost mile-long hike from Round Island to the end of the sand spit. "I was starting to get a little nervous," Ricketts recalled, "but the flats at the far end, where they go off into the deep channel suddenly, were so interesting we couldn't pull ourselves away." They reached the far end and quickly scooped a bounty from the sands, becoming intensely preoccupied by their fruitful labors.

The sandbar is a sort of golden land bridge almost connecting Round Island to Deadman Islet, a stone's throw across Deadman Pass, "the deep channel" that Ricketts mentioned. At high tide, the treacherous bar disappears; it is a hidden barrier and hazard to navigation between Tofino and Stubbs Island. Many novice or careless navigators, and even a few experienced skippers of the *Maquinna,* have run their vessels high and dry on the sandbar.

The tip of the long spit is an especially perilous place (as its proximity to Deadman Pass suggests) for anyone who hungrily craves clams, but carelessly forgets time—and tide. Once their sacks were heavy with mollusks, Ricketts and his son eventually noticed the seawater nipping at their heels. They looked back toward Round Island and were astonished at what they *didn't* see: the entire strip of sand, their land bridge, had disappeared. The sea completely surrounded them.

Over in Tofino, the four-year-old daughter of a Clayoquot settler looked out into the water and saw something most peculiar. She had actually heard the miraculous story before, on Sundays at the picturesque Saint Columba Anglican Church on Second Street in Tofino. Yet the little girl couldn't believe her eyes. Between two islands, Round and Deadman, about a mile apart, in the middle of the sound, she saw a man walking on water.

Pointing seaward, she gently tugged at her mother's hem. "Mommy, is that Jesus walking on the water over there?" she asked.

The mother looked out and quickly realized what was happening: two men were caught out on the sand spit in the racing tide. She sent someone running down to the lifeboat station where the skipper frantically prepared the vessel for launching. He also called Bill White at the Clayoquot Hotel to have him ready his runabout, the *Beegee*, for an imminent rescue. Time—and tide—was of the essence.

Ricketts and his son started back immediately as the tidal waters rose to their ankles, shins, knees, then thighs. The current was vicious, running at more than three knots. Both men were secretly frightened to death, but they kept up the appearance of calm. They slogged forward as icy seawater rose around them. They had half a mile to go and soon became almost panicky. They considered throwing away their heavy clam collections and stripping off their clothes to swim to safety. "It's slow going when you're wading almost up to your hips," Ricketts later recalled, "and your morale is ruined by realizing there are deeper crossings yet ahead." Soaking wet, they patiently waded back to Round Island, where the kicker was well moored. Ricketts figured, however, that if they had waited another fifteen or twenty minutes out on the spit, a full-scale rescue would have ensued.

*   *   *

FOR two weeks, Ed, Toni and Ed Jr. kept up a steady pace of collecting. The next day they headed out to Wickaninnish Island and Echachis Island, on the open coast. A phenomenally low tide revealed a hidden world of bright corals, sea squirts, hydroids, bryozoans and encrusted sponges plastered on rocks. Ricketts took a "magnificent haul," collecting or noting more than 125 species, including an enormous octopus and a river otter, *Lutra canadensis*. (According to Ricketts, there was "just one chance in a thousand" that it was a sea otter, *Enhydra lutris*, a species brought almost to extinction by native hunters and European fur traders in the late 1700s.) They also went out to Devil's Rock on Stubbs Island to see a legendary octopus that lived elusively in a rocky cavern. Ricketts figured it would take a crowbar and some dynamite to flush it out. They did more clam digging, once with Betty who wanted to show Ricketts her prowess at burrowing for the bivalves. There were more tide pools to poison, too. By June 5, after nine full days of collecting, Ricketts figured he had about two hundred containers full of specimens and his notebook was brimming with zoological data.

When reviewing his notebook one evening, however, he couldn't figure out why he'd failed to note all the specimens taken on Thursday, June 6. It was uncharacteristic of him to be so negligent. He then realized, with some amusement, the probable cause of his delinquency: the *Maquinna* called at Clayoquot between three and four o'clock that afternoon and Captain MacKinnon "made a beeline for my place, and we had as many fast ones as he cared to keep the vessel docked there for." One imagines a warm whiskey fog clouding Ricketts' usually clear mind that day.

Liquor was a natural comfort for sailors and fishermen who endured the coast's frequent bursts of intemperate weather. Even though it was summer, Ricketts was outside routinely in his feather-stuffed coat, plastic raincoat and sou'wester. The day after their arrival the sea was so stormy that a seventy-five-foot trawler, the *Western Ranger*, had sought shelter behind Stubbs Island. Most of the time the weather was overcast, dreary, drizzling or pouring buckets of rain, day and night. Or worse: Ed and Bill had planned a trip to Estevan Point one

Sunday, but had to cancel it because Bill dropped some freight on his toe which brought on an attack of gout. "It was a lucky thing all around," Ricketts later said. A violent storm swept in with "rain in sheets such as I've seldom seen even here and wind in dangerous gusts." Another night was particularly frightening, too:

> Candles tonight. Last night darkness only, but tonight we were ready. The generator broke down. Bearing trouble. A severe storm. Rain, driving heavy rain that almost scares you. Makes you think of biblical stories of the flood. Makes you fearful to go out in it, thinking if you slip and fall you'll drown. Like a deluge. Occasional high wind. Some lightning. Most people have no conception of what rain and storm can be. The winters must be terrible here. Bill says he doesn't think he can last out any more. They take too much out of you. Not very cold. Just concentrated storm and wind, and darkness.

* * *

SAVAGE was the land and "savages" were those who lived here. Darkness flooded the sky, the sea and, if one were to believe the first missionaries, the minds of the natives. Sea squalls, the natives believed, were caused by Thunderbird, the mighty crypto-zoological bird, which swooped down into the brine to fight Whale. The ensuing battle created a thrashing sea, howling winds, great thunder and flashes of lightning. And a colorful rainbow made the "savages," as early missionaries called the Nuu-chah-nulth, bow or turn their heads away, fearing such sublimity would cause harm to befall them. To the missionaries, Clayoquot Sound was a godforsaken land, gripped by evil since time immemorial.

Then one day a surprise came to Clayoquot Sound—and in more ways than one. On April 22, 1874, the twenty-eight-ton schooner *Surprise* sailed into the sound and grounded, as one might expect, on the sand spit off Round Island. Aboard was a twenty-nine-year-old Catholic missionary who recorded in his diary descriptions of the local "heathens" and their superstitions, Devil worship and sea serpents. "The wolves were howling in the distance," he wrote one terrifying night, "and the Indian dogs were barking at the rising moon. The sea was breaking against the shore, but there was not a human soul to break the solemnity and the monotony of the midnight hour."

The young priest came alone but carried the charity and zeal of a hundred men. He would beat the Devil out of the native people and bring civilization, that is to say Christianity, to the "savages." His life story is a heroic testament to the power of one.

Reverend Augustin Joseph Brabant established the first mission on the West Coast of Vancouver Island since the Spanish had left Nootka in 1795. He located it in Hesquiat Harbor, about a four-hour boat ride from Tofino, on the western edge of Clayoquot Sound near Estevan Point. A small chapel was built out of timber, complete with a steeple and bell. It was, Brabant described, "the poorest church in Christendom."

Reading Brabant's published journals, *Reminiscence of the West Coast of Vancouver Island*, Ricketts must have been both appalled and awed: horrified by the extremely intolerant, racist attitude Brabant showed toward the Nuu-chah-nulth, and yet awed, even inspired, by the perseverance, courage and selflessness of a man—however misguided—who spent almost thirty solitary years in the wilderness dedicated to their supposed betterment. Almost single-handedly, Father Brabant transformed this ancient civilization. Within three generations, around the time of Ricketts' visit, the region's native population had changed virtually beyond recognition. Their pagan gods had been demystified, their villages devastated by disease, their once unfettered dominion restricted to little Indian reserves, their potlatch ceremonies outlawed, their children forbidden to speak their native tongue. It had not happened without resistance, however.

Shortly after Father Brabant arrived, the Hesquiaht Chief Matlahaw, rabid and deranged with smallpox and believing Brabant had infected his people, shot the priest. Brabant was hit in the right hand. The chief then fired a second round, spraying buckshot into the priest's shoulder and back as he cleaned his mangled hand in a nearby creek. A bloodied Brabant barely survived the attack. A British man-of-war, H.M.S. *Rocket,* rescued him and took him to Victoria to recover. Undaunted by this uncharitable welcome, Brabant returned and became, according to a fellow priest, "a superman in the eyes of the heathens because he could not be killed."

Brabant spoke the local native dialect and held Mass, performed baptisms and burials, and taught the Lord's Prayer each Sunday. Day by day, he debunked their pagan mythology. "The Indians tell their yarns with such conviction of truth that it is almost painful to have to contradict them," Brabant wrote. Many Hesquiaht loathed the missionary. He was threatened with death several times, and initially found great opposition to his Christian teachings, especially among the shamans. After six years, he had converted only one of the villagers to Christianity. "As regards the spiritual state of the tribe," Brabant recorded in his journal, "it is worse than ever. They blame me for the absence of food. They laugh at the doctrine which I teach. I gain nothing by making the sign of the Cross. I am neither a white man nor an Indian. I am the *Chigha,* the devil."

He was undeterred, however, and continued to chip away at the ethos of this ancient civilization. "It is slow work," Brabant admitted, "but one after another the dark spots in the Indians' minds are being cleared." He finally usurped the shamans, sending a posse of thugs to break up a séance and scatter his nemeses. Father Brabant eventually converted almost the entire village—or what was left of it after waves of smallpox, measles and whooping cough brought on widespread death.

Yet he could not rest on his laurels after twenty-five years of soul saving, for a most scurrilous creed had started to menace the coast. Presbyterians and Methodists were arriving, he wrote with great sectarian zeal, "to give us trouble and pervert our Indian children." His legacy was in peril and so he resolved to build, in a central part of the coast, an Indian school for young boys and girls. "If we could keep the children from perversions," he wrote, "our position [would be] safe."

* * *

ED Ricketts visited Christie Indian Residential School on Thursday, June 13, after almost two weeks of collecting. The previous summer he had briefly met its principal, who asked him to visit. Ricketts accepted reluctantly, since he found the very idea of missionaries repugnant. But the priest seemed friendly and genuine about the invitation.

The school, which Brabant named after Alexander Christie, bishop of Vancouver Island, was located about two miles from Clayoquot on the western shore of Meares Island and was, as one priest described, "nestled at the hem of the skirt of Lone Cone, a mountain soaring high into the sky." The Nuu-chah-nulth called the area Kakawis, meaning "place of berries." There was a fine bay out front—St. Mary's Bay, Brabant named it—which at low tide became a hard-packed beach of more than twenty acres. Brabant thought it would be "a magnificent playground for children." It was close to a creek, a clam bed and good salmon fishing grounds—essential staples for maintaining the health of native children.

Old black-and-white photographs make the boarding school (which burned to the ground in 1983) look quaint and idyllic, if somewhat forlorn against the dramatic backdrop of Lone Cone. The original building was a white, two-and-a-half-story structure that housed an ornate chapel, schoolrooms and dormitories. A tiny steeple bearing the Cross crowned the building. Two wings were soon added, then a cow barn, running water, electricity and a gymnasium. To young native children, however, the residential school looked imposing. It was the largest building they had ever seen—far grander than any chief's longhouse. It loomed on a hilltop fifty feet above the beach. A huge crucifix bearing the emaciated body of Christ stood out front, like some sinister warning to those who misbehaved.

Kakawis was modeled on similar schools in the United States. Brabant envisioned it as an "industrial school," an apt description for the dehumanizing process that masqueraded as aboriginal education at the time. Native children were first removed from their home villages, forcing a physical, cultural and spiritual wedge to be driven between parent and child. Next came socialization—"to kill the Indian in the child." The little "savages" were stripped of their clothes and personal belongings, cleaned, their long hair cut, dressed in uniforms and assigned a number. Life was terribly regimented, with strict rules and schedules: half the day was dedicated to studies and the other half to chores—sewing, laundry, carpentry, farming. The kids were forbidden to "talk Indian" and punishment was often severe—strapping, public ridicule, confinement or missed meals. The final stage—assimilation—failed miserably, in part because the students' education was shoddy (few actually graduated) and because many native pupils, trained in modern vocations, were denied jobs by a racist society.

Christie Indian Residential School at Kakawis on Meares Island, circa 1919.
COURTESY OF THE HAMILTON FAMILY, KEN GIBSON COLLECTION.

The Canadian Royal Commission on Aboriginal Peoples has since denounced schools such as Kakawis as "contagion of colonization . . . a particularly virulent strain of that epidemic of empire, sapping the children's bodies and beings." There are currently some eighteen thousand lawsuits over Indian residential schools in Canada. Hundreds of criminal cases allege widespread emotional, physical and sexual abuse by clergy and teachers. Consequently, the historical archives of the Oblates of Mary Immaculate, which took over the school from the Benedictine Order in 1938, have been sealed until 2030, limiting knowledge of what life was like at these schools to testimonials of ex-pupils and court documents. Although no criminal charges were brought against those at the Christie School, a supervisor at the United Church School in Port Alberni was convicted of eighteen charges of sexual abuse over twenty years. The residing B.C. Supreme Court justice called the Indian residential school system "nothing more than institutional pedophilia." (Only a few months before visiting Kakawis, Ricketts too had heard that the "satyr" caught up to an Episcopalian priest in his mother's church in Carmel. "He got [caught] fooling around with little boys," Ricketts told Steinbeck.)

LEFT: *Reverend Augustin Joseph Brabant.* RIGHT: *Reverend James Philip Mulvihill.*
BOTH PHOTOS: RARE BOOKS AND SPECIAL COLLECTIONS, UNIVERSITY OF BRITISH COLUMBIA LIBRARY.

While Ed Jr. stayed behind on Stubbs Island, his dad and Toni took the kicker over to St. Mary's Bay to visit Kakawis. They could see a group of pupils coming down to the beach to greet them. "The shy little Indian children . . . look so terribly grave and dignified," Ricketts recounted, "they look so wooden you'd think they could never smile or cry." The principal of the Christie School, Reverend James Philip Mulvihill, received his visitors warmly. They climbed the school's front steps and were led to a private dining room. Some very competent nuns were at work in the kitchen and Ricketts could smell freshly baked bread.

They sat eating a snack and the Father showed his American visitors the mission's official record book. Its pages were yellow and brittle with age. They saw all the marriages, baptisms, burials and confirmations dating back to 1875 in what Ricketts described as "the clear old fashioned hand of beautiful, stern Father Brabant." A portrait of the legendary Brabant hung overhead. He was a handsome man with a broad nose and a severe gaze.

Ricketts viewed the Catholic Church sceptically. He disagreed with the narrow-mindedness and "slightly ridiculous framework" of Catholicism and had fought a very conservative priest on the questions of sex education and liberalism in the local high school in Monterey. Father Mulvihill brought out a bottle of scotch and they began to chat. Ricketts probably expected fiery proselytizing to ensue.

"It's a curious darn business that I always seem to get into such a spot," Ricketts recalled. "I automatically reject the reactionaryism that's so often associated with the Catholic church. And I especially object to the idea of missionaries. Yet in a place like [the West Coast of Vancouver Island] I find myself liking most of all the man who is at once the missionary and a Catholic. Well, I suppose it's to some extent the man rather than the Catholic I like."

When Father Mulvihill had come out into the schoolyard upon their arrival, wearing his long black frock, the native children spontaneously gathered around him. As Ricketts described, they were "laughing, taking hold of his hand, pulling at his gown, laughing, laughing just so happy you don't see how the world holds it." It was immediately clear to Ricketts that Mulvihill loved the children dearly. He was an avuncular, warm-hearted man with soft, rounded features. He wore wire-rim glasses and was balding considerably and thus looked older than his forty-one years.

The Father told Ricketts that anything that adds to the value or beauty of life and doesn't hurt man or break God's law—"I forget even if he includes God," Ricketts noted, "he's a pretty sensible guy"—is okay. He liked to drink about as well as any man living, he explained, but he'd given it up because of the natives. "If they see me do it they'll go out and do likewise," Mulvihill sighed, "and they carry it notoriously poorly."

Toni and Mulvihill sat smoking cigarettes. Their conversation drifted on an increasingly friendly current. Ricketts seemed especially impressed by the Father's sense of equality toward the Nuu-chah-nulth and his respect for their ways. The priest told him stories about the shamans—"he really believes in them," Ricketts wrote—and complained about the intolerant piety of the Shantymen, a sect of local medical missionaries. Once, Mulvihill told Ricketts, a Shantyman saw him smoking and sent him a "blistering letter" telling him that men of the cloth shouldn't "go around making chimneys of ourselves, smelling up God's good air."

One lovely looking nun—"and I mean she is really lovely too," Ricketts noted rather naughtily in his journal—explained how they tried to encourage the kids in their own native art. She said the simple, repetitive shapes of Northwest native art and earthly colors weren't better or worse than the white man's art with its "gaudy Rainbow dyes" that the Nuu-chah-nulth children were so crazy for. Their native art, the Sister insisted, should be encouraged rather than scorned. "It does only limited good for us to encourage them here in their own sturdy primitive art," Father Mulvihill lamented. "When they get back out what tourists they see will search out and buy the shoddy gaudy highly colored things." The children responded well nonetheless and even gave Ed and Toni a few of their paintings.

The missionary never did ask the scientist about religion, about whether Ricketts practiced any of the denominations. Ricketts was definitely not a religious man, at least not in a conventional sense. According to Steinbeck, he "distrusted all formal religions, suspecting them of having been fouled with economics and power and politics." He was an intensely spiritual man nevertheless. His beliefs were elemental, pantheistic and rooted more in the Oriental than Occidental—the Tao and Zen Buddhism being the spiritual springs on which he drew the deepest. He was on his own personal odyssey, constantly searching for the pathway between intellect and intuition, faith and reason, in order to *break through* to a transcendent view of the natural world.

Ed Ricketts understood that with every scientific discovery, from Galileo to genetics, from evolution to $E = mc^2$, a great chasm had grown between science and religion. The Bible's historical and literal *truths* proved, after close examination through the telescope and under the microscope, not to be *truthful* at all. Science began to erect its own cosmology about the nature and origins of life and the universe, one that clearly conflicted with Scripture. "The god hypothesis is rather discredited," the discoverer of DNA has said. Such blasphemy raised the ire of the church, which denied the science and condemned it bombastically at times.

Ed Ricketts, however, was actually setting about to create a rapprochement between science and religion. It was, in fact, a central theme of *Sea of Cortez*. Throughout the ages, Steinbeck and Ricketts explain, saints and scientists have been on a common, indeed universal, quest:

And it is a strange thing that most of the feeling we call religious, most of the mystical outcrying which is one of the most prized and used and desired reactions of our species, is really the understanding and the attempt to say that man is related to the whole thing, related inextricably to all reality, known and unknowable. This is a simple thing to say, but the profound feeling of it made a Jesus, a St. Augustine, a St. Francis, a Roger Bacon, a Charles Darwin, and an Einstein. Each of them in his own tempo and with his own voice discovered and reaffirmed with astonishment the knowledge that all things are one thing and that one thing is all things. . . .

With his non-teleological thinking, Ricketts even discovered interesting parallels to "the Christian ideas of trinity." Ricketts believed that what people called God or the Holy Spirit is actually "greater than Man but it arises through Man. The god in man." God was simply a symbol for humanity's collective soul, which was greater than the sum of all human relationships. So when Ricketts would use the phrase "all that lives is holy," from William Blake's "Visions of the Daughters of Albion," what he meant, metaphorically, was "all that lives is *holistic*."

Over the decades, Ed Ricketts has developed a certain Christ-figure aura—and not just on Vancouver Island where that little girl mistook him for the Messiah during his "Jesus walk" across the churning waters of Clayoquot Sound. "Ed was a prophet or spokesman for nature," Joel Hedgpeth has said. "One always felt when talking to him that there were reserves beyond the conversation of the moment. And so there were." And many have said that Steinbeck dipped deepest into those reserves.

The writer is largely responsible for creating Ricketts' messianic persona. He described the biologist, who had a beard for much of the 1930s, as "half-Christ and half-goat." It was a description Steinbeck repeated in *Cannery Row*: Doc "wears a beard and his face is half Christ and half satyr." (Literary scholars also refer to Doc as a "local deity" in the novel.) One of Steinbeck's most famous and controversial characters is also "loosely patterned" on a combination of Ed Ricketts and Jesus Christ. The character Jim Casy in *The Grapes of Wrath* is important to our understanding of not only how the ideas and personality of Ed Ricketts informed the writing of

John Steinbeck, but how the two men were ultimately trying to come to grips with the growing rift between science and religion.

The Grapes of Wrath, as many literary scholars have pointed out over the sixty years since its publication, is imbued with biblical imagery, symbols, vocabulary, tones, and religious motifs. The poor migrant farm workers are metaphorically the Hebrew people of Egypt. The Joads, like Judah exiled from the land of bondage and plagues, are driven from their farm by tenement landowners and drought. An exodus ensues. The Joads go west in search of the Promised Land, where Grandpa Joad dreams of squashing Californian grapes in his mouth and letting the sweet nectar run down his jowls. Yet the glimmering stories of the Golden State turn out to be an alchemist's yarn. There is no sweet salvation upon their arrival—just scorn and hatred from Californians.

Jim Casy, an ex-preacher who abandons Christian teachings, awakens the Joads to their innate salvation. After wandering the countryside—just as Ricketts did as a "vagabond through Dixie"—the preacher has what amounts to an epiphany, a "breaking through." He tells the Joads:

> I ain't sayin' I'm like Jesus. But I got tired like Him, an' I got mixed up like Him, an' I went into the wilderness like Him, without no campin' stuff. Night-time I'd lay on my back an' look up at the stars; morning I'd set an' watch the sun come up; midday I'd look out from a hill at the rollin' dry country; evenin' I'd foller the sun down. Sometimes I'd pray like I always done. On'y I couldn't figure what I was prayin' to or for. There was the hills, an' there was me, an' we wasn't separate no more. We was one thing. An' that one thing was holy.

Unfrocking himself, Casy renounces doctrinaire religion and its teleological concepts of good and evil—"There ain't no sin and there ain't no virtue," he says. "There's just stuff people do. It's all part of the same thing"—and preaches a new gospel:

> I figgered about the Holy Sperit and the Jesus road. I figgered, "Why do we got to hang it on God or Jesus? Maybe," I figgered, "maybe it's all men an' all women we love; maybe that's the Holy Sperit—the human spirit—the whole shebang. Maybe all men got one big soul ever'body's a part of."

Casy's is a holistic philosophy that binds him to the land and his fellow human beings. He echoes Ricketts' belief that the Holy Spirit is humanity's collective soul. Casy, like Ricketts, even quotes Blake: "Herd a fella tell a poem one time, an' he says, 'All that lives is holy.'"

Religious leaders attacked the novel vehemently, and especially the ex-preacher Jim Casy. Father Arthur D. Spearman of Loyola University condemned it in a prominent review printed in the *San Francisco Examiner* and other Hearst newspapers across the United States. Published on a Sunday, the review was a veritable sermon from the pulpit. "The objectives of the writer are revealed in the reflective psychoses of the ex-Preacher Casy," Spearman wrote, "who is the principle vehicle for Steinbeck's radical and deracinate propaganda."

The novel is full of "profanity," "sexual underflow" and "cursing and blasphemy," Spearman charged. Casy rejects Christianity and accepts "true religion's antithesis, the easy phallic indulgence, reminiscent of lustful paganism." Further, Steinbeck used the novel to "discredit religion, to honor and encourage lechery, and to inculcate contempt for the law enforcement officers of America, whom he depicts one and all as the dishonest and cruel bravos of a universally Frankensteinish group of large owners, bankers, and capitalists." And more: the novel was "an embodiment of the Marxist Soviet propaganda," "a highlighted appeal for the behavioristic philosophy of sexual indulgence," "an animated cartoon of the useless" and "a summons to revolution" from the "fevered brain of Mr. Steinbeck."

Father Spearman was right about one thing, if nothing else: *The Grapes of Wrath*, largely through the Ricketts-inspired Casy, was an affront to the teachings of the church and its power and privilege. Jim Casy is indeed a heretic, as Spearman claimed. But he's an ecologist, not an ideologue. The novel effectively renounces Christianity for its role in creating the Western pathology, which in turn was destroying the earth. "And God said . . . let them have dominion over the fish of the sea, and over the fowl of the air, and over the cattle, and over all the earth, and over every creeping thing that creepeth upon the earth," states Genesis. The church, in its anthropocentric interpretation of Scripture, had given mankind *carte blanche* to reconstruct Eden on earth — often with destructive consequences. Steinbeck seemed to be saying that by destroying

nature we ultimately destroy the good in human nature. Far from recon-
ciling or balancing man and nature, religion was part of the problem.

Deep suspicion of nature certainly imbued many missionaries on
the coast. Reverend H. P. Bessette, Kakawis assistant principal in 1946,
saw Eden in the "rough beauty" of Clayoquot Sound. "On a quiet, clear
day, the calm waters of the ocean reflect the beauty of the heavens," he
wrote in a booklet celebrating Kakawis' jubilee. Yet he quickly reminds
us that the ocean and rainforests are still Paradise Lost:

> When nature changes her mood and breaks out in wild rebellion, danger
> and death lurk for the unwary. The winds roar, the waves surge high, even
> higher so that only the most powerful craft can hope to survive. Even on
> land there is danger. The giants of the forest which seem so harmless and
> so inviting are now lashed about in fury and become instruments of
> destruction as torn from their moorings they crash to earth.

The missionaries were ultimately trying to bring order and enlightenment to this dark land, to beat the Devil out of the native people and
to restore Eden. It was this messianic drive to tame and ultimately
exploit nature that consequently destroyed it. And it was this same zeal
that ultimately tore apart indigenous cultures. "I think that we missionaries made many mistakes in our relations with the Indian people,"
Mulvihill later admitted. "[W]e tried to destroy their culture instead of
building on it."

Despite his contempt for missionary work and his misgivings about
Christian theology, Ed Ricketts actually came away from Kakawis
enlivened by his hours of discussion. He made copious notes about his
visit with the Father. On this languid afternoon in a poor missionary
school, with good Scotch whiskey in hand, an unlikely friendship was
born between the scientist and the priest, one that would soon help to
spark a radically new idea in Ed Ricketts about religion and what can
best be described as ecological salvation.

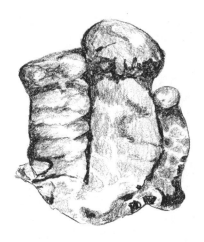

PALYTHOA RICKETTSI, SEA ANEMONE, NEW SPECIES COLLECTED BY
ED RICKETTS ON APRIL 3, 1940, IN GULF OF CALIFORNIA, MEXICO.

CHAPTER TEN

A HERO'S JOURNEY

The adventure of the hero represents the moment in his life when he achieved illumination — the nuclear moment when, while still alive, he found and opened the road to the light beyond the dark walls of our living death.

—JOSEPH CAMPBELL, *The Hero with a Thousand Faces*

THE day after his visit with Father Mulvihill, Ed Ricketts and his son collected in "a very curious and very lovely" cove plugged full of kelp between Mission and Schindler Points on Meares Island. Ricketts' notebook contains no collecting reports over the next two days. He was working hard, however, planning his most extraordinary journey yet on the outer shores.

Around 11 A.M. on June 17, Ed and Bill delicately loaded Ed's big chest of collecting equipment onto the *Beegee* at the Clayoquot wharf. They made the quick run to Tofino, where Ed, Toni and his son caught a "funny local bus" to the tiny fishing village of Ucluelet, twenty-six miles away. They ate lunch in Ucluelet and then boarded the *Uchuck No. 1*, a seventy-foot "coaster," for a seventy-five-mile run through the Broken Group Islands of Barkley Sound and up the Alberni Inlet. They arrived in Port Alberni at nine o'clock that evening and had a good steak dinner at the Somas Hotel. They would continue to Nanaimo, on the island's East Coast, the next day via train.

They climbed aboard the E&N Railway passenger train at 9:20 for the three-hour journey to Nanaimo. Ricketts was awed by the "spectacular scenery." For several miles the railway hugged sheer cliffs a few hundred feet above Cameron Lake, which was itself located high in densely forested mountains. They ate a "hardy and not good lunch" in Nanaimo and then transferred to a Canadian Pacific steamship bound for Vancouver. They arrived three hours later, partook in yet another "hardy and bad dinner," and then went to the Union Steamship Company's ticket office to collect their boarding passes. They were about to depart on a seven-hundred-mile voyage to the Queen Charlotte Islands, a remote offshore archipelago on the North Coast.

The S.S. *Cardena* was the 1,578-ton flagship of the Union Steamship Company and was said to have the most beautiful lines of any ship on the coast. The *Cardena* was "terribly crowded" that night, according to Ricketts—her decks were strewn with cargo, native people, Chinese cannery workers, missionaries and pioneers. They set sail at nine o'clock and at 12.5 knots the *Cardena* would make the journey up the majestic Inside Passage to Prince Rupert in four days. They would then transfer to a second, smaller steamer to the Queen Charlotte Islands.

It was a long, languorous trip. Ricketts used the time to ruminate on some things that were bothering him. The old-fashioned train ride from Port Alberni had sparked some thoughts about the emotional power of nostalgia. He shared his musings with Toni. "Oh, you've often talked about that," she said, "you discovered that a long time ago." Ricketts was unnerved by her dismissive reaction, as though his supposed new idea "wasn't so consequential after all." He scribbled a few pages of nearly illegible notes about how "some women have almost a pure genius for deflating a person." Evidently there were still unresolved tensions in their relationship.

As the *Cardena* sailed up the Inside Passage, it took the same route that Ricketts had taken fourteen years before with Jack Calvin and Joseph Campbell aboard the *Grampus*. The *Cardena* stopped at many of the same port calls, including Pender Harbor, Refuge Cove, Shoal Bay, Shushartie Bay, Port Hardy, Alert Bay, Bella Bella, Klemtu, and Lowe Inlet. As one would expect of a person in a nostalgic mood, Ricketts' journey northward unleashed a flood of memories about his first trip in 1932.

* * *

IT had been an "epochal voyage," according to Joseph Campbell. The 1932 trip brought about "one of the primary personal transformations of a life dedicated to self-discovery." Many of the philosophic conclusions reached during this voyage would resonate in the future work of both the marine ecologist and mythologist.

For both Campbell and Ricketts, the trip had also been an escape. The voyage started out in a mess of conflict and confused emotions. Campbell thought Steinbeck had dramatically overblown his relationship with Carol. Both Campbell and Carol secretly agreed that he should leave town before a row ensued with her jealous, melodramatic husband. The trip would succeed in taking Campbell's mind off Carol. His new romance would be with the Pacific Northwest and its totems, rainforests and coastal fjords shrouded in silvery mist.

Ed Ricketts was running from his own marital meltdown, which had been triggered by his affair with Xenia, Sasha's teenage sister. But for the biologist, the expedition was also a scientific endeavor. Ricketts hoped to conduct a "hurried ecological reconnaissance" of the Inside Passage from Puget Sound to Juneau and collect a variety of specimens, including some fifteen thousand *Goionemus vertens* (jellyfish), for commercial sale.

Ricketts and Campbell left Monterey for Tacoma, Washington, where Jack and Sasha Calvin were waiting aboard the *Grampus*. On June 29, they set off under Jack's steady and experienced captaincy. The year before, Jack and Sasha had paddled and sailed the same thousand-mile route to Juneau in a seventeen-foot canoe called "Nakwasina"; that same canoe was now stowed on the roof of the *Grampus*. The story of their intrepid voyage in such a tiny craft, powered only by paddle and sail, appeared in the July 1933 issue of *National Geographic*. Calvin wrote a lively narrative and took the photographs, too.

During the first two days, the *Grampus* sailed to Friday Harbor on the San Juan Islands and then to Nanaimo on Vancouver Island. They planned to cross the Strait of Georgia to Pender Harbor on the Sunshine Coast, but nature had other plans. "A fresh sou'easter blowing out in gulf, so back to anchorage," Calvin wrote in the *Grampus*'s log. They completed the journey over a "light rolling sea" the following day and made an emergency stopover at Refuge Cove to repair an overheated engine. Then they headed north up Johnstone Strait where Ricketts took great jellyfish hauls.

Whereas Johnstone Strait is narrow with sunken rocks, whirlpools and powerful tidal currents, Queen Charlotte Strait at the northern tip of Vancouver Island opens wide to the Pacific. The *Grampus* made a five-

TOP: *Joseph Campbell (center), Ed Ricketts (far right), and others on the* Grampus *at Refuge Cove, B.C., during 1932 summertime trip to Juneau, Alaska.* COURTESY OF THE JOSEPH CAMPBELL & MARIJA GIMBUTAS LIBRARY, SANTA BARBARA, AND JOSEPH CAMPBELL FOUNDATION.

BOTTOM: *Ed Ricketts sorting collections while young boys watch during* Grampus *trip, 1932.* COURTESY OF THE JOSEPH CAMPBELL & MARIJA GIMBUTAS LIBRARY, SANTA BARBARA, AND JOSEPH CAMPBELL FOUNDATION.

hour run across this strait through "rather heavy swells," Calvin recorded in his log. They arrived at the mouth of Fitz Hugh Sound and anchored for the night at Safety Cove.

Fitz Hugh Sound is the entrance to a labyrinth of interconnected inlets, channels, fjords and narrows that make up the most spectacular part of the voyage along the Inside Passage. Thanks to environmentalists who are trying to protect it from industrial logging, the area is known around the world today as the "Great Bear Rainforest." It was a little-known region back in 1932, of course. No scientist, according to Ricketts, had yet done a general ecological survey of its marine fauna. Hydrographical charts were shoddy, too. "The main steamer routes only have been adequately charted—the land almost not at all," Ricketts noted. "Dotted lines on the charts mark the approximate position of many small rivers and inland lakes, small islands and minor passages." One of Calvin's charts even carried the troubling disclaimer: "This chart should not be depended upon for navigating this area, pending its recharting from recent surveys."

It was a breathtaking journey up winding channels and into hidden bays and inlets. The Coast Mountains rose vertically out of the sea like thousand-foot skyscrapers. Ricketts saw a "striking resemblance" to Yosemite National Park with the same rugged, steep slopes, heavy foresting of conifers and snow-capped summits. It was, Ricketts described, "a most strict and spare land of the extreme of erosion." Grenville Channel was probably the most dramatic spot. It is a forty-five-mile-long fracture in the earth's crust with mountains rising to 3,500 feet and waters plunging as deep as 1,600. Passengers would often crowd a ship's top deck, hoping to catch a glimpse of a deer or Kermode "spirit" bear, a unique white subspecies of the black bear, as steamers passed dangerously close to shore in the narrow channels.

"The attenuated dawns and twilights, the continued drizzly rain, and the thrushes singing for hours at night and morning from the wet and steep hillsides—the only sound in this quiet region aside from the rush of waterfalls—are the things I remember chiefly from this country," Ricketts later recalled.

Yet even against this heavenly backdrop, far away from Pacific Grove and its associated troubles, Campbell felt a gnawing. A dark

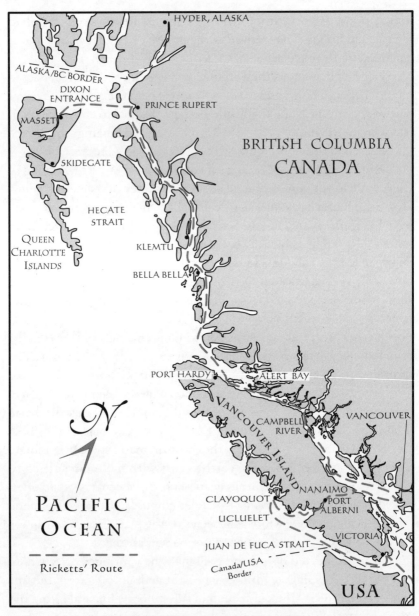

INSIDE PASSAGE
1946 Voyage to the Queen Charlotte Islands

shadow loomed over his thoughts. They continued up the coast, stopping occasionally to do specimen collecting, boat maintenance or calling into port for water and fuel. The growing distance from Pacific Grove mattered little to Campbell, however.

At Wrangell, Alaska, Campbell woke at six o'clock in the morning to find Ed already gone. The biologist came back shortly after eleven with two buckets full of starfish, hermit crabs and other animals, which he laid out in trays. After sorting through the specimens, they sat down to discuss Ed's troubles. (Campbell wasn't the only one suffering from pangs of the immediate past.) Ricketts was distraught about his infidelity and marital breakup. Campbell told Ricketts that he was also feeling torn apart inside and that his hatred for Steinbeck made him physically quiver at times.

Campbell's thoughts would grow even darker as the *Grampus* ventured deeper into the wilderness coast. At Petersburg, a Norwegian-settled fishing village, the next day, he wrote in his diary that he thought Carol was getting the "dirty end of the stick: John is giving her almost literally nothing except a chance to be intensely interested in his own confounded progress!" Campbell became blinded by rage against Steinbeck, making intemperate entries in his diary that he most surely regretted years later. "Marriage without children is a farce," he wrote about the Steinbecks. (Campbell would be happily married for almost fifty years without children.)

They arrived in Sitka two days later. The dock stank like fish and they could see the green cupola of St. Michael's Russian Orthodox Cathedral from the harbor. They whittled away almost three weeks here, canoeing, reading, listening to Stravinsky, snapping photographs and taking long walks through the totem park. Ricketts kept working and typing up his collecting reports while Campbell read Dostoyevsky's *The Idiot*. They had quiet dinners aboard the *Grampus,* followed by listening to records, drinks and long philosophical discussions into the dim hours of the morning. Ricketts and Campbell grew close; they admired each other immensely, shared common interests in music, art, philosophy and literature, and bonded over their personal travails.

On August 2, a "frantic" letter arrived in Sitka from Carol. Ed read the letter first and then passed it to Joe. "I felt suddenly sick inside,"

Joseph Campbell's photograph of Northwest Coast totem poles during Grampus *trip, 1932.* COURTESY OF THE JOSEPH CAMPBELL & MARIJA GIMBUTAS LIBRARY, SANTA BARBARA, AND JOSEPH CAMPBELL FOUNDATION.

Campbell wrote in his diary, "and there was again that old ripped-open feeling in my gut." They talked for awhile afterward: Ed and Joe agreed that John was a "prime damn fool." He had apparently disappeared, fleeing to the Sierra Nevada Mountains. Campbell thought that Steinbeck was trying to "demonstrate to Carol how violently unhappy his sensitive soul's reactions will be to her most little peccadillo."

"I wouldn't be surprised," Ed told Campbell, "if he stopped the publication of his novel!" (In 1932, Steinbeck published *The Pastures of Heaven*.)

There was nothing any of them could do from Sitka, thousands of miles away. They tried to keep busy. Over the next few days they did considerable specimen collecting, including a haul of five hundred jellyfish, and stayed up till three o'clock one morning discussing Spengler and sociology. Campbell spent a morning reading the first draft of *Between Pacific Tides* and making some grammatical corrections.

There were other distractions too: Xenia was now in Sitka and had been spending a lot of time aboard the *Grampus*. "I wasn't crazy about my sister or my brother-in-law," Xenia later reminisced. "Ed was no longer my lover, and there was a glamorous man aboard." She took a liking to Joe. Once she found him skinny-dipping in the sea. She sat sunning herself bare-breasted on a big rock and gazed at Campbell's athletic physique "glistening with cold icy water." Sasha feared that Xenia was making a mistake by flirting with an unattached man. She admonished her younger sister, but to no avail. One night Xenia and Campbell ended up sleeping on the roof of the *Grampus*. "It was a beautiful thing," Xenia recalled.

The next day the *Grampus* left for Juneau, taking Xenia along. They arrived on the afternoon of Saturday, August 20. Father Kashevaroff, a Russian Orthodox priest and father of Sasha, Tal and Xenia, hosted a dinner for the *Grampus*'s crew. They went to Mass on Sunday at the Russian Orthodox Cathedral. Father Kashevaroff presided over a service delivered partly in the native Tlingit language. They spent several more days taking it easy—berry picking, walking, partaking in fine dinners, visiting the local museum and other tourist attractions, and listening to Father Kashevaroff recount Alaskan history.

One evening, Joe and Xenia went for a long walk in a light mist. Eventually they came to a little stream where they talked for an hour. They agreed to maintain a strictly platonic relationship. On the walk back, in the dusk, they spotted a flashlight in the distance along the seashore. It was Ed out hunting jellyfish. A few days later Campbell decided to bring closure to his relationship with Carol, too. He stayed aboard the *Grampus* that morning to write a farewell letter to her. We know nothing about its contents, except that it would be Campbell's last known communication with her. They would never meet or talk again.

On the morning of August 26, everyone awoke feeling groggy and tired. The night before they had stayed up till one o'clock talking and smoking cigarettes. They had toast and coffee in the morning, and a taxi came to pick up Ed, Joe, Jack and Sasha, along with their pile of baggage. They drove to the steamship terminal, where Xenia stood waiting. After a sleepy good-bye, Campbell and Ricketts climbed the gangway onto a large Canadian Pacific passenger liner. The steamer departed Juneau at 8 A.M.

For almost three months, Ricketts and Campbell had lived the life of "metaphysical vagabonds" aboard the *Grampus*. Their conversations often revolved around the greatness of Goethe's *Faust* or Jeffers's "Roan Stallion," the pure genius of Bach or the implications of Spengler's *Decline of the West*. For entertainment, Campbell would recount mythic tales, "Sir Gawain and the Green Knight" or an "Old Man" story from American Indian lore. They pondered the totems of the Coast Salish, Kwakiutl, Heiltsuk and Tlingit, which they saw along the shore. The days of their thousand-mile journey were also filled with the duties of shipboard life and seamanship, navigating the treacherous waters, occasional squalls, fog, hidden shoals and racing currents. The men had experienced the rawness of this wilderness coast, satisfying a primal longing for nature and the sea.

It came to an abrupt end when Ed and young Joe stepped aboard the S.S. *Princess Louise*. The luxurious liner had a 125-seat dining room with fine linen tablecloths and polished silver. The ship's social halls and staircases were ornate and elegant, and the best staterooms had their own baths and eiderdown bedding. The juxtaposition with their life aboard the *Grampus* was jarring. "Shoes, instead of the naked earth. Stiff clothes, instead of the sun and the wind. A constriction about your shoulders, instead of an open expansion of chest," Campbell wrote in his diary. "Formal games in courts and gyms, instead of the flinging of an anchor from a boat into the sea." The young men felt wholly out of place among the well-groomed passengers and fanciful décor.

Ricketts' log from the 1932 journey was destroyed in his lab fire. His only surviving record was a copy of an unpublished scientific paper, thoroughly titled "Notes and Observations, Mostly Ecological, Resulting from Northern Pacific Collecting Trips Chiefly in South Eastern Alaska, with Especial Reference to Wave Shock as a Factor in Littoral Ecology," which was either with a friend or perhaps with scientists at Hopkins Marine Station the morning of the devastating fire. Jack Calvin kept a perfunctory logbook, mostly noting dates, weather, tides, distances, boat maintenance and terse personal asides. Campbell, however, kept an exacting diary written in a highly narrative, even literary, style. On Saturday, August 27, Campbell began recording days of philosophic discourse with Ricketts aboard the *Princess Louise*.

"Conventionally dressed, having stepped aboard a liner filled with those who live in the normal ways, I have felt clicking around me again the old unadventurous crust," Campbell wrote, followed by a quote from Robinson Jeffers: "Humanity is the mold to break away from, the crust to break through, the coal to break into fire, the atom to be split."

Campbell and Ricketts began discussing the difference between the forces that had originally shaped the human species versus the forces molding modern man. The wilderness, through natural selection, was the primary force that influenced the development of the human physique and psyche over thousands of years. Modern man was a city dweller, however, divorced from elemental forces. In the city, a person became a cog in a mass machine and life became constricted by social mores. An individual was forced to fit into the rigid pattern of industrial society. Thus, Campbell reasoned, city values left a person feeling spiritually unfulfilled. The secret, Campbell wrote, was to break through the crust of urban life to reach "the life breathing beneath," to tap the earth below the asphalt.

A well-rounded person, Campbell believed, needed to harness values from both the city and the country. The former gave humans the fruits of civilization: science, art, philosophy, politics, music and literature. And the latter provided life values: physical exertion, freedom, individuality and vitality. "There are certainly values to be squeezed from each," Campbell concluded.

The young men were exploring the tension—Ricketts later called it "hi-tension"—between civilization and nature, the modern and the primitive, which was tearing at the fabric of contemporary society. Both agreed that the path to happiness was to integrate the various values. For Ricketts, it would be about "breaking through," transcending the dualities of wilderness and civilization. Campbell summed up his own approach to life in a similar way: "To be without principles; to be free-thinking; to be sceptical of all dogmas—to break, whenever possible, the rule of the Golden Mean; to exercise restraint only for the fear of feeling formal—these are a few of the keys to a civilized primitiveness!" Whether in the city or country, one should balance the values from each. This new life-philosophy would guide both men on their respective journeys ahead.

When they finally arrived in Seattle, Campbell helped Ricketts load his huge preserved collections into his car, an old Packard limousine, and the two started on a nonstop drive south. When they reached the San Francisco Bay area, Campbell heard that his father's business had collapsed, a casualty of the deepening Depression. He decided not to go back to Pacific Grove. He had little reason to return anyway; his tormented relationship with Carol was finished and he had no work. He bade farewell to Ed and headed east to face his future. He made only a short note in his diary: "Return trip in Model T. $300 in debt, mostly to Ed Ricketts, but with a view ahead."

Over the next decade, the two men would each immerse themselves in separate spheres. Campbell would begin a life centered in the urban bustle of New York City. He took up teaching humanities in college and delved into scholarly research on world mythologies and religions. He became a learned, metropolitan man. Ricketts, on the other hand, eschewed the city and extended his scientific research to the uncharted coast of the Pacific. "Protean Ed, the man of the sea," as Campbell described him. Ricketts would focus all his energies on deciphering nature's design.

Joseph Campbell had only been on the Pacific Coast for little over eight months, of which three were spent crammed aboard the *Grampus*. During that short time, Ricketts became "not quite a guru, but a special teacher of consciousness as well as natural science" for Campbell. For both men the insights hatched on that journey up the Inside Passage would reverberate and unfold through their decades of scholarship. Although they sped off down separate roads that day in 1932, they were both beginning intellectual journeys that would eventually—perhaps surprisingly, considering their divergent disciplines—bring them together again.

* * *

IN August of 1939, Ricketts received a letter from Campbell asking if he and his new wife, Jean Erdman, could drop by the lab for a visit on their way to Honolulu. "Every time I see a rocky coast I think of you in your boots," Campbell wrote Ricketts. "Jean has heard more about you than about any single experience of my wander-years." They had fallen out of touch for an incredible seven years, in part because Campbell's address was lost in the lab fire. Excited at the prospect of rekindling their friendship, Ricketts dispatched his three philosophical essays to his long-lost friend. Campbell was overwhelmed by what he read, especially in "The Philosophy of Breaking Through." He immediately wrote back:

I am even a little glad, now, that seven years went by with hardly an exchange of words between us; for, if we had been discussing our problems as we encountered them, nothing quite as pretty as this could have taken place! You begin with the Jeffers quotations that I tried to memorize while driving across the continent, after our year of crazy beginnings. Then you present a series of ideas that corresponds essentially with the series that I too have encountered in following the Jeffers lead. You cannot imagine what a profoundly gratifying experience it has been to discover that we have been walking parallel ways.

Through their respective disciplines, mythology and marine ecology, Campbell and Ricketts, since parting ways in 1932, had essentially been tackling the same fundamental question: What is the meaning of life and the nature of things in a world in which the pieties of the past have been rendered falsities by modern science? They were both trying to develop a "unified field theory" to integrate science and spirituality in order to better understand and more deeply participate in the world around them.

When *Sea of Cortez* was published two years later, in 1941, Campbell realized, again with considerable delight, that their expedition in 1932 had essentially been a precursor, even a prototype, to the Gulf expedition. Campbell immediately recognized the "marvelous form of living" and the dominant theme in *Sea of Cortez* that they had first experienced aboard the *Grampus*:

[W]e understand that society itself is an organism, that these little intertidal societies and the great human societies are manifestations of common principles; more than that: we understand that the little and the great societies are themselves units in a sublime, all inclusive organism which breathes and goes on, in dream-like half-consciousness of its own life-processes, oxidizing its own substance yet sustaining its wonderful form. Suddenly, then, the life goes out of the trip and we are on our way back to the laboratory to follow this great thing through in a more exact set of terms, linking it into the fantastic thought-net of the modern scientific workers, whose thoughts somehow (as mysteriously as possible) duplicate the marvels of the fact world, and reveal in their own way the prodigious yet profoundly intimate mysteries of "that which simply is because it simply is." Ed, it's a great great book—dreamlike and with no end of implications—sound implications—all-sustaining implications: everything from the beer cans to the phyletic catalogue is singing with the music of the spheres.

At this time, Campbell had just begun work on his own scholarly tome. "During the past six months the world of the myths has been revealing to me those simple, wonderful forms that underlie and sustain the bewildering pell-mell," he told Ricketts. "I hope, within the next few years, to be able to send you a few papers, written in the jargon of another science, to supplement the discoveries of your lab!"

His book was, in effect, the mythological equivalent of *Between Pacific Tides*—a seminal treatise in a new field that Campbell himself was pioneering: comparative mythology. Although he would state it in greater detail and more directly in a 1951 essay, "Bios and Mythos," the book's thesis was clear: Campbell used the biological concepts and ideas first explored with Ed Ricketts, combined with psychoanalysis, the modern science of reading dreams, to explain that myth was a "biologically necessary spiritual organ."

Mythology actually performed life-supporting functions, helping the human species to survive and prosper in a hostile environment. "Every organ of the body has its energy impulse, an impulse to action, and the experience of the conflicts of these different energies inside is what constitutes the psyche. It's nature talking," Campbell would later explain. "And mythology is the expression in personified images of these energies." These energies percolate up into the psyche as dreams that, in turn, collectively and subconsciously manifest themselves as the myths of societies over generations. "Dream is the personalized myth, myth the depersonalized dream," Campbell wrote in his seminal book. "But in the dream the forms are quirked by the peculiar troubles of the dreamer, whereas in myth the problems and solutions shown are directly valid for all mankind."

After years of studying African tribal lore, Lao Tsu, Viking sagas, Eskimo fairy tales, the Upanishads, Saint Thomas Aquinas, and many other ancient texts, Joseph Campbell discovered a "marvellously constant story" in all the myths of the world. Borrowing a word from James Joyce, Campbell called it the *monomyth*—the universal structure that underlies every myth, every belief system, on earth. Its pattern of separation, initiation and return is the story of humanity's universal struggle. He referred to it as the "hero's journey." According to Campbell: "A hero ventures forth from the world of common day into a region of supernatural wonder: fabulous forces are there encountered and a decisive victory is won: the hero comes back from this mysterious adventure with the power to bestow boons on his fellow man."

Of course the hero's face may change from place to place, from culture to culture, depending on the influence of local history, climatic-geological factors and ethnic ideas, but the journey is a timeless tale. Its iterations are multitudinous. Thus, Campbell titled his book *The Hero with a Thousand Faces.*

During their reunion in September 1939 at the lab, Campbell shared his ideas with Ricketts and talked about James Joyce's "root word." After reading Ricketts' essays, he immediately wrote to say that they were clearly "proof that our thoughts have been following parallel ways since our discoveries of old time." He recognized the pattern of the hero's journey in Ricketts' "Philosophy of Breaking Through." Campbell lamented, however, that he had written no statement expressing his own thinking at the time. He seems to have inspired Ricketts to put pen to paper, however.

The next month the biologist typed a one-page introduction to a new essay entitled "Hi-tension or the Universality of Duality," which contained the first rudimentary description of the hero's journey. "In one sense," Ricketts wrote, "this quest is the most real and primitive in the world. It reappears continually. It seems to have been the primary desideratum of Lao Tsu, the Upanishads, Buddha, Plato, Christ." Ricketts would never finish this essay; it was Campbell who would complete it with *The Hero with a Thousand Faces.*

As Ricketts' *Between Pacific Tides* is a guide to the seashore, Campbell's book is a guide to the gods. The book's early working title was, in fact, *On How to Read a Myth.* Campbell first explains the "symbolic language" of myth and then collects examples in oral lore and sacred texts from every corner of the world. He identifies and catego-

Diagram of the "key" to the hero's journey in Campbell's The Hero with a Thousand Faces. COURTESY OF PRINCETON UNIVERSITY PRESS.

rizes the various archetypes of the hero—warrior, lover, emperor, tyrant, world redeemer, saint—and describes the morphology of myth with a "key" that illustrates the hero's cyclical path from the temporal world to the supernatural realm and back again. And like *Between Pacific Tides,* Campbell's guidebook would initially be rejected by publishers for being unconventional.

Campbell started writing it in 1941 and by September 1944 gave a manuscript to his publisher, Simon and Schuster, who hemmed and hawed about its publication. He redrafted his "myth book" in 1945, but just before he left for Honolulu on a second trip in June 1946, he found out that they did not intend to publish the book. The rejection stung bitterly.

The Hero with a Thousand Faces would eventually be published under the Bollingen Foundation imprint by Princeton University Press in 1949. It would have vast staying power—again, like *Between Pacific Tides*—becoming a classic in its field. *The Hero* is still in print today and was most recently on the *New York Times* Bestseller List in 1989, forty years after its first publication. It has been said that no book has impacted modern storytelling more than *The Hero*; a generation of Hollywood screenwriters would become indebted to Campbell's masterful and poetic telling of the hero's journey. To understand the phenomenal global popularity of J. K. Rowling's *Harry Potter*, J. R. R. Tolkien's *Lord of the Rings* or George Lucas's *Star Wars*, one needs only to examine how the universal motifs Campbell first identified resonate at a primal, biological level in the human species. "[T]he story may never be told dully," Ricketts once said.

In the early 1970s, in fact, George Lucas "stumbled" upon *The Hero with a Thousand Faces*. He would later befriend Campbell and invite him to his Skywalker Ranch in northern California to watch the original *Star Wars* trilogy. "It is possible," Lucas once said, "if I hadn't run across [Joseph Campbell] I would still be writing *Star Wars*. . . . He has become my Yoda."

Lucas modeled his trilogy on the hero's journey, recreating the classical mythological motifs in a modern context. Lucas said he was "telling an old myth in a new way" by giving the ancient struggle of good against evil a futurist form: man versus the machine. It was a theme that Campbell and Ricketts initially discussed on the *Princess Louise* in 1932 — the battle between the freedom of "primitive" man in the wilderness and the sublimation of modern man to the machine. "Is the machine going to crush humanity or serve humanity?" Campbell once said of *Star Wars*. "Humanity comes not from the machine but from the heart."

In his *Star Wars* films, Lucas also takes up a theme that was central to Ricketts' tide pool trilogy. Luke Skywalker is the young hero of a diverse alliance of intergalactic organisms who ban together to fight the Empire — the techno-army of cloned Storm Troopers and their robo-human leader Darth Vader. Lucas expounds an essentially ecological worldview about the oneness of the universe. "The Force is an energy field created by all living things," Ben Kenobi explains to Luke in the movie. "It surrounds us, it penetrates us, it binds the galaxy together." Lucas's world is intergalactic, not intertidal, but the struggle is the same.

Taking the advice of Ricketts and Steinbeck in *Sea of Cortez* — "it is advisable to look from the tide pool to the stars and then back to the tide pool again" — one can even trace the origins of Lucas's thinking back to marine ecology. "One of the main themes in *The Phantom Menace*," Lucas has said of his *Star Wars* prequel, "is of organisms having to realize they must live for their mutual advantage." Of course it was the esteemed ecologist Dr. W. C. Allee, Ricketts' professor at the University of Chicago, who pioneered this concept of "mutual aid among animals." As an eager graduate student, Allee had first discovered this principle while studying *Asellus communis,* an aquatic sow bug, in the tide pools of the Atlantic Coast.

With *The Hero* rejected by his publisher, Campbell wrote Ricketts in August of 1946 that he was on his way to Honolulu again. While passing through California, he hoped to visit Monterey to talk with his good friend, who had suffered similar troubles with publishers and reviewers. Campbell also knew that Ricketts would be just returning from his voyage up the Inside Passage. The reunion in September would bring their friendship full circle.

Fourteen years had passed since they first met in Pacific Grove. Although they had only seen each other once in the intervening years, the brief visit in 1939, Campbell often thought about Ricketts. "[A]nything from Ed's lab has fetish value in my life," Campbell once joked.

For a time in the early 1930s, he even made plans to turn his Monterey diaries into a play or novel entitled "The Grampus Adventure"; he later made notes for a dramatic work that compared Ed Ricketts' life to the hero's journey.

In 1932, both men were only beginning research in their respective fields. By 1946, their work was starting to bear fruit for both of them. Their "parallel ways" were about to come to a remarkable confluence during Campbell's mid-September visit. "There should be a lot for us to talk about," Campbell wrote to Ricketts. "All my time has been devoted to the mythological, and I am beginning to feel somewhat at home with the gods," he added. "The ramifications of this mythological matter into all departments of life and art now seem to me the great world-redeeming marvel to be brooded. I am sure that the laws of mythology are the laws of 'spiritual biology,' and that a good confab with yourself will make this quite clear to me."

* * *

AS the *Cardena* sailed into Prince Rupert around midnight on June 21, 1946, Ed Ricketts could simultaneously see the sunset blushing in the northwest and the sky freckled with incipient starlight. It was the longest day of the year, the summer solstice—a truly magical time in the North Pacific. In Prince Rupert they transferred to a second steamer, destined for the Queen Charlotte Islands.

Ed Ricketts would soon witness firsthand the battle between the "primitive" and the modern, and its devastating consequences on the islands' indigenous people. With the help of Campbell, he would also come to understand ecology and mythology as part of a seamless continuum "from the tide pools to the stars."

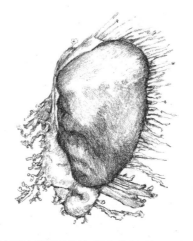

POECILLASTRA RICKETTSI, SEA SPONGE, NEW SPECIES
COLLECTED BY ED RICKETTS IN JULY 1930 IN CALIFORNIA.

CHAPTER ELEVEN

GALAPAGOS OF THE NORTH

I am strongly induced to believe that as in music, the person who understands every note will, if he also possesses a proper taste, more thoroughly enjoy the whole, so he who examines each part of a fine view, may also thoroughly comprehend the full and combined effect.

—CHARLES DARWIN, *The Voyage of the Beagle*

THE Queen Charlotte Islands are a lush, mountainous archipelago remotely perched on the edge of the continental shelf eighty miles out in the wind-swept North Pacific. The some 140 islands, strung in an arrowhead-like formation pointing southward, are known as the "Islands at the Edge," "Misty Isles" and "Canadian Galapagos."

Millions of years of tectonic uplift formed the islands at the point where the Pacific and North American plates collide. The outlying islands are thought to have been partially ice-free beginning about fifteen thousand years ago, when glaciation reached its peak on the continent, thus providing biota a livable refuge. Scientists believe that as glaciers receded, the archipelago's surviving species dispersed and colonized the North Pacific region. The ice-free islands may have also been one of *Homo sapien*'s first stepping-stones into North America from Asia.

Inhabited by many unique species of plants and subspecies of animals, the islands, according to one contemporary zoologist, are "an evolutionary showcase . . . a biological treasure that is not duplicated elsewhere in the vastness of Canada."

At the time of Ricketts' voyage, the Queen Charlotte Islands, often shrouded for days in thick summertime fog or battered weeks on end by fierce winter squalls, were a menacing place—at least to townsfolk in Vancouver. Few people had any reason—or even dared—to venture to their treacherous shores. Of the 150 passengers who departed Vancouver aboard the *Cardena,* Ricketts, his son and Jackson were the only ones traveling to this "bleak desolate country."

"Everybody's certainly upset about [the] Queen Charlottes," Ricketts confided to his notebook. "Of all the dire forebodings!"

* * *

SPANISH explorer Juan Perez was the first European to discover the Queen Charlotte Islands, although there is evidence that Sir Francis Drake visited the area on his "secret voyage" in 1579. Perez spotted the largest of the group, now called Graham Island, on July 17, 1774. Perez traded with the natives but didn't land ashore. Fur traders came in the 1780s, most notably Captain George Dixon, a former mate on Cook's final round-the-world voyage. He named the islands after his vessel *Queen Charlotte.* It would take another hundred years before a scientist, George Dawson, conducted the first concerted scientific investigation for the Geological Survey of Canada, including the collection of some marine invertebrates. Dawson was impressed by the islands' biological diversity and geology, and named a sound and a point after Charles Darwin, suggesting a comparison, perhaps, to the Galapagos.

The next sixty years were relatively quiet, scientifically, with smaller surveys by the U.S. Fish Commission, the Smithsonian Institution, Pacific Biological Station and the University of British Columbia (UBC), among others. Dr. C. McLean Fraser of UBC's zoology department conducted the first major observation of marine habitats since Dawson, spending two months there in 1935. Ricketts corresponded with Dr. Fraser and sent him many of the specimens he collected in 1946.

Ricketts' own expedition is significant in an historical context because his field notes and collecting data were the first to be sufficiently detailed so that comparative surveys can be conducted in the same area today. He created the first baseline of marine biodiversity in the region. In fact, the published proceedings of the First International Scientific Symposium on the Queen Charlotte Islands, held in 1984, are titled *The Outer Shores.* The symposium's organizers wanted to pay tribute to Ricketts and Steinbeck and "the spirit of independence and exploration embodied in their work."

In exploring this "Canadian Galapagos," Ricketts modeled his collecting methods and scientific thinking after Charles Darwin, a scientist whom both he and Steinbeck respected considerably. "In a way, ours is the older method, somewhat like that of Darwin on the *Beagle*," they wrote in *Sea of Cortez*. "He was called a 'naturalist.' He wanted to see everything, rocks and flora and fauna; marine and terrestrial." They admired how Darwin, by studying individual species, came up with a general theory of evolution, the process of natural selection. It was an inductive method that they closely associated with non-teleological thinking. "[T]he modern process—that of looking quickly at the whole field and then diving down to a particular—was reversed by Darwin," they wrote. "Out of long long consideration of the parts he emerged with a sense of the whole."

Ricketts shared this view and eschewed the scientific specialization in vogue during his own era. By studying individual organisms, as Darwin did, the marine biologist hoped to more thoroughly comprehend the whole. He wanted to develop a set of general principles or laws to describe ecology and to illuminate the underlying design of the natural world. This inductive method was at the heart of the Pacific trilogy. "[I]t seems that some of the broader, more general aspects of the tie-in of all animal species with one another has been lost since Darwin went out of the picture," Steinbeck said upon their departure to the Sea of Cortez. "We are trying in our small way to get back to a phase of that broader view." Even stylistically—in tone, language and structure—*Sea of Cortez* bears semblance to Darwin's *Journal of Researches into the Natural History and Geology of the Countries Visited during the Voyage of H.M.S. "Beagle"*. They thought Darwin's writing and thinking reflected "the slow heave of a sailing ship, and the patience of waiting for a tide." Their book, subtitled *A Leisurely Journal of Travel and Research*, reflected a similar pace.

Ricketts had kept a detailed travel log, handwritten in field notebooks, during their explorations of the Gulf of California. He later edited them into a typescript that was used by Steinbeck to write the book's narrative section. On February 28, 1941, Ricketts penned a letter telling Toni about their collaboration: "I have just been reading what John wrote today. It's so damn beautiful I can hardly stand it. He takes my words and gives them a little twist, and puts in some of his own beauty of concept and expression and the whole thing is so lovely you can't stand it."

Ricketts used similar oversize black field notebooks in the Queen Charlottes. Each day he jotted down scientific observations, tides, lists of species collected, sketches, impressions, speculations, descriptions of local people, quirky anecdotes and tall tales, just about anything that crawled, scampered or swam across his path. He then edited these notes into a typescript. Steinbeck would use this typed travelogue as reference material to write the narrative section of *The Outer Shores*.

* * *

SATURDAY, June 22. At 2 A.M. the S.S. *Cassiar II* departed from Prince Rupert under a sky awash with red sunrise in the northeast. At this northern latitude tinges of dusk and dawn give the horizon a warm hue at all hours of a midsummer's night.

The *Cassiar* was a 905-ton vessel, a dinosaur really. The men's toilets looked like gigantic porcelain thrones — "funny old things" Ricketts called them — and the great marble washbasins came from Scotland, where the ship was built in 1910. The hallways and rooms looked bygone, with high ceilings and secondary wiring running down narrow corridors. Originally christened the *Amethyst* and renamed *Prince John*, it sank on April Fools' Day of 1920. The ship was salvaged and re-christened *Cassiar II* in 1940. She had a reputation for being sturdy and dependable. Ricketts was charmed by the vessel and noted in his travelogue that she looked and smelled "delightfully old fashioned."

From Prince Rupert, the steamer crept across Hecate Strait to the remote settlement of Masset on its regular eighty-four-mile overnight journey. Ed, Toni and his son awoke that morning with great anticipation of landing on a biologically luxuriant region. On deck, however, Ricketts could see very little. Damp sea air stung his nostrils and white fog muffled sight and sound for miles. The ship crept toward the "Misty Isles" and soon slowed to half-speed. Then it slowed even further, stopped for a while and finally backtracked cautiously. The ship prowled about blindly. "Very evidently the skipper doesn't know where we are close

S.S. Cassiar II *at Masset in the Queen Charlotte Islands or Haida Gwaii, 1946.*
COURTESY OF ED RICKETTS JR.

enough to chance the narrow channel through the shoals," Ricketts scribbled in his notebook. The steamer lay adrift off the archipelago. They were lost at sea.

It mattered little to Ricketts and the rest of the passengers, however. Everyone ate a fine lunch and waited for the fog to lift. They were far from shore and there was no rush to risk a landing. By mid-afternoon, the steamer was behind schedule by more than six hours. The captain grew impatient and ordered a sounding, which was done by hand. Ricketts watched the crew drop a weighted rope into the sea to measure the depth. Ricketts guessed, quite correctly, the depth to be about thirteen fathoms. He then unrolled his own hydrographic chart and perused it for thirteen-fathom depths. He found their approximate location with some surprise: They had overshot the entrance to Masset by nine to ten miles. It was worse than even "the poorest of dead reckoning" in Ricketts' opinion.

Too close to land and completely lost in fog, the *Cassiar* headed back out to the safety of the deep water, backtracking a ways. The captain then swung her toward land—which he still couldn't actually see—hoping to hit the narrow entrance to Masset Inlet. Ricketts soon spotted some *Fucus* (seaweed) and jellyfish floating by and realized land was near. When the fog finally cleared, the island revealed itself in breathtaking sunlight. It was, Ricketts recorded in his diary, "as beautiful [a] place as you could hope ever to see. Pure paradise." They arrived at the dock in Masset at five o'clock, almost nine hours overdue. The scene was chaotic.

The wharf was crowded with natives, pioneers, passengers and welcome parties, reuniting and rejoicing. The entire town had shown up. Ship's officers barked orders at the crew who hauled cargo, "His Majesty's mails" and supplies ashore. Fish products and lumber waited to be loaded into the emptying hold. There was a desperate dash for fresh meat too, since no homes had refrigeration; people rushed to the village's two stores to buy every bit of meat coming off the ship. Amidst this dockside melee, Ricketts' heavy supply chest went missing. Some "local snooty superior people" suggested the natives had stolen it, but Ricketts gave little credence to their story.

To Ricketts, Masset was a solitary village. In 1946, it consisted of only a few hundred people and no more than seventy homes. (There were some empty houses, too, since the military had scaled down its wartime operations on the island.) Still, it had a post office, a general store, a co-op store, a school, a small hotel, a policeman, an Indian agent, a telegraph operator and a road superintendent (a fifteen-mile-long wooden plank road led to a wonderful beach on the island's northern shore). There were only two cars, both owned by the "taxi man," and several trucks, primarily used by clam diggers. Ricketts, however, seemed more impressed with what they didn't have: "there is no central power, there's no water works, no sewage. The community has no doctor, no dentist, no baker, no shoe repairman, no barber. . . . The community isn't incorporated, apparently it just runs itself." It was also a seaside community with no kickers or runabouts. Ricketts saw only one small skiff, which the owner eagerly lent to him.

People were either homesteaders or fishermen, either of Scandinavian, British or aboriginal descent. A local co-op cannery processed clams and was run by natives and non-natives working side by side. There were hook-and-line salmon trollers at the dock and a sawmill in Delakatla Slough, tucked just behind the village. Some pioneers lived out on the plank road and rode bicycles into the village through the dense rainforest and muskeg. "Masset, which to us seemed the last lonely outpost is to them a metropolis and their trips to town . . . must be a great event," Ricketts wrote. In winter, food was scarce, especially if storms prevented the steamer from sailing. People were forced to hunt for food, often flouting gaming rules. "It's a hungry country so why shouldn't they?" Ricketts figured.

Toni had arranged to rent a fine house for twenty dollars a month just a few doors down from the dock. At 1930 Harrison Street, the beachside bungalow was a comfortable place, brand new in fact. The house had a sink and a flushing toilet fed by fifty-gallon rain barrels on the roof. Naïvely, they flushed the toilet with rainwater and soon ran out. From then on, they ran down to the shore with a bucket to fetch saltwater for the toilet. Given the damp weather, they kept the kitchen stove stoked with firewood at all times. Ed Jr. listened to jazz being broadcast from Ketchikan on a battery-powered radio. By all accounts, their accommodations couldn't have been much better.

After settling in, the trio went for a walk two or three miles seaward along the inlet's shore to Old Masset, the local Indian reservation. Along the village's waterfront road, Ricketts saw a small monument to Chief Albert Edward Edenshaw. He was apparently the richest, most flamboyant chief to ever lead the natives, and one of the first to convert to Christianity. He became a pious man and a force for change among his people. In 1852, according to one historical account, he saved the crew of the trading schooner *Susan Sturgis* from being slaughtered by fellow native warriors. A small stone cenotaph was erected in "grateful remembrance" of the grand chief. A plaque informed Ricketts that the chief was "a staunch friend to the white man."

Ricketts saw an abandoned house nearby. The doors were ajar and the living room was full of rainwater. The beds were covered in rotting cloths. There was china in the dining room and utensils still in the kitchen. The bookcase was filled with molding Nelson encyclopedias. It was an eerie sight. A passerby told them it was the home of Chief Edenshaw. "[It's] a wonderful monument to the original chief Edenshaw, a great queer wooden house, completely furnished, all open to the wind," Ricketts wrote. "[H]e was so much loved that when he died, they left his house just as it was. You don't touch a thing like that. You don't even go in it." (Ricketts was actually mistaken: there's no aboriginal custom of leaving houses as monuments. Rather, mortuary or memorial poles serve this purpose.)

They continued on past the native village into a trail that led to a graveyard in a thinly wooded area. The fog started to creep in again and a cold wind blew, rustling the conifers that shaded the tombstones. They continued beyond into the woods. The forest floor was thick with moss and ferns. Darkness and mist began to set in. Suddenly, they came out on a "desolate gravel beach" facing the North Pacific. It was a haunting experience for Ricketts. An "alien" feeling overcame him. In his words:

> The Indian thing is terribly important here. If ever there was a place where you're surrounded by the ghosts of a powerful people now dead or changed, here it is. Not in New Masset so much. But in old Masset everywhere and all the time, and on the road en route, and above there particularly out in the wonderful Indian graveyard. A crazy place, because the graveyard thing is I think entirely after white men showed up. So there are the hopes and the disillusionments of the most powerful and significant Indian on the whole Pacific coast. The Haidas.

To their ancient indigenous people, the Queen Charlotte Islands are called *Haida Gwaii*, or in their classical native language *Xhaaydla Gwaayaay*—the "Islands on the Boundary between Worlds." Ricketts was visiting one of the greatest indigenous civilizations of the North Pacific, if not North America. It was a society whose food, art, architecture, oral literature, belief system and entire cultural ethos were shaped by the ecology of the seashore.

Human beings, in classical Haida, are called *xhaaydla xhaaydaghaay* or "surface people" and live at the conjuncture of at least three distinct realms—the world of the forest, the sea and the sky. These zones are mysterious and are frequently described in the oral narratives of the Haida, who live largely—but by no means exclusively—on the *xhaaydla*, or intertidal zone. This thin edge—between forest, sea and sky—is the human zone. For thousands of years, the Haida lived here in post-and-beam cedar longhouses. They embellished this world with elaborate totem poles and homes carved with the images of crypto-zoological animals such as Thunderbird, Bear Mother and Sea Wolf. They lived along the seashore, drawing sustenance and more from the sea and its creatures. "Manna falls only rarely from the heavens; it emerges daily from the waves," explains one poet and scholar of Haida texts. "And the primary realm of the gods, in Haida cosmology, is not celestial; it is submarine."

Myth, or *qqaygaang* in Haida, describes not their struggle against nature, but rather their sublimation to it. Besides food and clothing, the Haida sought guidance and inspiration from nature, from animal-deities. For primitive hunting peoples, Joseph Campbell explains in *The Hero with a Thousand Faces,* animals were both "the source at once of danger, and of sustenance—the great human problem was to become linked psychologically to the task of sharing the wilderness with these beings. An unconscious identification took place, and this was finally rendered conscious in the half-human, half-animal figures of the mythological totem-ancestors. The animals became the tutors of humanity."

To the Haida, a trickster-creator known as Raven, for instance, symbolized the oneness of the natural and the supernatural. The Haida's story of creation, an oral saga known as *Raven Traveling,* was recorded in 1900 by John Swanton, a graduate student of the great German-American anthropologist Franz Boas. (Ricketts most surely had discussed Boas with Joseph Campbell, who had attended Boas' lectures at Columbia University and who was reading the "Indian shelves" of the Carmel Library in 1932. Ricketts also read and took notes on Swanton's research on the Tlingit, the Haida's neighbors in Southeast Alaska whose myths recount similar Raven stories.) *Raven Traveling,* which describes the origins of the world and the supernatural age before the first humans, reveals the primal importance of the seashore in Haida cosmology. The oral saga begins:

> *Hereabouts was all saltwater, they say.*
> *He was flying all around, the Raven was,*
> *looking for land that he could stand on.*

After a time, at the toe of the Islands, there was one rock awash.
He flew there to sit.

Like sea-cucumbers, gods lay across it,
putting their mouths against it side by side.
The newborn gods were sleeping, out along the reef,
heads and tails in all directions.

Ed Ricketts had great interest in the Haida's social customs, beliefs and totems. He understood their deeply spiritual relationship to nature. He had observed this same connection in the Baja's indigenous people. "They seemed to live on remembered things, to be so related to the seashore and the rocky hills and the loneliness that they are these things," Ricketts and Steinbeck wrote in *Sea of Cortez*. "To ask about the country is like asking about themselves."

The day after his arrival, on his very first collecting trip, Ricketts explored a tidal region on the ancient shores of Haida Gwaii that was a veritable holy land to the Haida and is protected today as the Tow Hill Ecological Reserve.

It was a Sunday. At 1:30 P.M., after church service, some locals invited Ed, Toni and his son to the beach. Everyone piled into the back of an old pickup truck, women, children and grandmothers included. They grinned at each other in the pouring rain, and those without rain hats pulled papers, clothes or rags overhead to keep dry. They drove some fourteen miles, mostly over the creaking plank road through the rainforest. Tree branches brushed the cab of the truck, where three or four lucky people rode. The rain came down in torrents, Ricketts recalled, but did not dampen the hardy smiles of the island's residents.

The immense northeastern corner of Graham Island is lowland of muskeg, stunted pines and small lakes and rivers. A sandy beach trimmed with gnarled, wind-sculpted trees swoops out for more than twenty miles along the coast and ends at a sand spit in the shape of a buccaneer's sword. A great many mariners have perished on this point, known as Rose Spit or *Naay Kun* to the Haida. The truck came out of the dark forest onto the beach, its tires catching and spitting sand into the air. They drove for several miles to a rocky promontory known as Yakan Point on

Tow Hill in the distance, Queen Charlotte Islands or Haida Gwaii, 1946.
COURTESY OF ED RICKETTS JR.

the southwest side of Tow Hill. The region is simply and unremarkably called South Beach, though its natural history is anything but.

Tow Hill is a massive five-hundred-foot outcrop that rises out of nowhere in an otherwise lowland region. There are several legends that explain its existence, including one about an "outcast cripple" who saves the chief's daughter from a gluttonous ogre. Geologists, however, explain that this columnar mass of black basalt was created by a vertical lava flow that burst the earth's surface two million years ago. The boiling lava also oozed into the sea, where it cooled and made billowy, smooth rocky pools. The region looks strikingly like the seashore that Charles Darwin first landed upon in the Galapagos and described as "a broken field of black basaltic lava, thrown into the most rugged waves."

Like Darwin, Ricketts was thrilled by the experience of exploring a region where "in the history of marine biology, no scientist, no naturalist, no book-learning trained observer had ever collected before." He collected many specimens that day—crabs, periwinkles, tubeworms, starfish, clams and chitons—and took special note of the unique fauna on what is, at least to the Haida, a sacred shore.

This region is the setting of one of the Haida myths of the first humans. After a great flood—the deluge motif is common to almost all world religions—the waters receded, exposing the glimmering sands of Rose Spit. Flying about, Raven swooped down and gorged himself on intertidal delicacies. His hunger quenched, the trickster-creator now had other appetites to satisfy: lust and curiosity. After stealing light from a box in an old man's house and scattering it into the sky, he flew to the shore near Tow Hill. He found it lifeless and boring. He cried out and was surprised to be answered by a muffled squeak. He spotted a flash of light on the beach that turned out to be a clam with tiny creatures cowering inside. He coaxed and cajoled them to come out and play. When they finally did, the first humans stepped into the world.

Raven's playmates were all male and having an especially short attention span he quickly grew bored with them. He collected the men on his back and flew them to North Island, the most northern spot on the archipelago. Filled with mischievous and lewd thoughts, Raven pried some red gumboot chitons (*Cryptochiton stelleri*) from the rocks and threw these mollusks at the men's groins. The men became overwhelmed with sensations and unknown impulses, squirming and feeling the rush of a great storm and then calm. The chitons eventually went back to the low-tide rocks and after many moons grew enormous, their shells of articulated plates near bursting. A great wave then swept the chitons up onto the beach and out emerged more humans, both male and female, to populate the world.

The Haida were very much people of the seashore. In Old Masset, Ricketts saw rows of houses with their fronts to the ocean and their backs to the forest. Dugout canoes were pushed up on the pebble beach out front. It was a homely village, however. Mostly standardized Western-style housing stood on the Indian reserve. The homes were largely devoid of the enormous house poles that served as coats of arms for families and often depicted mythic stories. So much had changed in Haida society in only a few generations.

Even before the arrival of the first missionary in 1876, one chief had started to lose faith in his society's ancient ways. The shamans' supernatural powers and medicines seemed useless against smallpox and the wrath of "fire-water" (whiskey). The population of Haida Gwaii collapsed from more than twelve thousand prior to European contact to barely six hundred in 1900. Entire villages, such as Skung'gwaii, T'anuu and K'uuna, were destroyed by disease. The Christian missionary soon became the "Medicine Man from the Iron People," and systematically tore down totem poles, considered to be heretic symbols of paganism. Many were also carted off to museums.

Scientists were actually complicit in the pillaging. "They are a doomed race," a curator said of the Haida at a lecture at Chicago's Field Museum in 1897. "Wars, smallpox, gross immorality, a change from old ways to new ways—their fate is the common fate of the American, whether he sails the sea in the North, gallops over the plain in the West, or sleeps in his hammock in the forests of Brazil." As late as 1920, scientists who thought they were collecting "specimens" of a dying race robbed hundreds of Haida graves. They sent the bones, which are only beginning to be repatriated today, to the same museums—the Field Museum in Chicago, the Natural History Museum in New York and the Smithsonian in Washington, D.C.—where Ricketts was sending many of his own marine specimens.

All around him, Ricketts saw the remnants of spiritual and social decay:

> Now the Indian girl in the co-op cannery wears glasses and uses lipstick, she isn't very pretty and she used to work in a bank in Prince Rupert and she doesn't look very happy to me but maybe these people never were; they're sort of sober and grave. Most of the totems are down and no one bothers with them. They're rotting on the ground. You can't cart them away; that's forbidden by law, but no one does anything about them, even the Indian agent who mourns but has no action. And they're the finest totems certainly in the whole world. They were real, not for tourist show. At Yan, a deserted village across the sound (and it might as well be across the world; in this region of heavy tidal currents across the inlet is across the ocean) you can see it from the steamer but no one goes there. The forest of totems is a shambles of windfalls now.

TOP: *Old Masset in 1890.* BOTTOM: *Old Masset in 1922. Within one generation, museums and missionaries had torn down most of the totem poles in the village.*

TOP PHOTO: BRITISH COLUMBIA ARCHIVES PHOTO D-09210.

BOTTOM PHOTO: BRITISH COLUMBIA ARCHIVES PHOTO A-05341.

The rotting totems were evidence of the deliberate and wanton destruction of the Haida's belief system, which had sustained them for thousands of years. (Many Haida took their spirituality underground, away from the eyes of the church; as a result the Haida are today undergoing a cultural renaissance.) Ironically, just as missionaries were tearing down the totems and debunking pagan myths, scientists were laying siege to the Christian faith. In his research at the time, Joseph Campbell was coming to the conclusion that the same fate that befell the Haida was now befalling modern society. "We have seen what has happened, for example, to primitive communities unsettled by the white man's civilization," Campbell later said. "With their old taboos discredited, they immediately go to pieces, disintegrate, and become resorts of vice and disease. Today the same thing is happening to us."

For thousands of years, history, art, music, literature, science and politics sprang from the "sanctified cosmic images" of myth and religion. But with every new scientific discovery from the Enlightenment onward, this ancient system slowly began to disintegrate. The Bible became, in light of the discoveries of Galileo and Darwin, an anthology of absurdities. Science had effectively slain the gods. As Campbell wrote in *The Hero*:

> It is not only that there is no hiding place for the gods from the searching telescope and microscope: there is no such society any more as the gods once supported. The social unit is not a carrier of religious content, but an economic-political organization. Its ideals are not those of the hieratic pantomime, making visible on earth the forms of heaven, but of the secular state, in hard and unremitting competition for material supremacy and resources. Isolated societies, dream-bounded within a mythologically charged horizon, no longer exist except as areas to be exploited. And within progressive societies themselves, every last vestige of the ancient human heritage of ritual, morality, and art is in full decay.

As evidence of this decay, Campbell pointed to the "rapidly rising" incidences of neuroticism, mental disorders, suicides, dope addictions, shattered homes, impudent children, violence, murder and despair in modern society.

Instead of abandoning old belief systems, Campbell wanted to breathe life back into the timeless myths and religions of the world. He was attempting to render "the modern world spiritually significant." He saw no inherent conflict between science and spirituality. The secret, he believed, was to pierce the apparent fiction of pagan superstitions, aboriginal lore, ancient Chinese texts and biblical tales to understand their inner meanings. The purpose of writing *The Hero* was "to uncover some of the truths disguised for us under the figures of religion and mythology." Myth had to be read metaphorically, not literally. Campbell wanted to teach a "symbolic language" that would allow modern society to redis-cover the gods.

So, for example, although the Haida story of the first humans sounds preposterous when contrasted with the scientific facts, it is nevertheless true—metaphorically speaking. From Haida myth, we learn that at one time the earth was covered with water, and that the islands lurked below until the primal sea receded. It's a sequence of events that has been con-firmed by modern geologists. The Haida myth also describes life crawling up from this sea to land and man evolving from some lowly sea creature. The clam and the chiton are therefore metaphors for mankind's "common progenitor," which Darwin described.

What's more, the chiton with its fleshy, labial underside and the clam with its phallic siphon represent the female and male, respectively, and their union represents the act of procreation. Some Vancouver Island natives, in fact, associated the red chiton with female genitalia and called it *p'a7am*, which was considered a "bad word." Ricketts himself made a cheeky comment in his own notes about a clam, *Schizothaerus nuttallii*, being rather well endowed. "[T]he horse clam, short for horse-cock clam, tsk tsk . . . [has] great siphons bearded with moss." If under-stood as metaphor, Raven too takes on a meaning beyond a colorful and cantankerous character in a quaint fairy tale. Raven, according to one anthropologist, is "a metaphor of both inter-human relations and rela-tions between humans and nature."

Joseph Campbell knew the seashore intimately. He spent months studying the intertidal region with Ricketts. He considered it the "mother zone" and its creatures the "innumerable little children of the teeming shallows." He knew how the ecology of a given area colored and shaped the mythology of its indigenous people. According to Campbell, "mythology [was] a function of biology." It was also the metaphorical manifestation of a deep collective memory digging back to time imme-morial. With Campbell's insight and guidance, Ricketts too would come to understand the life-supporting nature of myth and religion. Later that summer, he would overcome his own prejudices about organized reli-gion to realize its ecological value.

* * *

FOLLOWING their collections near Tow Hill, Ricketts and his son kept up a steady pace of exploration for more than a week. The weather was mostly overcast and rainy. According to Ricketts, this was "a great benefit to the intertidal beasts, allowing them to occupy much higher levels than would be possible if the times of exposure coincided with dry air and hot sunshine." The awful weather did not slow his research, but by June 26, after three days of collecting, he became upset at his lack of laboratory supplies. "I was needing boots and jars and alcohol pretty pretty bad," he wrote. The Union Steamship Company had yet to wire him about the whereabouts of his biological supply chest. Still, he and Ed Jr. headed out in the wet weather and poor visibility once again, but their collecting efforts made for "many disappointments."

The next day they borrowed the village's only available skiff and rowed out on a flowing tide to Wimble Rocks, a mile seaward from Masset. They plucked about fifty species from the rocks including several new species of chitons. Their prospects seemed to be brightening. Indeed, sunshine broke through the rain clouds the next day. All work stopped in the community. "[W]hen the sun shines here it's pure paradise," Ricketts wrote. One by one, shops were closed, women put down their chores and men stopped fishing and logging. Families descended on the beach for picnics and finally "the community indulged in one great unplanned holiday."

Ricketts kept working though. At 6:30 A.M. the next morning he borrowed the local taxi and went back to South Beach to collect on "a very striking tide." He rounded up about a hundred different specimens, including a three-foot octopus that Ed Jr. photographed. "I dragged him out of his cavern," Ricketts wrote, "he swam, rocketed, and walked for us."

On Sunday, June 30, Ricketts returned to the beach for a "community crab feed" near Tow Hill. A truck brought the men out early. The area is incredibly rich with Dungeness crabs or *Cancer magister*. With a simple dip net and boots, one can venture into the surf and easily scoop up the big rusty brown crabs, which turn crimson when boiled. Within half an hour, four men netted forty-two crabs. The longest, Ricketts noted, was nine to ten inches. Rugs were laid out on the beach and the "wimmenfolks" came out to cook and prepare the feast. "We ate crab til it oozed out of our nostrils," Ricketts recalled. He did more collecting, of course, and captured

Captured octopus, Queen Charlotte Islands or Haida Gwaii, 1946. COURTESY OF ED RICKETTS JR.

another octopus, too. "I've often wondered if octopi ever bite," Ricketts wrote. "Today I found out. Yes, they do; they certainly do."

After ten days on the island, Ricketts' supply chest finally showed up on the first of July. It turned out that on the hectic day of their arrival, careless freight handlers had accidentally loaded it back onto the *Cassiar*, which then headed back to Prince Rupert. Unfortunately, this good news came with more bad weather. "[T]he wind and the rain were so bad we could hardly see," Ricketts complained in his journal. Violent gusts of wind swept in from the ocean, creating tempests in the tide pools and making it impossible to see the animals below the surface. While out collecting, Ricketts could barely stop the tears streaming out of his eyes because of the wind.

He recorded his last collecting entry in his "New Series Notebook No. 4" on Wednesday, July 3. He spent most of the day searching for small chitons to send to "old Jinglebollix." (This was apparently an unflattering nickname for Dr. William A. Hilton of Pomona College in Claremont, California.) He and his son collected sixty-one specimens of eight different species. These included a new species that Jinglebollix later said he'd call *Mopalia rickettsi*. (There is, in fact, no such species designation today, suggesting it turned out not to be a new species after all.) They spent their last three days on the island busily preserving and packing specimens. Ricketts also reflected on the "biological curiosities" of the island and pondered the environmental factors that conditioned its human inhabitants—notably its geographic isolation, old plank road, strong tidal currents and heavy rain.

* * *

ON July 6, Ricketts wrote his last notebook entry from the Queen Charlotte Islands. The nearly illegible jottings were apparently made aboard the *Cassiar* while journeying back to Prince Rupert in the early evening. As the steamer sailed out of the inlet into Dixon Entrance, it passed Old Masset on its starboard side. Ricketts remembered his visit to the Haida cemetery:

> Since projections are the only "true" things, at least the only things in the world we can really know, it's not a figure to speak of ghosts in these Indian graveyards. I think of them forming a group soul, now wiser than 200 years ago, less fierce, kind, but pretty sad. Now that [collective being] *knows* how *terrible* the coming of the white man has disoriented the Indian from his land. [The white man] not only disposed him economically, but killed him spiritually.

The *Cassiar* continued out past the abandoned village of Yan, which was nestled in a small cove on the west side of Masset Inlet. In 1881, it was recorded to be a thriving village of some twenty longhouses with as many beautifully carved totem poles. But by the end of the decade it was abandoned, left to rot on the misty seashore. Ricketts could vaguely see the remnants of the village. His last image of Haida Gwaii was a haunting one. "On the way out," he wrote, "in the distance, the deserted Yan, a few totems still standing black against the dark land."

* * *

IN *Parallel Expeditions: Charles Darwin and the Art of John Steinbeck,* literary scholar Brian E. Railsback documents how Darwin's ideas and the biological perspective were the most important hallmark of John Steinbeck's writing. It's a point largely lost on literary critics. "Darwin takes fire from the creationists," Railsback writes, "and Steinbeck gets it from the humanists."

Railsback makes one unfortunate error in an otherwise interesting comparison, however. Through a narrow analysis of Ricketts' daily log from which Steinbeck wrote the narrative portion of *Sea of Cortez*, he wrongly concludes that it was Steinbeck who brought Darwin's ideas into the book—and so by extension into the trilogy. "To some extent," he writes, "the parallel expeditions of Darwin and Steinbeck leave even Ricketts behind." A more thorough review of Ricketts' philosophical and scientific writing—and especially his outer shores notebooks— reveals that Railsback's assertion is manifestly false.

At the end of his published journal, Charles Darwin provided the reader with "a short retrospect of the advantages and disadvantages, the pains and pleasures" of his five-year circumnavigation of the world. He warned that the cost was great, the hardships many, the isolation unbearable. For this reason, he cautioned, one should possess some branch of knowledge in order "to look forward to a harvest, however distant that may be, when some fruit will be reaped, some good effected" from a far-flung expedition.

Darwin did not fully understand the meaning of what he saw on the Galapagos Islands until long after H.M.S. *Beagle* sailed away. The harvest reaped would be revolutionary. His scientific observations on the Galapagos, as he wrote in his masterpiece of 1859, "seemed to throw some light on the origins of species—that mystery of mysteries."

In *Origins of Species*, Darwin hesitated to specifically apply his theory of natural selection to humans. He feared it would "thus only add to the prejudices against my views." It took him another dozen years to publish *The Descent of Man* (1871). Man, Darwin concluded, "with all his noble qualities, with sympathy which feels for the most debased, with benevolence which extends not only to other men but to the humblest living creature, with his god-like intellect which has penetrated into the movements and constitution of the solar system—with all these exalted powers—Man still bears in his bodily frame the indelible stamp of his lowly origin." It took Darwin nearly forty years from first stepping foot on the deck of H.M.S. *Beagle* to write these shattering words.

According to Darwin, what separated man from beast and set him above all other species in the animal kingdom was his moral being. Darwin explained that man was "capable of reflecting on his past actions and their motives—of approving of some and disapproving of others." Morality, Darwin continued, was derived from social instincts common to other animals, but highly developed in humans. A belief in God was mankind's "greatest distinction" and "apparently follows from a considerable advance in man's reason, and from a still greater advance in his faculties of imagination, curiosity and wonder." Social instincts such as love and sympathy—cornerstones of the Christian faith—are "highly beneficial to the species," he wrote, and thus "they have in all probability been acquired through natural selection." And the Christian God, who had made humans in His own image, was certainly the highest evolved in the pantheon of gods. He was certainly more advanced than the lowly animal-deities of "primitive" peoples such as the Haida.

Darwin seemed torn, however. He knew that the Church would attack his evolutionary theory, especially if applied to humans. He was obviously at odds with a *literal* interpretation of Scripture. He even admitted that Christianity was not "supported by evidence." Yet he believed a man could undoubtedly be "an ardent Theist and an Evolutionist." He had "never been an Atheist in the sense of denying the existence of God." He liked to point out to colleagues that he was agnostic; the existence of God was simply unknown or unknowable, scientifically anyway.

In *The Descent of Man,* Darwin attempted to bridge the gap between science and religion or perhaps mollify critics. He wrote that a belief in God was evidence of advanced evolution. It was a matter of scientific fact, he stated. But some questions went unanswered. How, for instance, did a belief in God benefit the survival of the human species? Why would believers be naturally selected over nonbelievers in the struggle for existence?

Ed Ricketts clearly modeled his scientific methodology on Charles Darwin. Indeed, the Queen Charlottes were to Ricketts what the

Galapagos were to Darwin. They were intellectual departure points. After decades of expeditions and rigorous fieldwork, both men left their respective archipelagos and made inductive leaps into the theoretical. By the summer of 1946, Ricketts had been observing and describing marine fauna for a quarter-century. He now felt confident enough to develop some general principles of marine ecology, which would be informed by his readings of other scientists and his own research and speculation. He was also convinced, as was Darwin, that his biological theories must apply equally to human beings. "The laws of animals," Ricketts once wrote, "must be the laws of men."

Ricketts would also discuss with Joseph Campbell in the following months how a belief in God (or gods) had contributed to the survival of the human species. They would pick up where Darwin left off in *The Descent of Man*. So as the *Cassiar* plied the dark waters away from the Queen Charlotte Islands, Ed Ricketts was indeed voyaging in the mighty wake of Charles Darwin—and perhaps even beyond.

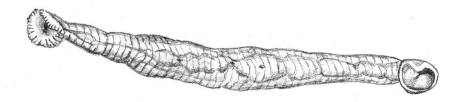

MARSIPOBDELLA SACCULATA, MARINE LEECH, NEW SPECIES
COLLECTED BY ED RICKETTS IN MARCH 1929 IN CALIFORNIA.

CHAPTER TWELVE

FAREWELL PARTY

The nature of parties has been imperfectly studied. It is, however, generally understood that a party has a pathology, that it is a kind of an individual and that it is likely to be a very perverse individual. And it is also generally understood that a party hardly ever goes the way it is planned or intended.

—JOHN STEINBECK, *Cannery Row*

AS the *Cassiar* crossed Hecate Straits to the mainland, Ed Ricketts slipped below deck to get some rest. They would be in Prince Rupert by early morning and he was exhausted. He'd had a fruitful, though grueling, two weeks of collecting in the mist, rain and blinding squalls that constitute summer in the North Pacific. His travel trunks were chock-full of critters. Ricketts figured many were probably new to taxonomy. Yet he also knew that he had in his possession only a relative few. He had barely even begun to systematically survey the islands.

The archipelago was vast. Ricketts believed there were many remote regions that probably contained a unique fauna: Yan, Wiah Point, Naden Harbor and North Island to the west; Masset Inlet, a veritable inland sea fifteen miles southward; and Skidegate, a native village on a narrow channel on the southern end of Graham Island. In his journal, he listed these as "places we should go," meaning places he and John Steinbeck should visit on their return voyage.

The *Cassiar* arrived in Prince Rupert on July 7 and made a hasty turnaround, heading back out to sea by ten o'clock that morning. Prince Rupert was a town of unrealized dreams. Charles Melville Hays, tycoon, visionary and president of the Grand Trunk Railway—and according to some a heartless, cruel and tyrannical man—envisioned and built Prince Rupert. He willed it into existence as an instant town in 1910. It was the western terminus of his transcontinental railway and would become a "super-port" to rival Vancouver. After a successful fund-raising trip to

England, on April 10, 1912, Hays stepped aboard a luxurious ocean liner on its maiden voyage to New York. Neither Hays nor his great scheme for Prince Rupert would survive the sinking of the *Titanic*. A financial disaster, the railway went bankrupt in 1919. Prince Rupert has been floundering ever since. There was a fevered shipbuilding boom during the war, but by 1946 Ricketts had happened upon a decidedly quiet fishing community.

This being a Sunday—and a sunny day at that—Ricketts found everything from the cinema, library, and museum to the marine terminal closed "tighter than a drum." The *Cardena*, which would take them southbound, wasn't due until the afternoon and actually arrived well overdue late that night. So they whiled away several hours collecting in a little land-locked cove drained by a sewer pipe, probably near Cow's Bay in the harbor. It was an extremely protected and polluted environment, or as Ricketts euphemistically described, "highly specialized." He found a new species of freshwater sand flea, but not much else. The water was too contaminated to support much life. They also explored the town, walking through the gravel streets of pioneer homes set on rolling hills.

When the *Cardena* finally arrived, everyone boarded the vessel and cargo was unloaded in the pitch dark. The steamer departed, not southbound, but northbound for Alaska to her final port of call before the return journey to Vancouver. The ship stopped at the native village of Port Simpson in the morning and then Wales Cannery and Arrandale Cannery in the mouth of Portland Canal, a natural boundary separating B.C. and Alaska. The coast was incredibly majestic, but contrasted sharply with the sordid conditions Ricketts saw in the cannery towns:

> The native village at Arrandale is as filthy a place as I've ever seen anywhere. No one to look after these people who are children at least in civilization (in Western civilization). I went across a creek where some friendly Indian people were living in smiling squalor; even the dogs were filthy. There was shit and salmon entrails and maggots and flies and for all I know human vomit mixed up with washing and drying clothes and buckets for hauling water and rottenly dried fish in the most awful stink you ever [smelled] and I'm not squeamish about those things. I suppose no church to look after this place.

Portland Canal also seemed a "little bit terrible" to Ricketts, but for different reasons. It leads seventy miles inland to the Misty Fjords and the twin border towns of Hyder and Stewart, in the United States and Canada, respectively. The canal is barely a mile wide in places, with massive coastal mountains topped with glaciers flanking each side. As the steamer sailed inland, the mountains grew higher and higher, the canal deeper and deeper. It was so sheltered that Ricketts figured it got "sun (what little there is) so very seldom." He felt daunted by nature's monumental design. "To the eagles watching high over Portland Canal," Ricketts wrote in his log, "the steamer that's so great to us must seem like a dot at the bottom of a great trough."

These inland waterways differed markedly from the outer shores. "We found the most fantastic fauna I've ever seen," Ricketts wrote. It wasn't particularly lush, however. To the contrary, there were no fish, crabs or flatworms. The mussel and snail fauna were quite modest. At Arrandale Cannery, he only found marine pseudo-scorpions and sea centipedes, along with several species of pill bugs, beach hoppers and fleas. The fauna was "fantastic," according to Ricketts, because it was "so highly specialized." Farther inland, the glacial and rainforest runoff was so great that it formed a fifteen- to twenty-foot freshwater glaze—a "milky" and "emulsified" effect—on the surface of the deep canal. This freshwater condition effectively eliminated the truly salt-loving animals, allowing the hardy insects to penetrate their ecological niche.

Ricketts collected wherever the *Cardena* stopped. He speculated that he had enough material for a half dozen books, but later told Steinbeck that this research from the inner shores should be excluded from *The Outer Shores*. He suggested that it would be fun to do another summertime expedition, similar to his 1932 trip with Jack Calvin and Joseph Campbell, specifically up the Inside Passage; he shied away from suggesting yet another book to his friend, however.

Ricketts would certainly need a coauthor for such a volume. He was capable of great elucidation and touching eloquence at times. Henry Miller had said as much. Yet often his grammar and sentence structure were as tangled as a kelp bed. His writing was, according to one reviewer, "clumsy and oblique," and his style was "very awkward and in places the syntax breaks down." Even Campbell, who greatly admired Ricketts' ideas, found his language "obscure." "What is the meaning of 'holistic tenderness'?" Campbell asked in one case. Steinbeck even complained that his "use of words was unorthodox and, until you knew him, somewhat startling." Editors at *Harper's, Atlantic Monthly, Cosmopolitan* and *Reader's Digest* repeatedly rejected his submissions. He loved to write and did so prodigiously. The struggle was in reading his often awkward, introspective prose. He knew he wasn't a strong writer and therefore recruited friends either to serve as coauthors or editors.

From his 1932 expedition to Juneau, he wrote a forty-three-page research paper on the Inside Passage. He even drafted a succinct "statement" of the unique ecology of these inland shores:

> Given, originally, an equal distribution of animals, the tendency would be (a) for inlet conditions to favor the survival of species better fitted to withstand a considerable annual and diurnal temperature range, occasional fresh water, stagnation, and the deposition of silt, and (b) for surf conditions to favor the survival of species better fitted to withstand persistent wave shock....
>
> Thus, progressively, the tendency would be for environmental factors to select out a society of species physically fitted to survive the imposed conditions, and for the consequently established society itself to reinforce its own supremacy by crowding out and eating exotic creatures adapted to other conditions.

An asterisk beside the statement points to an intriguing footnote at the bottom of the page:

> * I have to thank Mr. Joseph Campbell of New York for this clear and concise statement of the situation all of us observed and discussed.

So beside coauthors Calvin and Steinbeck, it seems that Campbell too had helped give voice to Ed Ricketts' ideas. Ricketts even thanked his "constant and interested companion, for clarifying and outlining in some detail certain conclusions attained en route." Campbell was more than just a mere helper to Ricketts. He was, like Steinbeck, a student and collaborator engrossed in all aspects of the biologist's work.

* * *

HYDER, Alaska, is a painfully sleepy town. The defunct mining community today claims to be "the Friendliest Ghost Town in Alaska." Besides viewing black bears and grizzlies on the local Bear Glacier, the only other activity of note is being "Hyderized." The stomach-wrenching initiation involves drinking shots of pure grain alcohol at the Glacier Inn's bar.

Apparently, little has changed in fifty years. The only "excuse" for Hyder's existence, Ricketts observed in 1946, was alcohol. The community straddled the border between "liberal Alaska," where you could buy American cigarettes and unlimited whiskey, and "strict Canada," where the pubs "close on the dot" and "hard stuff" was rationed. At 10 P.M., the *Cardena* docked at the end of a long causeway in Canadian territory. The causeway actually ran across the American border to a general store and some "lousy saloons" along the shore. "This place is the end of the line," Ricketts wrote.

Passengers and the ship's stewards made their way to the clean and tidy general store to buy cheap cigarettes and limitless liquor. The customs officer, who was also the owner of the store, turned a blind eye to the lucrative duty-free trade. Passengers shuffled back over the border with cigarette cartons and bottles of liquor obviously stuffed under their coats.

Ricketts went ashore too. He stopped at one of the many seaside saloons. A "funny sad guy" who "lives here cheerlessly" ran the bar. Ricketts ordered a beer from the guy, who bragged about their local blue-glacier bear. There was little else to boast about. Ricketts found Hyder to be altogether "vile." He thought it was a town built on "wickedness and cupidity." He sipped his beer, but when the bartender started to recount old war stories, he politely excused himself and walked out. It was, Ricketts wrote in his journal, just "too sad to stay here." He went outside and looked up at the dusky sky and snow-capped mountains. The scenery was, Ricketts remembered, "as lovely as I've ever seen." He heard birds singing in the distance, but that wasn't all.

The "sad rather than vicious old town whore," Ricketts wrote, had picked up a group of men at the saloon and took them back to her shack on the edge of town. Ricketts could hear them in there drinking and singing. "She doesn't want to be screw[ed] particularly," Ricketts went on in his journal, "she just wants the money and much much more she wants the companionship." She was a sad, fattish middle-aged woman, who was being "sentimental and palsywalsy and crying into her beer." Hell, Ricketts figured, she'd even give you "the fat contents of her whoring purse if you'd once in her life clasp her face honestly, pat her on the back. Well, and how that all contrasts with the smell of the clean country on the good gravel road, mountains with snow right almost down to the sea level."

The steamer departed around midnight, and perhaps not soon enough for Ed Ricketts. The trip southward was uneventful. Ricketts took few notes. He prepared specimen packages and letters to send to Dr. Schmitt at the Smithsonian Institution and to Dr. Carlgren at Lund University in Sweden. It was a restful time, all in all. "These inland passages are the quietest places you've ever seen," he later reflected. "Nothing but the drip of rain, the sound of waterfalls and the songs of the thrushes; at dawn and dusk the hillsides ring with their whistles, and maybe no other sound. Russet backed thrush, sound of the wilderness."

On Wednesday, July 10, the steamer slipped out of Fitz Hugh Sound on B.C.'s Central Coast, crossed the exposed waters of Queen Charlotte Strait and arrived in Port Hardy on the northeast end of Vancouver Island. From here they continued down Johnstone Strait, arriving in Campbell River at 3 A.M. the following day. Ed and Toni disembarked to travel via train to Port Alberni. The shortcut would shave twenty-four hours off a return journey via Vancouver. Ricketts' son, however, was lured back to the big city; Ed Jr. had met a beautiful young nurse and decided to travel back to Vancouver, where she worked at the general hospital.

In Campbell River, a female taxi driver was the lone soul to meet the *Cardena* that early morning. "I never saw such seamanship," Ricketts recalled. The woman skillfully hooked one hawser until a deckhand hopped ashore and fastened it tight. She helped Ed and Toni with their specimen trunks and baggage, and drove them to an inn. The couple got little sleep. They woke before nine o'clock and took a "jerky" bus ride to Courtenay, less than an hour away. They had to catch the 10:40 A.M. train from there to Port Alberni.

Daylight revealed a shocking scene: Campbell River and Courtenay, according to Ricketts, looked like "they were hit by a cyclone." About three-quarters of the chimneys in Campbell River had tumbled down. Windows were cracked and shattered. There were huge cracks and tears in the road en route to Courtenay, whose downtown was in disarray. A brick wall of the post office was nothing but rubble; the roof of the elementary school was caved in; and the Bank of Commerce looked like it had been bombed. It soon became apparent what had wreaked such indiscriminate devastation, especially to two Californians.

On June 23, about nineteen seconds after 10:13 A.M., according to one witness, "we thought the world was coming to an end." "I saw the whole ground moving like waves in the ocean," said another, "and there was a noise like a rumble." In the Alberni Valley, a farmer saw his pastureland roll "like ocean swells." Aboard the *Cardena*, which was leaving Shushartie Bay en route to Port Hardy at the time, a passenger felt the vessel shudder, as though it were grating on rocks. The frightened helmsman reported to his captain that the ship's compass was trembling inexplicably.

At 7.3 on the Richter scale, the earthquake was "one of the most severe which has been recorded in Canada within historic times," according to the Dominion Seismological Division. Campbell River and Courtenay bore the brunt of it. The epicenter was only ten miles south-southwest of Campbell River. The tremor triggered landslides, shifted the depth of the ocean floor by more than a hundred feet in places, and drowned a man when a wave, lashed up by the quake, swamped his boat. Several barrels of broken glass were hauled out of the liquor store in Courtenay, which must have been especially troubling for Ricketts. Did his hundreds of specimens in glass jars and vials at Clayoquot meet a similar fate?

Their jerkwater train ride through the mountains and across the island was "a pure delight," according to Ricketts. At the quay in Port Alberni, Captain Young greeted them "like old timers" and invited them into the pilothouse of the *Uchuck*. From the bridge, Ricketts saw how the quake had damaged the West Coast. The transpacific telegraph cable at Bamfield had been severed and at the cannery town of Kildonan part of the wharf had collapsed, casting an ice-crusher into the sea.

The voyage became trying as they neared the outer shores. The *Uchuck* rolled badly coming across the exposed entrance to Barkley Sound. In the passenger lounge, people were vomiting from seasickness. "We hear that during the winter," Ricketts wrote, "the sitting room below is a mess of sick and crying Indian children and grown whites; the floor runs ankle deep in vomit swishing from side to side as the boat rolls—the Bone Crusher." The *Uchuck* finally arrived in Ucluelet, where Ricketts and Jackson caught a bus to Tofino.

The earthquake had done serious damage to buildings on Stubbs Island. An English war bride living on the island told Ruth White it reminded her of the bombing of London. The shaker knocked down most of the chimneys, threw dishes crashing to the floor and scared everyone pretty badly. Bill White went into the storage attic to see how Ricketts' specimens had fared. Some jars and bottles were knocked over, but only a few were broken.

Betty Farmer told Ricketts that shortly after the earthquake some natives had come over to the store to tell her that their beaches were mysteriously full of dead pink crawfish. No one had ever seen such a phenomenon. Ricketts also noticed that thousands of burrowing ghost shrimp lay dead on the island's sand spit. The biologist had no explanation for this uncanny occurrence. In his 1934 scientific paper on tides, Ricketts had noted that earthquake seiches (popularly known as "tidal waves") from the devastating quakes of San Francisco in 1906, Santa Barbara in 1925, and Long Beach in 1933 had no appreciable effect on marine fauna. Ricketts did wonder about the relationship between quakes and tides. About a month before leaving for Clayoquot, he mentioned in a letter to Jack Calvin that the "year of the big tides" could also be subjected to "earthquake activity larger than usual." Scientists have yet to prove, to this day, any connection between tidal forces and earthquake occurrences, however.

Normalcy soon came back to the lives of the island's residents. Broken windows were replaced, smashed china and glass swept up, and chimneys repaired. Ricketts too was able to salvage his few broken specimens. In his final week, he continued his collecting around Clayoquot Sound, traveling up to the native village of Ahousat to find more chitons for "Old Jinglebollix." He also went inland ten miles to Tsapee Narrows, on the south side of Meares Island. One Friday, July 19, everyone went out in the *Beegee* to a place called Elbow Bank near Maurus Island. Many of the islanders, especially Betty, Bill, Ruth and Pete Ackley, the army captain, had become good friends with Ricketts, and they enthusiastically helped with his work. In pursuit of a coral specimen, Pete even stripped off his clothes and valiantly dove under the boat into the cold sea. Ricketts was "very tickled" by his heroic efforts to fetch a specimen.

* * *

LIKE a scene out of Steinbeck's *Cannery Row*, Ricketts staged a farewell party the next day "of such a quality" that Captain MacKinnon got involved. Late Saturday afternoon, Ed and Toni carted their specimen trunks and luggage along the wooden trestle to the *Princess Maquinna* moored at the end of the Clayoquot wharf. A ship's derrick swung over to load their belongings. The couple settled into their stateroom and then Betty, Bill, Ruth, Pete and several others joined them in the *Maquinna*'s aft lounge for drinks during the ten-minute sail to Tofino.

Having heard that his good friend "Doc" was aboard on his farewell voyage, Captain MacKinnon abandoned his duties on the bridge to join in the revelry below deck. The captain got so caught up in the occasion that he kept the ship moored in Tofino for an extra half hour. Although Ricketts was "a little mixed up" on the details, he later believed that MacKinnon was taken off the West Coast route after, or perhaps as a result of, this trip. (The ship's official logbook, under "report on character," recorded MacKinnon's ability and conduct during this trip as "V.G." or very good.) "Everyone including Capt. MacKinnon got quite swacko," Ricketts recalled. "We drank up all but one or two bottles of the saved liquor." Eventually the first officer blew the *Maquinna*'s whistle. He was frustrated by MacKinnon's behavior and sent the cabin boy down after him.

"Tell 'em I'll be right up," the merry master assured the cabin boy, who was later sent back down a second time.

Ricketts remembered the "fine drunken" Captain MacKinnon "actually staggering" up to the bridge around six o'clock. The Clayoquot partygoers stumbled onto the wharf. Ed and Toni hugged and kissed everyone farewell. They would visit next summer, Ricketts assured

Ed Ricketts and Toni Jackson wave farewell to Clayoquot Sound, 1946.
COURTESY OF ED RICKETTS JR.

them, and he'd drag along John Steinbeck, too. Climbing back aboard, Ricketts turned on the gangway and waved good-bye.

The *Maquinna* set sail for Victoria in the twilight. They'd be in the provincial capital in two days, where Ed Jr. was waiting penniless, having spent all his money impressing the young nurse in Vancouver. MacKinnon steered the *Maquinna* through Templar Channel, past the Lennard Island lighthouse and onto the Pacific. As they headed onto the high seas, an evening fog rolled in. The crew navigated by dead reckoning and after awhile a squabble erupted on the bridge about the ship's coordinates. Ricketts remembered the officer on duty being "so young and gold braid and trim and disapproving" of the captain. The young officer thought they should have changed course, but MacKinnon overruled him. Ricketts stayed up past midnight to see who would be correct: "The drunken Captain, by this time cold sober, was right," Ricketts wrote, "and the precise, sober young officer was minutes and a half mile off. The Captain was on the nose."

AIPTASIOMORPHA ELONGATA, SEA ANEMONE, NEW SPECIES COLLECTED
BY ED RICKETTS ON APRIL 4, 1940, IN THE GULF OF CALIFORNIA, MEXICO.

CHAPTER THIRTEEN
IN TOTO

*All things are one thing and that one thing is all things—plankton, a
shimmering phosphorescence on the sea and the spinning planets and an
expanding universe, all bound together by the elastic string of time.*

—JOHN STEINBECK & EDWARD F. RICKETTS,
Sea of Cortez: A Leisurely Journal of Travel and Research

ON September 11, 1946, the "wheels of destiny," as Joseph Campbell described, brought him and his wife Jean rolling into Monterey on their way back from a holiday in Honolulu. Ed and Toni met the couple with open arms at the lab. They hadn't seen each other for seven years, since a similar visit in 1939. Robert Rossen, the Hollywood director who later made *The Hustler* with Paul Newman, also unexpectedly dropped by the lab. Toni had worked with him on a film starring Errol Flynn in Monterey years before. Ricketts thought he seemed lonely that night. He had just finished filming *Body and Soul*. Rossen knew he could always find a friend and interested listener in the lab on Cannery Row.

It must have been a philosophical roller coaster ride for Rossen, trying to keep up with Ricketts and Campbell. They had much to discuss, not having seen each other for so long. They dove into James Joyce's *Finnegan's Wake*. Ricketts agreed with Campbell that "those last few pages are among the best . . . in modern literature." Campbell had coauthored *A Skeleton Key to Finnegan's Wake* in 1944, deciphering Joyce's cryptic prose. "You're blossoming out as a writer at a great rate," Ricketts said. That winter Campbell would also start his last revision of *The Hero with a Thousand Faces*. By this time, he felt like he had been working on it "since the fall of Man."

Ricketts recounted his own summertime travels along British Columbia's outer shores, and his efforts to complete the trilogy with Steinbeck. They also talked about the perilous sardine situation, which had made Cannery Row conspicuously quiet and "very downcast." It was, Ricketts later told Campbell, "[j]ust another instance of greed, lack of foresight, lack of seeing beyond a narrow individual segment of a large picture."

If the cannery owners continued to ignore the larger picture, Ricketts insisted, the sardines would soon be exterminated. "Our policy of insisting on taking everything at the moment," he told a friend the next month, "free enterprise at its freest, hurts only us." Ricketts seemed at a loss about what to do. How could he convince the fishermen that the only way to save the dwindling sardine industry, and ultimately themselves, was through conservation? How could he show that selfish individualism would lead to what we now call the tragedy of the commons?

"The ecologist who is accustomed to whole pictures, to such ideas as balance, and integration, and relationship, isn't likely to countenance any action based on pure selfishness," he wrote in a short essay titled "Sociology and Ecology" around this time. "He won't be a party to the extermination for instance of any natural resource such as food, fish or lumber. A sense of proportion is one of the primary requisites of his work, he looks at everything from the standpoint of 'greater-than-any-one-of-its-units.'" Yet fishermen knew little of ecology and were suspicious of any science calling for catch reductions.

Ed Ricketts thus began to think of another way to convince the fishing industry to heed science's call for conservation. The biologist distrusted organized religion. To him, the church was spirituality corrupted by power politics and economics. He had seen firsthand what the missionaries had done to the indigenous peoples in Mexico and Canada. Just after returning from Vancouver Island, he told Steinbeck, "Religion is deadish or cultish or wishful." Yet shortly after his meeting with Campbell, as he struggled to make sense of the sardine industry's suicidal behavior, his outlook changed—and quite radically.

His dialogue with Campbell that night, and their subsequent letter writing, brought about nothing short of an epiphany in Ed Ricketts. "Now I see one of the social values of organized religion," he told Campbell. "I've thought so little of them I never realized [it] before. If people won't of their own accord achieve a sense of balance with something suprapersonal, you beat it into them."

He now understood religion as being "pragmatically valuable," as having "social significance." The churches, with their insistence on values beyond the temporal and material, could sublimate or at least temper the thirsty individualism of the free market by "insisting on a regard for suprapersonal values." Perhaps a Sunday sermon could convince the fishing industry of salvation through conservation. "A good many religious ideas may not hold water intellectually and scientifically," Ricketts believed, "but they certainly do socially."

In *Sea of Cortez* and his philosophical essays, in his outer shores notebook and his conversations with Father Mulvihill, and now in his discussions with Joseph Campbell, Ricketts seemed to be searching for an integration of the scientific and the spiritual, a rapprochement of sorts. He was pioneering a new mode of thinking that contained all the primary elements of what would become "deep ecology" in the 1970s. The movement elevated the ecologist to the status of prophet and took on "the quality of a religious awakening." Deep ecology would offer a bio-centric worldview. The ancient Greek Goddess of the Earth would be reborn, through modern science, as the "Gaia hypothesis," which viewed the planet as a single vast, almighty and self-regulating being. Through ecology, science would atone for its sins against nature. Yet it would take another two decades for religion to do the same.

In 1989, Pope John Paul II made a historic speech, "On the Ecological Crisis." The destruction of the environment, said the pontiff, was "contrary to the order of creation, an order which is characterized by mutual interdependence." Since his historic pronouncement, there has been an explosion of ecological evangelism worldwide. Inspired by the biblical notion of Jubilee—"You shall hallow the fiftieth year and proclaim liberation in the land for all its inhabitants. You shall make this your year of Jubilee"—a coalition of thirty churches created the Canadian Ecumenical Jubilee Initiative to promote social justice, peace and ecological integrity. Likewise, the U.S. Conference of Catholic Bishops launched its own Environmental Justice Program in 1993. An evangelical network also fought the weakening of the U.S.'s Endangered Species Act, accusing Congress of trying to sink the act, which the group described as the "Noah's Ark of our day."

In 2002, the Worldwatch Institute, a global environmental watch-dog group, came to the same conclusions that Ricketts did half a century before. Regarding religion and environmentalism, its report, "Invoking the Spirit," stated: "Both look at the world from a moral perspective, stressing obligations that extend beyond the individual to other people, distant places, and future generations. Both generally see the natural world as having value that transcends economics. And both oppose the excessive consumption that drives industrial economies." The report identified "a budding rapprochement" among religious leaders, scientists and environmental activists that could be of historical significance. "Should it blossom," concluded the report, "it could help to heal the centuries-old rift in the West between religion and the sciences" and "help reunite our civilization's head and heart, re-engaging religion in the quest for a new cosmology, a new worldview for our time." Finally, the churches took up the call that Ed Ricketts had made a half-century before: "I say let's have more of the moral insistence of the Catholic Church, and the Salvation Army, and the hard-shell Baptists. At least they have regard for more than their temporal physical selves."

Ricketts saw both ecologists and mythologists as "integrators." From what we can read of his later writing, Campbell certainly believed this and in all probability inspired Ricketts' religious speculations. Campbell would go much further in explaining the crucial function myth plays to the human species. "[I]n the nineteenth century sociological anthropologists had the idea that myths and rites were an attempt to control nature. Totally wrong," Campbell thought. "They are not to control nature, they are to control the society and put it in accord with nature."

In the past, mythological and religious systems helped to integrate the individual, society and nature. Myth served four primary functions, Campbell explained:

First, the mystical or metaphysical function linking up regular waking consciousness with the vast mystery and wonder of the universe. Any part can be a symbol for the whole....Second, the cosmological function of presenting some intelligible image or picture of nature. In primitive cultures the relationship between man and woman is frequently seen as a mirror of nature: the universe is created by a union of Father Sky and Mother Earth. Third, the sociological function [as Ricketts had identified] of validating and enforcing a specific social and moral order. The example that comes to mind is the Ten Commandments and the Deuteronomic Law which were believed to have been revealed directly to Moses by God. And, finally, the psychological function of providing a marked pathway to carry the individual through the stages of life: the dependency of childhood, the responsibility of adulthood, the wisdom of old age, and the ultimate crisis of death. Every culture has rites of passage and related myths that serve this need.

Myth had worked its magic for thousands of years. Darwin had suggested that the belief in God was beneficial to the human species. It was, as Campbell described, "a spiritual organ" that had evolved—that is to say, had been naturally selected in the human species—over thousands of years. It helped the species maintain a sense of community and balance with nature that ultimately led to its survival and, arguably, its climb to the top of the evolutionary tree.

Yet Campbell believed, as did Ricketts, that over centuries Christian teachings had been perverted and twisted, creating a religion of exile from nature. Zen master Daisetz T. Suzuki described the state of mankind following the Fall from Eden this way: "God's own likeness (Man), God's own creation (Nature) and God himself—all three are at war." Campbell also thought Occidental theology pitted man, nature and God against one another in an eternal struggle. And science became mankind's ultimate weapon, slaying the gods and creating technology to conquer every habitat on earth.

In the American Indian, Campbell saw an ancient way of life and mythology that fostered intimacy and harmony with nature from which modern society could learn. "We have today to learn to get back into accord with the wisdom of nature," Campbell said years later, "and realize again our brotherhood with the animals and with the water and the sea."

As a child, Campbell was fascinated with stories of Buffalo Bill and the Wild West. But unlike most young boys, he became enamored not with the cowboys, but with the Indians. "I have Indian blood in me," he said as a young child. At nine years old, his diary was full of drawings of teepees, totems, native warriors and thunderbirds. By thirteen, he had read the fourteen-volume report on the American Indian by the Bureau of American Ethnology. Decades later, as a renowned scholar, he maintained this fascination. He once invoked the famed 1855 speech of Chief Seattle, after whom the city is named, to illustrate the need to integrate God, mankind and nature:

> What befalls the earth befalls all the sons of the earth. This we know. The earth does not belong to man. Man belongs to the earth. All things are connected like the blood that unites us all. Man did not weave the web of life, he is merely a strand in it. Whatever he does to the web he does to himself. One thing we know, our God is also your God. The earth is precious to Him. And to harm earth is to heap contempt on its creator.

Ricketts shared similar views about the value of native mythology. For most of his life, the biologist had been deeply suspicious of organized religion, but now, provoked by Campbell, he came to realize its redemptive possibilities. Their evening of conversation also seems to have convinced Ricketts of the application of his ecological work to the great problems of humanity. A few days after Campbell left, Ricketts excitedly wrote to Steinbeck: "I am interested now more than ever in comparing the action of human society as is—and how it got there—with the presence of societies in the tidepools."

* * *

ARGUABLY more than any scientist of his time, Ed Ricketts saw the tide pool as the place where celestial and worldly forces interacted most vividly—with the tides ebbing and flowing according to the moon's pull. It was in this truly cosmic niche, Ricketts reasoned, where one could see most clearly the relationships between all things, living and nonliving, earthly and interplanetary, aquatic and terrestrial, biological and spiritual.

Recognizing Ricketts' pioneering work in his field, the John Simon Guggenheim Memorial Foundation in New York encouraged him to

SPECIES NAMED AFTER ED RICKETTS AND JOHN STEINBECK

SCIENTIFIC NAME	COMMON NAME	COLLECTING LOCATION	DATE*	IDENTIFIED BY
Pentactinia rickettsi	sea anemone	California, USA	1930	M. De Laubenfels
Poecillastra rickettsi	sea sponge	California, USA	1930	M. De Laubenfels
Panoploea rickettsi	sand flea	California, USA	1931	Clarence R. Shoemaker
Pycnogonum rickettsi	sea spider	California, USA	1934	Waldo L. Schmitt
Nephtys rickettsi	polychaete worm	Alaska, USA	1938	O. Hartman
Lampanyctus steinbecki	longfin lampfish	California, USA	1939	Rolf Bolin
Mesochaetopterus rickettsi	polychaete worm	California, USA	c. 1930s	C. Berkeley & Berkeley
Siphonides rickettsi	peanut worm	Baja California, Mexico	c. 1941	W. K. Fisher
Thalassema steinbecki	spoon worm	Baja California, Mexico	c. 1941	W. K. Fisher
Hypsoblenniops rickettsi	blenny	Mexico	1942	Leonard P. Schultz
Palythoa rickettsi	sea anemone	Sonora, Mexico	1951	Oskar Carlgren
Isometridium rickettsi	sea anemone	Baja California, Mexico	1951	Oskar Carlgren
Phialoba steinbecki	sea anemone	Sonora, Mexico	1951	Oskar Carlgren
Longiprostatum rickettsi	flatworm	Baja California, Mexico	1953	L. H. Hyman
Polydora rickettsi	polychaete worm	Baja California	1961	K. H. Woodwick
Aclesia rickettsi	sea slug	Baja California, Mexico	1966	MacFarland
Catriona rickettsi	sea slug	California, USA	1984	David W. Behrens
Eubranchus steinbecki	sea slug	California, USA	1987	David W. Behrens
Mysidium rickettsi	opossum shrimp	Baja California, Mexico	1987	E. B. Harrison and T. E. Bowman

* year of publication of new species

apply for a fellowship to finance a second trip to the Queen Charlotte Islands in 1947 and a trip to the Gulf of Alaska in 1948. Ricketts explained that once he completed his trilogy he would assemble a "manual of the invertebrates of the entire Pacific Coast" that would provide a zoological key to 1,500–2,000 of the most common shore animals. It would be the culmination of almost a quarter-century of research.

An eminent array of international scientists sponsored his fellowship: the esteemed Dr. W. C. Allee, professor of zoology, University of Chicago; Dr. S. F. Light, professor of zoology, University of California, Berkeley; Dr. W. K. Fisher, professor emeritus of zoology, Stanford University; Dr. Enrique Rioja, professor of zoology, University of Mexico, Casa de Lago; Dr. Torsten Gislén, professor of zoology, Lund University, Sweden; Dr. Karl Schmidt, director, National History Museum, Chicago; Dr. W. G. Van Name, director, American Museum of Natural History, New York; Dr. C. McLean Fraser, professor of zoology, University of British Columbia, Vancouver; and Dr. G. E. MacGinitie, professor of zoology, California Institute of Technology, Pasadena. At the top and bottom of this list of distinguished scholars, Ricketts added two names, which stood out like bookends: Harold Guinzberg, publisher of Viking Press, and John Steinbeck, author.

In the fellowship application, Ricketts outlined an inductive methodology that strikingly paralleled Darwin's. The significance of his work, the biologist explained, was threefold: First, he would provide "the layman, traveler or student, as well as the scientist with a clear, nontechnical handy guide to a specific (and in this particular case little known) region" of the world. He had already uncovered some twenty new species in the Queen Charlottes and more than a hundred in the course of researching the trilogy.

Second, his seashore research would "cast light on the laws governing the distribution of animals"—a phrase that is remarkably similar to Darwin's statement that his Galapagos research "seemed to throw some light on the origins of species." Ricketts said he would now start to work up some general principles or laws from his fieldwork. This theoretical research would "contribute towards new zoo-geographical and ecological concepts regarding the mutual relations between the animals and their environments." He would focus on what Dr. Gislén called "marine sociology," and on concepts such as biological integration and cooperation. "I am at one with Dr. Allee," Ricketts wrote, "who [rates] these concepts among the most significant biological developments of recent years."

And third, Ricketts explained, his research and the resulting theoretical conclusions could have far-reaching implications, well beyond tide pools. As Darwin had applied his theory of evolution to humanity in *The Descent of Man*, Ricketts would begin to speculate about the importance of biological cooperation to human communities. With an anonymous quote probably taken from Allee, Ricketts explained:

> The great problems facing mankind today are social problems. "From the lowest to the highest forms in the series, all animals are at some time in their lives immersed in some society; the social medium is the condition necessary to conservation and renewal of life . . . social facts are subject to laws and these are the same everywhere that such facts appear, so that they constitute a considerable and uniform domain in nature, a homogenous whole thoroughly integrated in all its parts." Light may well be shed on the social problems of *Homo sapiens* by a consideration of the social adaptations achieved on the humbler group levels.

On October 9, Ricketts posted his application for a Guggenheim Fellowship. Steinbeck sent a supporting letter describing how "extremely enthusiastic" he was about the project, "which while it adds greatly to our knowledge, has no application to the making of money." He spoke glowingly of Ricketts "as a scholar, as a scientist, as a writer, and as a man." With such prestigious scientific sponsors, a stellar reference from a Pulitzer Prize–winning author, a publisher lined up and even encouragement from the foundation itself, Ricketts was certain that he'd get the funding. His money troubles would be over, his magnum opus soon complete.

* * *

NOT long after he returned from Vancouver Island, on August 24, Ed Ricketts' mother died. He admittedly never liked his parents "too well." Her death seemed to come and go with almost perfunctory mourning.

Then Kay, Toni's daughter, also became ill. She was hospitalized once again and underwent brain surgery in San Francisco. Toni began to spend most of her time there, traveling home to the lab only on occasion, such as for Campbell's visit. The separation and stress of a sick child added to their domestic woes. It would only get worse as Kay's health deteriorated. The little girl came back to the lab shortly after Campbell's visit. Her prognosis wasn't good.

Medical bills started to pile up, and in January Kay had a couple more attacks, as the pressure welled in her head. She lay in the back room of the lab squirming in pain. Ed and Toni administered phenobarbital, a sedative, to calm her down. Toni, though exhausted from a sleepless night, was "so cheerful and affectionate" throughout, Ricketts remembered.

Then came more bad news. In April, Ricketts found out that he did not, in fact, get a Guggenheim Fellowship. "A pity," he told Campbell. "I was counting on it." It was a terrible blow. His summertime trip back to British Columbia had to be postponed indefinitely. He made a second revision to *Between Pacific Tides*—"a big big job," he said—to keep himself busy. Some twenty friends also held a "fabulous" surprise party for his fiftieth birthday to cheer him up. They even created hilarious mock birthday cards from the American Legion, other "reactionary outfits" and the United Brotherhood of Cats. John Steinbeck visited with his wife and seemed "to be his old self." His friends rallied around. Ricketts also made a short trip to the Oregon coast in July to do some collecting.

Things were looking up. In September, a giant in the world of marine biology visited the lab. Dr. T. A. (Alan) Stephenson and his wife Anne were on a collecting expedition throughout North America. The esteemed British scientist had been in the Florida Keys earlier in the year and had spent the summer on the East Coast of Vancouver Island at the Pacific Biological Station in Nanaimo. They stayed in Pacific Grove for two months, before moving on to collecting spots in La Jolla.

Dr. Stephenson first became convinced of the scholarly merits of the ecological approach during his participation in the Great Barrier Reef Expedition of 1928–29. He spent the next decade conducting an ecological survey of the South African coast. Ricketts considered his South African work "the most significant detailed ecological study of all time." Stephenson had compiled five or six general scientific papers, eight geographic summaries and dozens of systematic reports. He was now attempting to travel to the rocky shores of every continent to conduct a global comparative study of marine life. Dr. Stephenson was, Ricketts thought, "one of the world's greatest zoologists, probably *the* greatest ecologist."

Ricketts had followed his work for years—everyone did—but he'd only recently begun to correspond with him, telling him about his work on Vancouver Island's West Coast. Ricketts was ecstatic to hear that he'd be in Pacific Grove. They not only shared a love of marine life and ecology, but they also had similar philosophical outlooks. Dr. Stephenson agreed that if scientific information was presented "in a very impartial and impersonal manner" it became "merely colorless and dull." A scientist should certainly weigh all the facts, he believed, but then he should provide his own interpretation of the results. Another quality also endeared him to Ed Ricketts: "[E]very time I fill his glass with beer, he empties it," Ricketts told Steinbeck.

"I know *Between Pacific Tides* perhaps as well as any living person," Dr. Stephenson told Ricketts. He said he had read "every word." For months, he constantly mentioned the book to the point where his wife started to complain. "I was sick of it," she said. While at Hopkins Marine Station, Dr. Stephenson had heard "more and more fantastic stories" about Ricketts. He had just missed a huge party at the lab attended by scientists from Berkeley, Stanford and Davis. At one point, the small lab had more than sixty people in it. The party finally burned itself out around dawn.

Dr. Stephenson said he regarded Ricketts as a "legend"—and not just for the wild yarns that Steinbeck or the Hopkins scientists told about him. He knew that Ed Ricketts' ecological survey of the entire Pacific Coast of North America and the completion of the trilogy would eclipse his own South African survey. In the competitive world of academia, Dr. Stephenson joked, Ed Ricketts was "a dragon to be slain." Finally, after a quarter-century of research, Ricketts was receiving the recognition he deserved—and from no less than the world's preeminent marine ecologist.

It was the best of times and, alas, the worst of times for Ed Ricketts. Kay lay in the back room of the lab for months. She was heavily sedated. Her eyesight was blurry and she seemed only half awake at times. Doctors had actually cut a small hole in her skull to release the pressure from the tumor. A little bump formed on her forehead and soon swelled to the size of a golf ball. By summer's end, her health had declined even more, and Ricketts feared the worst. She would spend her last few days in the hospital.

It was torture for Toni to watch her daughter's brain being eaten by the tumor. As Kay's health deteriorated, so did her relationship with Ed. He had already felt that they were drifting apart the year before. Toni also harbored insecurities about their relationship. She felt an "emotional impediment" in Ricketts and knew exactly what it was. "The real love of his life was Jean Ariss," she said. Jean was the wife of Ricketts' friend Bruce Ariss. Their affair was an open secret on Cannery Row. When Toni moved into the lab, Jean started coming by for visits. "No way!" Toni snapped at Ed. "Absolutely no way is she going to be in this lab while I'm here." Jean stopped coming around, but that didn't stop Ricketts from dreaming about her, and recording the dreams in his journals.

Ed and Toni's relationship effectively unraveled in the summer of 1947. Each struck up a new relationship: Toni with Ben Volcani, a marine biologist at Hopkins Marine Station who would later discover life in the Dead Sea, and Ricketts, now fifty, with a twenty-five-year-old Berkeley student, Alice Campbell, who shared a passion for music and psychology. He had always loved women with big lips and owlish eyes, and she had both, along with irresistible youth.

In early October, on the day Kay died, Toni packed her bags and left Cannery Row forever. She moved to Pasadena for a while, then to New York. When Joseph Campbell visited Toni in a slum apartment in New York, he was aghast. "You can't stay here," he told her. Campbell immediately called Steinbeck, who hired Toni to work at a film production company he owned. Years later, Toni thanked Campbell for rescuing her. "I was extremely depressed, almost out of money, without a job, and might in that awful, dirty, tiny box have just gone through the window...," she told him. Eventually, she married Volcani and moved to Palestine.

Ricketts was equally devastated by their separation. He tried to apply his detached, scientific eye to understand what went wrong. "The relation between Ed and Toni, both of whom are really quite good people I am convinced has been a tragedy of errors when it wasn't an equal comedy," he wrote Steinbeck, in an odd third-person voice. Ricketts also felt somewhat responsible for pushing Toni away. "This whole thing fills me with the most poignant regret," he confided to Steinbeck.

* * *

SOMETIME after 6 P.M. on New Year's Eve, Ed Ricketts and his stunning young girlfriend packed his old car and went on a road trip to Las Vegas. With the exception of his trip to Mexico City in 1940, Ricketts hadn't ventured more than ten or twenty miles from the sea in twenty-five years. "I won't go inland," he once told Steinbeck. They arrived on the second of January and stayed at the Gateway Auto Court; they left the next day. On the way back, they made a stop in Death Valley. In his collecting notebook, Ricketts made some ecological observations in the desert and listed some highlights of the trip, "besides from getting married." They had apparently eloped to Las Vegas. (Ricketts was never actually divorced from his first wife, Nan, so this second marriage was invalid.)

With a new year and a beautiful new wife, a renewed vitality soon came to Ed Ricketts. On Sunday, the first of February, John Steinbeck also swept into Cannery Row like a winter gale. It would take three or four days for the whirlwind to blow itself out. Ricketts and Steinbeck drank and talked far into the night. Steinbeck agreed to lend him a thousand dollars to finance their final voyage to the outer shores. Even so, Ricketts was forced to scale back his plans for financial reasons; Alaska and the Aleutians would have to wait. He would return to Vancouver Island and the Queen Charlotte Islands with Steinbeck that summer to complete his research. *The Outer Shores* would now focus primarily on the British Columbian coast.

They woke the next day to a quiet morning of reading that slowly, but surely, built up to another night of heavy drinking in the lab. Friends also came by to visit: Tal and Ritch Lovejoy, Ricketts' daughter Cornelia, and Toby Street, an old college buddy of Steinbeck's. The following morning Ricketts got up early to find Steinbeck coughing and smoking. Hearing that the novelist was in town scouting locations to film *Cannery*

Ricketts' new wife Alice in the lab, circa 1947–48. COURTESY OF ED RICKETTS JR.

Row, celebrity hunters badgered Ricketts throughout his friend's visit. Steinbeck wanted to use Pacific Biological Laboratories for the filming. He planned to buy Ricketts a new phonograph, pay him two thousand dollars cash and use the movie royalties to finance the outer shores expedition. (The project was eventually stymied because of a million-dollar nuisance lawsuit filed against Steinbeck about the novel's film rights.)

On Tuesday, Steinbeck came over for a quiet dinner. When they had finished eating, Steinbeck read a book, Alice played the phonograph and Ed worked in his notebook. Ricketts wrote a list of the greatest artistic achievements of all time: Goethe's *Faust*, Joyce's *Finnegan's Wake* (Joseph Campbell's influence), the first-century Sanskrit poem "Black Marigolds" (which Steinbeck quoted extensively at the end of *Cannery Row*), Walt Whitman's "Out of the Cradle Endlessly Rocking" and "When Lilacs Last in the Door-yard Bloom'd," Sir Thomas Malory's *Morte d'Arthur* (Steinbeck's favorite, too) and Homer's *Odyssey*. In music, he listed Stravinsky's *Song of the Nightingale,* William Byrd's *Mass for Five Voices,* Giovanni Pierluigi da Palestrina's *Missa Brevis,* Beethoven's *Quartette No. 16,* Mozart's *Don Giovanni* and Bach's *The Art of the Fugue.* He saw these works as manifestations of "breaking through." Of *The Art of the Fugue,* he once told Steinbeck: "Bach nearly made it. Hear now how close he comes, and hear his anger when he cannot. Every time I hear it I believe that this time he will come crashing through into the light. And he never does—not quite."

As the phonograph played, Steinbeck watched his friend scribbling intently in his notebook across the room. "He was walled off a little," Steinbeck once said of Ricketts, "so that he worked at his philosophy of 'breaking through,' of coming out through the back of the mirror into some kind of reality which would make the day world dreamlike. This thought obsessed him." At the bottom of the page, Ricketts wrote a curt conclusion to his evening's musings: "Humans aren't big enough to bear the visions they conceive."

During his stay, Steinbeck took several walks over the rolling countryside, along the riverbeds and through the fields, picking plants as he went. He also went collecting seashore specimens with Ricketts one early morning. He thought little had changed since his childhood. He was renting a small cottage and had been sleeping almost twelve hours a day, getting "superb rest."

On Sunday evening, February 15, Steinbeck again went over to the lab. He and Ricketts cracked open some beers and slid into a discussion about the trilogy, their plans for the summer and the new edition of *Between Pacific Tides.* Ricketts could barely contain his anger at Stanford University Press for repeatedly delaying the second edition of the book. "[T]hat cursed SU Press still hasn't published my book" and "damn that SU Press" had been common refrains for over a decade.

Steinbeck had written a foreword to the revised second edition in 1941 to help push up its sales, but Stanford delayed publication because of the war. With each gulp of beer, Ricketts and Steinbeck became more enraged. They finally plunked themselves down at the typewriter and allowed their outrage to spill onto a page:

February 15, 1948

Stanford University Press
Stanford University, Calif.

Gentlemen:
May we withdraw certain selected parts of "Between Pacific Tides" which with the passing years badly need revision? Science advances but Stanford Press does not.

There is the problem also of the impending New Ice Age.

Sometime in the near future we should like to place our order for one (1) copy of the forthcoming (1948, no doubt) publication, "The Internal Combustion Engine, Will it Work?"

Sincerely
John Steinbeck
Ed Ricketts

P.S. Good luck with "A Brief Anatomy of the Turtle"

Two days later, Ricketts wrote a letter of apology to Floris P. Hartog, manager of SUP's publishing department. He was embarrassed about their "slightly drunken but perhaps amusing epistle." He explained, "I had purposed writing more soberly but something quite the opposite happened." But the letter worked. Hartog immediately wrote back to say that the letter "made me feel even more ashamed about what we have been doing to you than I was before." Hartog proposed to come down to Monterey "to speed up matters so that the book will be out before the new 'ice age' is upon us." The second edition of the book would be published that summer, he assured Ricketts.

* * *

IT was a dry winter. What little rain had fallen had come and gone. The golden hills around the Salinas Valley were starting to shimmer, but only faintly, with a green patina. "The country is drying up as badly as the time I wrote about it in *To a God Unknown*," Steinbeck remembered. "It is the same kind of drought that used to keep us broke all the time when I was growing up."

Steinbeck knew the land vividly. It was the country of his birth. He had written about it in *To a God Unknown, The Pastures of Heaven, Tortilla Flat, In Dubious Battle, Of Mice and Men, The Red Pony, The Long Valley, The Grapes of Wrath* and *Cannery Row*. In 1948, almost his entire literary canon had been set in the hills, valleys and seashores of northern California.

After the drunken letter writing, Steinbeck woke the next morning and set off for Salinas. He spent part of the day at the city's newspaper office perusing old copies of the *Salinas-Californian*. In the afternoon, he went up into the hills and then over to San Juan, remembering hundreds of places from his childhood. He wanted to get "reacquainted with the trees and bushes." Steinbeck was researching what he believed would be his greatest novel yet. He called it "the whole nasty bloody lovely history of the world" and felt he had been training for this book all his life. "It may be my swan song," he wrote his wife from Monterey, "but it certainly will be the largest and most important work I have or maybe will do."

Steinbeck would finish the trilogy with Ricketts and then write his masterpiece, what would become *East of Eden*. He was determined to complete this even if it took the rest of his life.

* * *

AFTER Steinbeck's departure, Ricketts continued to plan their summertime trip, which he figured would cost him and Steinbeck about $10,000. By this time, Ricketts conceded that book royalties would never recover the full cost of his three expeditions to the outer shores. He became resigned to the fact that the trilogy was an unmitigated financial disaster. (Kay's medical and funeral bills made financial matters even worse.)

His work schedule was intense. He constructed an outline for the book and started reading histories of the region, including the journal of French explorer La Pérouse, who visited the North Pacific in the 1780s. He did some local collecting in the Great Tide Pool, checked the summer tides, got all the schedules for the steamers and trains, wrote various travel memos, and sent letters to Betty, Bill and Ruth, and to contacts in the Queen Charlotte Islands. He was so busy that he even had Pacific Biological Laboratories unlisted from the telephone directory to stop amateur collectors and tourists from bothering him with frivolous calls.

Ricketts also started to refine his ideas on ecology, which he defined as "the science of relationships. Of living relationships." He outlined four approaches, which largely chronicled the development of the science from its beginning. The first approach was the most "superficial" or "primitive"—an approach used by eighteenth- and nineteenth-century naturalists like Linné and Darwin. This involved "cataloguing the beasts of a given region," both the kinds and their quantities and describing where they live. The second approach focused on animal communities—aggregations, groupings, loose associations and bands of species. The community concept had grown out of the pioneering work of Midwestern plant ecologists and Scandinavian scientists, and was taken up enthusiastically by Victor E. Shelford in his Puget Sound work, and also by Allee. Shelford broadened ecology's scope by merging the study of plant and animal communities into a single "biotic community" or "biome." The third approach, which was favored by Dr. MacGinitie at Caltech, focused on an animal's life history. An animal might change its feeding habits, protective strategies and habitat throughout its life and even from day to day. Ricketts felt that MacGinitie had "a pure genius for that sort of stuff." It was highly specialized work and largely taxonomic in its organization. Dr. MacGinitie would publish his *Natural History of Marine Animals* in 1949.

The fourth approach was rooted in the law of ecological incompatibility and can best be described as comparative ecology. This method compared species that while widely separated geographically "are strikingly similar morphologically, and . . . occupy an identical niche." In his

Pacific Coast wanderings, Ricketts had noticed that different species of crab and starfish, for instance, occupied identical niches in British Columbia, California, the Tropics and even Europe. The revered Dr. Stephenson, in fact, had been attempting such a comparative study when he visited Ricketts in September. He would publish a paper on "The universal features of zonation between tide-marks on rocky coasts" in *The Journal of Ecology* in 1949.

Ricketts believed that the integration of all these approaches would give a true picture of ecology. "The toto-picture is the important thing," he wrote in his notebook. He believed that Dr. MacGinitie was wrong to write that the fundamental unit of ecology was the living organism. "The living organism is the fundamental unit of *biology,* not of ecology," Ricketts countered. The fundamental unit of ecology, Ricketts underscored, was the *"relationship."*

But how could a scientist measure something as intangible as relationships? Ricketts looked to mathematics and physics for the answer. Vector analysis, which deals with both magnitude and direction, could help him understand the complex relationships at work in nature. Ricketts' idea was to develop "an exact and a quantitative science in which the vectors representing these relationships, their direction, extension, and strength or intensity, would be considered and evaluated."

Through his own observation, experimentation and speculation, Ricketts was starting to move away from a concept of nature as a series of organic wholes or animal aggregations. He was beginning to conceive of nature as an *ecosystem.* That word, so commonplace today, was first coined in 1935 by British ecologist A. G. Tansley. Ed Ricketts never used the word *ecosystem,* nor is there any evidence that he was familiar with Tansley's concept or a groundbreaking paper published by Yale University student Raymond Lindeman in 1942. And yet he seemed to be coming to similar conclusions as these scholars.

Lindeman's classic definition of an ecosystem focused on energy flow in nature from the sun to plants to primary consumers (herbivores) to secondary consumers (carnivores) and eventually to decomposers that feed on decaying plant and animal matter. The concept of the food chain is key, and Lindeman wanted to measure the flow of energy between these different "trophic" levels. This quantification of the science, according to one historian, "marked ecology's coming of age as an adjunct of physical science."

In a new essay on plankton in the second edition of *Between Pacific Tides,* which he had finalized just before leaving for British Columbia, Ricketts wrote his most concise statement yet on ecology, describing a feeding hierarchy that contemporary scientists refer to as a series of trophic levels in the ocean ecosystem:

> Only one large thesis can be stated with any degree of certainty. The idea of hierarchy is implicit. Rank behind rank, societies stand in mutual interdependence. From the most minute and ephemeral bacteria and diatoms, clear up to the fish, seals, and whales, each rank is supported by the abundance of smaller and more transient creatures under it. Each in turn contributes to the series next above it. Ascending ranks have each a little more leeway in the matter of food storage, a little more resilience, a little more freedom of movement in the environment. Although the individuals are larger, their numbers are smaller. And their spores — the resting stages — are less significant in the life history. Finally, at the top of the hierarchy, the disintegrating body of the whale supports astronomical hordes of bacteria, busily engaged in breaking down the complex and slowly assembled proteins into simpler units which fertilize the waters for the oncoming crop of diatoms — James Joyce's *recorso* theme in its original manifestation.
>
> Each higher order, instead of ruling the ranks of individuals below, is actually ruled by them. Each rank is completely at the mercy of its subjects, dependent on their abundance or accessibility. All the schemes which our social order prides itself on having discovered have been in use by societies of marine animals far back into the dim geological past. The units comprising human society very commonly say one thing and be another. Not the least of the many values of marine sociology is the fact that the sea animals can be only themselves.

Ricketts turned the natural hierarchy on its head. Far from having dominion over nature, mankind was essentially in its servitude. This became obvious in his research on sea temperatures, plankton and the sardine fishery. Ricketts had constructed a rudimentary ecosystem model to understand the chain of events that caused the wild fluctuations, and ultimately the spectacular decline, of the fishery.

* * *

BY the end of April, Ed Ricketts had completed most of the research for *The Outer Shores*. He had written some 400 pages of notes covering his 1945 and 1946 trips, and he'd typed 180 pages of "revised collecting reports" for each collecting trip on Vancouver Island and the Queen Charlottes. He also amassed 350 pages of correspondence to and from experts who identified the many species, and he'd created 500 cards to index and catalog the species. The book could have been written with this material alone.

He had outlined a structure for *The Outer Shores* too, which reflected the method used in drafting *Sea of Cortez*. The first part would be a narrative written by Steinbeck, and it would include Ricketts' 1945 and 1946 trips, plus their 1948 trip. Ricketts also wanted Steinbeck to incorporate his thinking on ecology and vector analysis and perhaps some notes on his 1932 journey to Alaska with Calvin and Campbell. The second part would be a catalog of species, a bibliography, and a description of his research methodology.

To help Steinbeck with the narrative he also typed his handwritten journals into a coherent travelogue, which he embellished with his own memories, collecting reports, other jottings and his new thinking on ecology. Again, it was very much like the log Steinbeck used to assemble *Sea of Cortez*. The outer shores transcript was 143 pages of dense single-spaced text. He finished it around April 26 and sent it to Steinbeck in New York. The typed log was essentially a long, personal letter to his friend, containing many asides and words of advice to the writer. On its last page, Ed Ricketts typed his final words to Steinbeck before they'd meet in British Columbia: "Well Johnny boy this is it, this is [the end], the trips of 1945 and '46 are over, it's your book now and God bless you."

* * *

THE outer shores work pulled Ricketts out of the clutches of a deep depression. He was still haunted by memories of Toni. Steinbeck had always thought "there was a transcendent sadness in his love — something he missed or wanted, a searching that sometimes approached panic. I don't know what it was he wanted that was never there, but I know he always looked for it and never found it." During his Las Vegas trip, he had suffered from a "depression-neurosis-fear-anxiety" complex, but was able to hide this from Alice. He worried that his "depression or gloominess or (even outright) anger will communicate itself to Alice."

For years his bouts of depression went unbeknownst to friends and family. Few have any recollection of Ed Ricketts ever being morose or depressed. It seems that only one woman truly knew his anguish. She was a Jungian therapist and friend named Evelyn Ott, whom Ricketts saw professionally from time to time in Carmel. The Ricketts family has sealed their correspondence, which is stored today in the Stanford University archive. Still, there are no shortage of entries in Ricketts' journals that show just how emotionally and spiritually torn he was at various times in his life. One such entry, early in January of 1948, suggested that he delved into his work as a form of therapy. "I have to do something," he wrote in his notebook, "or I perish."

From the fictionalization of his life in *Cannery Row* and from his own letters and journals, a portrait emerges of Ed Ricketts sitting alone at night restless in his lab. It is silent but for the sea lapping outside and the scientist tapping on his typewriter, scribbling in his notebook or preparing a specimen downstairs. He is working with great efficiency and exactitude. His eyes are ablaze. He's tired but keeps focused. It is the portrait of a lone scholar striving for discovery.

Ricketts recognized that there was "an undertone of sadness and loneliness" to *Cannery Row* and felt that he too was traveling through life in his "own solitary way." He once told Steinbeck that he felt "a little cut off" from the world. Steinbeck agreed with his friend that "there is no creative unit in the human save the individual working alone." All creations and inventions in art, music and science were ultimately the result

Ed Ricketts poses on seashore in Monterey, 1948. COURTESY OF ED RICKETTS JR.

of lonely, individual pursuit. "Well of course that's it, isn't it, what you wrote about [in *Cannery Row*]," he told Steinbeck. "That feeling of aloneness." There was an insatiable striving in Ed Ricketts, an attempt even to overcome his own mortality. He thought Goethe had written about this in *Faust* and seemed to be heeding Goethe's dictum:

> *Rest not! Life is sweeping by; go and dare before you die.*
> *Something mighty and sublime, leave behind to conquer time.*

He would complete the ecological trilogy, but he did not know if at fifty years old he would have enough time to conduct the surveys in the Gulf of Alaska, Aleutians and Bering Sea, and then revise the first three books into a massive two-volume tome entitled *Contributions Toward a Natural History of the Pacific Coast.*

It would be his masterpiece, his legacy to the world. Volume I, *A Manual of Marine Biology*, would catalog between 600 and 1,500 common seashore animals from Baja to the Bering Sea. The first book would provide anatomical and structural drawings, brief descriptions and a zoological bibliography of all the animals contained in it. This systematic catalog of species would then be cross-referenced with Volume II, a revised edition of *Between Pacific Tides*. It would be both popular and inductive in its treatment, both an amateur collector's guidebook and a book of general theories and principles. The book's closing chapters would describe oceanography, ecology, animal communities and biological principles such as animal aggregation, population growth, crowding, the law of ecological incompatibility, evolution, parasitism, physiology and so on. He planned to spend the rest of his life assembling the *Natural History of the Pacific Coast*.

With the completion of the trilogy, Steinbeck too would turn to his lifetime's great masterpiece (though many critics would say that distinction belongs to *The Grapes of Wrath* and not *East of Eden*). Steinbeck had said he trained all his life for this book.

In what would be his final letter before meeting his friend in British Columbia, Steinbeck echoed the cautionary lines of *Faust* about mankind's desperate and illusory quest for absolute knowledge. "God help us all," Steinbeck wrote, "we go on trying to climb that miserable mountain and it is always higher than the last rise we scrabbled onto."

CATRIONA RICKETTSI, SEA SLUG, NEW SPECIES NAMED AFTER
ED RICKETTS AND IDENTIFIED BY DAVID W. BEHRENS IN 1984.

CHAPTER FOURTEEN

DEATH OR DEPARTURE

The last act in the biography of the hero is that of the death or departure. Here the whole sense of the life is epitomized.

—JOSEPH CAMPBELL, *The Hero with a Thousand Faces*

Twas only a few minutes past six o'clock in the morning and the sun was just about to break over the dusty ridge of the Gabilan Range with a lush Salinas Valley below and shine on the gentle waters of Monterey Bay. Cannery Row lay in a penumbra.

"Early morning is a time of magic in Cannery Row," John Steinbeck famously wrote. "In the gray time after the light has come and before the sun has risen, the Row seems to hang suspended out of time in a silvery light. The street lights go out, and the weeds are brilliant green. The corrugated iron of the canneries glows with the pearly lucence of platinum or old pewter. No automobiles are running then. The street is silent of progress and business. And the rush and drag of the waves can be heard as they splash in among the piles of the canneries. . . . It is the hour of the pearl— the interval between day and night when time stops and examines itself."

It was on such a morning, Saturday, May 8, 1948, that the Row awoke to another day. One of the first signs of life was a newspaper boy slinging rolled copies of the *Monterey Peninsula Herald* at the doorsteps of houses and shops. A brief article on the newspaper's society page told everyone in the Monterey area that Ed Ricketts would surely have a hectic day before him:

ALICE AND ED RICKETTS PLANNING

EXPLORATORY TRIP THIS SUMMER

Ed Ricketts, marine biologist whose Pacific Biological Laboratories on Cannery Row have figured in several of John Steinbeck's

stories, and his recent bride, the former Alice Campbell, are laying plans for an exploratory trip up into the Charlotte Islands this
summer. Here Ed will gather marine specimens and data for the
book in which he and Steinbeck plan to collaborate. This will be
their second of such text books, the first being "Sea of Cortez."

Mrs. Ricketts, daughter of Mrs. James Collyer of Paso
Robles and a former University of California music and philosophy major, has been doing extensive work in photography
recently and will take over all the camera work on the Charlotte
Islands expedition.

Ed Jr., who had enrolled at the University of California, Berkeley,
came down to Monterey that weekend to show Alice how to use her new
photography equipment. In just over a week, with train and steamship
tickets purchased, Ricketts and Alice would depart for the final expedition to the outer shores. John Steinbeck, who was recuperating in New
York from an operation to remove varicose veins in his leg, would join
them later that summer at Clayoquot.

There have been suggestions made in later years that Steinbeck
wasn't as enthusiastic as his friend about coauthoring *The Outer Shores*.
Steinbeck was certainly focused on writing his great book, *East of Eden*,
and his health problems had hampered his mobility, at least temporarily.
Still, no matter his ambivalence, poor health or busy writing schedule,
Steinbeck was willing to put aside any reservations, as one scholar has
suggested, "simply to avoid hurting his friend's feelings." He also seemed
committed to financing the expedition, as he had for the trip to the Gulf
of California.

"It was just one big parade of people in and out," Ed Jr. remembered
of that Saturday. Friends were visiting, drinking and wishing Ricketts
bon voyage. Rick Skahen, a bohemian medical student, came down from
Berkeley with a friend. Skahen and Ricketts became engrossed for much
of the day in his work on the statistics of the sardine fishery. Scientists
and postgraduate students from Hopkins Marine Station also dropped
by to inquire about the upcoming expedition and the second edition of
Between Pacific Tides, whose proofs had just been sent back to the press.
Ed Jr. and Alice left for most of the day, traveling over to the beautiful

Carmel Valley to take photographs. They returned in the late afternoon
to find Ricketts literally hopping and dancing around the lab with
excitement.

Sometime around 6:30 P.M., the phone rang in the lab. Ricketts
answered to find his sister, Frances, on the other end. They talked for a
few minutes and Frances, who lived with her husband Fred in Carmel,
immediately sensed that her brother was "feeling fine and very happy."
All preparations were made for the trip, her brother explained: travel
tickets were booked, letters were sent to Betty, Bill and Ruth in Clayoquot informing them of their date of arrival, supply lists and memos were
prepared and Steinbeck planned to meet them in British Columbia.
They would leave around May 22, a week after his birthday. Frances
thought her brother sounded like he was "just on top of the world."

The day quickly slipped by. Ricketts was working so hard that he
barely had time to partake in the lab's customary beer drinking. He was
hungry though. And so around 7:30 he stepped out of the lab to buy
some steaks and salad for dinner. It was his favorite meal.

His 1936 Buick stood in the gutter along the street. He'd nicknamed
it "Eyebrows" because of the peculiar look of the tie-racks above each
door. Steinbeck remembered that the car was tricky to start and that its
"ancient rusty motor coughed and broke into a bronchial chatter which
indicated that it was running." The bearings in the car were shot too,
which made the gears jagged and shifting noisy. Repairing the beast had
cost Ricketts a small fortune. Shortly after the New Year he was forced
to write the local garage, Bettie Motors Co., and explain why he was
unable to pay the small amount outstanding on his repair bills. "During
the past year, I have been forced to divert considerable sums to my personal needs," he explained apologetically. "We finally lost our 12 year old
daughter after a two year session with brain tumor and I'm still climbing
up slowly out of this."

The car snorted to life nonetheless, and Ed Ricketts started off
down Cannery Row. It was a quiet early evening. He drove past the sad-
looking fish-meal warehouse that used to be so flush with sex and money
when it was Flora's. (Madam would die penniless on August 1 that year.)
The car continued on, passing under the crossovers that connected the
seaside canneries to warehouses across the street. He drove by the Del

Mar Cannery, the Monterey Cannery, the Old Custom House Packing warehouse, the Carmel Canning Company facility and Cal Pack, where he worked. The reduction plants and canneries in Monterey had barely processed 18,000 tons that season, a spectacular collapse from the 237,000 tons of just three years before. It was thus an unusually quiet time on Cannery Row.

The sardine weighed heavily on Ed Ricketts' mind that night. He had amassed a huge volume of statistics on sea temperatures, plankton production and sardine landings in an attempt to understand the natural and man-made factors that led to their collapse. His son had compiled these statistics into tables, graphs and charts for *Between Pacific Tides.* That evening, he and Skahen had been poring over much of the data.

Ricketts had worked hard to dispel theories that the decline of the sardine was a result of munitions dumping at sea or the effects of the atom bomb—"the two most fantastic" explanations he had heard. "[T]he unpleasant fact stares us in the face that the industry is over-expanded," he wrote in the *Herald*'s "Sardine Edition" the month before. "If conservation had been adopted early enough, a smaller but stream-lined cannery row in all likelihood this month would be winding up a fairly successful season, instead of dipping as they must be now, deeply into the red ink of failure."

After three somber blocks, Cannery Row swung to the right, merging with Drake Avenue, which then crossed the Southern Pacific Railway track. Here the avenue began a steep climb up a hill. Ricketts made the turn and started up the hill. A corrugated-iron warehouse stood to his left, creating a blind corner with the railway crossing. There was no wigwag to warn of oncoming trains, either.

It is unclear exactly what happened in the next few moments. Perhaps the car stalled while Ricketts was shifting the grinding gears. Or perhaps the motor in the tired old car just coughed, sputtered and died of exhaustion on the hill. Or perhaps the car didn't stall at all and Ed Ricketts was just so preoccupied with the lowly sardine that he wasn't paying attention. Suddenly from around the blind corner swung the Del Monte Express, the evening train from San Francisco. The locomotive's engineer sounded the whistle, which echoed off the Row's corrugated buildings, and slammed on the brakes.

Photo in Monterey Peninsula Herald *shows Ed Ricketts being laid on a stretcher shortly after the train-car accident.* COURTESY OF THE NATIONAL STEINBECK CENTER AND MONTEREY PENINSULA HERALD.

It was too late. The whistle blast and shrieking brakes were followed by a thunderous crash. The train's iron cowcatcher buckled the car's side door, pinning Ricketts inside. It mangled and pushed the old Buick a hundred yards down the track before the whole screeching, tangled, smoking mess came to a stop. And Cannery Row was quiet again.

Many residents came out of their homes and bums crawled out of their boiler pipes to see what all the commotion was about. Word spread up and down the Monterey hillside. Some residents had heard the crash and knew it must be trouble. Shocked passengers and crew climbed down from the train. A ring of people quickly formed around the car. Everyone stood with their hands stuffed in their pockets looking dejected.

A policeman arrived and couldn't believe that Ed was conscious when they lifted him from the twisted metal heap and placed his limp body on the grass. The officer then rushed to the lab just down the hill. Rick Skahen, the young medical student, answered the door and heard the startling news. Quietly, unbeknownst to Ed Jr. and Alice, he and Ritch Lovejoy slipped out of the lab. When Rick arrived, he got down on one knee and leaned over Ed. The crowd of people fell silent.

"My God, Ed, what's happened?" he asked, aghast and out of breath.

"Rick, I was thinking about the work we were doing," Ed replied. "I hurt."

"Where do you hurt?"

Ed shifted his hand and placed it on his left side. Steinbeck later talked to Skahen who reportedly told him that "Ed's skull had a crooked look and his eyes were crossed. There was blood around his mouth, and his body was twisted, distorted—wrong, as though seen under an untrue lens."

Before he was loaded into the ambulance, the policeman took a brief "perfectly coherent" statement from him. "I didn't seen the train in time," Ricketts said. "The engineer was not to blame."

At two minutes past eight o'clock, the sun dipped below the Pacific's horizon. Cannery Row fell dark and the sound of an ambulance's siren could be heard speeding through the night.

* * *

THE phone rang in the lab. It was Frances calling again. Her voice was shaky. Had they heard the terrible news? No, replied Ed Jr., they hadn't heard one word. "Ed has been hurt, not badly, just some ribs broken," Frances explained. She and Fred would come by the lab in a few minutes to pick them up on their way to the Monterey Hospital.

Ricketts was in the emergency room when they arrived. Everyone heard in detail what had happened. Frances and Fred talked privately with the police officer who told them Ed had been entirely conscious and that he couldn't believe he was hit by a train and not injured far worse. Alice was devastated, breaking down in tears and hysteria. She was in no shape to see her husband. Ritch Lovejoy asked for Dr. John Gratiot, who had lived near Ricketts and his first wife in Pacific Grove. Ricketts considered Dr. Gratiot a friend and a good surgeon.

At first, the doctors did not realize that Ricketts was bleeding internally and that his lung had been punctured. The diagnosis soon changed. Dr. Gratiot and the surgical staff administered him ether and opened him up.

While they operated, Ed Jr., Alice and Tal Lovejoy gave blood. Ritch called everyone he knew who might be able to give a pint. A friend of Ricketts' came down from Fort Ord. There was no blood bank at the hospital and it was getting late. Frances worried they wouldn't have enough for the long operation through the night. Around midnight, with a list of blood donors from the Red Cross and two local hospitals, she called some fifty people in Carmel Valley and the Monterey Peninsula. Everyone wanted to help. They ended up with more blood than they could use.

Frances and Fred took Ed Jr. out for some food and brought back coffee for everyone. The operation was finished early the next morning. Rick was the only one who talked to Dr. Gratiot. Ricketts' spleen had been removed, Skahen told everyone. He spoke encouragingly. According to Steinbeck, "Ed was all messed up—spleen broken, ribs shattered, lungs punctured, concussion of the skull. It might have been better to let him go out under the ether, but the doctors could not give up, any more than could the people gathered in the waiting room of the hospital."

Friends and family went home around 5 A.M. and got a few hours' sleep. Frances awoke and called Dr. Gratiot, who informed her that there was some hope. The doctor apparently couldn't bear telling her the painful truth. Later, Dr. Gratiot told Steinbeck that when they had finished the operation "they knew it was hopeless." Ed was barely conscious. He was wasted from the ether and morphine, and he spoke with great difficulty.

"How bad is it?" Ricketts asked the doctor.

Dr. Gratiot had great respect for Ricketts and couldn't bring himself to say any "soothing nonsense" just to make him feel better. "Very bad," the doctor said.

"I think he realized that the end wasn't too far off," Dr. Gratiot remembered.

* * *

ON Monday morning, the *Monterey Peninsula Herald* ran a large photo of the train wreck splashed across its front page: the "Doc" of John Steinbeck's novel *Cannery Row* had been badly hurt in the accident. A sidebar headlined STEINBECK FLYING TO RICKETTS' SIDE told readers "author John Steinbeck, close friend of Edward Ricketts and collaborator of the book 'Sea of Cortez,' is arriving here by plane from New York tomorrow to be with the marine biologist who was seriously injured in a car-train accident Saturday."

On Monday night, before he was to fly to California, Steinbeck went to dinner with his close friend and fellow novelist Nathaniel Benchley. Steinbeck was drunk and weepy. "The greatest man in the world is dying," he told Benchley, "and there is nothing I can do." In New York, Steinbeck boarded a plane for a nightmare of a journey—delays, missed connections and a maddening stopover in San Francisco, where he waited hours for a flight to Monterey.

Early Tuesday morning, Dr. Gratiot told Frances that he felt a little encouraged. The doctor grasped at any faint signs of progress as hope for a miracle. But by 7:30 A.M. Frances was informed that Ricketts had "slipped back to no better, but no worse."

Ritch Lovejoy was overwhelmed with only one thought that day as he sat down at his desk to write his usual "Round and About" column for the newspaper. "[There's] nothing else that seems worth mentioning," he began the column. He told of Ricketts' tireless efforts cataloging the fauna of the Pacific Coast and how thousands of people came to him with their scientific and personal problems. "He has always given too generously of himself, even at times when he was deep in the problems of his profession," Lovejoy wrote. He also told readers of the filing system Ricketts was working on to make a comprehensive catalog of animals from the Gulf of California to Alaska. "It will be the first attempt of any scientist to create such a file," he boasted. He ended the article on an ironic note, informing readers that Ricketts was "one of the best car drivers I have ever known. I've always felt safe with Ed behind the wheel." Lovejoy, like so many others, was at a loss to explain what had happened to his friend. "It may sound corny but I can only conclude that Fate took a sock at Ed."

*　*　*

THAT Tuesday the *Princess Maquinna* sailed into Tofino in Clayoquot Sound. Cargo and mail were unloaded and villagers and natives in dugout canoes came out to greet Old Faithful. Captain Martin MacKinnon was surely at her helm. Bill White was there to pick up the post. There was a letter from Ed Ricketts. His spirits were lifted.

Bill and Ruth had moved to a large house on a hill on the peninsula in Tofino. Clayoquot Sound was changing. Pioneers were slowing moving away from Stubbs Island to settle in Tofino. When Betty sold Clayoquot Hotel and the entire island in 1964 and moved to Tofino, it marked the end of an era. The island would eventually be deserted, the hotel knocked down.

Bill had built a new home out of kiln-dried timber cut from the surrounding rainforest. It's a beautiful house, which still stands today, on a small knoll surrounded by rhododendrons overlooking the sound. Bill had sent a joking letter to Ricketts inviting him to stay in their "Royal Suite" with the "nicest view in Tofino," hot and cold running water, chambermaids, and two acres of land. "So don't go enquiring about hotel accommodation if you come up," Bill insisted. "We'd love to have you."

Bill arrived home and went into the living room to read the letter in the light of the bay windows. Ruth was in the kitchen preparing some food. A battery-powered radio droned with the hourly newscast in the background. Bill tore open the envelope and unfolded the letter. The businesslike "Pacific Biological Laboratories" letterhead belied the personal tone of the correspondence. There was a torrent of news: Kay was dead; he and Toni had split up and she had moved to New York; he had a young new wife; they'd be coming to Clayoquot in just over a week; and Steinbeck would join them as well.

Then the radio crackled and Bill and Ruth couldn't believe what they were hearing. Bill's eyes left the letter and they both stared breathlessly. Word had spread across North America, traveling from Cannery Row to the city newspapers, wire service and now finally to the radio in

Clayoquot Sound. The announcer repeated the shocking news: "Edward F. Ricketts, the real-life 'Doc' of John Steinbeck's novel 'Cannery Row,' died today. . . ."

* * *

ED Ricketts, echoing a Taoist proverb, liked to say, "When you are caught by the tide, don't fight it, drift with it and see where it takes you." After three days in Monterey Hospital, he stopped fighting for life just after noon on May 11—three days before his fifty-first birthday. Dr. Gratiot led Alice to an unoccupied room on the second floor where he gave her the news. "[A]s happens so often with men of large vitality," Steinbeck later said, "the energy and the color and the pulse and the breathing went away silently and quickly, and he died."

* * *

SOME people call it God. Joseph Campbell said that God was just a metaphor for the oneness and the mystery of the universe. Steinbeck called it a "phalanx emotion" and said Ricketts' own idea of God "could have been expressed by the mathematical symbol for an expanding universe." Ed Ricketts himself called it the Tao or "a spark, the deep thing, all—love, tenderness, unselfishness." But ultimately he believed "it's probably best that that thing be nameless, because as soon as it gets a name it gets constricted." God simply transcended all human thought and language.

A sense of immanence in nature, the synergy of living beings, a deep feeling of wonder, a symbol for humanity's collective soul—God was all these things to Ed Ricketts. His lifetime of scientific research had also confirmed that God was ultimately a mystery: there were simply unknown and unknowable phenomena in the world beyond humanity's grasp. "At the charge that I have inclinations toward mysticism," Ed Ricketts once said, "I say only that if in observable phenomena such as tides, earthquakes, growth patterns of animals, marine sociology, in the 'pre-natal' behavior pattern which impels grunions towards discharging their eggs on the shore at extreme high tide, that sends marine salmon back into perhaps parental fresh water for spawning—if in all this there is mysticism, then I'm of course a mystic."

Steinbeck said his friend was "suspicious of promises of an afterlife" and didn't believe in it "in any sense other than chemical." Ed Ricketts certainly believed that life was about living. He thought all of his philosophical essays could be placed under one simple title, "Participation." He ceaselessly strove most of his life to "break through" to a moment of divine rapture in which all the dualities and chaos of the natural world would dissolve into a unified whole. He was always on the quest to discover that hidden "matrix underlying the nature of things." This idea obsessed him.

He saw this "matrix" at work one early morning in Clayoquot Sound. On June 1, 1946, Ricketts went out on a reef on Wickaninnish Island, near Lennard Island and the entrance to the sound. It was the lowest tide he had ever seen. He had been collecting marine species for over a quarter of a century by this time. The reef seemed as spangled with stars as the heavens. Thousands of starfish were strewn about in brilliant colors: reds, oranges, tangerines, purples, burgundies, rusty browns. "There are more species here, and incomparably more individuals too, than anywhere else in the world," he observed. "They're everywhere, all colors, sizes, shapes."

Dr. Fisher at Hopkins had told him that along Canada's Pacific Coast there was such a "fantastic mixing" of species that even he, the world authority on starfish, found it near impossible to taxonomically differentiate many of the *Asteroidea* species. The picture of the evolutionary tree, with new species constantly branching off in every direction, was "pretty muddled" and "confused." On a fantastic island like Wickaninnish any scientist, Ricketts reckoned, "must either understand nothing, or through the muddle come to grips with one of the most ultimate and fundamental ideas: that of essential unity." The scientist later told Father Mulvihill at the Kakawis mission that his "idea of heaven was to be out on the reef near [Lennard Island] on the West Coast at low tide when the sun was rising and marine life was just teeming."

* * *

LATE Tuesday evening, Alice and George Robinson, who was a friend
of Ricketts' from Cal Pack, met Steinbeck at the Monterey Airport.
Upon hearing the news the writer became enraged and "wanted to tear
the town apart because he had been delayed and because Ed had been
allowed to die before he got there."

Alice, too, was stricken with grief. Before she was put to bed with
sedatives that night, she turned responsibility for the burial over to
Ritch Lovejoy. According to Frances, he made all the arrangements without consulting family or waiting for young Ed Jr., who had gone back to
San Francisco on Monday. There would be no funeral and no flowers. A
burial notice in the newspaper said the service was private. Only those
who were telephoned were invited to come for one hour to pay their
respects in a small chapel. Sarah Richards, a student at Hopkins, was
asked to inform all the scientists at the marine station. The service
would be held the next day and Ricketts' body would be cremated with
inurnment at the Monterey City Columbarium. "People wanted to get
rid of him quickly and with dignity so they could think about him and
restore him again," Steinbeck said.

Not far from the Great Tide Pool and across from the lighthouse
stands the Little Chapel by the Sea. Outside, a small group of friends and
family and colleagues gathered—Ritch and Tal Lovejoy, Remo and
Virginia Scardigli, Alice, Ed Jr., Fred and Frances, Ricketts' youngest
daughter Cornelia, John Steinbeck, George Robinson, several Hopkins
scientists, among others. At two o'clock, Steinbeck pushed open the
double swinging doors and he and Virginia led the procession into the
tiny chapel. At the end of an aisle stood a gray closed casket with an ugly
purple artificial wreath. Steinbeck stopped momentarily, then stepped
aside. People wandered in behind him.

Nobody spoke. Only the combers of the Pacific could be heard in
the distance. Some people in very raggedy clothes came in, too. They sat
in the back of the chapel and never said a word. They meant no disrespect by their poor attire; perhaps some were embarrassed and even
ashamed. They were cannery workers, probably from Cal Pack where

Ricketts had worked, and they had done their best to look tidy. But they were the working poor and had indeed worked very little that catastrophic sardine season. They sat quietly paying their last respects to a man much loved on Cannery Row. Jean Ariss, once the love of Ricketts' life, also came into the small, silent hall with its stubby wooden pews. Cornelia and Frances sat quietly on one. After a half hour, Frances whispered a quiet benediction and everyone got up and left. Howard and Emma Flanders, distant relatives, took up a collection from the family to donate in Ricketts' name to the local children's hospital. The service seemed over before it began.

Outside, Frances walked over to Ritch Lovejoy. She was terribly upset about the funeral arrangements and told him so. The private service was wrong, a bad mistake. Many friends and colleagues who weren't invited would feel slighted and hurt. "[Ricketts'] warmth and friendship were not for a select few," she told him, her eyes swollen with tears, "but for all his family and friends and all the bums up and down Cannery Row."

Steinbeck looked adrift. Everyone shuffled around aimlessly outside the chapel. Then someone started to descend the sandy trail that led down to the beach, to Ed Ricketts' favorite collecting spot. He once described it as "the most prolific zone in the world." One by one, people made their way to the Great Tide Pool. "No one wanted company," Steinbeck remembered. "Everyone wanted to be alone." Some sat in the sand by the rocky tide pools. Others walked along the beach. The tide crept in by the pull of the moon. Steinbeck just sat staring blindly out to sea.

"A kind of anesthesia settled on the people who knew Ed Ricketts," Steinbeck later said. "There was not sorrow really but rather puzzled questions—what are we going to do? how can we rearrange our lives now? Everyone who knew him turned inward. It was a strange thing—quiet and strange. We were lost and could not find ourselves."

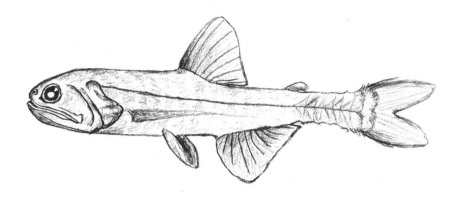

LAMPANYCTUS STEINBECKI, LONGFIN LAMPFISH, NEW SPECIES
NAMED AFTER JOHN STEINBECK AND IDENTIFIED BY DR. ROLF BOLIN IN 1939.

CHAPTER FIFTEEN
LAYING THE GHOST

There it is. That's all I can set down about Ed Ricketts. I don't know whether any clear picture has emerged. Thinking back and remembering has not done what I hoped it might. It has not laid the ghost.

—JOHN STEINBECK,
"About Ed Ricketts," *The Log from the Sea of Cortez*

THE sardine and Ed Ricketts were the body and soul, respectively, of Cannery Row—the fish very much its lifeblood, keeping the chimneys puffing and canning lines rolling, and Ricketts its "fountain of philosophy and science and art," as Steinbeck wrote in his novel.

Ricketts moved to the Monterey Peninsula when the sardine industry just started to take off in the early 1920s. He had his ups and downs and so did the sardine. The year 1936 was particularly bad for them both: Ricketts' lab burned to the ground in November, and the scientist would later discover that this was the year in which the sardine began its decline into oblivion. The Second World War then called them up for patriotic duty. The scientist served at the local army base and the sardine was drafted overseas in small tin cans to feed the troops. Ricketts was physically unscathed by the war, but not financially. His lab business virtually went bust. The sardine fared far worse. As Steinbeck explained, "The canneries themselves fought the war by getting the limit taken off fish and catching them all. It was done for patriotic reasons, but that didn't bring the fish back. As with the oysters in *Alice,* 'They'd eaten every one.'" The sardine ultimately became a casualty of war.

The fishing season after the war was the most disastrous in the history of the Monterey fishery. The value of the catch had plummeted to barely $4.5 million in 1946–47, down from almost $13 million the year before. In the *Monterey Peninsula Herald*'s annual 1947 "Sardine Edition," an official from the California Bureau of Marine Fisheries had paltry explanations for the abysmal season: Maybe the sardines were swimming offshore. Maybe they remained in deep waters away from fisher-men's nets. Or maybe it had something to do with oceanographic conditions. Or maybe, just maybe, he wondered, the "entire sardine population is so reduced in numbers that good fishing is not to be expected." The real answer was that he simply didn't know. The official admitted government scientists lacked information and complained that they had no research budget.

Dr. Robert C. Miller, director of the California Academy of Sciences and chairman of the Sardine Fisheries Commission for the State Chamber of Commerce, figured the fish just moved southward, although he admitted this was only a guess too. But he knew one thing for certain. "A decline of this magnitude is not due to overfishing," he told the *Herald*.

The scientific establishment of the State of California lacked any solid working hypothesis to explain the collapse. All the scholars, all their research, all the universities, marine stations and research vessels up and down the coast had come up with nothing but a few dubious speculations and vague musings about oceanographic conditions and fish stock migration. Even more astonishing, the spectacular collapse failed to dampen fishermen's faith. In its "Sardine Edition," the *Herald* actually reported that "everyone along famed Cannery Row and the Monterey waterfront looks forward to the coming season with optimism." That wasn't entirely true.

In the lab on Cannery Row, Ed Ricketts was outraged and not so optimistic. He had done his best to warn his community of the scientific facts: the sardine stocks were declining, precipitously so. In the final three years of his life, he had done a tremendous amount of research on the sardine, gathering fishery and oceanographic data from Baja California to British Columbia. "For years the canners and reduction plant operators and fishermen have been warned they were taking too many fish," he wrote to Joseph Campbell. "They refused to listen, selected their evidence, petitioned for more and more permits, put pressure on the Fish and Game Commission, lobbied the legislators, always got their way. And now so sad. No fish."

Ed Ricketts had few resources. His research lab was a glorified shack. His equipment was makeshift and antiquated. His entire scientific staff included only his bohemian friends, a very capable son who prepared readable graphs and charts, an occasional lab assistant and winos who did some specimen collecting. He never received a research grant. The Guggenheim Foundation passed him over and instead gave a fellowship to Dr. Rolf Bolin at Hopkins to go on an extravagant round-the-world expedition to study the lowly lantern fish. Bolin's "dream itinerary" included Sydney, Calcutta, Naples, Rome, Genoa, Monaco, Vienna, Berlin, Leningrad, Stockholm, Oslo, Bergen, Copenhagen, Amsterdam, Leiden, Brussels, Paris and London. All Ed Ricketts wanted to do was go to Alaska.

It's easy to understand why such a prestigious foundation would dismiss Ed Ricketts. He never even finished college. And the stories they had probably read in Steinbeck's *Cannery Row* about the bums, whores and wild parties in the lab probably made them squeamish about funding such an eccentric character. One graduate student at Hopkins was disgusted by some of the lowlifes who hung around the lab. "Ed had good and faithful friends," the student remembered, "but he was also surrounded by a circle of what I call 'pseudo-intellectuals,' people who abused his hospitality, sponged off him when they were down and out, used him as a sounding board for their own inane notions and knew that at the very least a visit to Ed's was good for one meal."

Yet on the front page of the *Herald*'s 1947 "Sardine Edition," Ed Ricketts published an article titled "Science Studies the Sardine" that was, by far, the most sophisticated and in-depth investigation of the sardine ever conducted. He applied everything he knew about fisheries, oceanography and ecology to this problem. It was the culmination of years of thinking and research. He had told Ritch Lovejoy he was working on a large project tentatively titled "The California Sardine: An Ecological Picture," which he hoped to publish in *National Geographic*. Lovejoy boasted in his *Herald* column the day Ricketts died that his friend had "completed to date, the most comprehensive study of sardine habits and migration ever compiled."

Ed's article was one of the first to apply a rudimentary ecosystem model to the ocean, though Ricketts had probably never even heard the word *ecosystem* before. The article is concise and clear, describing ecological concepts such as food chains, material and energy exchange, and the

Front page of the March 7, 1947, "Sardine Edition" of the Monterey Peninsula Herald *features a pioneering article by Ed Ricketts, "Science Studies the Sardine," on the ecology of the sardine and its collapse as depicted in the front-page graph.*

connection between sea temperatures, currents and ocean productivity. "It was certainly way before its time," one contemporary oceanographer has said of Ricketts' analysis. Indeed, in January 2003, an article in the journal *Science* described the fluctuation of the sardine in a similar manner, drawing connections between fish stock levels and oceanographic conditions over decade-long cycles. The coauthors ignored Ed Ricketts' seminal research in their article, but John Steinbeck warranted a mention for his "memorable novel."

How could Ed Ricketts explain the magnitude of the crisis? How could he explain to the fishermen and the public biological processes they couldn't see deep in the ocean? How could he convey the dire environmental and economic consequences of overfishing? How could he warn everyone that the unsustainable fishery would soon render Cannery Row a ghost town? Then it dawned on him: He would use a farming metaphor to explain how environmental factors combined with man-made factors—that is, industrial overfishing—were causing the collapse of the fishery. The public understood how drought and poor farming practices had caused the Dust Bowl. Many Americans experienced this firsthand; millions of others had read about it in horrifying detail in *The Grapes of Wrath*.

"[T]here's a long chain of events involved" in the collapse of the sardine, Ricketts explained. It wasn't just ocean currents or overfishing. The ocean was far more complex. "The result may be a labyrinth, but there's no way to avoid it," he added. He then described a series of links between sunlight, wind, sea temperatures and plankton levels in the ocean ecosystem that influenced the sardine stocks.

Plankton, he explained, consists chiefly of diatoms (microscopic plants). It is the "product of oceanic pastures, and like grain and grass and root crops, bears a direct relation to sunlight and fertilizer." In the spring, stronger sunlight creates plankton blooms that die off and form "a rain of particles [that] constantly enrich the dark deeper layers." Coastal winds then force surface water offshore, creating "upwellings" of nutrients from the cold deep layers. Lower sea surface temperatures also increase the upwellings, which fertilize the water with nutrients that increase plankton growth. According to Ricketts, "Some of these ocean pastures produce more [plankton] per acre than others. This is due to variations in the amount of fertilizer brought to the surface." The connection between sunlight, temperatures and wind to nutrients and plankton levels is the first link in the chain.

The sardines then feed on this plankton and grow fat. The fat is, in turn, converted into sperm and eggs when the fish swim to southern California and the Baja coast to spawn. This is the second link, connecting the plankton to sardine reproduction. Higher plankton levels in the ocean create fatter sardines that produce more sperm and eggs and thus more sardines. Ricketts reasoned he could forecast sardine stock productivity from plankton levels. He then drew a final link in this cycle of life. Since plankton levels were determined, in part, by sea surface temperatures, he figured he could forecast sardine stock production from these temperatures.

He published a chart showing warm water temperatures in 1941 and 1942. These were, in fact, later discovered to be years of El Niño currents. The warm water reduced upwellings of nutrients, which lowered plankton growth and thus food for the sardine. It was the oceanic equivalent of a dust bowl, and Ricketts suggested fewer fish should have been taken in those unproductive years for the sardine. "Instead," he wrote, "each year the number of canneries increased. Each year we expended more fishing energy pursuing fewer fish . . . each year we've been digging a little further into the breeding stock." It was like a greedy farmer eating his seed. He warned everyone not to disregard or sabotage conservation measures. Monterey, he insisted, could go the way of "ghost towns that faded when the sea otter or the lumber or the gold mining failed."

A year later, in the *Herald*'s 1948 "Sardine Edition," published on April 2, Ricketts continued to decry industry lobbyists who fought for larger catches. "Foolish men still threaten the goose with the golden eggs," Ricketts wrote in a draft of the article. He called on an international program of conservation and scientific research, headed by Canada, the United States and Mexico, to save the sardine. He said he was optimistic about the future of Monterey, if conservation were heeded.

The night of his accident Ed Ricketts drove down a Cannery Row that was eerily silent. It didn't have to be that way. He had forewarned that too many canneries had been built. In a rush to meet the wartime demand and feed the troops, a massive cannery and warehouse was built on the corner of Drake and Ocean View Avenues. It only took the Oxnard Canning Company five months to construct the large facility, which opened in October 1942. It was poorly and hastily planned, both in terms of fisheries conservation and urban planning. The corrugated iron warehouse obscured the sight of the right of way. It was impossible for motorists to see oncoming trains on the railroad track that traversed Drake Avenue. There wasn't even a wigwag at the railway crossing.

That cannery would spell the end of Ed Ricketts and ultimately the sardine. When the Del Monte Express swung around that blind corner on the evening of May 8, 1948, one of the strongest voices for conservation and one of America's pioneering ecologists would be silenced. And this tale becomes a ghost story, about a man, a fish and one of the most famous streets in America.

* * *

AFTER the funeral service, most of Ed's friends and family went to a small Mexican restaurant in a home on the hill overlooking Cannery Row. A place was set for Ed, or for his spirit, at one of the tables. Steinbeck sat without speaking or even moving. He was full of rage and whiskey.

Steinbeck stayed in the lab that night and a student from Hopkins Marine Station, Raghu Prasad, was asked to watch over him. Steinbeck went wild and threatened to burn down the lab. Prasad called a fellow student, Sarah Richards, for help. Prasad sounded "rather frantic" and so she came at once. Richards found a much-harassed Prasad and a half-asleep Steinbeck on the bed. Richards sat on the bed ready to hold down the huge, drunken writer if he tried to get up while Prasad combed the lab for matches. He had already removed the box with the pistol, which was under the shelf next to Ricketts' desk. Steinbeck roused himself twice, but the two Hopkins students "persuaded" him to stay put. To Prasad's relief, the writer woke the next morning rather subdued.

For three days, Ed Jr., Cornelia, Alice, Steinbeck, Ritch and Tal stayed at the lab, drinking beer, commiserating and going out for dinner. Other friends came and went. Steinbeck resented some of the visitors, especially the ones he'd never met. "Who are you? What right have you to be here at all?" he blasted. He had always been possessive about his friendship with Ed Ricketts. One night they were laughing and story-telling when one of them suddenly said, "We'll have to let him go! We'll have to release him and let him go." It wouldn't be so easy for John Steinbeck.

Many struggled to find meaning in the death of Ed Ricketts. Others desperately tried to find the proverbial silver lining. "The only thing that seems good to me about this disaster," Frances wrote to Nancy the Sunday following her father's death, "is the fact that your father was happier in these last two or three months with Alice than I have ever seen him. We can't know what the future would have held for him and to go out quickly while at the peak of life may be the happiest for him everything considered." Steinbeck agreed: "It is good that he was killed during the very best time of his life with his work at its peak and with the best girl he ever had. I am extremely glad for that."

A few days later, Steinbeck and George Robinson, a cannery man-ager and a colleague of Ricketts', went to the lab to clear it out. Robinson went over to Wing Chong's grocery across the street and got as many empty cartons as he could. Steinbeck sifted through a mountain of papers, notebooks and journals, and handed Robinson anything that should be put in the cartons for trash. Steinbeck threw away galley proofs—one was for his book *A Russian Journal*, published that year—and research papers from the departments of agriculture and labor, which Robinson believed were used to write *The Grapes of Wrath*. In the lab also stood the huge empty safe that had survived the 1936 fire. The safe's interior compart-ment was locked, and none of Ed's keys would open it.

"What should we do?" Robinson asked.

Steinbeck shrugged. "I guess we'd better have it opened."

A locksmith came and picked the lock. Inside was a little bottle of Haig & Haig scotch and a dusty yellow note, a veritable message from the grave: "What the hell do you expect to find in here? Here's a drink for your trouble." It was classic Ed Ricketts.

Steinbeck took Ricketts' notebooks to his cottage in Pacific Grove and read through them. He later claimed to have found references to sui-cide, which he immediately tore out of the books. Sarah Richards also remembered a time, about a month before his death, when Ricketts came to her lab at the marine station. He seemed very depressed and sat on a bench telling her about "the necessity of having a funeral after a person dies, not to celebrate his death, but rather to convince the living that the end had come, and that nothing would change the fact of his death." He also talked about Toni's departure. Sarah remembered that afternoon well, "because it seemed prophetic in light of the events two or three weeks later." She later suggested that a psychoanalyst would wonder about the suspicious circumstances surrounding his death, since Ed knew that the evening train always came through at 7:30 P.M.

There is little evidence to support this gossip that swirled around Monterey, including one rumor that Ricketts was drunk when the train hit him. There were certainly references to suicide in his journals. "Suicide perhaps a way out of a terribly complicated and almost hopeless situation," he wrote on December 5, 1945, about his deteriorating relationship with Toni. Yet it seems less a desperate cry for help than a man thinking freely as Ricketts often did. Besides, he had spent a lifetime poisoning animals and had a lab full of toxic chemicals, including a canister of cyanide. A train crash was just too crude, too sloppy and too haphazard a suicide for Ed Ricketts. "I don't believe this," Robinson said of the suicide rumors. "It's absolutely ridiculous."

Among his collecting notes and zoological observations, Steinbeck also claims to have found "the most outspoken and indelicate observation from another kind of collecting." Steinbeck said he tore out a "great number" of entries about Ricketts' sex life that could be considered "blackmail material on half the female population of Monterey." Ricketts' last three notebooks, covering the years 1942 to 1948, only contain two missing pages. Perhaps Steinbeck was being facetious. Still, such quips and exaggerations only served to reinforce Ricketts' reputation as a legendary womanizer.

The rest of Ricketts' belongings were distributed among friends and others. His collecting notes, species index cards and other materials went to Hopkins Marine Station. Ricketts had almost no money to speak of and, as Steinbeck pointed out, the "laboratory without Ed is just a run down piece of real estate" and "any attempt to maintain it or hold it together is . . . a piece of morbid wishful thinking." Alice burned some books on the beach behind the lab. And although Steinbeck never burned down the lab, he did burn almost every letter between the two of them. Today, only a scattering of letters remain out of what must have been hundreds.

John Steinbeck packed up Ed's microscope and quickly left for New York City. Before departing, however, he made a final entry into Ricketts' outer shores notebook, on page 261, just after a page of notes in which Ricketts outlined the structure of the book they were to coauthor.

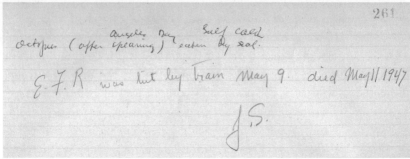

Perhaps in haste and surely with great sorrow, maybe even clouded by sedatives or alcohol, Steinbeck made this erroneous inscription. The train hit Ed Ricketts on May 8, not 9, and he died in 1948, not 1947.

* * *

WHAT would be the fate of *The Outer Shores?* In a holograph will dated February 28, 1940, Ricketts left to his best friend his personal notebooks, papers and manuscripts in progress which, according to the will, contained a great deal of "conceptual material for a system of metaphysics." Ricketts hoped that the materials could be arranged by "one competent and sympathetic mind, such as John's, into quite significant work."

Back at the Bedford Hotel in New York, Steinbeck sat alone and dull with pain. On May 24, a week after returning from Monterey, he wrote both Mr. Hartog at Stanford University Press and Dr. Joel Hedgpeth, who would become an editor of later editions of *Between Pacific Tides.* "There is nothing to say about Ed, not yet anyway," he told Hedgpeth. "It is going to take time for rearrangement." He promised, however, to try to put Ricketts' collecting notes in order for *The Outer*

Shores and to edit "his intimate journals for some future use." To Mr. Hartog on June 3, he wrote:

> It will be a very long time I am afraid before I can get to work on Ed's Journals. Indeed I should like to leave them for some future leisure when I can go over them in quiet and also when some time will have given me more perspective than I now have. I think these journals will prove to be almost the clinical development of the best mind I have ever known. It was a mind that knew itself and yet was apart from itself. Its observations of its own times and of the events that went on about it will be of value I am sure. But that is something I am not going into in a hurry.

Steinbeck wanted to go back to the Monterey Peninsula and sit quietly reading these journals. He seemed committed to publishing his friend's work. It would be up to John Steinbeck, and him alone, to publish *The Outer Shores* and complete the trilogy that Ricketts had started.

*   *   *

THE second edition of *Between Pacific Tides*—after nearly nine years of delay and stalling by Stanford University Press—came out shortly after Ricketts' death. The publisher wrote an addendum to the new preface, which was terse, yet surprising, in its content:

PUBLISHER'S NOTE

The tragic death of Edward F. Ricketts on May 12 [actually May 11], following an automobile accident near his home in Pacific Grove, prevented his final check of the second edition. Dr. Ricketts had just finished the revision of page proofs and returned it to the Press with his copy for the new index. It is the task of the Press staff to prepare the pages for press without benefit of the author's further approval.

STANFORD UNIVERSITY PRESS

June 8, 1948

After years of shabby treatment, after having peer reviewers denigrate him as simply a "collector of considerable experience," after seeming to lack confidence in the credentials of the author, Stanford University Press awarded Edward F. Ricketts, however informally, the distinction of "Dr."

* * *

JOHN Steinbeck remained deeply confused after the death. "How much was Ed and how much was me and which was which?" he wondered in a letter to Ritch and Tal Lovejoy on May 27, 1948. He limped around aimlessly as though part of his body had been severed. "[Ed Ricketts] was my partner for eighteen years—he was part of my brain," Steinbeck later said. "At one time a very eminent zoologist said that the two of us together were the best zoologists in America, and when he was killed I was destroyed." He told the Lovejoys that he had "a great feeling of life again," but described it as "vital and violent."

Toni Jackson had always felt, from the first time she met Steinbeck in the lab, that he was under the surface a "very angry man." A petite woman, Toni remembered Steinbeck with his hulking, broad shoulders looming over Ricketts' bookshelves. On some level she was afraid of him. She recalled how Steinbeck hated the people of Salinas and wrote a chapter for *Cannery Row*, which was later cut from the book, about the town's streets being overrun by mad dogs. By the time Ricketts was killed, Toni had left New York for Palestine with Volcani. She later heard through a friend what happened when Steinbeck went to Mexico to work on the film *Viva Zapata!* in June. "His anger came out after Ed died," Toni recalled. "He went on terrible rampages in Mexico, devastated with anger. He got drunk and busted things up."

When Steinbeck returned he wrote a friend saying he was "out of sadness and into fierceness now. That is natural to the organism that feels under attack I guess." He was drinking heavily and felt a need for "violent work" and "violent play." When he got back to New York he finally had a "crack-up," which, he admitted, was "a little frightening." Adding to his pain, his wife Gwyn asked for a divorce.

Steinbeck had depended on Ricketts' unconditional friendship during his most trying times—during his search for a philosophical voice in his writing, the controversies around *The Grapes of Wrath* and his romantic travails. Steinbeck admitted that Ricketts had been a sort of emotional and intellectual "prop" for him. He would have to write *East of Eden* without the support of Ricketts or even a wife. He now felt "times of cold terror about doing it alone."

In September, Steinbeck moved back to the small cottage in Pacific Grove where he first lived in 1930 and met Ed Ricketts. The cottage would be his protective shell and he'd crawl into it "like a hermit crab." His father had built the three-room bungalow. It was clad in shingles and had a little rock garden in the backyard. Over the years, successive occupants had pillaged its furniture. Steinbeck had only a bed, some old work chairs and a card table to write on. From the living room, he could hear the sea lions, surf and bell buoy bobbing off China Point. He hoped the damp sea fog would seep into him like medicine. He was restless and lonely and confused—missing Ricketts one moment and then dismissing him the next. He had sleepless nights during great thunder storms. One night he wrote "a little story that was so evil, so completely evil that when I finished it I burned it."

Friends who visited found him "deeply disturbed and frightened about his work." One old friend from Los Gatos found "the atmosphere bizarre, with John Steinbeck in a kind of melancholy stupor and Ed Ricketts's microscope enshrined under glass and set in a position of reverence in the center of the room." The writer was still clinging to his "prop."

A year after Ricketts' death, Steinbeck had barely written a word of *East of Eden*. He was forlorn and sought sexual release with several women. "One is really a whore," he told a friend, "and she's the sweetest and most lady like of the lot." Concerned friends tried to help him, but Steinbeck pushed them away. "Everyone tries to get me married," he complained.

Then, in May 1949, he met Elaine Scott, who would become his third and final wife. They moved back to New York at Christmastime. His emotional wounds were healing, but the ghost of Ed Ricketts still haunted him.

He wrote a play-novella that winter called *Burning Bright*, about a woman who commits adultery in order to give her sterile husband a child. A character called Friend Ed helps to reconcile the troubled couple. It was a bizarre artistic experiment, broken into three acts with the character-archetypes transposed into three discordant settings: a circus, a farm and the sea. (The settings must have held meaning to Steinbeck: he apparently heard the news of Ricketts' accident while at the circus and buried him by the sea.) It was supposed to be a morality play written as a parable. The theatrical and literary reviewers were excoriating. It closed after only thirteen performances. "[I]t was dead the first night," admitted its coproducer. It was becoming clear, as one literary scholar has noted, that John Steinbeck "was becoming a novelist without a vision."

* * *

WITH a new edition of *Between Pacific Tides* in distribution, Steinbeck decided on a small project that would prepare him for editing Ricketts' unpublished notes and journals into a book. He decided to reissue *Sea of Cortez* with a sixty-page prologue titled "About Ed Ricketts." It would be his eulogy to his best friend. New editions of *Between Pacific Tides* and *Sea of Cortez* would be the perfect segue for a final volume, edited by Steinbeck, on Ed Ricketts, his ecological philosophy and his North Pacific expeditions.

Instead of demystifying "Doc," as Ricketts was popularly known across North America, and celebrating him as a pioneering ecologist, the eulogy painted the same caricature of Ed Ricketts as in *Cannery Row*. Steinbeck seemed to lift, almost verbatim, descriptions from the novel. In *Cannery Row*, he wrote:

> Doc is rather small, deceptively small, for he is wiry and very strong and when passionate anger comes on him he can be very fierce. He wears a beard and his face is half Christ and half satyr and his face tells the truth. . . . Doc would listen to any kind of nonsense and change it for you to a kind of wisdom. His mind had no horizon—and his sympathy had no warp. He could talk to children, telling them very profound

things so that they understood. He lived in a world of wonders, of excitement. He was concupiscent as a rabbit and gentle as hell. Everyone who knew him was indebted to him. . . .

And seven years later, in "About Ed Ricketts," he wrote:

Everyone near him was influenced by him, deeply and permanently. Some he taught how to think, others how to see or hear. Children on the beach he taught how to look for and find beautiful animals in worlds they had not suspected were there at all. He taught everyone without seeming to. . . . Such things were said of him as, "He was half-Christ and half-goat." He was a great teacher and a great lecher—an immortal who loved women. . . . He was gentle but capable of ferocity, small and slight but strong as an ox. . . .

The eulogy is episodic, without structure or any real chronology. It is a series of touching, even hilarious, anecdotes and some dubious facts. Steinbeck said he died in April of 1948 and had a Bachelor's of Science—both untrue. The essay is flooded with idiosyncrasies. We learn that Ricketts affectionately nicknamed women, including his daughters and Toni, "Wormy," and that he hated to get his hair wet so much that he wore an oilskin sou'wester into the shower—a fact that seems hardly believable. Steinbeck recounts how Ricketts once attacked a cop who was pistol-whipping a drunk for no reason. There's the story about the "The Snake" and descriptions of Wing Chong's and Flora's. Steinbeck also tells us about how the bums tried to hustle Ricketts: Once Ed went across the street to buy beer at Wing Chong's and return empty bottles. A bum was sitting in the gutter in front of the store.

"Say Doc," he said, "I'm having a little trouble peeing. What's a good diuretic?"
　　Ed fell into that hole. "I never needed to think beyond beer," he said.
　　The man looked at the bottles in Ed's hand and raised his shoulders in a gesture of helplessness. And only then did Ed realize that he had been had. "Oh, come on in," he said, and he bought beer for both of them.

This type of silly storytelling goes on for pages and pages. Steinbeck even boasts about Ricketts' "sexual output," going on ad nauseam about his liaisons with women. It sounds just like "Doc" in *Cannery Row*. Yet no matter the inaccuracies, exaggerations or, in places, ridiculousness of the eulogy, it certainly described the Ed Ricketts that Steinbeck knew.

"Yes, *Cannery Row* is a true story," Joel Hedgpeth and Jack Calvin would later say of the novel, "but it is not the whole truth. The laboratory, the phonograph records, the beer milkshake, and the establishment across the street—these details are true. And Ed was really like Doc, but Doc is only a one-dimensional portrait of Ed. Who would know from *Cannery Row* that Ed was the devoted father of three children, and that he was a hard-working biologist who managed to get a great deal done between his records and that solemn procession—Ed would have called it a lovely procession—of wine jugs? We mean no criticism of John in suggesting that the Doc of *Cannery Row* is half Ricketts the man and half Steinbeck the author."

In sixty pages, there is only one brief paragraph in which Steinbeck tells us that Ricketts' "scientific interest was essentially ecological and holistic." There is no mention of *Between Pacific Tides*. No discussion of his friend's unparalleled ecological survey of the Pacific Coast. No mention of his research on zonation, tides or plankton. No boasting about Ricketts' attempts to save the sardine. He does, however, mention their work on *The Outer Shores*.

At the time of Ed's death our plans were completed, tickets bought, containers and collecting equipment ready for a long collecting trip to the Queen Charlotte Islands, which reach so deep into the Pacific Ocean. There was one deep bay [Masset Inlet] with a long and narrow opening where we thought we might observe some changes in animal forms due to a specialized life and a long period of isolation. Ed was to have started within a month and I was to have joined him there. Maybe someone else will study that little island sea. The light has gone out of it for me.

Ed Ricketts' trilogy of the Pacific would be left unfinished. His three years of research—a thousand pages of notes, correspondence and collecting reports—to write *The Outer Shores* would be filed away in a dusty archive and forgotten for decades. And worse: the new edition of *Sea of Cortez* appeared in 1951 under the title *The Log from the Sea of Cortez* and without the zoological bibliography—which took Ricketts months of research to construct—and without his name as coauthor.

Prodded by Viking editor Pascal Covici, Steinbeck pressured Ed Jr. to sign over the exclusive copyright for the narrative portion of *Sea of Cortez,* which would allow Viking to drop Ricketts' name from its authorship. Covici suggested 15 to 20 percent as a fair share of royalties. "At that time it was widely believed that the only contribution that Ricketts had made was the scientific portion, which would now be eliminated," remembered Ed Jr. "Knowing that Ricketts had indeed contributed to the narrative portion, I objected and said that I thought at least 25 percent would more nearly represent the Ricketts share in such a book. Anything less would seem disrespectful to his memory." With *Sea of Cortez* out of print and monies still owing the publisher for the advance, Ed Jr. felt "this was the only way for things to proceed." Covici finally got what he had always wanted: Edward F. Ricketts was removed as coauthor.

The episode isn't very flattering to John Steinbeck. He meant no disrespect to his friend and always maintained, even a few years before his own death in 1968, that *Sea of Cortez* was "a true collaboration"—a fact that has been well noted in Steinbeck scholarship. (A long-lost typescript of Ricketts' log made public in 2003 also proves that Steinbeck kept "a lot of Ricketts' wording and that huge chunks [were] simply cut and pasted" from his log.) It was a peculiar way to honor his best friend, though. Perhaps Steinbeck just thought it didn't matter since his friend was dead. Nevertheless, the continued omission of Ed Ricketts' name from the book's cover remains, to this day, a slight against one of America's great ecologists and conservationists. This and the colorful, though very skewed essay "About Ed Ricketts" would continue to obscure the real Ed Ricketts and his contribution to science. In its place, the legend of Doc would grow larger than life. Ricketts would become increasingly known as the "John Steinbeck character." Today, *The Outer Shores* and Ricketts' attempt to complete a trilogy of the Pacific are all but forgotten.

* * *

STEINBECK'S literary reputation declined after Ricketts' death. With the exception of *East of Eden,* there is little of note in the Steinbeck canon after 1948. Critics were ruthless. In reviewing *The Winter of Our Discontent* in 1961, *Newsweek* noted, "Any critic knows it is no longer legal to praise John Steinbeck." The next year Steinbeck won the Nobel Prize in Literature, a laurel that would usually elicit exaltation from a nation celebrating one of its own. Not so for Steinbeck. An editorial in the *New York Times* went out of its way to attack the Nobel committee, questioning their choice of the winner: "[W]e think it interesting that the laurel was not awarded to a writer—perhaps a poet or critic or historian— whose significance, influence and sheer body of work had already made a more profound impression on the literature of our age."

Of course, the *New York Times* and most of the Eastern literary establishment never really understood the essentially ecological message Steinbeck was making. Science was largely outside the purview of the literati. Despite ecological themes imbuing *In Dubious Battle* and *The Grapes of Wrath*, one reviewer noted that prior to *Sea of Cortez*, Steinbeck's "previous writings had given little indication of a scientific propensity."

In 2002, upon Steinbeck's centennial, the *New York Times* reported that his popularity (Steinbeck still sells about two million copies a year) was "more about sociology and history than about literature." Students were reading Steinbeck to understand the radicalism of the thirties. Picking up where Edmund Wilson left off, Harold Bloom, described as "a sort of chancellor of the Western literary canon," has even omitted Steinbeck from the canon's American division. Bloom describes *The Grapes of Wrath* as a "flawed but permanent American book," and thinks Steinbeck's philosophy of "radical and naturalistic humanism" is confused: "do his characters fall into animal-like behavior because of society's oppressions, or because they simply revert to their true identity when they are uprooted?" Steinbeck wasn't saying that humans are "animal-like"; he was saying that humans *are* animals and thus are *one* with nature. "Why do we so dread to think of our species as a species?" Steinbeck and Ricketts wrote in *Sea of Cortez*. "Can it be that we are afraid of what we may find? That human self-love would suffer too much and that the image of God might prove to be a mask?" (Joseph Campbell would later title his four-volume magnum opus, which laid out his theories of the history of myth and religion, *The Masks of God*.)

Bloom and many other literary scholars completely missed the point of Steinbeck's writing. As for Steinbeck's Nobel Prize and its measure of his greatness, Bloom told the *Times*: "The people in Stockholm often seem to have a dusty file on people no one ever heard of that they pull out when making the awards."

Steinbeck's message was not lost on everyone, however. Only a few years after his death in 1968, ecology began to ignite the popular imagination. In 1970, *Newsweek,* one of Steinbeck's harshest critics, printed a special report on "The Ravaged Environment." Bookstores carried such titles as *Before Nature Dies, Silent Spring, Our Precarious Habitat* and *The Endangered Planet.* The American media heralded the 1970s as the "Age of Ecology." As a result, one of Steinbeck's greatest contributions to American literature—his ecological message—finally began to resonate with the culture at large. It would be recognized and celebrated by both literary academics and scientists. And as scholars sifted through Steinbeck's old papers and letters for evidence of his scientific influences, the trail inevitably led to Ed Ricketts.

On May 4, 1974, Dr. Joel Hedgpeth and literary scholar Dr. Richard Astro organized a conference at the Marine Science Center in Newport, Oregon, called "Steinbeck and the Sea." There was a groundswell of interest in both Steinbeck and Ricketts. Astro had published a book entitled *John Steinbeck and Ed Ricketts: The Shaping of a Novelist* the year before. And Hedgpeth had edited many of Ricketts' essays and travel logs into a two-volume paperback entitled *The Outer Shores*, a task that Steinbeck had once promised to undertake. Stanford University Press, of course, refused to publish the book. "There is *nothing* conventional about this project," the press told Hedgpeth, which ironically was the same criticism originally leveled at *Between Pacific Tides.* Hedgpeth's *The Outer Shores* finally came out in 1978 in a paperback edition by Mad River Press. Few copies were sold and it has long been out of print.

The scholars at the Newport conference confirmed what many of Ricketts' friends and family had been saying for years. Jack Calvin, who never liked Steinbeck, told Astro that "Ed was a reservoir for John to draw on" and that "in Ed he found an endless source of material—or call it inspiration, if you like—and used it hungrily." When Ricketts died, Calvin concluded, the "fountain had been turned off."

Jean Ariss had her own curious ideas about why Steinbeck burned all his letters to and from Ed Ricketts. "He never wanted anyone to know what a tremendous influence Edward had on his thinking and his work," she told Hedgpeth. "Edward said sometimes that he only acted as a catalyst, but it was a necessary function as the decline in the essential Steinbeck philosophy after Ed's death plainly indicates."

The academics agreed. In 250 pages of scholarship, Astro dissects Ricketts' influence on Steinbeck and how the biologist served as the author's personae in six novels and novellas (*In Dubious Battle, The Grapes of Wrath, The Moon Is Down, Cannery Row, Burning Bright* and *Sweet Thursday*) and in one short story ("The Snake"). It is an exhaustive study, describing the complex relationship of ideas, influences, emotions and personal discoveries that resulted from the two friends. "No, it hardly seems coincidental that Steinbeck's fictional genius declined after Ricketts' death," Astro concluded. "Rather, it seems apparent that the train that killed Ricketts set off a series of reactions that helped kill Steinbeck as a serious novelist."

Others at the conference reached the same conclusion. Dr. Fred Tarp was a marine biology professor who had been a student at Hopkins Marine Station in the late 1940s and often frequented the lab. He said he followed Steinbeck's career with great interest, particularly the public adulation and honors that culminated with the Nobel Prize in 1962. "Despite this successful period of his life," he told the conference, "it was as if... an era had ended when he lost his friend in 1948." Dr. Tarp then read out a short passage from Steinbeck's foreword to the second edition of *Between Pacific Tides*: "There is in our community an elderly painter of seascapes who knows the sea so well that he no longer goes to look at it while he paints. He dislikes intensely the work of a young painter who sets his easel on the beach and paints things his elder does not remember having seen."

By 1948, Ricketts was Steinbeck's only real connection to his native California. After his death, the writer's lifeline to the Pacific Coast was severed. Steinbeck no longer looked to the seascape, which he had known so intimately, for inspiration. "To some of us," Tarp lamented, "in the years following Monterey, Ricketts, and the sea, Steinbeck had become that elderly painter."

* * *

STEINBECK'S second to last book did bring him back to California in late 1960. His nostalgic three-month odyssey across the United States, from his home in Sag Harbor, New York, to Monterey, seemed to confirm that he was no longer the man he once was. He bought a pickup truck with a camper, and despite his frailty he drove across the country with his French poodle, Charley. He wanted to be "a wandering ear and eye," to gauge the pulse of the people, the temper of the times. It was a quixotic farewell tour, recorded in full lamentation in *Travels with Charley*.

He was aghast at what he saw in Monterey. It was his first visit since Ricketts' death, and his wife Elaine had joined him by this time. She was elated to be with her husband in the place he had made famous. "Oh, isn't that Ed's lab over there? Is that where the Chinese grocery store was?" she asked. "Look! Look, there's a movie theatre called the John Steinbeck Theatre! Can't we go in and see it?" "No," he groaned, "let's don't do that. I don't want to do that."

The adulation Steinbeck saw on Cannery Row was shocking. Only fifteen years earlier he had basically been run out of town. Many in Monterey hated him for what he had written about them in *Cannery Row*; Steinbeck had exposed the unseemly underbelly of their community—the whores, pimps and winos. He had called Monterey's townspeople "pure poison" during his short "homecoming" in 1944. So it must have seemed rather fitting that now, years later, he got mild food poisoning when he went for dinner at one of the tourist restaurants on Cannery Row.

Alone one night, he also went to Johnny Garcia's bar to seek out old friends and acquaintances. He had "a touching reunion . . . with tears and embraces, speeches and endearments." He asked about his friends. "Where's Pilon, Johnny, Pom Pom, Miz Gragg, Stevie Field?"

Tourists walk by Ed Ricketts' old lab on Cannery Row, 1999. PHOTO BY AUTHOR.

"Dead, dead, dead," Johnny said.

"Ed Ricketts, Whitey's Number One and Two, where's Sonny Boy, Ankle Varney, Jesús Maria Corcoran, Joe Portagee, Shorty Lee, Flora Wood, and that girl who kept spiders in her hat?"

"Dead—all dead," Johnny moaned. "It's like we was in a bucket of ghosts."

But Steinbeck knew that wasn't the case. "I [am] the ghost," he told Johnny.

"When I went away I had died," he wrote in *Travels with Charley*, "and so became fixed and unchangeable. My return caused only confusion and uneasiness. Although they could not say it, my old friends wanted me gone so that I could take my proper place in the pattern of remembrance—and I wanted to go for the same reason. Tom Wolfe was right. You can't go home again because home has ceased to exist except in the mothballs of memory."

As Steinbeck took on a revisionist persona among locals, as Monterey's businessmen manufactured him and his fabled characters into

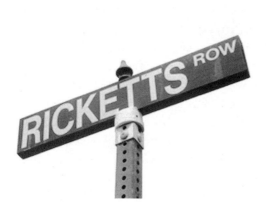

LEFT: *Ricketts Row in Pacific Grove, located along the alley where Ed Ricketts' first lab stood.* PHOTO BY AUTHOR.

RIGHT: *Bust of Ed Ricketts at the corner of Drake Avenue and Cannery Row in Monterey, 1999.* PHOTO BY AUTHOR.

consumable products for the tourist trade, the remarkable life and achievements of Ed Ricketts became inadvertently, and increasingly, overshadowed. By the Newport conference in 1974, Cannery Row was well on its way to becoming a Steinbeck amusement park. (The last cannery closed in 1973.) And Ed Ricketts was packaged and sold as a fictional icon, simply the "Doc" of *Cannery Row*, just another gimmicky tourist prop.

Recognition would come slowly and sparingly to Ed Ricketts. Joel Hedgpeth took up the work of revising *Between Pacific Tides* and published some of Ricketts' letters, scientific papers, and other miscellanea, but no other scientist stepped forward to publish Ricketts' extensive research of the Pacific Coast. Many of his papers at Hopkins also went missing for years, in a shameful display of scholarly hoarding.

Almost thirty years would pass from the time of his death before Ed Ricketts was given his due. In 1978, the Moss Landing Marine Laboratory named a small research vessel R.V. *Ed Ricketts.* They christened it with a beer milkshake, supposedly a drink Ricketts had once tried. Then in 1986, the Monterey Bay National Marine Sanctuary inaugurated an annual Ed Ricketts Memorial Lecture delivered by Dr. Hedgpeth. By the early 1990s, attempts were being made to create a Ricketts Marine Park in Monterey Bay (supporters are still waiting for the government to create the park) and in 1994 Pacific Grove renamed an alley off Fountain Avenue, where Ricketts' first lab stood, Ricketts Row. A bronze bust of Ed Ricketts was also erected at the corner of Drake Avenue and Cannery Row, the site of his tragic accident. The lab, of course, sat for decades like a perfectly preserved specimen, but received a rigorous historical restoration in the 1990s. There would also be several local exhibitions on Ricketts and an annual party celebrating his birthday. In 2002, a collection of Ricketts' letters would be published in a superb book, *Renaissance Man of Cannery Row*.

And finally, after more than sixty years, a writer, Jon Christensen, and a Hopkins marine biologist, Dr. Bill Gilly (who's studying the intelligence of marine invertebrates), left Monterey in March 2004 with an enthusiastic crew to retrace the voyage of Ricketts and Steinbeck to the Sea of Cortez. They chartered an old seine boat, the *Gus-D*, and departed in the same spirit as the first voyage, with some seventy cases of beer aboard that had been donated by a California brewery.

✶ ✶ ✶

STEINBECK wrote "About Ed Ricketts" with one goal in mind. "Maybe if I write down everything I can remember about him, that will lay the ghost," he said. "It is worth trying anyway."

He had received so many letters from Ricketts over the years. They were usually, Steinbeck remembered, "so much in the style of his speech that I could hear his voice over the neat page full of small elite type." Reading the letters, Steinbeck felt like he was back at the lab. A haunting picture became etched in his mind. "It is the time just before dusk," he wrote. "I can see Ed finishing his work in the laboratory. He covers his instruments and puts his papers away. He rolls down the sleeves of his wool shirt and puts on his old brown coat. I see him go out and get in his beat-up old car and slowly drive away in the evening. I guess I'll have that with me all my life."

In 1954, Steinbeck wrote his final "Doc" novel, *Sweet Thursday*. It was the sequel to *Cannery Row*. He wrote to Gabe Bicknell, whom he fictionalized as Mack in both books: "I've just finished another book about the Row. It is a continuation concerned not with what did happen but with what might have happened. The one can be as true as the other. I think it is a funny story, and sad too because it is what might have happened to Ed and didn't. I don't seem to be able to get over his death. But this will be the last piece about him."

As in *Cannery Row*, an ecological thread runs through *Sweet Thursday*. "To a casual observer," Steinbeck wrote, "Cannery Row might have seemed a series of self-contained and selfish units, each functioning alone with no reference to the others. There was little visible connection between La Ida's, the Bear Flag, the grocery (still known as Lee Chong's Heavenly Flower Grocery), the Palace Flophouse and Western Biological Laboratories. The fact is that each was bound by gossamer threads of steel to all the others—hurt one, and you aroused vengeance in all. Let sadness come to one, and all wept."

A malaise about the world imbues the novel. Doc is even overcome with a deep sense of failure. There is a recurring image of him sitting for hours at his desk hunched over a blank yellow notepad. He is "deeply, grievingly unhappy" and is incapable of writing a scientific paper on octopi. "The beckoning yellow pages became his enemies," Steinbeck wrote. Doc is just as lost and confused while out collecting on the seashore. As Steinbeck described in one scene:

> The pains that came to Doc were like a stir of uneasiness or the flick of a skipped heartbeat. Whisky lost its sharp delight and the first long pull of beer from a frosty glass was not the joy it had been. He stopped listening in the middle of an extended story. He was not genuinely glad to see a friend. And sometimes, starting to turn over a big rock in the Great Tide Pool—a rock under which he knew there would be a community of frantic animals—he would drop the rock back in place and stand, hands on hips, looking off to sea, where the round clouds piled up white with pink and black edges. And he would be thinking, What am I thinking? What do I want?

Voices are whispering in Doc's ear as he searches the tide pools. One voice asks, "What are you looking for, little man? Is it yourself you're trying to identify? Are you looking at little things to avoid big things?" And deep down inside, another melancholy voice sings, "Lonesome! Lonesome!"

Doc is angry, full of self-hatred, and he quarrels viciously with friends. "Deep in himself Doc felt a failure," Steinbeck wrote. The voices haunt him; the empty yellow pads taunt him. "Everybody's laughing at you behind your back—and you know why?" asks one of the working girls. "Because everybody knows you're kidding yourself. You ain't never going to write that paper because you can't write that paper."

Nobody believed that this despondent Doc character was Ed Ricketts, a man who constantly tried to savor "the hot taste of life." Despite his occasional psychological pangs, Ed Ricketts was at the peak of his life when he died. He was producing his best scientific thinking ever. In researching his book, Richard Astro stayed up late one night poring over all of Ricketts' writing. He wrote Hedgpeth the next morning about the materials. "They're fascinating—particularly since they conclusively prove that Ed never lost his drive—his scientific energy. The impression Steinbeck gives of him in *Sweet Thursday* is, of course, quite the contrary."

Superficially, the Doc character looked like Ricketts, but his anguish was Steinbeck's. It was Steinbeck who was dating tramps and who complained about everyone trying to get him married after he moved back to Pacific Grove in 1948. (*Sweet Thursday*'s plot revolves around Cannery Row's misfits trying to marry Doc to one of the working girls at the brothel across the street.) It was Steinbeck who wrote his manuscripts on yellow ledgers, not Ricketts, who largely used bound notebooks. (Steinbeck also wrote many handwritten letters to Ricketts on yellow ledgers.) And it was Steinbeck who was full of doubts about his writing and seemed lost after his friend's death. The image of Doc in *Sweet Thursday* is one of a forlorn, troubled John Steinbeck despairing about his writing of *East of Eden*.

"A novelist, perhaps unconsciously, identifies himself with one chief or central character," Steinbeck once wrote. "You will find one in every one of my books. . . . I suppose my own symbol character has my dream wish of wisdom and understanding." Throughout Steinbeck's writing, the "symbol character" was always an idealized Ed Ricketts—always the

Doc character. But with Ed Ricketts dead, he now fictionalized his own life. He became his own "symbol character." "It was an act of reconciliation, of integration, that may be unparalleled in literature," Steinbeck's biographer, Jackson J. Benson, wrote. "Steinbeck had learned, at last, to like himself well enough to speak as himself and to project a possible version of Steinbeck based on what he actually was, as well as what he would wish to be or become." By abandoning Ricketts as his "symbol character," Steinbeck finally brought closure to the tragic death of his friend.

The final scene of *Sweet Thursday* is a familiar one. It is just before twilight. Cannery Row's misfits buy Doc a gift—the biggest "microscope" they can find. Unbeknownst to them, it is actually a telescope to explore the stars. Just before dark, Doc loads his old car with supplies, a microscope and the gigantic telescope, preparing to leave on a collecting trip. The scene hauntingly echoes that fateful evening when Ricketts left his lab and drove his old car down the Row and up Drake Avenue, where the warehouse stood by the railway tracks. Steinbeck wrote:

> Doc turned in the seat and looked back. The disappearing sun shone on his laughing face, his gay and eager face. With his left hand he held the bucking steering wheel.
>
> Cannery Row looked after the ancient car. It made the first turn and was gone from sight behind a warehouse just as the sun was gone.

With those final words, John Steinbeck laid to rest the ghost of Ed Ricketts in the "hour of the pearl" on Cannery Row. It was, Steinbeck described, "a time of great peace, a deserted time, a little era of rest."

EPILOGUE

To finish is sadness to a writer—a little death. He puts the last word down and it is done. But it isn't really done. The story goes on and leaves the writer behind, for no story is ever done.

—JOHN STEINBECK,
personal letter, *Steinbeck: A Life in Letters*

FOR three years, I lived in an abandoned fish camp at the end of a pier in the lonely harbor of Ucluelet on Vancouver Island. In the early mornings, seagulls dropped clams on my roof, trying to break open the shells. Harbor seals barked like neighborhood dogs. Schools of herring bubbled to the glassy ocean surface, creating ripples like rain falling on water.

Down the harbor sat five other fish packers that form a veritable "Fish Camp Row" along the waterfront. The camp buildings look like huge corrugated aluminum boxes stacked atop each other, three or four stories high. Each camp contains ice-making machines, freezers, a two-story icehouse, unloading stations, an office and a small apartment for the "campman." That's where I lived.

My grandfather Gordon Edwards moved to Ucluelet from Harbor Le Cou, Newfoundland, in 1938. He was one of a group of fishermen who founded the Ucluelet Fishing Company and built this camp. Old-timers tell me he was a hard-drinking, competitive man and a highliner. For more than twenty years, he sold his daily catches of salmon to the company and when he died his ashes were spread over the fishing grounds of the outer shores. Thanks to men like him, the company became a pillar of the community. Its profits were divvied up among the fishermen who owned or sold fish to the company, and some were given to the local fish hatchery to ensure stable salmon runs for the future. The company even gave me a scholarship to go to college. During summer breaks, I returned to fish with my father on our family's hook-and-line troller, the *Tribute*. Then, in 1994, the company manager offered me the job of campman.

I ran the ice-making machines, filled the boats with tons of salted ice and graded the silvery catches of pink, coho, chinook, chum and sockeye salmon when the boats would return from a week at sea. The docks bustled with fishermen whose personalities were as colorful as their nicknames: Snakebite, The Lord, Jumbo, Mountain (my uncle), Crazy, Captain Crunch, George the Greek. But that summer was my last working on the decks and docks of B.C.'s salmon fishing industry.

Two years later, salmon stock depletions and a government program to downsize the fishing fleet turned Ucluelet into a ghostly harbor. No fishing and no fish boats. My father retired, finally, at the age of seventy.

When I finished college that year, Dan Edwards, a local fisherman and a cousin of mine, suggested I come home to work with coastal communities and aboriginal tribes that were fighting the government's plan to buy out many small-boat fishermen. Back home again and looking for a place to stay, I inquired about the vacant apartment in the fish camp, which was now virtually bankrupt. It was available and cheap, so I moved in immediately.

The camp is much like Ed Ricketts' lab, except it sorted, packed and shipped salmon instead of scientific specimens. And like the lab, accommodations were upstairs and business operations were below. When I first moved in, I discovered the sewage pump was broken. Then the water line burst. For a month I showered in a nearby motel and washed my dishes with bottled water.

Nineteen ninety-seven was an especially bad year for Ucluelet. It was one of the windiest winters on record. Terrifying squalls rocked the camp on its old creosote-soaked pilings. On Easter Sunday, wind gusts reached 130 kilometers per hour. The hurricane-force winds blew rain through every crack in the building. My bedroom, living room and kitchen sprang leaks. The downstairs office was flooded. The entire building was either rotting or rusting. The docks were half-sunk. The gangway teetered and eventually collapsed.

The following winter scientists recorded the strongest El Niño in history in the tropical Pacific. Energy from the warm water current (about four degrees Celsius above average) was affecting the jet stream, the high-altitude, swirling river of air, causing extreme weather patterns, including torrential floods and violent winds. As El Niño moved northward through Mexico and California, it left a wake of death and destruction. One climatologist called it "the El Niño of the century."

Around this time, ocean survival rates for some North Pacific salmon stocks mysteriously declined by 60 to almost 90 percent. In one northern B.C. river, scientists discovered almost no coho salmon survived their ocean migration back to their natal river. And like the collapse of the sardines half a century before, solid explanations eluded everyone. Habitat degradation, high-seas poaching or pollution could be causes. Global warming could also be affecting the marine ecosystem. Some scientists talked of an environmental "regime" shift in the ocean. Many fishermen pointed to El Niño and the rapacious schools of mackerel, which follow the warm water and eat juvenile salmon, as the culprit. Whatever the explanation, the severe storms and collapsing salmon stocks spelled doom for many fishermen. The United Nations declared 1998 the International Year of the Ocean, but there was little to celebrate. The entire outer coast of Vancouver Island closed to commercial salmon trolling—the first time in the hundred-year history of the fishery.

Living in the fish camp that winter, I couldn't help but draw a parallel between the severe storms, long dark days and the chaos in the ocean ecosystem and the dust storms of the Dirty Thirties and their catastrophic affect on farming. I bought a dog-eared copy of *The Grapes of Wrath*. "The dawn came, but no day," Steinbeck wrote. "In the gray sky a red sun appeared, a dim red circle that gave a little light, like dusk; and as that day advanced, the dusk slipped back toward darkness, and the wind cried and whimpered over the fallen corn."

And just like during the Dust Bowl, it would be rural working families and native people—those at the economic margins of society—
who'd pay the greatest price for this crisis, which the government blamed
on forces beyond its control: environmental conditions and depressed
global salmon prices. The reality was that the Canadian government had
grossly mismanaged the fishery with unsustainable catch levels and
lacked the political will to protect the salmon from industrialists and
developers. Urban sprawl, highways, pollution from mining, farming and
pulp mills, hydroelectric dams and especially industrial logging or "clear-
cutting" destroyed river and stream habitats critical to salmon.

Even though purse seine boats—which had wiped out Monterey's
sardines in the 1940s—posed the greatest threat to the industry and
were also the most overcapitalized, it was the smaller hook-and-line and
gillnet fishermen who were targeted with the biggest cuts. According to
one fisheries economist, the government's policy was "a clear threat to
smaller fishing communities." The native village of Ahousat (which
Ricketts visited in 1945), for example, lost half its jobs as a result of this
skewed policy. The big fish companies, merging into even bigger food
conglomerates with supermarket chains, would weather this storm.

By 2001, the cumulative effect of fish stock depletions, fleet down-
sizing and downturns in the coastal forestry industry caused the largest
population decline on the rural coast in modern history. Several coastal
communities lost more than a quarter of their citizens. I actually met
fishermen—and in one case an entire family—who lost their homes.
They piled their worldly possessions onto their fishing boats to wander
the coast like marine "Okies." Down on the docks, other fishermen,
forced out of the inshore salmon fishery, were strapping huge fuel drums
to the decks of their small vessels. They were traveling 100–200 miles
off the coast to go tuna fishing. It was a desperate, even deadly, act since
their forty-foot boats weren't designed to weather offshore storms.

One day a fisherman who had bought my grandfather's boat, the
Terry Wayne (named after my uncles Terry and Wayne), arrived in Ucluelet on a refitted North Sea trawler. He had sold his small salmon fishing
boat and bought this larger vessel, which he converted to a tuna boat. He
gave me a tour of the freshly painted ship with its new freezers and an
engine so spick-and-span you could cook steak on its manifold. He

looked bug-eyed and spoke anxiously, though. He knew there was no future for small-boat fishermen on the coast. He bought a big boat and was leaving his family and going west. He was going so far west that it sounded like the Far East to me. "I'm going to Midway and the South Pacific," he said. He was heading to the new Wild West, a largely lawless realm of unfettered opportunity and unclaimed bounty—the high seas.

*　*　*

THE ocean is humanity's last frontier. Nearly two hundred years ago, Lord Byron wrote these words:

> *Roll on, thou deep and dark blue Ocean—roll!*
> *Ten thousand fleets sweep over thee in vain;*
> *Man marks the earth with ruin—his control*
> *Stops with the shore.*

Ruin indeed. In the past four centuries, human conquest has extirpated some 750 animal species worldwide. The rate of extinction is between one hundred and two hundred times higher than in geologic times. Yet only now are we beginning to understand the consequences of our exploitation of the sea. "People can, in fact, ruin the sea as surely as they can ruin the land," explains a group of international fisheries scientists. "The only difference is that ecological destruction in the ocean is harder to see, particularly when the damage is inflicted on the delicate and largely invisible web of marine life."

Ed Ricketts, as we have read, was one of the first to understand this "invisible web" at work in the ocean. On their Gulf of California trip in 1940, he and Steinbeck came across a Japanese fishing fleet working the Mexican coast. There were six shrimp dredgers and a 10,000-ton factory ship anchored farther offshore. They went aboard one of the boats and were aghast at what they saw. The Japanese fishermen were scooping up everything in the ocean, scraping the seafloor clean. They threw the unwanted fish or "bycatch" overboard, keeping only the shrimp.

"We liked the people on this boat very much," Steinbeck and Ricketts wrote in *Sea of Cortez*. "They were good men, but they were caught in a large destructive machine, good men doing a bad thing. With their many and large boats, with their industry and efficiency, but most of all with their intense energy, these Japanese will obviously soon clean out the shrimps of the region. And it is not true that a species thus attacked comes back. The disturbed balance often gives a new species ascendancy and destroys forever the old relationship."

The vicious cycle that Ricketts first identified in the sardine fishery, and also saw in the shrimp fishery, would eventually repeat itself in every ocean on earth. "In the good years," Ricketts wrote of the sardine industry, "tons and tons of fish are being reduced, the canneries get larger, there are more of them, they spread out to the west coast of Vancouver Island, to the Oregon coast, to Ensenada, the fishing boats get larger and finer, there are more of them, they're better equipped, and the fishermen themselves become more skillful. So finally an industry gets built up that not only can handle these bumper crops, but that has to have them in order to operate."

In the decades after Ricketts' death in 1948, massive industrial fleets of seine boats, factory ships and bottom trawlers would be built and plough the ocean, scouring it of life. World fish harvests would soar from twenty million tonnes in 1950 to more than ninety million in 2000.

Scientists are only now coming to realize that overexploitation of the world's fisheries may, in fact, be changing the very structure of marine food webs in the ocean. Researchers are employing the same basic methodology that Ed Ricketts used in his seminal sardine study. They are combining decades of fishery and environmental data with models of marine food webs to understand the natural and man-made factors depleting global fisheries. It is exactly what Ricketts did, except their databases are far more comprehensive and they are using complex computer modeling to spew out their dire analysis.

An influential study, "Fishing Down Marine Food Webs," published in the journal *Science* in 1998, showed that since 1950 global catches have shifted away from species high on the food web, such as tuna, swordfish and cod, to species lower on the food web, such as anchovies and shrimp. Another study of global catch data published in 2003 also found that the number of large, predatory fish species in the world's oceans declined by 90 percent since 1950. "From giant blue marlin to mighty bluefin tuna and from tropical groupers to Antarctic cod, industrial fishing has scoured the global ocean," said one of the study's authors. "There is no blue frontier left."

Yet the serial depletion of species went unnoticed until recently because catches stayed high as fleets fished down the food web and as aquaculture production—the so-called "blue revolution"—flooded fish markets from San Francisco to Tokyo. From 1996 to 2000 alone, marine aquaculture production jumped by 40 percent worldwide.

Having depleted the ocean, we are now trying to domesticate it by "farming" fish. The U.S. government is even proposing new legislation to privatize the ocean within the two-hundred-mile Exclusive Economic Zone by promoting fish farming in much the same way that pioneers settled the West. In the words of one newspaper reporter, who obtained a draft of the proposed legislation, "Look out at the boundless ocean, and envision a new Iowa—homesteaded by fish farm colonies . . . with row upon row of undersea cages roiling with swimming livestock."

Today, the outer shores of the North Pacific represent a tragic microcosm of the world at large. In British Columbia, pristine inlets are being turned into the aquatic equivalent of industrial feedlots with thousands of fish crammed into tiny floating pens. The fish are particularly susceptible to disease and sea lice infestation, are fed pellets and dyes to color their flesh, and contain a level of toxic PCBs seven times higher than in wild salmon. Production from this type of industrial salmon farming soared from 15,500 tonnes in 1990 to 89,000 tonnes in 2002, while wild salmon catches plummeted.

What remains of the wild fisheries, including groundfish, black cod and halibut, among others, are being privatized. The fish in the ocean are being divvied up into individual quotas owned by corporations and so-called "arm chair" fishermen who trade and lease their quotas for profit. Tenant fishermen, not unlike the tenant farmers depicted in *The Grapes of Wrath*, often pay usurious "rents" equivalent to 70 percent of the revenue from their catches to the quota owners. Poorer rural and aboriginal fishermen have been pushed off the sea, as quota holdings are consolidated in the hands of a rich few. Of the 1,006 quota licences in B.C., for example, only thirteen are owned by people living on the outer shores of Vancouver Island. A billionaire businessman, Jimmy Pattison, now owns more fishing licences than all these communities combined.

Coastal and aboriginal people are losing their connection to the sea. With declining populations, high unemployment and associated social problems such as suicide, alcoholism and domestic violence, coastal communities have now become expendable in the eyes of corporations and a royalty-hungry government pushing for industrial fish farms and petroleum exploration on the seafloor. This "wave of the future" has overwhelmed many. Most people feel helpless in the face of this economic tsunami promising billions in investment and thousands of jobs.

Are we slaves to a great industrial machine, or "monster" as Steinbeck called it, or are we a species living in mutual dependence with our natural environment? It seems we have failed to heed the one biological truth so evident in the various writings of Ricketts, Steinbeck and Campbell: humans, like other animals, live in communities. Our traditional knowledge, connection to place, dependence on clean air and water, and intergenerational bonds are part of a lifecycle that has allowed us to thrive in nature and persevere despite history's travails. Destroy this organic entity or try to replace it with the harsh mathematics of a corporate ledger or sever a community's connection to the land and sea, and you'll ultimately destroy what makes us human. We will become the brutal machines we have created.

We are industrializing, domesticating and ultimately privatizing the ocean with the same folly with which we settled the Great Plains: preemption by pioneers turned native territory into private property. Trees were cut, minerals extracted and wilderness cleared for family farms, which were later consolidated by banks, agribusiness and food conglomerates infatuated with the efficiency of industrial feedlots, hormone-enhanced milk production and genetically modified crops. Steinbeck first lashed out against this system, foretelling today's backlash by organic farmers and local farmers' markets. "Men ate what they had not raised, had no connection with the bread," Steinbeck wrote in *The Grapes of Wrath*, about our growing disconnection with nature and obsession with the machine. "The land bore under iron, and under iron gradually died; for it was not loved or hated, it had no prayers or curses."

In the Gulf of California, Ricketts and Steinbeck saw the sea bear under the iron of industrial fishing with similar consequences. The waste and overexploitation of the sea was, they thought, "a true crime against nature and against . . . the eventual welfare of the whole human species."

* * *

IN the late 1990s, a strange phenomenon occurred on the Pacific Coast. After an absence of almost fifty years, sardines started reappearing in the waters off Vancouver Island and Monterey. "They're most definitely back," a biologist for the California Department of Fish and Game told the *Monterey County Herald.* "The population of sardines off the coast is well into the realm of a recovered fishery." In 1999, the first new sardine boat in over half a century arrived at Moss Landing in Monterey Bay and a new cannery was built in Salinas. (Bylaws prohibit new canneries on Cannery Row.) And a small, pilot fishery with seven seine boats began fishing for sardines off Vancouver Island. Ed Ricketts had predicted that the sardine would bounce back—though he never imagined it would take half a century.

With the return of the sardine comes a time for reflection. That silvery little fish has become synonymous with Steinbeck's famous novel, which scientists even quote occasionally and perfunctorily in their research. With the exception of *Between Pacific Tides*, citations of Ricketts' pioneering ecological research are few and far between since he was never published in scholarly journals. In an odd twist of fate, there is more of Ed Ricketts in John Steinbeck's canon than probably all the scientific journals of the twentieth century. A man who dedicated his life to gathering facts about the natural world has become, himself, a fiction.

Yet whether you hear his voice directly—in *Between Pacific Tides, Sea of Cortez*, or even this book—or whether you hear it echo in a Steinbeck novel or in bits of Joseph Campbell's mythological musings, you'll realize that Ed Ricketts was a man before his time. Or perhaps, as Steinbeck said, Ricketts simply had "a timeless mind, not modern and not ancient." His ideas seem as contemporary today as when he first wrote them half a century ago. His ecological approach and ethic, and espe-cially his warnings about the excesses of humanity's material pursuit and technological mania, have become more relevant than ever to a genera-tion now waking to full environmental consciousness. Ed Ricketts, it seems, is bouncing back with the sardines.

NOTES

BY and large, I have attempted to piece together this book through primary sources, principally letters, journals, ships' logs, unpublished and published essays, research papers, official records, and taped and personal interviews. Materials pertaining to Ed Ricketts are scattered in several archives, including the Monterey Public Library, the National Steinbeck Center in Salinas, the Joseph Campbell & Marija Gimbutas Library in Santa Barbara, Hopkins Marine Station in Monterey, San José State University, and several personal collections. The vast majority of Ricketts' papers, however, are housed within the Department of Special Collections of Stanford University Libraries, including some three hundred personal letters. I have quoted generously and extensively from all these collections.

Ricketts' writing, according to those who knew him, was very much like his speech. He wrote in a colloquial style and often used abbreviations, such as "thru" for through, "PG" for Pacific Grove or "JS" for John Steinbeck. Many of his letters and unpublished papers also contain errors in punctuation, grammar and spelling. When quoting from these texts, I have corrected small mistakes and replaced abbreviated words for clarity. All other modifications are noted in brackets.

Finally, the word *Indian* is falling out of usage in Canada because of its colonial connotations. It is still used by some, however, such as the Union of B.C. Indian Chiefs. I have used the word *Indian*, in places, because it accurately reflects the vernacular of the period, if not necessarily my personal preference.

PROLOGUE
PAGE

xii. **"Man's greed killed off the fish"**: Quoted in Hedgpeth. *The Outer Shores: Part II*, p. 45.

CHAPTER I
PAGE

1. **Campbell epigraph**: Campbell, Joseph. *The Hero with a Thousand Faces,* Princeton: Princeton University Press, 1949, p. 3.
3. **"One look into his mild but goatish eyes"**: Steinbeck, Carol. Transcript of interview with George Robinson, 1977. Courtesy of the National Steinbeck Center, Salinas.
3. **"Double crotches or a skirt"**: See Monterey County Historical Society website for Pacific Grove's early history: http://users.dedot.com/mchs/pacific-grove.html.
4. **There was even gossip circulating**: Ricketts, Edward F. "Ed Ricketts Covers the Waterfront for 20 Years," *Monterey Peninsula Herald.* Monterey, Feb. 27, 1942, pp. 1–2.
4. **The person immediately suspected the worst**: Ricketts, Anna. "Anna Ricketts Recollections," unpublished, July 4, 1984, p. 16. Courtesy of Ed Ricketts Jr.
4. **The laboratories had been moved**: "A brief chronology of ownership of the property at 800 Cannery Row, compiled from public documents." Courtesy of the California History Room, Monterey Public Library.
5. **The corner of Ocean View and Irving**: Shillinglaw, Susan. "Introduction," in Steinbeck, John. *Cannery Row,* New York: Penguin Books, 1995, p. xxiii.
5. **"A queer and secretive business"**: Ricketts, Edward F. Letter to Dick Albee, March 4, 1938. Courtesy of the Department of Special Collections, Stanford University Libraries.
6. **"It was rather a startling figure"**: Steinbeck, John. "About Ed Ricketts," *The Log from the Sea of Cortez,* New York: Penguin Books, 1995, p. 236.
6. **"An abortion"**: Benson, Jackson J. *The True Adventures of John Steinbeck, Writer,* New York: Penguin Books, 1990 (first edition 1984 by Viking Press), p. 151.
7. **Meeting at dentist's office**: See Rodger,

Katharine A. (ed.). *Renaissance Man of Cannery Row: The Life and Letters of Edward F. Ricketts,* Tuscaloosa: University of Alabama Press, 2002, p. xxiii. Also, according to *Polk's Salinas, Monterey, Pacific Grove and Carmel City Directory* of 1930, Dr. Curry's office and home were in Pacific Grove and not New Monterey as Steinbeck wrote in his essay "About Ed Ricketts" in *The Log from the Sea of Cortez.*
7. **"A bloody molar"**: Steinbeck. "About Ed Ricketts," *The Log from the Sea of Cortez,* p. 229.
7. **"From birth, a child of intelligence and rare charm"**: Rodger, p. xv.
8. **"At the age of six"**: Rodger, p. xv.
8. **"The proverbial solitary and self-reliant pathfinder"**: See Cowles, H. C. "The ecological relations of the vegetation on the sand dunes of Lake Michigan," *Botanical Gazette,* 27: 95–117, 167–202, 281–308, 361–391, 1899. The quote is from Worster, Donald. *Nature's Economy: The Roots of Ecology*, San Francisco: Sierra Club Books, 1977, p. 208.
8. **"The economy of nature"**: Haeckel's definition quoted in Worster. *Nature's Economy,* p. 192.
9. **"An underlying pervasive element"**: Allee, Warder Clyde. *The Social Life of Animals,* Chicago: University of Chicago Press, 1938, p. 49.
9. **"[T]he principle of co-operation"**: Allee, Warder Clyde. *Animal Life and Social Growth,* Baltimore: The Williams and Wilkins Co., 1932, pp. 148–149.
9. **"A member of a small group of 'Ishmaelites'"**: Allee, Warder Clyde. Letter to Joel W. Hedgpeth, September 18, 1950. Quoted in Hedgpeth. *The Outer Shores: Part I,* p. 5.
9. **A year later Ricketts' first and only son**: Rodger, p. xxi.
9. **"[I]t was a sunny day"**: Ricketts, Anna. "Anna Ricketts Recollections," unpublished, July 4, 1984, p. 1. Courtesy of Ed Ricketts Jr.
10. **One of the first scientists, along with Victor E. Shelford**: Shelford studied at the Minnesota Seaside Station on Vancouver Island around 1905 and at Friday Harbor Laboratories in Puget Sound between 1914 and 1930. See Benson, Keith R. "Experimental Ecology on the Pacific Coast: Victor Shelford and His Search for Appropriate Methods," Seattle:

Department of Medical History and Ethics, University of Washington, unpublished paper, undated. Courtesy of the Keith R. Benson.

10. **"Ed was not a rebel against society"**: Hedgpeth. *The Outer Shores: Part II*, p. 38.

10. **"Ricketts didn't know how to lie"**: Ricketts, Ed Jr. Interview, June 12, 1999. Ed Jr. attributes this comment to Jean Ariss.

10. **"Knowing Ed Ricketts was instant"**: Steinbeck. "About Ed Ricketts," *The Log from the Sea of Cortez*, p. 230.

10. **Campbell's early life**: Larsen, Stephen and Robin Larsen. *A Fire in the Mind: The Life of Joseph Campbell*, New York: Doubleday, 1991, p. 50

11. **"I have been living aloof"**: Larsen and Larsen, p. 149.

13. **"John has a fine, deep, living quality"**: Larsen and Larsen. p. 166.

13. **"[Ed] developed a theory"**: Steinbeck, Carol. Transcript of interview with George Robinson, 1977. Courtesy of the National Steinbeck Center, Salinas.

13. **"[H]e had no subject of his own"**: Benson. *The True Adventures of John Steinbeck, Writer*, p. 174

14. **"That was my party to start me out on life"**: Campbell, Joseph. Transcript of interview with Pauline Pearson, November 28, 1983. Courtesy of the National Steinbeck Center, Salinas.

14. **"Really, I've got the message of 'Roan Stallion,' "**: Campbell, Joseph. Transcript of interview with Pauline Pearson, November 28, 1983. Courtesy of the National Steinbeck Center, Salinas.

15. **"Took something home from Carol's gift"**: Larsen and Larsen, p. 181.

15. **"She was resilient and alive"**: Campbell, Joseph. Transcript of interview with Pauline Pearson, November 28, 1983. Courtesy of the National Steinbeck Center, Salinas.

15. **"She looked particularly sweet"**: Larsen and Larsen, p. 182.

15. **The situation came to a head**: Larsen and Larsen, p. 189.

15. **The thirty-four-year-old biologist found himself**: Larsen and Larsen, p. 175.

16. **"When I first met him"**: Steinbeck. "About Ed Ricketts," *The Log from the Sea of Cortez*, p. 259.

16. **"How they stayed together"**: Ricketts, Nancy. Interview, July 16, 2002.

16. **"Don't try to change me"**: Ricketts, Nancy. Interview, July 19, 2002.

16. **On June 26, 1932, Ed sent a wire**: Calvin, Jack. "Grampus Log 1932," Courtesy of Mary Purvis (granddaughter of Jack Calvin).

16. **"With a noble, manly handshake"**: Larsen and Larsen, p. 200.

17. **"Not quite a guru"**: Larsen and Larsen, p. 204.

17. **"I have still a deep nostalgia"**: Campbell, Joseph. Letter to Edward F. Ricketts, October 1, 1944. Courtesy of the Department of Special Collections, Stanford University Libraries.

17. **"Coffee-house conviviality"**: Ariss, Bruce. *Inside Cannery Row*, Pacific Grove: Lexikos, 1988, p. 14.

18. **"I never heard anything like it"**: Toni Volcani (Jackson). Interview, June 15, 2002.

18. **"Smiled sweetly and waved two fingers"**: Steinbeck, John. "About Ed Ricketts," *The Log from the Sea of Cortez*, p. 253.

18. **This other Bruce**: Cook, Andrew. "Original Bond's life of Reilly," *Times Online*, November 23, 2002, http://www.timesonline.co.uk/article/o,,1178-488420,00.html

18. **"His nose exploded"**: Ariss, p. 91.

18. **He was a colleague of Sidney Reilly**: Cook, Andrew. "Original Bond's life of Reilly," *Times Online*, November 23, 2002, http://www.timesonline.co.uk/article/o,,1178-488420,00.html

18. **The Scotsman was a womanizer**: Young, Kenneth (ed.). *The Diaries of Sir Robert Bruce Lockhart, 1915–1938*, London: MacMillan, 1973, pp. 7–21 and pp. 286–288.

19. **But according to his detailed diaries**: Lockhart, Sir Robert Bruce. Diaries. Courtesy of the House of Lords Record Office, London, United Kingdom.

19. **"Beat the shit out of 007"**: This boast was made by Bruce Ariss to Ed Ricketts, who relayed it to his friend, Don Henry, in an e-mail on June 7, 2000. Courtesy of Ed Ricketts Jr.

19. **"It was to have been the lone child"**: Steinbeck, John. "About Ed Ricketts," *The Log from the Sea of Cortez*, p. 236.

19. **He would drain their blood**: Ariss. *Inside Cannery Row*, p. 75.

19. **INJECT RICKETTS**: Ricketts, Edward F. Letter to Evelyn Ott, early 1940. Courtesy of Ed Ricketts Jr.

19. **"It saddened Ed a little"**: Steinbeck.

"About Ed Ricketts," *The Log from the Sea of Cortez*, p. 237.

20. **"The people of the Row really loved Ed"**: Steinbeck. "About Ed Ricketts," *The Log from the Sea of Cortez*, p. 241.

20. **"Cats, unlimited number"**: Ricketts, Edward F. "Pricelist given Gabe Bicknell Febr. 25, 1937." Courtesy of the Department of Special Collections, Stanford University Libraries.

21. **"I don't know what you guys do with all the money"**: Ricketts, Edward F. Letter to Harold "Gabe" Bicknell, October 26, 1937. Courtesy of the Department of Special Collections, Stanford University Libraries.

21. **"Almost invariably"**: Ricketts, Edward F. Letter to Harold "Gabe" Bicknell, January 28, 1939. Courtesy of the Department of Special Collections, Stanford University Libraries.

21. **"Financial jam"**: Ricketts, Edward F. Letter to Harold "Gabe" Bicknell, January 28, 1939. Courtesy of the Department of Special Collections, Stanford University Libraries.

22. **"Are so related to their parts"**: Ritter, William Emerson and Edna W. Bailey. "The Organismal Conception: Its Place in Science and Its Bearing on Philosophy," *University of California Publication in Zoology*, XXXI (1931), p. 307.

22. **"All life forms"**: Quoted in Astro, Richard. *John Steinbeck and Edward F. Ricketts: The Shaping of a Novelist*, Minneapolis: University of Minnesota Press, 1973, p. 65.

22. **"The artist is simply the spokesman"**: Steinbeck, John. Letter to George Albee, 1933. Quoted in Steinbeck, Elaine and Robert Wallsten (eds.). *A Life in Letters*, New York: Penguin Books, 1989, pp. 80–81.

23. **Doc is, in fact, modeled directly on Ed Ricketts**: Astro, p. 122.

23. **"I want to watch these group-men"**: Steinbeck, John. *In Dubious Battle*. New York: Bantam Books, 1966 edition (1936), p. 104.

CHAPTER 2
PAGE

25. *Sea of Cortez* **epigraph**: Ricketts, Edward F. and John Steinbeck. *Sea of Cortez: A Leisurely Journal of Travel and Research*. Mount Vernon, NY: Paul P. Appel, 1941, p. 73. (*The Log*, p. 61.)

27. *Of Mice and Men* **was one of his favorites**: Ricketts, Ed Jr. Interview with author, June 6, 2002.

27. **"A sort of cottage industry"**: Astro, p. 6.

28. **By 1931, a typescript was taking shape**: Hedgpeth. *The Outer Shores: Part I*, p. 25.

28. **"Ed had no talent for systemic zoology"**: Hedgpeth. *The Outer Shores: Part I*, p. 29.

28. **"I am rather averse to setting down on paper"**: Fisher, W. K. Letter to William Hawley Davis, Stanford University Press, December 2, 1931. Courtesy of Joel W. Hedgpeth.

29. **"Knife edge"**: Ricketts, Edward F. "Zoological Introduction," quoted in Hedgpeth. *The Outer Shores: Part I*, p. 26.

29. **"I have found few, very few"**: Fisher, W. K. Letter to William Hawley Davis, Stanford University Press, February 29, 1936. Quoted in Hedgpeth. *The Outer Shores: Part I*, p. 27.

29. **"Startling perception"**: Hedgpeth. *The Outer Shores: Part I*, p. 28.

29. **"May well have delayed progress"**: Hedgpeth. *The Outer Shores: Part I*, p. 28.

29. **"He was a little pixie"**: Steinbeck, Carol. Transcript of interview with George Robinson, 1977. Courtesy of the National Steinbeck Center.

30. **"Impressed with a sense of stillness"**: Ricketts, Edward F. Letter to Mr. Erickson, December 16, 1936. Courtesy of Stanford University Special Collections.

31. **He almost wept from the generosity**: Ricketts, Edward F. Letter to C. E. S. Wood, December 26, 1936. Courtesy of the Department of Special Collections, Stanford University Libraries.

31. **"This is a book for laymen"**: Steinbeck, John. "Foreword," Edward F. Ricketts and Jack Calvin. *Between Pacific Tides*. Stanford: Stanford University, 2nd ed., 1948, p. vi.

32. **"The first work of its kind"**: McCosker, John E. "Ed Ricketts: A Role Model for Marine Biologists," *Steinbeck Newsletter*, Fall 1995, p. 12.

32. **"The pleasant and absurd hermit crabs"**: Ricketts, Edward F. and Jack Calvin. *Between Pacific Tides*, 3rd ed., Stanford: Stanford University Press, 1962, p. 21.

32. **"May conceivably make understandable"**: Ricketts and Calvin, p. 40.

32. **"Confronted with a mystery"**: Ricketts and Calvin, p. 155.

32. **"Great fleas have little fleas"**: Ricketts and Calvin, p. 68.

33. *"Between Pacific Tides* **was a great depar-**
ture": Tiffney, Wesley N. "Introduction: A
Scientist's Perspective," Beegel, Susan F.,
Susan Shillinglaw and Wesley N. Tiffney Jr.
(eds.). *Steinbeck and the Environment,*
Tuscaloosa: University of Alabama Press,
1997, p 6.
33. **"Some importance for the course of**
Steinbeck's life": Benson. *The True*
Adventures of John Steinbeck, Writer, p.396.
34. **"They can't shoot me":** Steinbeck, John.
Letter to Carlton A. Sheffield, June 23,
1939. Quoted in *Steinbeck: A Life in Letters,*
p. 187.
34. **In 1984, a newspaper:** "FBI spied on
Steinbeck, file shows," *Oakland Tribune,*
June 16, 1984, p. A6.
35. **"Grew largely from his interest":** Astro,
Richard. *John Steinbeck and Edward F.*
Ricketts: The Shaping of a Novelist.
Minneapolis: University of Minnesota
Press, 1973, p. 119.
35. **"Print a small edition":** Steinbeck, John.
Letter to Elizabeth Otis, 1938. Quoted in
Steinbeck: A Life in Letters, p. 173.
35. **After one month:** Parini, Jay. *John*
Steinbeck: A Biography, London: Random
House, 1997, p. 226.
35. **"If only a couple of million":** Parini, p.
219.
35. **"Shockingly low":** Steinbeck, John. Letter
to Pascal Covici, January 1, 1939. Quoted in
Steinbeck: A Life in Letters, p. 174.
35. **"A nightmare all in all":** Steinbeck, John.
Letter to Elizabeth Otis, October 1939.
Quoted in *Steinbeck: A Life in Letters,* p. 189.
35. **Hollywood stars quickly came knock-**
ing: Benson. *The True Adventures of John*
Steinbeck, Writer, p. 416.
36. **"This whole thing is getting me down":**
Steinbeck, John. Letter to Elizabeth Otis,
June 22, 1939. Quoted in *Steinbeck: A Life in*
Letters, p. 185.
36. **"A secluded canyon":** Cameron, Tom.
"The Grapes of Wrath Author Guards Self
from Threats at Moody Gulch," *Los Angeles*
Times, July 9, 1939, pp. 1–2.
36. **In late July:** Benson. *The True Adventures of*
John Steinbeck, Writer, p. 412.
36. **"Once, when I had suffered":** Steinbeck,
John. "About Ed Ricketts," *The Log from the*
Sea of Cortez. p. 255. Steinbeck does not
mention the date of this incident, but it
probably occurred shortly after he left
Hollywood and stayed with Ricketts for
several days. He had certainly suffered an
"overwhelming emotional upset" at the
time. Also see Benson. *The True Adventures*
of John Steinbeck, Writer, p. 413.
37. **"The last two days":** Quoted in Benson.
The True Adventures of John Steinbeck, Writer,
p. 424.
37. **"Dear Dook":** Steinbeck, John. Letter to
Carlton A. Sheffield, November 13, 1939.
Quoted in *Steinbeck: A Life in Letters.* pp.
193–194.
38. **"A sort of sea anchor":** Benson. *The True*
Adventures of John Steinbeck, Writer, p. 401.
39. **"Mr. Steinbeck almost always":** Wilson,
Edmund. "The Californians: Storm and
Steinbeck," *The New Republic.* December 9,
1940, pp. 785–787.
39. **One event effected a sea-change:**
Worster. "Chapter 12: Dust Follows the
Plow," *Nature's Economy,* pp. 219–254.
40. **"The land bore under iron":** Steinbeck.
The Grapes of Wrath, New York: Bantam
Book, 1966, p. 30.
40. **"The only major literary figure":**
Benson. *The True Adventures of John*
Steinbeck, Writer, p. 431.
40. **Proclaiming Steinbeck a conservation-**
ist: See Beegel, Susan F., Susan Shillinglaw
and Wesley N. Tiffney, Jr. (eds.) *Steinbeck*
and the Environment. Tuscaloosa: University
of Alabama Press, 1997.
40. **"The study of animal communities":**
Quoted in Hedgpeth. *The Outer Shores: Part*
I, p. 35.
40. **"Our fingers turned over the stones":**
Ricketts and Steinbeck. *Sea of Cortez,* p.
270. (*The Log,* p. 224.)
41. **On the side of the truck:** Quoted in
Benson. *The True Adventures of John*
Steinbeck, Writer, p. 428.
41. **"I can't tell you":** Steinbeck, John. Letter
to Elizabeth Otis, December 15, 1939.
Quoted in *Steinbeck: A Life in Letters,* p. 197.
41. **Ricketts first collected:** Hedgpeth, Joel.
W. "John Steinbeck: Late Blooming
Environmentalist." Beegel *et al* (eds.).
Steinbeck and the Environment, Tuscaloosa:
University of Alabama Press, 1997, p. 299.
43. **"Perhaps the strangest crew":** Costello,
Jimmy. "Steinbeck, Ricketts Embark on
Cruise," *Monterey Peninsula Herald,* March
11, 1940, pp. 1–2.
43. **A published picture:** Enea, Sparky and
Audry Lynch. *With Steinbeck in the Sea of*
Cortez. Los Osos: Sand River Press, 1991, p.
9.
43. **"Like a perplexed and mournful bull":**

Ricketts and Steinbeck. *Sea of Cortez*, p.29. (*The Log*, p. 25.)

43. **"The first rule of life is living"**: Ricketts and Steinbeck. *Sea of Cortez*, p.29. (*The Log*, p. 26.)

45. **"Speculative metaphysics"**: Steinbeck, John. "About Ed Ricketts." *The Log from the Sea of Cortez*, p. 256.

46. **By this point Ricketts:** Enea and Lyn. *With Steinbeck in the Sea of Cortez*, p. 61.

46. **"I had kept up in good spirits"**: Quoted in Hedgpeth. *The Outer Shores. Part II*, p. 151.

46. **A longing for love and companionship:** Ricketts, Nancy. Interview, July 16, 2002.

46. **Others attacked Steinbeck:** See Benson. *The True Adventures of John Steinbeck, Writer*, p.420.

46. **"The painting Steinbeck made"**: Benson. *The True Adventures of John Steinbeck, Writer*, p. 418

46. **"I have never believed"**: Benson. *The True Adventures of John Steinbeck, Writer*, p. 422.

47. **"Ed did not like his sex uncomplicated"**: Steinbeck. "About Ed Ricketts," *The Log from the Sea of Cortez*, p. 260.

47. **"This morning when I awakened Toni"**: Ricketts, Edward F. "New Series Notebook No. 4," p. 179. Courtesy of the Department of Special Collections, Stanford University Libraries.

48. **"He's hated or idealized"**: Ricketts, Edward F. "New Tidepool book," undated, p. 86. Courtesy of the Department of Special Collections, Stanford University Libraries.

48. **Ricketts gave the writer:** Ricketts, Edward F. Letter to Henry Miller, July 2, 1941. Courtesy of the Department of Special Collections, Stanford University Libraries.

48. **"I saw Ed real and whole"**: Miller, Henry. Letter to Toni Jackson, July 15, 1941. Courtesy of the Department of Special Collections, Stanford University Libraries.

48. **"The country is vast and empty"**: Miller, Henry. Letter to Ed Ricketts, June 26, 1941. Courtesy of the Department of Special Collections, Stanford University Libraries.

48. **"It would be an understatement"**: Ricketts, Edward F. Letter to John Steinbeck, August 22, 1941. Courtesy of Ed Ricketts Jr.

49. **"I find your suggestion outrageous"**: Quoted in Hedgpeth. *The Outer Shores: Part II*, p. 8.

49. **"We worked together"**: Steinbeck, John. "About Ed Ricketts," *The Log from the Sea of Cortez,* p. 256.

49. **"Undue attention"**: Ricketts and Calvin. *Between Pacific Tides.* 3rd ed., 1952, p. 9.

49. **"Bleeding the laboratory"**: Steinbeck, John. "About Ed Ricketts," in *The Log from the Sea of Cortez*, p. 271.

50. **"My study of the marine invertebrates"**: Ricketts, Edward F. Letter to Stanford University Press, February 11, 1942. Quoted in Astro, "Footnotes," p. 236.

50. **"Not only is 'Sea of Cortez' the record"**: Hyman, Stanley Edgar. "Of Invertebrates and Men," *The New Republic,* February 16, 1942.

51. **"All last week"**: Quoted in Benson. *The True Adventures of John Steinbeck, Writer*, p. 518.

51. **"The commanding officer of the unit"**: Steinbeck. "About Ed Ricketts," *The Log from The Sea of Cortez*, p. 251.

51. **"Physical decrepitude"**: Ricketts, Edward F. Letter to Remo Scardigli, January 14, 1944. Courtesy of the Department of Special Collections, Stanford University Libraries.

53. **"The feeling of persecution"**: Benson. *The True Adventures of John Steinbeck, Writer*, pp. 557–558.

53. **"Pure poison"**: Steinbeck, John. Letter to Pascal Covici, Spring 1945. Quoted in *Steinbeck: A Life in Letters*, p. 280.

53. **"The old easy relation"**: Steinbeck refers to Sheffield's letter in which he says he's afraid of the writer. See *Steinbeck: A Life in Letters*, p. 198.

53. **"You remember how happy"**: Steinbeck, John. Letter to Pascal Covici, Spring 1945. Quoted in *Steinbeck: A Life in Letters*, p. 280.

53. **"This isn't my country anymore"**: Steinbeck, John. Letter to Pascal Covici, Spring 1945. Quoted in *Steinbeck: A Life in Letters*, p. 280.

54. **"Closer than most friends"**: Benson. *The True Adventures of John Steinbeck, Writer*, p. 197.

CHAPTER 3
PAGE

55. **Campbell epigraph:** Campbell. *The Hero with a Thousand Faces*, p. 217.

57. **So loud was the ring:** Abraham, Dorothy. *Romantic Vancouver Island: Victoria Yesterday and Today*, Victoria: Acme-Buckle Printing Co. Ltd., 1964, p. 58

57. **Headlines:** *Daily Colonist.* Victoria, B.C. May 24–June 2, 1945.

58. **"The *Maquinna* is an ugly ship":** Maiden, Cecil. "Maquinna Makes Coast History." *Victoria Times.* March 24, 1951, p. 11.

58. **"Graveyard of the Pacific":** Scott, R. Bruce. *"Breakers Ahead!" on the Graveyard of the Pacific,* Sidney, B.C.: Review Publishing House, 1970.

58. **"One of the charms":** Ricketts. "Transcript" p. 1

59. **Grounded at Pachena Point:** Scott. *"Breakers Ahead!" on the Graveyard of the Pacific,* pp. 97–113.

59. **"An ocean without its unnamed monsters":** Steinbeck and Ricketts. *Sea of Cortez.* p. 31 (*The Log,* p. 27).

59. **"They that go down to the sea":** King James Bible. Psalm 107.

59. **"I have no idea":** This quote is attributed to an anonymous captain of the *Maquinna,* who was probably Captain MacKinnon. See Robertson, Neil. *The Good Ship Maquinna,* undated, p. 44. Courtesy of Special Collections, Vancouver Public Library.

59. **Long-lost brothers:** Volcani (Jackson), Toni. Interview. June 15, 2002.

59. **"Capt. MacKinnon, scotch as the country he came from":** Ricketts. "Transcript," p. 5.

60. **"Worst Run in the World":** "Worst Run in the World," *Daily Colonist,* March 13, 1977, p. 23.

61. **Maps:** See Hayes, Derek. *Historical Atlas of the North Pacific Ocean,* Vancouver: Douglas & McIntyre, 2001.

63. **"Safe landing":** Nicholson, George. *Vancouver Island's West Coast 1762–1962,* Victoria: Morriss Printing Company, 1962, p. 286.

63. **"When the tide was out":** Scott, R. Bruce. *People of the Southwest Coast of Vancouver Island,* Victoria: Morriss Printing Co., 1974, p. 61.

63. **"They are like the Gulf Indians":** Ricketts. "Transcript," p. 4.

64. **"I would read and eat and sleep":** Ricketts. "Transcript," p. 3.

65. **"One day":** Abraham, Dorothy. *Lone Cone: A Journey of Life on the West Coast of Vancouver Island,* Victoria: Tiritea, 1945, p. 62.

66. **"The flashpoint":** Kennedy, Robert F. Jr. "Foreword," *Clayoquot Mass Trials,* Ron MacIsaac and Anne Champagne (eds.),

Gabriola Island, B.C.: New Society Publishers, p. vii.

66. **"Chainsaw massacre":** Stone, Oliver. "Hollywood and our woods," *Vancouver Sun,* June 26, 1996, p. A13.

66. **The newfound waters and their creatures:** See Clemens, W. A. and G. V. Wilby. "A History of Marine Ichthyological Collections on the Pacific Coast of Canada," *Fishes of the Pacific Coast,* Ottawa: Fisheries Research Board of Canada, 1961, pp. 11–14.

67. **"The great resource":** Johnstone, Kenneth. *The Aquatic Explorers: A History of the Fisheries Research Board of Canada,* Toronto: University of Toronto Press, 1977, p. 68.

67. **The eager Americans:** Scott, R. Bruce. "Chapter 5-Botanical Beach," *People of the Southwest Coast of Vancouver Island,* Victoria: Morris Printing, 1974.

67. **Almost two-thirds of the species:** Hart, L. J. "Development of Ichthyology in the Region," *Pacific Fishes of Canada,* Bulletin 180, Ottawa: Fisheries Board of Canada, 1973, p. 5.

67. **"[T]he fever of seashore study":** Hedgpeth, Joel W. (ed.). *Treatise on Marine Ecology and Paleoecology,* Washington, D.C.: Geological Society of America, 1957, p. 3.

68. **Ricketts came up with but a trifle:** Ricketts found two articles, one by Dr. John B. Tully, director of the Pacific Biological Station, on the oceanography of Nootka Sound in the *Journal of the Fisheries Board of Canada* (1937) and another on marine invertebrates by John Macoun, who'd collected in Barkley Sound, published in *Canadian Field Naturalist* (1924).

68. **Little in the way of ecological work:** Croker, Robert A. *Pioneer Ecologist: The Life and Work of Victor Ernest Shelford, 1877–1968,* Washington: Smithsonian Institution Press, 1991, p. 55.

68. **"The cataloguing of what we've got":** Ricketts. Transcript, p. 26.

68. **"The average expedition":** Ricketts, Edward F. Letter to John Steinbeck, August 22, 1941. Courtesy of Ed Ricketts Jr.

CHAPTER 4
PAGE

71. **Ricketts epigraph:** Ricketts, Edward F. "Transcript of summer 1945 and 1946 notes based on trips to the outer shores, W

Coast Vanc Id., Queen Charlottes etc," p.
14. Courtesy of the Department of Special
Collections, Stanford University Libraries.

73. **Selling beer and hard liquor:** Guppy,
Walter. *Clayoquot Soundings: A History of
Clayoquot Sound, 1880s–1980s*, Tofino, B.C.:
Grassroots Publication, 1997, p. 8.

73. **"The liquor situation":** Ricketts.
Transcript, p. 14.

73. **Clayoquot Hotel:** White, Ruth. Interview
by author, May 26, 2002.

75. **"People rushing ashore":** Ricketts. "New
Series Notebook Number 3," June
1944–July 1945, p. 65. Courtesy of the
Department of Special Collections,
Stanford University Libraries.

75. **"He had very penetrating":** Ricketts,
Edward F. New Series Notebook Number
3, pp. 58–60; and White, Ruth. Interview
by author, May 20, 1999.

76. **"In 1945":** Ricketts. Transcript, p. 6.

76. **"To blaze the trail":** Ricketts, Edward F.
"Racism with esp re to Japanse," undated.
Courtesy of the Department of Special
Collections, Stanford University Library.

76. **"The anonymous ad":** Ricketts, Edward
F. "Letter to the editor," *Monterey Peninsula
Herald*, April 26, 1945.

77. **"All Orientals be excluded":** Bossin, Bob.
Settling Clayoquot, Victoria: Province of
British Columbia, Sound Heritage Series
Number 31, 1981, p. 71.

77. **"[A]ctually he'd reported too little":**
Ricketts. Transcript, p. 9

77. **"This whole island":** Ricketts. Transcript,
p. 8.

77. **"I almost fell down from surprise":**
Ricketts. Transcript, p. 8.

78. **"Little Kremlin":** Guppy, Walter.
Interview by author, April 21, 2002.

78. **"The name Clayoquot":** Walbran, John T.
British Columbia Coast Names, 1592–1906,
Vancouver: Douglas & McIntyre, 1971, p.
94

78. **In 1874, Frederick Christian Thornberg:**
For the island's history read: Bossin, Bob.
Settling Clayoquot, Victoria: Province of
British Columbia, Sound Heritage Series
Number 31, 1981; Guppy, Walter. *Clayoquot
Soundings: A History of Clayoquot Sound,
1880s–1980s*, Tofino, B.C.: Grassroots
Publication, 1997, p. 8.; and Nicholson,
George. "Clayoquot Sound" and "Trader
Thornberg," *Vancouver Island's West Coast,
1762–1962*. Victoria, Morris Printing
Company Ltd., 1962, pp. 86–92.

79. **Last great tribal war:** The story of this
battle, the chief and the skulls on Stubbs
Island is also recounted in Nicholson.
Vancouver Island's West Coast, pp.78–81.

79. **"Of good size":** Ricketts. Transcript, p.21

79. **"Quite easy":** Hammer, Les. "Bleached
Skulls Recall Wicked Kyuquot Raid," *Daily
Colonist*, Victoria, July 7, 1974, pp. 4, 5 and
13.

79. **"A fierce and warlike tribe":** Ricketts.
Transcript, p. 8.

81. **Similarities between Clayoquot and
Monterey:** Hemp, Michael Kenneth.
*Canny Row: A History of Old Ocean View
Avenue*. Pacific Grove: The History
Company, 1986, pp. 34–35.

81. **Sardine statistics:** Heimann, Richard
F.G., and John G. Carlisle. *The California
Marine Fish Catch for 1968 and Historical
Review 1916–1968*, Department of Fish and
Game, Fish Bulletin No. 149, 1970.

81. **Huge schools suddenly appeared:**
Nicholson. pp. 244–247.

81. **"Predictions of some value":** Ricketts,
Edward F. Essay on sardines, dated
December 4, 1946. Courtesy of the
Department of Special Collections,
Stanford University Libraries.

82. **"Had reached the very back of beyond":**
Abraham. *Lone Cone*, p. 18.

82. **"Old Testament weather":** Montgomery,
Charles. "Storm Coast," *Canadian
Geographic*, Ottawa: Royal Canadian
Geographic Society, pp. 58–70.

82. **"A nice young Indian woman":** Ricketts.
Transcript, p. 8.

CHAPTER 5
PAGE

83. *Sea of Cortez* **epigraph:** Steinbeck, John
and Edward F. Ricketts. *Sea of Cortez*.
Mount Vernon, NY: Paul P. Appel, 2nd
rep., 1982, p. 85.

85. **"It is a fabulous place":** Steinbeck.
Cannery Row, pp. 31–32.

86. **"The fusion point":** Ricketts, Edward F.
"Foreword," *Biological Material Catalogue*.
Pacific Grove: Pacific Biological
Laboratories, 1925. Courtesy of the
Department of Special Collections,
Stanford University Libraries.

86. **"A world under a rock":** Steinbeck and
Ricketts. *Sea of Cortez*, p. 38. (*The Log*, p.
33.)

86. **"An unknown and probably unknow-**

able": Ricketts. Transcript, p. 22.

86. **"Possibly the most prolific zone":** Ricketts, Edward F. and Jack Calvin. "Preface," *Between Pacific Tides.* Stanford: Stanford University Press, 1939.

86. **"A very rich region":** Ricketts. Transcript, p. 18.

86. **List of supplies:** Ricketts provided a more detailed breakdown of his equipment in his New Series Notebook No. 4 for his 1946 trip on page 56.

87. **Rain hat and magnifying glass:** Ricketts' Bausch and Lomb magnifying glass and his rain hat are on permanent display at the National Steinbeck Center in Salinas, California.

87. **"He used the glass constantly":** Steinbeck, John. "About Ed Ricketts," in *The Log from the Sea of Cortez,* p. 266.

87. **3.6-foot tide:** According to Ricketts, "The Canadian Pacific Coast tides are figured from a unique datum, the mean of all the lowest 'normal' waters, a datum about 2 feet below mean lower low water of US charts. So [3.6 feet] was about plus 1.5' [by U.S. standards]." See Ricketts. Transcript, p. 9.

87. **"Ed Ricketts had the best eyes":** De Roos, Robert. "This World," *San Francisco Chronicle.* Quoted in Hedgpeth. *The Outer Shores: Part I,* p. 42.

87. **"He would see things in tide pools":** Ruth White. Interview by author, May 20, 1999.

87. **Dropped it in a jar of Formalin:** Ricketts did not mention his preservation techniques in his "Outer Shores" notebooks. Instead, see Steinbeck and Ricketts. "A Note on Preparing Specimens," *Sea of Cortez* pp. 272–277.

88. **"The almost universal cry":** Steinbeck and Ricketts. *Sea of Cortez,* p. 275.

88. **"A fairly good method":** Steinbeck and Ricketts. *Sea of Cortez,* p. 273.

89. **"They are so delicate":** Steinbeck and Ricketts. *Sea of Cortez,* p. 274.

89. **"Sorting, laying out, preserving":** Ricketts. Transcript, p. 10.

90. **"The crowning work":** Agassiz, Louis. *Methods of Study in Natural History* (1863), New York: Arno Press, rep. 1970, p. 71.

90. **First seaside collecting trips:** Hedgpeth, Joel W. "Introduction," *Treatise on Marine Ecology and Paleoecology,* Washington, D.C.: Geological Society of America, rep. 1971, p. 5.

90. **"All these treasures of nature":** Linné quoted in Worster. *Nature's Economy,* p. 36.

91. **"[I]t seems apparent":** Steinbeck and Ricketts. *Sea of Cortez,* p. 216. (*The Log,* p. 178.)

91. **"Three co-ordinate and interlocking factors":** Ricketts and Calvin. *Between Pacific Tides,* p. 3.

92. **"[S]uch men are not really biologists":** Steinbeck and Ricketts. *Sea of Cortez,* p. 29. (*The Log* p. 25)

92. **"Vulgar sense of wonder":** Steinbeck and Ricketts. *Sea of Cortez,* pp. 68 and 73 (*The Log,* pp. 58 and 62).

92. **"So that it can be used":** Quoted in Astro, Richard. "Introduction," in John Steinbeck. *The Log from the Sea of Cortez.* p. xiv.

92. **"Ecological arrangements":** Ricketts. "Zoological Introduction," *The Outer Shores: Part I,* p. 27.

92. **"Art is a harmony parallel to nature":** Quoted in Osbon, Dian K. (ed.). *A Joseph Campbell Companion,* New York: HarperPerrenial, 1991, p. 250.

92. **"[T]he abstractor is concerned":** Ricketts, Edward F. "Scientist writes about art and defines 'abstraction,' " *Monterey Peninsula Herald,* October 31, 1941, p. 10.

92. **Ricketts ordered new reproductions:** Ricketts, Edward F. Letter to Metropolitan Museum of Art, February 15, 1937, and Letter to Museum of Modern Art, April 7, 1937. Courtesy of Department of Special Collections, Stanford University Libraries.

93. **"A radical departure":** Tarp, Fred. "John Steinbeck: Some Reflections," Richard Astro and Joel W. Hedgpeth (eds.) Steinbeck and the Sea: Proceedings of a Conference held at the Marine Science Center Auditorium, Newport, Oregon, May 4, 1974, Newport: Oregon State University, 1975, p. 30.

94. **This environmental crisis:** Worster. *Nature's Economy,* p. 253.

94. **"It is an inherent characteristic":** Quoted in Worster. *Nature's Economy,* p. 231.

94. **The earth was but water:** This account of the origin of life on Earth comes from Thurman, Harold V. *Introductory Oceanography,* 8th ed., Upper Saddle River, NJ: Prentice Hall, 1997, p. 24.

95. **"With the littoral associations":** Ricketts, Edward F. "The tide as an environmental factor chiefly with reference to

ecological zonation on the Californian coast (1934)," *The Outer Shores: Part II*, p.68.

95. **"But it was an intact":** Ricketts, Edward F. and Jack Calvin. *Between Pacific Tides.* Stanford University Press, Stanford, 1948, p. 12–13.

95. **"Some species of *Littorina*":** Ricketts and Calvin. 1948, p. 12–13.

96. **"The higher up these beasts occur":** Ricketts. Transcript, p. 11.

96. **"Phenomenal staying powers":** Ricketts and Calvin. 1948, p. 159.

97. **"Horizon makers":** Ricketts and Calvin. 1948, p. 165.

97. **One modern ecological survey:** Jamieson, G. S., S. Dixon and R. Lauzier. "Initial Evaluation of Community Structure in Goose Barnacle (*Pollicipes polymerus*) and Sea Mussel (*Mytilus californianus*) Beds off the West Coast of Vancouver Island, British Columbia," Ottawa: Canadian Science Advisory Secretariat Research Document 2001/24, 2001.

97. **"Climax community":** Hedgpeth. "Intertidal zonation," *Between Pacific Tides*, 3rd ed., p. 367.

97. **"Animals manage to survive":** Ricketts. Transcript, p. 9.

98. **"Weather so far cold":** Ricketts. "New Series Notebook No. 2," p. 73.

98. **"Triton is a fruitful deity":** Ricketts and Calvin. *Between Pacific Tides*, 3rd ed., p. 50.

100. **"The good, kind, sane little animals":** Ricketts and Calvin. *Between Pacific Tides*, 3rd ed., pp. 21, 70, 73, 192, 306.

100. **"Every generation":** Worster. *Nature's Economy*, p. 292.

101. **"Dismal science":** Worster. *Nature's Economy*, p. 114.

101. Truly **"Victorian":** Ricketts and Calvin. *Between Pacific Tides*, 3rd ed., p. 41.

101. **"Into a reflection":** Worster. *Nature's Economy*, p. 292.

101. **"The present system of international relations":** Allee, Warder Clyde. "Chapter 7: Some Human Implications," *The Social Life of Animals*, Chicago: University of Chicago, 1938.

102. **"Even the two chief philosophies":** Ricketts. "Zoological Preface to San Francisco Bay Guidebook," 1939. Quoted in Hedgpeth. *The Outer Shores: Part I*, p. 35.

102. **"A field biologist's slant":** Ricketts, Edward F. "One Man's Approach to the Problems of International Understanding,"

and cover letters to *Harper's Magazine, Atlantic Monthly, Cosmopolitan* and *Reader's Digest* dated from September 13 to December 3, 1942. Courtesy of the Department of Special Collections, Stanford University Libraries.

CHAPTER 6
PAGE

103. **Ricketts epigraph:** Ricketts, Edward F. "The Philosophy of Breaking Through." California History Room, Monterey Public Library. All the quotes in this chapter regarding this philosophical essay come from this draft, unless otherwise noted.

105. **"A marvel of skilled workmanship":** "Fine Product of Local Yard," *Daily Colonist,* Victoria, May 6, 1913.

105. **"[A] boat, above all":** Steinbeck and Ricketts. *Sea of Cortez.* p. 16 (*The Log* p. 14).

106. **"It was at Tofino":** Turner, Robert D. *Those Beautiful Coastal Liners.* Victoria: Sono Nis Press, 2001. p. 85.

107. **"Self-consciously":** Ricketts. Transcript, p. 18.

107. **"Very alert pleasant young fellow":** Ricketts. Transcript, p. 18.

107. **"When the *Princess Maquinna* was approaching":** Dr. Richard Atleo, Chief Umeek of Ahousaht. Quoted in Turner. *Those Beautiful Coastal Liners*, Contents page.

107. **"This is one of the sad":** Ricketts, Transcript, p. 18.

107. **"Saw one of those things":** Ricketts. Transcript, p. 18.

108. **"Pretty well sum up the world outlook":** Ricketts, Edward F. Letter to Joseph Campbell, October 7, 1939. Courtesy of the Department of Special Collections, Stanford University Libraries. Also see Astro, p. 14.

108. **"I think that in the [essays] you succeeded":** Ricketts, Edward F. Letter to Henry Miller, July 2, 1941. Courtesy of the Department of Special Collections, Stanford University Libraries.

109. **"The whole is necessarily everything":** Ricketts, Edward F. "Non-teleological thinking," undated, p. 20. Courtesy of the Department of Special Collections, Stanford University Libraries.

109. **"Took life and the world as they were":** Suzuki, Daisetz Teitaro. *Essays in Zen Buddhism.* London: Luzac and Company,

1933, p. 140. In *Renaissance Man of Cannery Row*, Rodger states that Ricketts' idea of "participation" which comes from non-teleological thinking "is derived from the Taoist concept of 'quietism,' in which surrendering oneself to the temporal world's limitations brings enlightenment." Ricketts himself felt that Zen Buddhism was largely derived from the teachings of the Tao brought over to Japan.

110. **"The greater the struggle"**: Suzuki, p. 16.

110. **"The deep thing"**: Ricketts. New Series Notebook No. 2, p. 222. Courtesy of the Department of Special Collections. Stanford University Libraries.

112. **"Other missionaries think the Indian"**: Ricketts. Transcript, p. 18

112. **"You must have been with Indians"**: Ricketts recorded this brief conversation in the transcript of his travel log. I've changed the wording only slightly, replacing a few pronouns.

112. **"They sat in the canoe"**: Steinbeck and Ricketts. *Sea of Cortez*, p. 74. (*The Log*, p. 63.)

112. **Back in June of 1940**: Benson. *The True Adventures of John Steinbeck, Writer*, p. 455.

113. **"A new experience for me"**: Ricketts, Edward F. Letter to Ritch and Tal Lovejoy, June 18, 1940. Courtesy of the Department of Special Collections, Stanford University Libraries.

113. **"I don't think it's much good"**: Ricketts, Edward F. Letter to Toni Jackson, March 7, 1941. Quoted in Astro, p. 136.

113. **"Anti-script"**: Ricketts, Edward F. "Thesis and Materials for a Script on Mexico," 1940. Courtesy of the Department of Special Collections, Stanford University Libraries.

113. **Yet the story is also about**: Steinbeck, John. *The Forgotten Village: With 136 Photographs from the Film of the Same Name*. New York: Viking Press, 1941.

113. **"The only heroes left"**: Quoted in Benson. *The True Adventures of John Steinbeck, Writer*, p. 401–402.

114. **"Try to bludgeon"**: Ricketts. Transcript, p. 120.

115. **"As our material prosperity increases"**: Lane, Robert E. "The Loss of Happiness in Market Democracies," *Miami Herald*, May 8, 2000.

115. **Nuu-chah-nulth phrases**: Department of Fisheries and Oceans Canada, "Backgrounder: West Coast of Vancouver Island Aquatic Management Board Terms of Reference," Ottawa: Government of Canada, (BG-PR-01-009E), February 26, 2001.

116. **"Back from the land of the dead"**: Walbran. *British Columbia Coast Names, 1592–1906*, pp. 172–174.

116. **"Examine the coast"**: Quoted in Nicholson. *Vancouver Island's West Coast, 1762–1962*, p. 35.

116. **Named after William Bligh**: Walbran. *British Columbia Coast Names, 1592–1906*, p. 54.

117. **A Chinese cook gave her**: Ricketts. Transcript, p. 17.

117. **"A monument, a table"**: Jackson, Toni (by-line "tj"). "Forgotten Nootka: Two Silver Spoons in Power Politics," *What's Doing*, Monterey, August 1946, Vol. 1 (5), p. 30.

117. **"[T]he threads connecting"**: Jackson. "Forgotten Nootka," p. 46.

118. **"Clean and well ordered"**: Ricketts. Transcript, p. 19.

118. **"Shake the fillings out of your teeth"**: Turner. *Those Beautiful Coastal Liners*, p. 87.

118. **They arrived at 7:41 P.M.**: "Official Log Book and List of Crew," S.S. *Princess Maquinna*. Ottawa: Department of Transportation, April 7, 1945 to October 17, 1945. National Archives of Canada, Ottawa.

119. **"Nothing"**: Ricketts. Transcript, pp. 20–21.

120. **The *Maquinna* squeaked and groaned**: Turner. *Those Beautiful Coastal Liners*, p. 87.

CHAPTER 7
PAGE

123. ***Cannery Row* epigraph**: Steinbeck. *Cannery Row*, pp. 6–7

125. **"They look black"**: Ricketts. Transcript, p. 12.

126. **The novel had been published**: Benson. *The True Adventures of John Steinbeck, Writer*, p. 561.

126. **"Cannery Row in Monterey in California"**: Steinbeck. *Cannery Row*, p. 5.

126. **"The book is only fiction"**: Steinbeck, John. Letter to John Forman, June 3, 1958. Quoted in *Steinbeck: A Life in Letters*, p. 585.

127. **"It's mostly about me"**: Ricketts, Edward F. Letter to Ed Ricketts. Jr, October 23, 1944. Courtesy of the Department of Special Collections, Stanford University Libraries.

127. **"A crazy kind of a book"**: Steinbeck, John.

Letter to Tal and Ritch Lovejoy, July 1944. Quoted in Benson. *The True Adventures of John Steinbeck, Writer*, p. 553.

127. **"Through the magic"**: McCosker, John E. "Ed Ricketts: A Role Model for Marine Biologists," *Steinbeck Newsletter*, San José: San José State University, Fall 1995, pp. 12–14.

127. **The author actually said as much**: Steinbeck, John. "About Ed Ricketts," *The Log from the Sea of Cortez*, p. 266.

127. **"I dislike the publicity"**: Ricketts, Edward F. Letter to Ed Ricketts. Jr, November 15, 1944. Courtesy of the Department of Special Collections, Stanford University Libraries.

127. **By January 1945**: Ricketts, Edward F. Letter to Xenia Cage, February 9, 1945. Courtesy of the Department of Special Collections, Stanford University Libraries.

127. **"I imagine Cannery Row"**: Ricketts, Edward F. Letter to Ed Ricketts Jr., May 10, 1945. Courtesy of the Department of Special Collections, Stanford University Libraries.

128. **"Once when Doc"**: Steinbeck. *Cannery Row*, pp. 99–100.

128. **However strange, the facts**: Benson. *The True Adventures of John Steinbeck, Writer*, p. 190.

128. **He even wrote about the experience**: Ricketts, Edward F. "Vagabonding Through Dixie," *Travel*, June 1925, pp. 16–18, 44, 48.

129. **Ruth White thought Ricketts was a great storyteller**: White, Ruth. Interview by author, May 20, 1999.

129. **"The lady with snake eyes"**: White, Ruth. Interview by authory, May 20, 1999.

129. **"Very briefly, this is the incident"**: Steinbeck, John. "About Ed Ricketts," *The Log from the Sea of Cortez*, pp. 238–239.

129. **"He seemed to like that story"**: White, Ruth. Interview by author. May 26, 2002.

129. **Fed everyone's curiosity**: I have drawn from two very good sources of information about Cannery Row's denizens and their connection to Steinbeck's novel: Knox, Maxine and Mary Rodriguez. *Steinbeck's Street: Cannery Row*, San Rafael, California: Presidio Press, 1980; and Mangelsdorf, Tom. *A History of Steinbeck's Cannery Row*, Santa Cruz: Western Tanager Press, 1986.

129. **"Monterey's largest, most genteel"**: Steinbeck. "About Ed Ricketts," *The Log from the Sea of Cortez*, p. 240.

130. **Her gowns had to be custom made**: Knox and Rodriguez. *Steinbeck's Street: Cannery Row*, p. 76.

130. **She opened the Lone Star Cafe in 1923**: Shillinglaw. "Introduction," *Cannery Row*, p. xxiv.

130. **"What a wonderful woman"**: Shillinglaw, "Introduction," *Cannery Row*, p. xxiv.

130. **"She's one hell of a woman"**: Steinbeck. "About Ed Ricketts," *The Log from the Sea of Cortez*, p. 241.

130. **"Dora is a great woman"**: Steinbeck. *Cannery Row*, p. 19.

130. **Won Yee opened the store in 1918**: Shillinglaw. "Introduction," *Cannery Row*, p. xxiii.

130. **"Lee Cong is more than a Chinese grocer"**: Steinbeck. *Cannery Row*, p. 17.

131. **Gabe was even looking after the lab**: Edward F. Ricketts. Letter to Bill and Ruth White, and Betty Farmer, July 16, 1945. Courtesy of the Department of Special Collections, Stanford University Libraries.

131. **"To get anything on Steinbeck"**: "Interview with Peter Stackpole, photographer," *Steinbeck Newsletter*, San José: San José State University, Fall 1995, pp. 19–23.

132. **"The ones you left out"**: Benson. *The True Adventures of John Steinbeck, Writer*, p. 562.

132. **"A trivial and seemingly meaningless"**: Quoted in Lisca, Peter. *The Wide World of John Steinbeck*, New York: Gordian Press, 1981, p. 198.

132. **He professed to have written it**: Steinbeck, John. Letter to Carlton A. Sheffield, September 27, 1944. Quoted in *Steinbeck: A Life in Letters*, p. 273; and Steinbeck, John. Letter to Pascal Covici, January 5, 1945, quoted in Lisca, p. 208.

132. **"The superficialities"**: Ricketts, Edward F. Letter to Pat Stevens, May 1, 1945. Courtesy of the Department of Special Collections, Stanford University Libraries.

132. **The reviewers chortled**: Sexias, Antonia (Toni Jackson). "John Steinbeck and the Non-teleological Bus," reprinted in Tedlock, E. W. Jr. and C. V. Wicker (eds). *Steinbeck and His Critics*, Albuquerque: University of New Mexico Press, 1969, p. 276.

133. **"Cannery Row after hours"**: Shillinglaw. "Introduction," *Cannery Row*, p. ix

133. **"Soft and brilliant flowers"**: Steinbeck. *Cannery Row*, p. 32.

133. **"It never mentions the war"**: Steinbeck, John. Letter to Carlton A. Sheffield,

September 27, 1944. Quoted in *Steinbeck: A Life in Letters*, p. 273.

133. "A nostalgic thing": Quoted in Shillinglaw. "Introduction," *Cannery Row*, p. xxvi.

133. "Where men hungering for love": Steinbeck. *Cannery Row*, p. 18.

133. "A strange duality": Steinbeck. *Cannery Row*, p. 134.

133. "The sale of the souls": Steinbeck. *Cannery Row*, p. 135.

134. "Enlarged his scientific German": Steinbeck. "About Ed Ricketts," *The Log from the Sea of Cortez*, p. 255.

134. "The peak of an age": Ricketts, Edward F. Letter to Heinz, May 2, 1942. Courtesy of the Department of Special Collections, Stanford University Libraries.

134. "About 45 minutes": Ricketts. Transcript, p. 24.

135. Ricketts mentioned to the Clayoquot pioneers: White, Ruth. Interview by author. May 20, 1999.

135. Steinbeck wrote the novella: Steinbeck and Ricketts. *Sea of Cortez*, pp. 102–103.

135. "Dream Isle": Bossin. *Settling Clayoquot*, p. 44.

136. "The aftermath of your departure": White, Bill. Letter to Ed and Toni Ricketts, July 26, 1945. Courtesy of the Department of Special Collections, Stanford University Libraries.

136. "Devote that money and thought": Ricketts. Transcript, p. 2

136. "Prejudice blown into intolerances": Ricketts, Edward F. "What's wrong with the world," undated, p. 1. Courtesy of the Department of Special Collections, Stanford University Libraries.

136. "I got to thinking": Ricketts. Transcript, p. 26.

137. You could find any scientific discovery: Steinbeck, John. Letter to George Albee, 1933. Quoted in *Steinbeck: A Life in Letters*, p. 80.

137. "Race riot": Ricketts, Edward F. "Atom Bomb Experiment," two pages of undated notes. Courtesy of the Department of Special Collections, Stanford University Libraries.

137. "We are an engineering world": Ricketts, Edward F. "What's wrong with the world," undated essay. Courtesy of the Department of Special Collections, Stanford University Libraries.

137. The "Age of Ecology began": Worster. *Nature's Economy*, p. 339.

137. Largest underground nuclear bomb: Miller, Pam and Norman Buske. *Nuclear Flashback*. Greenpeace, 1996, http://archive.greenpeace.org/-usa/reports/nuclear/amchitka/.

138. "Fear and hatred of strangers": Ricketts. Transcript, p. 22.

138. "In the remote field of marine biology": Ricketts, Edward F. "What's wrong with the world," undated essay. Courtesy of the Department of Special Collections, Stanford University Libraries.

CHAPTER 8
PAGE

139. Steinbeck epigraph: Steinbeck, John. "About Ed Ricketts," *The Log from the Sea of Cortez*, p. 230.

141. "[T]he canneries started up": Ricketts, Edward F. Letter to Xenia Cage, October 9, 1939. Courtesy of the Department of Special Collections, Stanford University Libraries.

141. "Flora is staging": Ricketts, Edward F. Letter to Virginia Scardigli, 1941. Courtesy of the Department of Special Collections, Stanford University Libraries.

142. "The money's coming in so fast": Ricketts, Edward F. Letter to Toni Jackson, October 1940. Courtesy of the Department of Special Collections, Stanford University Libraries.

142. "Monterey is changing": Ricketts, Edward F. Letter to Cornelia Ricketts, June 20, 1941. Courtesy of the Department of Special Collections, Stanford University Libraries.

142. "Sometimes even I can't drink": Ricketts, Edward F. Letter to Cornelia Ricketts, March 16, 1942. Courtesy of Ed Ricketts Jr.

142. "There were times when we were hungry": Ricketts, Nancy. Interview by author. July 16, 2002.

143. "Spiteful on the part of the draft board": Steinbeck. "About Ed Ricketts," *The Log from the Sea of Cortez*, p. 250.

143. "I suspect somehow": Ricketts, Edward F. Letter to "Sparky" Enea, August 28, 1942. Courtesy of the Department of Special Collections, Stanford University Libraries.

143. Took up a collection for her: Ricketts, Edward F. Letter to Joseph Campbell, September 23, 1945; letter to "Sparky" Enea, September 16, 1942; and letter to Jack Calvin, April or May 1946. Courtesy of

the Department of Special Collections, Stanford University Libraries.

143. **"Kaleidoscopically"**: Ricketts, Edward F. "Ed Ricketts Covers the Waterfront for 20 Years," *Monterey Peninsula Herald*, February 27, 1942, pp. 1–2.

144. **"Ed was fuming"**: Ricketts, Anna. "Recollections," July 4, 1984, p. 55. Courtesy of Ed Ricketts Jr.

144. **"Sober for a change"**: Ricketts, Edward F. Letter to Bill and Ruth White, and Betty Farmer, July 16, 1945. Courtesy of the Department of Special Collections, Stanford University Libraries.

144. **"The fact that the institution survived"**: Steinbeck. "About Ed Ricketts," *The Log from the Sea of Cortez*, p. 271.

144. **"So, PBL is going to pieces"**: Ricketts, Edward F. Letter to Jack Calvin, April 28, 1943. Courtesy of the Department of Special Collections, Stanford University Libraries.

146. **"I am devising some printed forms"**: Ricketts, Edward F. Letter to Ed Ricketts Jr., October 5, 1945. Courtesy of the Department of Special Collections, Stanford University Libraries.

146. **Prepared a long-term program**: Ricketts, Edward F. New Series Notebook No. 3, p. 152. Courtesy of the Department of Special Collections, Stanford University Libraries.

147. **Details of costs to build lab**: Ricketts, Edward F. Letter to Bogard. December 16, 1936. Courtesy of the Department of Special Collections, Stanford University Libraries.

147. **"It is a low building"**: Steinbeck. *Cannery Row*, pp. 28–29.

149. **"A good residence and lab"**: Ricketts, Edward F. Letter to Ed Ricketts Jr., October 23, 1944. Courtesy of the Department of Special Collections, Stanford University Libraries.

150. **"We have in mind a combination"**: Ricketts, Edward F. Letter to L. R. Blinks, November 11, 1944. Courtesy of the Department of Special Collections, Stanford University Libraries.

150. **Up to $18,000**: Ricketts, Edward F. Letter to L. R. Blinks, August 11, 1945. Courtesy of the Department of Special Collections, Stanford University Libraries.

150. **"A fairly detached office"**: Ricketts, Edward F. Letter to L. R. Blinks, July 24, 1945. Courtesy of the Department of

Special Collections, Stanford University Libraries.

151. **"There was no hope"**: Ricketts, Edward F. Letter to Ed Ricketts Jr, October 5, 1945. Courtesy of the Department of Special Collections, Stanford University Libraries.

151. **"A modern miracle"**: Ricketts, Edward F. Letter to Bill White, October 22, 1945. Courtesy of the Department of Special Collections, Stanford University Libraries.

151. **"Party gal"**: Ricketts, Ed Jr. Interview by author, June 6, 2002. Ed Jr. said that Toni "liked to party and it was too much for dad" who would often go downstairs to the basement to get work done.

151. **Ricketts left at 1 A.M.**: Ricketts, Edward F. New Series Notebook No. 4, p. 21. Courtesy of the Department of Special Collections, Stanford University Libraries.

152. **The deal . . . fell apart**: Ricketts, Edward F. Letter to Xenia Cage, March 3, 1946. Courtesy of the Department of Special Collections, Stanford University Libraries.

152. **Plummeted by almost 40 percent**: Heimann, Richard F. G. and John G. Carlisle. *The California Marine Fish Catch for 1968 and Historical Review 1916–1968*, Department of Fish and Game, Fish Bulletin No. 149, 1970.

153. **Ricketts wrote a "progress" report**: Ricketts, Edward F. New Series Notebook No. 4, p. 23. Courtesy of the Department of Special Collections, Stanford University Libraries.

153. **He hired Gabe**: Ricketts, Edward F. Letter to Jack Calvin, April or May 1946. See also page 24 of Ricketts' New Series Notebook No. 4 for reference to Gabe's collecting trips.

153. **"Lay a good foundation"**: Ricketts, Edward F. Letter to Joseph Campbell, April 1946. Courtesy of the Department of Special Collections, Stanford University Libraries.

153. **"Let it go that way"**: Steinbeck, John. "About Ed Ricketts," *The Log from the Sea of Cortez*, p. 266.

154. **"We had last Sunday"**: Ricketts, Edward F. Letter to John Steinbeck, April 9, 1946. Courtesy of the Department of Special Collections, Stanford University Libraries.

155. **"It's rumored up here already"**: Ricketts. Transcript, p. 101.

CHAPTER 9
PAGE

159. **"I never saw so many unappetizing women"**: Ricketts. Transcript, p. 101.
160. **"Very quiet night"**: Ricketts, Edward F. New Series Notebook No. 4, p. 64. Courtesy of the Department of Special Collections, Stanford University Libraries.
160. **"After half hour or so"**: Ricketts. Transcript, p. 102.
161. **"Vivid burnt orange"**: Ricketts. Transcript, p. 103.
161. **Ricketts had discovered another new species**: Ricketts. Transcript, p. 103.
162. **"I was starting to get a little nervous"**: Ricketts. Transcript, p. 104.
163. **"Mommy, is that Jesus"**: This story is confirmed in Ed Ricketts' Transcript notes on p. 104 as well as in an interview with Ruth White, May 20, 1999.
164. **"Made a beeline for my place"**: Ricketts. Transcript, p. 112.
164. **Even though it was summer**: Ricketts. Transcript, p. 114.
165. **"It was a lucky thing"**: Ricketts. Transcript, p. 113.
165. **"Candles tonight"**: Ricketts. Transcript, p. 109.
165. **"The wolves were howling"**: Brabant, Rev. A. J. "Reminiscences of the West Coast of Vancouver Island," in *Mission to Nootka, 1874–1900*, Charles Lillard (ed.), Sidney, BC: Gray's Publishing Ltd., 1977, p. 113.
166. **Almost single-handedly**: Lillard, Charles (ed.). *Mission to Nootka, 1874–1900*, Sidney, B.C.: Gray's Publishing Ltd., 1977, p. 5.
166. **"A superman in the eyes"**: *Golden Jubilee of Christie Indian Residential School, 1900–50*, Kakawis, Vancouver Island. Department of Special Collections, University of British Columbia. No page number.
167. **"The Indians tell their yarns"**: Brabant. "Reminiscences of the West Coast of Vancouver Island," *Mission to Nootka, 1874–1900*, p. 50.
167. **"As regards the spiritual state"**: Brabant. "Reminiscences of the West Coast of Vancouver Island," *Mission to Nootka, 1874–1900*, p. 70.
167. **"It is slow work"**: Brabant. "Reminiscences of the West Coast of Vancouver Island," *Mission to Nootka, 1874–1900*, p. 87.
167. **"If we could keep the children"**: Brabant. "Reminiscences of the West Coast of Vancouver Island," *Mission to Nootka, 1874–1900*, p. 112.
168. **Kakawis was modeled**: Canada. Royal Commission on Aboriginal Peoples. "Chapter 10: Residential Schools," *People to People, Nation to Nation: The Report of the Royal Commission on Aboriginal Peoples*. Ottawa: Government of Canada, 1996, p. 2.
168. **"Industrial school"**: *People to People, Nation to Nation: The Report of the Royal Commission on Aboriginal Peoples*, p. 8.
168. **"To kill the Indian in the child"**: *People to People, Nation to Nation: The Report of the Royal Commission on Aboriginal Peoples*, p. 24
169. **"Contagion of colonization"**: *People to People, Nation to Nation: The Report of the Royal Commission on Aboriginal Peoples*, p. 33.
169. **"Nothing more than institutional pedophilia"**: Platiel, Rudy. "Natives want Ottawa to make amends for abuse at schools," *Globe and Mail*, June 18, 1996, p. A10.
169. **"He got [caught] fooling around"**: Ricketts, Edward F. Letter to John Steinbeck, August 1946. Courtesy of the Department of Special Collections, Stanford University Libraries.
170. **"The shy little Indian children"**: Ricketts. Transcript, p. 116.
171. **"Blistering letter"**: Ricketts. Transcript, p. 117.
172. **The missionary never did ask**: Mulvihill, Rev. J. P. Letter to Joel W. Hedgpeth, February 9, 1971. Courtesy of Ed Ricketts Jr.
172. **"Distrusted all formal religions"**: Steinbeck. "About Ed Ricketts," *The Log from the Sea of Cortez*, p. 255.
172. **"The god hypothesis"**: Highfield, Roger. "50 years on, it's still science vs. God," *Vancouver Sun*, March 21, 2003, p. A15.
173. **"And it is a strange thing"**: Ricketts and Steinbeck. *Sea of Cortez*, pp. 216–217. (*The Log*, pp. 178–79.)
173. **"The Christian ideas of trinity"**: Ricketts and Steinbeck. *Sea of Cortez*, p. 148. (*The Log*, p. 123). Also see Ricketts essay on "non-teleological thinking."
173. **"Greater than Man"**: Ricketts. Transcript, p. 121.
173. **"Ed was a prophet"**: Hedgpeth. *The Outer Shores: Part II*, p. 57.
173. **"Local deity"**: Lisca. *The Wide World of John Steinbeck*, p. 214.
173. **"Loosely patterned"**: Astro. *The Shaping of a Novelist*, p. 128.

174. **Imbued with biblical imagery:** For a discussion of religious imagery and allusions in *The Grapes of Wrath* see: Owens, Louis. *The Grapes of Wrath: Trouble in the Promised Land*, Boston: Twayne Publishers, 1989; Hayashi, Tetsumaro. *Steinbeck's The Grapes of Wrath: Essays in Criticism*, Muncie, Indiana: Ball State University, Steinbeck Essay Series, No. 3, 1990; Bloom, Harold. *Bloom's Notes: John Steinbeck's* The Grapes of Wrath. Broomall: Chelsea House Publishers, 1996; and Slade, Leonard A. Jr. "Biblical Imagery in *The Grapes of Wrath*," Bender, David L. *et al* (eds.). *Readings on* The Grapes of Wrath, San Diego: Greenhaven Press, 1999, pp. 104–110.

174. **"I ain't sayin' I'm like Jesus":** Steinbeck. *The Grapes of Wrath*, p. 71.

174. **"There ain't no sin":** Steinbeck. *The Grapes of Wrath*, p. 19.

174. **"I figgered about the Holy Sperit":** Steinbeck. *The Grapes of Wrath*, p. 20.

175. **"Herd a fella tell a poem":** Steinbeck. *The Grapes of Wrath*, p. 127.

175. **Condemned it in a prominent review:** Spearman, A. D. "Steinbeck's Grapes of Wrath Branded as Red Propaganda," *San Francisco Examiner*, June 4, 1939, p. 12.

176. **"I think that we missionaries":** Mulvihill, Rev. J. P. Letter to Joel Hedgpeth, February 9, 1971. Courtesy of Ed Ricketts Jr.

CHAPTER 10
PAGE

177. **Campbell epigraph:** Campbell. *The Hero with A Thousand Faces*, p. 259.

179. **"A very curious and very lovely":** Ricketts. Transcript, p. 117.

179. **"Spectacular scenery":** Ricketts. New Series Notebook No. 4, p. 92.

180. **"Epochal voyage":** Campbell, Joseph. Letter to Edward F. Ricketts, December 26, 1941. Courtesy of the Department of Special Collections, Stanford University Libraries.

180. **"One of the primary personal transformations":** Larsen and Larsen, p. 172.

181. **"A fresh sou'easter":** Calvin, Jack. *Grampus* logbook. Courtesy of Mary Pervis.

183. **"The main steamer routes":** Ricketts, Edward F. "Notes and Observations, Mostly Ecological, Resulting From Northern Pacific Collecting Trips Chiefly in Southeastern Alaska, with Especial Reference to Wave Shock as a Factor in Littoral Ecology," 1932. Courtesy of Joel W. Hedgpeth.

183. **"This chart should not be depended upon":** Calvin, Jack. " 'Nakwasina' Goes North," *National Geographic,* July 1933, Vol LXIV, No. 1, p. 16.

183. **"Striking resemblance":** Ricketts. Transcript, p. 121.

183. **"The attenuated dawns and twilights":** Ricketts, Edward F. "Notes and Observations, Mostly Ecological, Resulting From Northern Pacific Collecting Trips Chiefly in Southeastern Alaska, with Especial Reference to Wave Shock as a Factor in Littoral Ecology," 1932 (no page number). Courtesy of Joel W. Hedgpeth.

185. **"Dirty end of the stick":** Larsen and Larsen, p. 205.

185. **"Marriage without children":** Larsen and Larsen. p. 205.

185. **"I felt suddenly sick inside":** Larsen and Larsen, p. 207.

186. **"I wouldn't be surprised":** Larsen and Larsen, p. 207.

186. **"I wasn't crazy about my sister":** Larsen and Larsen, p. 206.

187. **"Glistening with cold icy water":** Larsen and Larsen, p. 206.

187. **"Metaphysical vagabonds":** Larsen and Larsen, p. 209.

188. **"Shoes, instead of the naked earth":** Larsen and Larsen, p. 209

188. **"Conventionally dressed":** Larsen and Larsen, p. 209

189. **"The life breathing beneath":** Larsen and Larsen, p. 209

189. **"There are certainly values":** Larsen and Larsen, p. 209

189. **"To be without principles":** Larsen and Larsen, p. 209

190. **"Return trip in Model T":** Larsen and Larsen, p. 210.

190. **"Protean Ed":** Campbell, Joseph. Letter to Ed Ricketts, December 10, 1939. Courtesy of the Department of Special Collections, Stanford University Libraries.

190. **"Not quite a guru":** Larsen and Larsen, p. 204.

190. **"Every time I see a rocky coast":** Campbell, Joseph. Letter to Edward F. Ricketts, August 22, 1939. Courtesy of the Department of Special Collections, Stanford University Libraries.

191. **"I am even a little glad":** Campbell, Joseph. Letter to Edward F. Ricketts,

September 14, 1939. Courtesy of the Department of Special Collections, Stanford University Libraries.

191. **"Unified field theory"**: Campbell uses the phrase, "unified field theory," in a letter to Ricketts dated September 14, 1939. The phrase most likely comes from Ricketts, who used it repeatedly in his writing.

191. **"Marvelous form of living"**: Campbell, Joseph. Letter to Edward F. Ricketts, December 26, 1941. Courtesy of the Department of Special Collections, Stanford University Libraries.

192. **"During the past six months"**: Campbell, Joseph. Letter to Edward F. Ricketts, December 26, 1941. Courtesy of the Department of Special Collections, Stanford University Libraries.

192. **"Biologically necessary spiritual organ"**: Campbell, Joseph. "Bios and Mythos," Joseph Campbell Foundation, rep. 2001 (1951), p. 10.

192. **"Every organ of the body"**: Quoted in Cousineau, Phil (ed.). *The Hero's Journey: Joseph Campbell on His Life and Work*, San Francisco: Harper & Row Publishers, 1990, p. 159.

192. **"Dream is the personalized myth"**: Campbell. *The Hero with A Thousand Faces*, p. 19.

192. **"Marvelously constant story"**: Campbell. *The Hero with a Thousand Faces*, p. 3.

193. **"A hero ventures forth"**: Campbell. *The Hero with A Thousand Faces*, p. 30.

193. **"Proof that our thoughts"**: Campbell, Joseph. Letter to Edward F. Ricketts, December 10, 1939. Courtesy of the Department of Special Collections, Stanford University Libraries.

193. **Campbell lamented, however**: Campbell, Joseph. Letters to Edward F. Ricketts, September 14, 1939 and December 10, 1939. Courtesy of the Department of Special Collections, Stanford University Libraries.

193. **"In one sense"**: Ricketts, Edward F. "Possible Introduction to Essay IV (or V) 'Hi-Tension' or 'The Universality of Duality,' " October 29, 1939. Courtesy of the Department of Special Collections, Stanford University Libraries.

193. **"Symbolic language"**: Campbell. *The Hero with a Thousand Faces*, pp. vii–viii.

194. **They did not intend to publish the book**: Larsen and Larsen, p. 336.

195. **No book has impacted modern story-telling more**: Cousineau. *The Hero's Journey: Joseph Campbell on His Life and Work*, pp. 180–82.

195. **"[T]he story may never be told dully"**: Ricketts. "Possible Introduction to Essay IV (or V) 'Hi-Tension' or 'The Universality of Duality.' "

195. **"It is possible"**: Cousineau. *The Hero's Journey: Joseph Campbell on His Life and Work*, p. 182.

195. **Lucas modeled his trilogy**: Moyers, Bill and George Lucas. "Of Myth and Men," *Time*, April 26, 1999 (Vol. 153, No. 16), p. 1.

195. **"Is the machine going to crush"**: Campbell, Joseph, and Bill Moyers. *The Power of Myth*, New York: Doubleday, 1988, p. 18.

196. **"One of the main themes"**: Moyers, Bill and George Lucas. "Of Myth and Men," *Time*, April 26, 1999 (Vol. 153, No. 16), p. 1.

196. **"Mutual aid among animals"**: Allee, W. C. *The Social Life of Animals*, Chicago: University of Chicago, 1938, p. 49.

196. **Allee had first discovered**: Allee. *The Social Life of Animals*, p. 20.

196. **"[A]nything from Ed's lab"**: Campbell, Joseph. Letter to Edward F. Ricketts, April 3, 1947. Courtesy of the Department of Special Collections, Stanford University Libraries.

196. **He later made notes**: Larsen and Larsen, p. 171. Campbell also once told a newspaper reporter: "I was keeping a meticulous diary at that time, so I have a play-by-play of the Cannery Row (of that era), everything that went on. Some fine day when everyone's dead, I may think of publishing that." See Goodman, Al. "Scholar recalls friendship with Steinbeck," *Monterey Peninsula Herald*, December 4, 1983, p. 3B.

196. **"There should be a lot"**: Campbell, Joseph. Letter to Edward F. Ricketts, April 21, 1946. Courtesy of the Department of Special Collections, Stanford University Libraries.

CHAPTER 11
PAGE

199. **Darwin epigraph**: Darwin, Charles. *The Voyage of the Beagle*, Ware, Hertfordshire: Wordsworth Classics, 1997, p. 476.

201. **As glaciers receded**: Koppel, Tom. "How new discoveries are rewriting the history of our continent," *Vancouver Sun,* December 10, 2001 p. B4.

201. **"An evolutionary show case"**: Scudder, G.

G. E. "The Queen Charlotte Islands: overview and synthesis," Scudder, Geoffrey G. E. and Nicholas Gessler. *The Outer Shores*, Proceedings of the Queen Charlotte Islands First International Scientific Symposium, University of British Columbia, August 1984, Queen Charlotte Islands Museum Press, 1989, p. 319.

202. "Bleak desolate country": Ricketts. New Series Notebook No. 4, p. 97. Department of Special Collections, Stanford University Libraries.

202. "Everybody's certainly upset": Ricketts. New Series Notebook No. 4, p. 97.

202. "Secret voyage": Bawlf, Samuel. *The Secret Voyage of Sir Francis Drake 1577–1580*. New York: Walker & Company, 2003.

202. Dawson...named a sound and a point after Charles Darwin: Dalzell, Kathleen E. *The Queen Charlotte Islands: Volume 2 Places and Names*, Queen Charlotte City: Bill Ellis Publisher, 1973, p. 200.

202. Comparative surveys can be conducted in the same area today: Sloan, N. A. et al. *Living Marine Legacy of Gwaii Haanas: Marine Invertebrate Baseline to 2000 and invertebrate related management issues*, Ottawa: Parks Canada, Report 35, 2002, p. 51.

202. "The spirit of independence": Scudder and Gessler. *The Outer Shores*, p. i.

203. "In a way, ours is the older method": Steinbeck and Ricketts. *Sea of Cortez*, p. 61. (*The Log*, p. 51.)

203. Closely associated with non-teleological thinking: Steinbeck and Ricketts. *Sea of Cortez*, p. 135. (*The Log*, p. 112.)

203. "[I]t seems that some of the broader": Quoted in Hedgpeth. *The Outer Shores: Part II*, p. 2.

203. "I have just been reading": Ricketts, Edward F. Letter to Toni Jackson, February 28, 1941. Quoted in Hedgpeth. *The Outer Shores: Part II*, p. 7.

204. *Cassiar* description: Twigg, A. M. *Union Steamships Remembered 1920–1958*, Campbell River, B.C.: A. M. Twigg, 1997, pp. 110–112.

204. "Very evidently the skipper": Ricketts. New Series Notebook No. 4, p. 98.

205. "The poorest of dead reckoning": Ricketts. Transcript, p. 122.

206. "As beautiful [a] place": Ricketts. New Series Notebook No. 4, p. 98.

206. Almost nine hours overdue: Ricketts. New Series Notebook No. 4, p. 98.

206. People rushed to the village's two stores: Ricketts. Transcript, p. 124.

206. "Local snooty superior people": Ricketts. Transcript, p. 125.

206. "There is no central power": Ricketts. Transcript, pp. 123–124.

208. "The Indian thing is terribly important": Ricketts. Transcript, p. 135.

208. "Islands on the Boundary": Bringhurst, Robert. *A Story as Sharp as a Knife*, Vancouver: Douglas & McIntyre, 1999, p. 20.

208. These zones are mysterious: Bringhurst. *A Story as Sharp as a Knife*, p. 155.

208. This thin edge: Bringhurst. *A Story as Sharp as a Knife*, p. 372.

209. "Manna falls only rarely": Bringhurst. *A Story as Sharp as a Knife*, p. 65.

209. Rather their sublimation to it: Bringhurst. *A Story as Sharp as a Knife*, p. 27.

209. "The source at once of danger": Campbell. *The Hero with a Thousand Faces*, p. 390.

209. Ricketts also read and took notes: Ricketts made some references to and notes on *Social Conditions, Beliefs and Linguistic Relationships of the Tinglit Indians* (1908) by John R. Swanton and *Indians of the Northwest Coast* by Pliny Earle Goddard in his New Series Notebook No. 4 on p. 243, which were probably made in March or April of 1948.

209. "Hereabouts was all saltwater": Bringhurst, p. 224.

210. "They seemed to live": Steinbeck and Ricketts. *Sea of Cortez*. p. 75. (*The Log*, p. 63.)

211. "Outcast cripple": Dalzell, Kathleen E. *The Queen Charlotte Islands: Volume 2, Places and Names*, Prince Rupert: Cove Press, 1973, pp. 368–369.

211. "A broken field of black basaltic lava": Charles. *The Voyage on the Beagle*, p. 355.

212. One of the Haida myths: This summary of the Haida myth of the first humans is taken from Bill Reid and Robert Bringhurst. *The Raven Steals The Light*, Vancouver: Douglas & McIntyre, 1984, pp. 26–30.

212. The shamans' supernatural powers: Dalzell, Kathleen E. *The Queen Charlotte Islands: Volume I, 1774–1966*, Queen Charlotte City: Bill Ellis Publisher, 1968, pp. 85–89.

213. The population of Haida Gwaii: Dalzell. *The Queen Charlotte Islands: Volume I, 1774–1966*, p. 309.

213. **"They are a doomed race"**: Mullen, William. "After century at museum, Indian remains go home," *Chicago Tribune*. October 17, 2003, p. 1.
214. **"We have seen what has happened"**: Campbell, Joseph. "The Impact of Science on Myth," *Myths to Live By*, New York: Arkana, 1993, p. 10.
215. **"Sanctified cosmic images"**: Campbell, Joseph. "The Impact of Science on Myth," in *Myths to Live By.* p. 4.
215. **"It is not only that there is no hiding place"**: Campbell, Joseph. *The Hero with A Thousand Faces*, pp. 387–88.
215. **"Rapidly rising"**: Campbell, Joseph. "The Impact of Science on Myth," *Myths to Live By*, pp. 10–11.
215. **"The modern world spiritually significant"**: Campbell. *The Hero with a Thousand Faces*, p. 388.
216. **"Symbolic language"**: Campbell, *The Hero with a Thousand Faces*, p. vii.
216. **"Bad word"**: Ellis, David W. and Luke Swan. *Teachings of the Tides*, Nanaimo: Theytus Books, 1981, pp. 38–39.
216. **"[T]he horse clam"**: Ricketts. Transcript, p. 16.
216. **"A metaphor of both"**: Boelscher, Marianne. *The Curtain Within: Haida Social and Mythical Discourse*, Vancouver: UBC Press, 1988, p. 178.
216. **"Mother zone"**: Campbell, Joseph. Letter to Edward F. Ricketts, December 26, 1941. Courtesy of the Department of Special Collections, Stanford University Libraries.
216. **"Mythology [was] a function of biology"**: Quoted in Cousineau, Phil. (ed.) *The Hero's Journey: Joseph Campbell on His Life and Work*, San Francisco: Harper & Row Publishers, 1990, p. 159.
217. **"A great benefit to the intertidal beasts"**: Ricketts. Transcript, p. 128.
217. **"I was needing boots and jars"**: Ricketts. Transcript, p. 130.
217. **"[W]hen the sun shines"**: Ricketts. Transcript, p. 131.
217. **"We ate crab"**: Ricketts. Transcript, p. 133.
218. **Violent gusts of wind**: Ricketts. Transcript, p. 133.
218. **"Old Jinglebollix"**: Hedgpeth, Joel W. Letter to Edward F. Ricketts, December 13, 1940. Courtesy of the Department of Special Collections, Stanford University Libraries.
219. **"Since projections are the only 'true' things"**: Ricketts. New Series Notebook No. 4, p. 125.
219. **A thriving village**: MacDonald, George F. *Chiefs of the Sea and Sky*, Vancouver: UBC Press, 1989, pp. 78–79.
219. **"On the way out"**: Ricketts. Transcript, p. 135.
220. **It's a point largely lost on literary critics**: As Railsback comments, Richard Astro, Jackson Benson and Peter Lisca—along with Susan Shillinglaw—are among the few literary scholars who have written about the importance of science in Steinbeck's writing.
220. **"Darwin takes fire from the creationists"**: Railsback, Brian E. *Parallel Expeditions: Charles Darwin and the Art of John Steinbeck*, Moscow, ID: University of Idaho Press, 1995, p.9.
220. **"To some extent"**: Railsback. *Parallel Expeditions*, p. 9.
220. **"To look forward to a harvest"**: Darwin. *The Voyage of the Beagle,* p. 475.
220. **"Seemed to throw some light"**: Darwin, Charles. *The Origin of Species*, New York: Avenel Books, 1979, p. 65.
220. **"Thus only add to the prejudices"**: Darwin, Charles. *The Descent of Man*, Princeton: Princeton University Press, 1981, p. 1.
220. **"With all his noble qualities"**: Darwin. *The Descent of Man*, p. 405.
221. **"Capable of reflecting on his past actions"**: Darwin. *The Descent of Man*, pp. 391–392.
221. **Morality, Darwin continued**: Darwin. *The Descent of Man*, p. 393.
221. **"Greatest distinction"**: Darwin. *The Descent of Man*, p. 394.
221. **"Highly beneficial to the species"**: Darwin. *The Descent of Man*, p. 391.
221. **"Supported by evidence"**: Desmond, Adrian and James Moore. *Darwin*, London: Michael Joseph, 1991, p. 658.
221. **"An ardent Theist and an Evolutionist"**: Desmond and Moore. *Darwin*, p. 636.
222. **"The laws of animals"**: Astro. *The Shaping of a Novelist*, p. 11.

CHAPTER 12
PAGE

223. *Cannery Row* epigraph: Steinbeck. *Cannery Row*, p. 172.
225. **"Places we should go"**: Ricketts. New Series Notebook No. 4, p. 126.

226. **"The native village at Arrandale"**: Ricketts. Transcript, p. 137.
227. **The fauna was "fantastic"**: Ricketts. Transcript, p. 137.
227. **"Clumsy and oblique"**: Astro. *The Shaping of a Novelist*, p. 27.
228. **"What is the meaning"**: Campbell, Joseph. Letter to Edward F. Ricketts, May 19, 1940. Courtesy of the Department of Special Collections, Stanford University Libraries.
228. **"Use of words was unorthodox"**: Steinbeck. "About Ed Ricketts," *The Log from the Sea of Cortez*, p. 233.
228. **"Given, originally, an equal distribution"**: Ricketts. "Notes and Observations, Mostly Ecological, Resulting from Northern Pacific Collecting Trips Chiefly in Southeastern Alaska with Especial Reference to Wave Shock as a Factor in Littoral Ecology," p. 39. Courtesy of the Department of Special Collections, Stanford University Libraries.
228. **"Constant and interested companion"**: Ricketts. "Notes and Observations," p. 4.
229. **"Sad rather than vicious"**: Ricketts. Transcript, p. 139.
230. **"These inland passages"**: Ricketts. Transcript, p. 139.
231. **"We thought the world"**: Ross, Irene. Interviews about the 1946 earthquake. Courtesy of the Campbell River Museum, Campbell River.
231. **"I saw the whole ground moving"**: "Earthquake 1946," *Musings*, Campbell River: Campbell River and District Museum and Archives Society, Newsletter Vol. V, No. 2, July 1986, p. 3.
231. **"Like ocean swells"**: "Port Alberni Feels Force of Big Quake," *Daily Colonist*, Victoria, June 25, 1946, p. 2.
231. **The ship's compass was trembling**: Hodgson, Ernest A. "British Columbia Earthquake, June 23, 1946," *Journal of the Royal Astronomical Society of Canada*, Vol. XL, No. 8, October 1946, pp. 293–4.
231. **"One of the most severe"**: "That B.C. 'Quake No Mere Tremor," *Vancouver Sun*, November 29, 1946.
232. **"We hear that during the winter"**: Ricketts. Transcript, p. 141.
232. **Reminded her of the bombing of London**: White, Ruth. Interview by author. May 26, 2002.
232. **In his 1934 scientific paper**: Ricketts. "The Tide as an Environmental Factor Chiefly with Reference to Ecological Zonation on the Californian Coast," 1934, pp. 20–21. Courtesy of Joel W. Hedgpeth.
232. **"Year of the big tides"**: Ricketts, Edward F. Letter to Jack Calvin, April or May 1946. Courtesy of Ed Ricketts Jr.
234. **Ed Jr. was waiting penniless**: Ricketts. Transcript, p. 140.
234. **"The drunken Captain"**: Ricketts, Transcript, p. 143.

CHAPTER 13
PAGE

235. *Sea of Cortez* **epigraph**: Steinbeck and Ricketts. *Sea of Cortez*, p. 217. (*The Log*, pp. 178–79.)
237. **"Wheels of destiny"**: Campbell, Joseph. Letter to Edward F. Ricketts, April 21, 1946. Courtesy of the Department of Special Collections, Stanford University Libraries.
237. **He had just finished filming**: Ricketts, Edward F. Letter to Nancy Ricketts, September 13, 1946; and Ricketts, Edward F. Letter to John Steinbeck, September 15, 1946. Courtesy of the Department of Special Collections, Stanford University Libraries.
237. **"Those last few pages"**: Ricketts, Edward F. Letter to Joseph Campbell, October 25, 1946. Courtesy of the Department of Special Collections, Stanford University Libraries.
237. **"You're blossoming out"**: Ricketts. Letter to Campbell, October 25, 1946.
237. **"Since the fall of Man"**: Campbell, Joseph. Letter to Edward F. Ricketts, April 3, 1947. Courtesy of the Department of Special Collections, Stanford University Libraries.
238. **"Just another instance of greed"**: Ricketts, Edward F. Letter to Joseph Campbell, October 25, 1946. Courtesy of the Department of Special Collections, Stanford University Libraries.
238. **"Our policy of insisting"**: Ricketts, Edward F. Letter to Ritchie Lovejoy, October 22, 1946. Courtesy of the Department of Special Collections, Stanford University Libraries.
238. **"Religion is deadish"**: Ricketts, Edward F. Letter to John Steinbeck, August 1946. Courtesy of the Department of Special Collections, Stanford University Libraries.
238. **"Now I see one of the social values"**: Ricketts, Edward F. Letter to Joseph

Campbell, October 25, 1946. Courtesy of the Department of Special Collections, Stanford University Libraries.

239. "A good many religious ideas": Ricketts, Edward F. "Ecology and Sociology," undated. Courtesy of the Department of Special Collections, Stanford University Libraries.

239. Contained all the primary elements: Kelley, James C. "John Steinbeck and Ed Ricketts: Understanding Life in the Great Tide Pool," *Steinbeck and the Environment*, p. 28.

239. "The quality of a religious awakening": Worster. *Nature's Economy*, p. 344.

239. "Gaia hypothesis": Put forward by J. E. Lovelock in 1969 at a scientific symposium at Princeton, the Gaia Hypothesis is defined as "a complex entity involving the Earth's biosphere, atmosphere, oceans and soils; the totality constituting a feedback or cybernetic system which seems an optimal physical and chemical environment for life on this planet." See J. E. Lovelock. *Gaia: A New Look at Life on Earth*, New York: Oxford University Press, 1979, p. 11.

239. "You shall hallow the fiftieth year": Leviticus 25: 10.

240. "Both look at the world": Gardner, Gary. *Invoking the Spirit: Religion and Spirituality in the Quest for a Sustainable World*, Washington, D.C.: Worldwatch Paper No. 164, December 2002, p. 8.

240. "Should it blossom": Gardner, pp. 8, 20 and 51.

240. "I say let's have more": Ricketts. "Ecology and Sociology," undated.

240. "Integrators": Ricketts, Edward F. Letter to Joseph Campbell, October 25, 1947. Courtesy of the Department of Special Collections, Stanford University Libraries.

240. "[I]n the nineteenth century": Quoted in Cousineau (ed.). *The Hero's Journey: Joseph Campbell on His Life and Work*, p. 168.

240. "First, the mystical or metaphysical function": Keen, Sam. "Man & Myth: A Conversation with Joseph Campbell," *Psychology Today*, July 1971, p. 35.

241. "God's own likeness": Campbell. *Myths to Live By*, p. 194.

241. "We have today to learn": Campbell, Joseph, and Bill Moyers. *The Power of Myth*, New York: Doubleday, 1988, p. 31.

242. "I have Indian blood in me": Larsen and Larsen. p. 10.

242. "What befalls the earth": Campbell,

Joseph. *Transformations of Myth Through Time*, New York: Harper & Row Publishers, 1990, pp. 28–29.

244. "Seemed to throw some light on the origins of species": Charles. *The Origin of Species*, p. 65.

245. "I am at one with Dr. Allee": Ricketts, Edward F. Fellowship Application Form: John Simon Guggenheim Memorial Foundation, dated October 9, 1946. Courtesy of the Department of Special Collections, Stanford University Libraries.

245. "Extremely enthusiastic": Steinbeck, John. Letter to Guggenheim Foundation, November 20, 1946. Quoted in Hedgpeth. *The Outer Shores: Part I*, p. 45.

245. Perfunctory mourning: Ricketts, Edward F. Letter to John Steinbeck, August 1946. Courtesy of the Department of Special Collections, Stanford University Libraries.

246. "So cheerful and affectionate": Ricketts, Edward F. Letter to Theodore Seixas Solomans, January 22, 1947. Courtesy of the Department of Special Collections, Stanford University Libraries.

246. "A pity": Ricketts, Edward F. Letter to Joseph Campbell, April 11, 1947. Courtesy of the Department of Special Collections, Stanford University Libraries.

246. "A big big job": Ricketts, Edward F. Letter to Nancy Ricketts, Summer 1947. Courtesy of the Department of Special Collections, Stanford University Libraries.

247. "One of the world's greatest zoologists": Ricketts, Edward F. Letter to John Steinbeck, September 22, 1947. Courtesy of Joel W. Hedgpeth.

247. "In a very impartial": Stephenson, T. A. and Anne Stephenson. *Life Between Tidemarks on Rocky Shores*, San Francisco: W. H. Freeman and Company, 1972, p. 3.

248. Description of Kay's medical condition: Volcani (Jackson), Toni. Interview by author, June 15, 2002.

248. "The real love of his life was Jean Ariss": Volcani (Jackson), Toni. Interview by author, June 15, 2002.

248. "No way!": Volcani (Jackson), Toni. Interview by author, June 15, 2002.

248. But that didn't stop Ricketts: In his Presidio notes while in the Army, Ricketts wrote on January 19, 1943: "I closed my eyes for a minute. Jean went by, dressed in that black and white tweed coat, and with overalls or jeans. I got that strong flash of nostalgia." Ricketts also wrote to John

Steinbeck on November 25, 1947, about their breakup and mentioned "Toni's Jean insecurity."

248. **"I was extremely depressed"**: Volcani (Jackson), Toni. Letter to Joseph Campbell, March 5, 1979. Courtesy of the Joseph Campbell and Marija Gimbutas Library, Santa Barbara.

249. **"This whole thing fills me"**: Ricketts, Edward F. Letter to John Steinbeck, November 25, 1947. Courtesy of the Department of Special Collections, Stanford University Libraries.

249. **"I won't go inland"**: Ricketts. Letter to Steinbeck, November 25, 1947.

249. **"Besides from getting married"**: Ricketts. New Series Notebook No. 4, p. 218.

249. **John Steinbeck also swept into Cannery Row**: Ricketts, Edward F. Letter to Toni Jackson, February 4, 1948. Courtesy of the Department of Special Collections, Stanford University Libraries.

250. **Steinbeck wanted to use**: Ricketts, Edward F. Letter to Virginia Scardigli, no date, but in response to an April 6 letter. Courtesy of the Department of Special Collections, Stanford University Libraries.

250. **The project was eventually stymied**: Benson. *The True Adventures of John Steinbeck, Writer*, p. 610; and see Ricketts, Edward F. Letter to Bob Stephens, March 8, 1948. Courtesy of the Department of Special Collections, Stanford University Libraries.

251. **"Bach nearly made it"**: Steinbeck. "About Ed Ricketts," *The Log from the Sea of Cortez*, p. 263.

251. **"He was walled off a little"**: Steinbeck. "About Ed Ricketts," *The Log from the Sea of Cortez*, p. 263.

251. **"Humans aren't big enough"**: Ricketts. New Series Notebook No. 4, p. 229.

251. **"[T]hat cursed SU Press"**: Ricketts, Edward F. Letter to G. E. MacGinitie, February 16, 1938. Courtesy of the Department of Special Collections, Stanford University Libraries.

252. **Letter to SUP**: Steinbeck, John and Edward F. Ricketts. Letter to Stanford University Press, February 15, 1948. Courtesy of California History Room, Monterey Public Library, E. F. Ricketts Papers.

252. **"Slightly drunken"**: Ricketts, Edward F. Letter to Floris P. Hartog, manager of SUP's publishing department, February 17, 1948. Courtesy of California History Room, Monterey Public Library, E. F. Ricketts Papers.

252. **"Made me feel even more ashamed"**: Hartog, Floris P. Letter to Edward F. Ricketts, February 20, 1948. Courtesy of California History Room, Monterey Public Library, E. F. Ricketts Papers.

253. **"The country is drying up"**: Steinbeck, John. Letter to Pascal Covici, February 1948. Quoted in *Steinbeck: A Life in Letters*, p. 304.

253. **"The whole nasty bloodying lovely history"**: Steinbeck. Letter to Covici. February 1948. Quoted in *Steinbeck: A Life in Letters*, p. 304.

253. **"It may be my swan song"**: Steinbeck, John. Letter to Gwyndolyn Steinbeck. February 17, 1948. Quoted in *Steinbeck: A Life in Letters*, p. 308.

254. **Unlisted from the telephone directory**: Ricketts, Edward F. Letter to Braun-Knecht-Heimann Company, January 17, 1948. Courtesy of Department of Special Collections, Stanford University Libraries.

254. **"The science of relationships"**: Ricketts. Transcript, p. 26.

254. **"Biotic community"**: Worster. *Nature's Economy*, p. 214.

255. **Ed Ricketts never used the word *ecosystem***: Lindeman, Raymond. "The Trophic-Dynamic Aspect of Ecology," *Ecology*, Vol. 23 (October 1942): pp. 399–417. Ricketts once wrote the word *trophisms* in a list of scientific concepts, but this is most likely a spelling error. He probably meant *tropism*, which he defined in *Sea of Cortez* as "innate involuntary movement of an organism or any of its parts toward (positive) or away from (negative) a stimulus."

256. **"Marked ecology's coming of age"**: Worster. *Nature's Economy*, p. 302.

256. **Only one large thesis**: Ricketts and Calvin. *Between Pacific Tides*, 1948, p. 283. This quote appears in a final section on "Marine Plankton of the Pacific Coast" which Ricketts added to the revised, second edition in 1948. Dr. Joel W. Hedgpeth, who revised later editions, subsequently removed this section because he felt it was based on out-of-date or poor data, which had made the plankton analysis "quaint" over time.

257. **He had outlined a structure**: Ricketts wrote some undated "notes on the next

book" in his New Series Notebook No. 4 on p. 224 which fall between other pages dated January 6 and February 3, 1948; however, below these "notes on the next book" are further notes titled "Present set-up apr 1948" which were apparently inserted a few months later.

257. **"Well Johnny boy this is it"**: Ricketts. Transcript, p. 143.

258. **"There was a transcendent sadness"**: Steinbeck. "About Ed Ricketts," *The Log from the Sea of Cortez*, p. 263.

258. **"Depression or gloominess"**: Ricketts. New Series Notebook No. 4, pp. 218–220.

258. **"I have to do something"**: Ricketts. New Series Notebook No. 4, pp. 218–220.

258. **"An undertone of sadness"**: Ricketts, Edward F. Letter to Ed Ricketts Jr., October 23, 1944. Courtesy of Ed Ricketts Jr.

258. **"There is no creative unit"**: Steinbeck. "About Ed Ricketts," *The Log from the Sea of Cortez*, p. 257.

259. **"Well of course that's it"**: Ricketts, Edward F. Letter to John Steinbeck, August 1946. Courtesy of Department of Special Collections, Stanford University Libraries.

259. **Revise the first three books:** Ricketts, Edward F. "Plans for 2 volume: Contributions towards a Natural History of the Pacific Coast, " (undated). Courtesy of Department of Special Collections, Stanford University Libraries.

260. **"God help us all"**: Steinbeck, John. Letter to Edward F. Ricketts, April 1948. Quoted in *Steinbeck: A Life in Letters*, p. 309.

CHAPTER 14
PAGE

261. **Campbell epigraph:** Campbell. *The Hero with a Thousand Faces*, p. 356.

263. **"Early morning is a time of magic"**: Steinbeck. *Cannery Row*, p. 81.

264. **Suggestions made in later years:** Astro. *The Shaping of a Novelist*, p. 22.

264. **"Simply to avoid"**: Astro. *The Shaping of a Novelist*, p. 228.

264. **"It was just one big parade"**: Ricketts, Ed Jr. Interview by author, June 12, 1999.

264. **Skahen and Ricketts became engrossed:** Hedgpeth. *The Outer Shores: Part II*, p. 26.

265. **Ricketts literally hopping:** Ricketts, Ed Jr. Interview by author, June 6, 2002.

265. **"Feeling fine and very happy"**: Ricketts,

Nancy. Interview by author, July 17, 2002. The account from Frances comes from a letter she sent to Nancy Ricketts, dated Sunday 1948, which was probably the Sunday, May 16, following Ricketts' death.

265. **They would leave around May 22:** Ricketts, Edward F. Letter to Joseph Campbell, April 1947. Department of Special Collections, Stanford University Libraries.

265. **"Just on top of the world"**: Ricketts, Nancy. Interview by author, July 17, 2002.

265. **Ricketts was working so hard:** Hedgpeth, Joel W. Notes on a telephone conversation with Dr. Richard Skahen, March 1, 1971. Courtesy of Joel W. Hedgpeth.

265. **He'd nicknamed it "Eyebrows"**: Hedgpeth. Notes on a telephone conversation with Dr. Richard Skahen, March 1, 1971.

265. **"Ancient rusty motor"**: Steinbeck. "About Ed Ricketts," *The Log from the Sea of Cortez*, p. 225.

265. **"During the past year"**: Ricketts, Edward F. Letter to Beattie Motors Co., January 14, 1948. Courtesy of the Department of Special Collections, Stanford University Libraries.

266. **Canneries in Monterey had barely processed:** Heimann, Richard F. G. and John G. Carlisle, Jr. *The California Marine Fish Catch for 1968 and Historical Review 1916–1968*, Department of Fish and Game, Fish Bulletin No. 149, 1970.

266. **"[T]he unpleasant fact"**: Ricketts, Edward F. "Scientists Report on Sardine Supply," *Monterey Peninsula Herald,* April 2, 1948, pp. 1–3.

268. **"My God, Ed, what's happened?"**: Hedgpeth. Notes on a telephone conversation with Dr. Richard Skahen, March 1, 1971.

268. **"Ed's skull had a crooked look"**: Steinbeck. "About Ed Ricketts," *The Log from the Sea of Cortez*, pp. 225–226.

268. **"Perfectly coherent"**: Ricketts, Nancy. Interview by author, July 17, 2002.

268. **"I didn't seen the train in time"**: Ricketts, Nancy. Interview by author, July 17, 2002.

269. **"Ed was all messed up"**: Steinbeck. "About Ed Ricketts," *The Log from the Sea of Cortez*, p. 226.

269. **"They knew it was hopeless"**: Steinbeck does not name Dr. Gratiot in his account, but Dr. Gratiot was the surgeon who

worked on Ricketts. See Steinbeck. "About Ed Ricketts," *The Log from the Sea of Cortez*, p. 226.

269. **"Very bad"**: Steinbeck. "About Ed Ricketts," *The Log from the Sea of Cortez*, p. 226.

269. **"I think he realized"**: Gratiot, John. Interview by George Robinson, April 15, 1975. Courtesy of the National Steinbeck Center, Salinas.

270. **"Author John Steinbeck"**: "Steinbeck Flying to Ricketts' Side," *Monterey Peninsula Herald*, May 10, 1948, p. 1.

270. **"The greatest man in the world"**: Benson. *The True Adventures of John Steinbeck, Writer*, p. 615. Richard Astro also received correspondence from Benchley in 1971 repeating this story. See Astro. *The Shaping of a Novelist*, p. 22.

270. **"[There's] nothing else that seems worth mentioning"**: Lovejoy, Ritch. "Round and About," *Monterey Peninsula Herald*, May 11, 1948.

271. **"Royal Suite"**: White, Bill. Letter to Ed "Doc" Ricketts, February 5, 1947. Courtesy of the Department of Special Collections, Stanford University Libraries.

271. **Bill arrived home**: White, Ruth. Interview by author, May 26, 2002.

272. **"Edward F. Ricketts, the real-life 'Doc' "**: "Steinbeck's 'Doc' Dies in Monterey," *San Francisco Chronicle*, May 11, 1948.

272. **"When you are caught by the tide"**: Hedgpeth. *The Outer Shores: Part II*, p. 24.

272. **Dr. Gratiot led Alice to an unoccupied room**: Gratiot, John. Interview by George Robinson, April 15, 1975. Courtesy of the National Steinbeck Center, Salinas.

272. **"[A]s happens so often"**: Steinbeck. "About Ed Ricketts," *The Log from the Sea of Cortez*, p. 227.

272. **"Could have been expressed"**: Steinbeck. "About Ed Ricketts," *The Log from the Sea of Cortez*, p. 255.

272. **Tao or "a spark, the deep thing"**: Ricketts. Undated and untitled essay. Courtesy of the Department of Special Collections, Stanford University Libraries.

272. **"It's probably best"**: Ricketts. Undated and untitled essay. Courtesy of the Department of Special Collections, Stanford University Libraries.

272. **"At the charge that I have inclinations toward mysticism"**: Ricketts. "Ecology and Sociology," undated. Courtesy of the Department of Special Collections, Stanford University Libraries.

273. **"Suspicious of promises of an afterlife"**: Steinbeck. "About Ed Ricketts," *The Log from the Sea of Cortez*, p. 228.

273. **"Matrix underlying the nature of things"**: Ricketts. Transcript, p. 22.

273. **"Must either understand nothing"**: Ricketts. Transcript, p. 108.

273. **"Idea of heaven"**: Mulvihill, Rev. J. P. Letter to Joel W. Hedgpeth, February 9, 1971. Courtesy of Ed Ricketts Jr.

274. **Late Tuesday evening**: Benson. *The True Adventures of John Steinbeck, Writer*, p. 615.

274. **"Wanted to tear the town apart"**: Hedgpeth. *The Outer Shores: Part II*, p. 26.

274. **He made all the arrangements**: Ricketts, Nancy. Interview by author, July 17, 2002.

274. **Sarah Richards...was asked to inform**: Richards, Sarah W. Letter to Joel W. Hedgpeth, June 27, 1972. Courtesy of Joel W. Hedgpeth.

274. **"People wanted to get rid of him"**: Steinbeck. "About Ed Ricketts," *The Log from the Sea of Cortez*, p. 227.

274. **Gray closed casket**: Benson. *The True Adventures of John Steinbeck, Writer*, p. 615.

275. **"The most prolific zone in the world"**: Ricketts and Calvin. "Preface," *Between Pacific Tides*, Stanford: Stanford University Press, 1939.

275. **"A kind of anesthesia"**: Steinbeck. "About Ed Ricketts," *The Log from the Sea of Cortez*, p. 227.

CHAPTER 15
PAGE

277. **Steinbeck epigraph**: Steinbeck. "About Ed Ricketts," *The Log from The Sea of Cortez*, p. 274.

279. **"Fountain of philosophy"**: Steinbeck. *Cannery Row*, p. 30

279. **Would later discover that this was the year**: Ricketts, Edward F. "Scientists Report on Sardine Supply," *Monterey Peninsula Herald*, April 2, 1948, p. 1.

279. **"The canneries themselves"**: Steinbeck, John. *Sweet Thursday*. New York: Penguin Books, 1996, p. 1.

280. **Government scientists lacked information**: Clark, N. Frances. "Division of Fish and Game to Intensify Sardine Study," *Monterey Peninsula Herald*, March 7, 1947, p. 3.

280. **"A decline of this magnitude"**: "Mystery of the Vanishing Sardine Puzzles Scientists as Much as Does the Fishermen," *Monterey Peninsula Herald*, March 7, 1947, p. 2.

280. **"Everyone along famed Cannery Row":** "Disastrous Season Fails to Dampen Optimism of Industry Here," *Monterey Peninsula Herald*, March 7, 1947.

280. **"For years the canners and reduction plant operators":** Ricketts, Edward F. Letter to Joseph Campbell, October 25, 1946. Courtesy of the Department of Special Collections, Stanford University Libraries.

281. **Bolin's "dream itinerary":** "Dr. Rolf Bolin Will Trace Lantern Fish Around World," *Monterey Peninsula Herald*, March 7, 1947, p. 2.

281. **"Ed had good and faithful friends":** Vishniac, Wolf V. Letter to Joel W. Hedgpeth, March 16, 1971. Courtesy of Joel W. Hedgpeth.

281. **The most sophisticated and in-depth:** Ricketts, Edward F. "Science studies the Sardine," *Monterey Peninsula Herald*, March 7, 1947, pp. 1–3.

281. **"Completed to date":** Lovejoy, Ritch. "Round and About," *Monterey Peninsula Herald*, May 11, 1948.

283. **"It was certainly way before its time":** Kelley, Jim. Letter to the author, November 3, 2003.

283. **"Memorable novel":** Chavez, Francisco P. et al. "From Anchovies to Sardines and Back: Multidecadel Change in the Pacific Ocean," *Science*, Vol. 299, January 10, 2003, pp. 217–221.

284. **He said he was optimistic:** Ricketts, Edward F. "Scientists report on sardine supply," *Monterey Peninsula Herald*, April 2, 1948, pp. 1, 3.

285. **It only took the Oxnard Canning Company:** Hemp, Michael Kenneth. *Cannery Row: The History of Old Ocean View Avenue*, Pacific Grove: The History Company, 1986, p. 123.

285. **After the funeral service:** Benson. *The True Adventures of John Steinbeck, Writer*, p. 615.

285. **Steinbeck sat without speaking:** Steinbeck, John. Letter to Bo Beskow, May 22, 1948. *Steinbeck: A Life in Letters*, p. 312.

285. **For three days:** Ricketts, Nancy. Interview by author, July 17, 2002. The account from Frances comes from a letter she sent to Nancy Ricketts, dated Sunday, 1948. Also see Steinbeck, "About Ed Ricketts" *The Log from the Sea of Cortez*, p. 228.

285. **"Who are you?":** Hedgpeth. *The Outer Shores: Part II*, p. 26.

286. **"We'll have to let him go!":** Steinbeck. "About Ed Ricketts," *The Log from the Sea of Cortez*, p. 228.

286. **"The only thing that seems good":** Ricketts, Nancy. Interview by author, July 17, 2002.

286. **"It is good":** Steinbeck, John. Letter to Bo Beskow, May 22, 1948. Quoted in *Steinbeck: A Life in Letters*, p. 312.

286. **In the lab also stood:** Hedgpeth. *The Outer Shores: Part II*, pp. 27–28.

287. **"The necessity of having a funeral":** Richards, Sarah W. Letter to Joel W. Hedgpeth, June 27, 1972. Courtesy of Joel W. Hedgpeth.

287. **"I don't believe this":** Gratiot, John. Interview by George Robinson, April, 15, 1975. Courtesy of the National Steinbeck Center, Salinas. The comment is made by Robinson during the interview.

287. **"The most outspoken and indelicate":** Steinbeck. "About Ed Ricketts," *The Log from the Sea of Cortez*, p. 262.

287. **"The laboratory without Ed":** Steinbeck, John. Letter to Webster F. Street, May 25, 1948. Quoted in *Steinbeck: A Life in Letters*, p 314.

288. **"Conceptual material":** Edward F. Ricketts' will is now held at Hopkins Marine Station, Monterey. It is dated February 28, 1940.

288. **"There is nothing to say about Ed":** Steinbeck, John. Letter to Joel W. Hedgpeth, May 24, 1948. Courtesy of the Center for Steinbeck Studies, San José State University.

289. **"It will be a very long time":** Steinbeck, John. Letter to Mr. Hartog, June 3, 1948. Courtesy of the Department of Special Collections, Stanford University Libraries.

290. **"[Ed Ricketts] was my partner for eighteen years":** Fensch, Thomas (ed.). *Conversations with John Steinbeck*, Jackson, MS: University Press of Mississippi, 1988, p. 68.

290. **"A great feeling of life again":** Steinbeck, John. Letter to Ritchie and Natalya Lovejoy, May 27, 1948. Quoted in *Steinbeck: A Life in Letters*, p. 316.

290. **"Very angry man":** Volcani (Jackson), Toni. Interview by author, June 15, 2002.

290. **"Out of sadness and into fierceness":** Steinbeck, John. Letter to Bo Beskow, June 19, 1948. Quoted in *Steinbeck: A Life in Letters*, p. 318.

291. **"Times of cold terror":** Steinbeck, John.

Letter to Ritch and Natalya Lovejoy, May 27, 1948. Quoted in *Steinbeck: A Life in Letters*, p. 316.

291. **"Like a hermit crab"**: Steinbeck John. Letter to Pascal Covici, September 1948. Quoted in *Steinbeck: A Life in Letters*, p. 330.

291. **"A little story that was so evil"**: Steinbeck, John. Letter to Mr. and Mrs. Joseph Henry Jackson, October 26, 1948. Quoted in *Steinbeck: A Life in Letters*, p. 336.

291. **"The atmosphere bizarre"**: Benson. *The True Adventures of John Steinbeck, Writer*, p. 624.

291. **"One is really a whore"**: Steinbeck, John. Letter to Bo Beskow, May 23, 1949. Quoted in *Steinbeck: A Life in Letters*, p. 355.

291. **"Everyone tries to get me married"**: Steinbeck, John. Letter to Bo Beskow, May 9, 1949. Quoted in *Steinbeck: A Life in Letters*, p. 352

292. **"[I]t was dead the first night"**: Astro. *The Shaping of a Novelist*, p. 183.

292. **"Was becoming a novelist without a vision"**: Astro. *The Shaping of a Novelist*, p. 177.

292. **"Doc is rather small"**: Steinbeck. *Cannery Row*, pp. 29–30.

293. **"Everyone near him"**: Steinbeck, "About Ed Ricketts," *The Log from the Sea of Cortez*, p. 228.

293. **Conversation with bum**: Steinbeck. "About Ed Ricketts," *The Log from the Sea of Cortez*, p. 243.

294. **"Sexual output"**: Steinbeck. "About Ed Ricketts," *The Log from the Sea of Cortez*, p. 259.

294. **"Yes, *Cannery Row* is a true story"**: Calvin, Jack and Joel W. Hedgpeth. "Preface: About this Book and Ed Ricketts (1952)," *Between Pacific Tides*, Stanford: Stanford University Press, 1962, p. x.

294. **"At the time of Ed's death"**: Steinbeck. "About Ed Ricketts," *The Log from the Sea of Cortez*, pp. 271–272.

295. **"At that time it was widely believed"**: Ricketts, Ed Jr. E-mail message to author. March 12, 2003.

295. **"A true collaboration"**: Steinbeck, John. Letter to John Bivins Jr., March 16, 1964. Courtesy of Joel W. Hedgpeth.

295. **"A lot of Ricketts' wording"**: Shwartz, Mark. "Credit where credit is due: The controversial decision to remove Ed Ricketts as co-author of *The Log from the Sea of Cortez*," *Stanford Report*, December 3, 2003.

295. **The "John Steinbeck character"**: "Christening a la Ricketts," *Monterey Peninsula Herald*, May 15, 1978.

296. **"Any critic knows"**: "The Old Steinbeck," *Newsweek*, June 26, 1961, p. 96.

296. **"[W]e think it interesting"**: Editorial, *New York Times*, October 26, 1962, p. 12.

296. **Steinbeck's "previous writings"**: Lyman, John. "Book Reviews," *American Neptune*, April 1942, Vol. II, No. 2, p. 183.

296. **"More about sociology and history"**: Arnold, Martin. "Of Mice and Men and Novelists," *New York Times*, February 7, 2002, p. B3.

296. **"Flawed but permanent"**: Bloom, Harold. *Bloom's Notes: John Steinbeck's* The Grapes of Wrath, Broomall, PA: Chelsea House Publishers, 1996, pp. 5–6.

296. **"Why do we so dread"**: Steinbeck. *The Log from the Sea of Cortez*, p. 219

297. **"The people in Stockholm"**: Arnold, Martin. "Of Mice and Men and Novelists," *New York Times*. February 7, 2002, p. B3.

298. **"Ed was a reservoir for John to draw on"**: Astro. *The Shaping of a Novelist*, p. 26.

298. **"He never wanted anyone"**: Ariss, Jean. Letter to Joel Hedgpeth, undated, although the Old Monterey Bicentennial Letterhead is stamped 1970. An accompanying letter to Ariss from Hedgpeth is dated August 17, 1970. Courtesy of Joel W. Hedgpeth.

298. **"No, it hardly seems coincidental"**: Astro. *The Shaping of a Novelist*, p. 228.

299. **"Oh, isn't that Ed's lab"**: Quoted in Benson. *The True Adventures of John Steinbeck, Writer*, pp. 887–888.

299. **"A touching reunion"**: Steinbeck, John. *Travels with Charley*. New York: Bantam Books, 1962, p. 198.

299. **"Where's Pilon"**: Steinbeck. *Travels with Charley*, p. 202.

300. **"When I went away I had died"**: Steinbeck. *Travels with Charley*, p. 205.

301. **The last cannery closed in 1973**: Shillinglaw. "Introduction," *Cannery Row*, p. viii.

301. **Many of his papers at Hopkins**: Hedgpeth. *The Outer Shores: Part II*, p. 28.

302. **"Maybe if I write down everything"**: Steinbeck. "About Ed Ricketts," *The Log from the Sea of Cortez*, p. 229.

302. **Back at the lab**: Steinbeck. "About Ed Ricketts," *The Log from the Sea of Cortez*, p. 263.

302. **"It is the time just before dusk"**:

Steinbeck. "About Ed Ricketts," *The Log from the Sea of Cortez*, p. 274.

302. **"I've just finished another book":** Quoted in *Steinbeck: A Life in Letters*, p. 474.

303. **"To a casual observer":** Steinbeck, John. *Sweet Thursday*, New York: Penguin Books, 1996, p. 55.

303. **"Deeply, grievingly unhappy":** Steinbeck. *Sweet Thursday*, p. 55.

303. **"The pains that came to Doc":** Steinbeck. *Sweet Thursday*, p. 56.

303. **"What are you looking for":** Steinbeck. *Sweet Thursday*, p. 21.

303. **"Deep in himself":** Steinbeck. *Sweet Thursday*, p. 63.

303. **"Everybody's laughing at you":** Steinbeck. *Sweet Thursday*, p. 20.

304. **"They're fascinating":** Astro, Richard. Letter to Joel Hedgpeth, July 30, 197(?). Courtesy of Joel W. Hedgpeth.

304. **Steinbeck also wrote many handwritten letters:** Robinson, George. Interview by Pauline Pearson, November 8, 1972. Courtesy of the National Steinbeck Center, Salinas.

304. **"It was an act of reconciliation":** Benson. *The True Adventures of John Steinbeck, Writer*, p. 890.

305. **"Doc turned in the seat":** Steinbeck. *Sweet Thursday*, p. 260.

305. **"A time of great peace":** Steinbeck. *Cannery Row*, pp. 81–82.

EPILOGUE
PAGE

307. **Steinbeck epigraph:** Steinbeck. *Steinbeck: A Life in Letter*, p. 523.

309. **In one northern B.C. river:** Canada. *Coho Salmon: Final Report of the Coho Response Team*, Vancouver: Fisheries and Oceans Canada, May 1998, p. 4.

309. **"The dawn came, but no day":** Steinbeck. *The Grapes of Wrath*, p. 2.

310. **"A clear threat":** Copes, Parzival. *Coping with the Coho Crisis*, Victoria: Ministry of Fisheries, April 1998.

311. **In the past four centuries:** United Nations. *Global Biodiversity Outlook*, Montreal: Secretariat of the Convention on Biological Diversity, 2001, pp. 70–71.

311. **"People can, in fact":** Pauly, Daniel, Villy Christensen, Rainer Froese and Maria Lourdes Palomares. "Fishing down aquatic food webs," *American Scientist*, Vol. 88, No. 1, January 2000, p. 46.

311. **"We liked the people on this boat":** Steinbeck. *The Log from the Sea of Cortez*, p. 206.

312. **"In the good years":** Ricketts, Edward F. Letter to Ritch Lovejoy, October 22, 1946. Courtesy of the Department of Special Collections, Stanford University Libraries.

312. **World fish harvests would soar:** United Nations. *State of the World Fisheries 2002*, Rome: Food and Agriculture Organization, 2002, p. 8.

312. **Since 1950 global catches:** Pauly, Daniel, Villy Christensen, Johanne Dalsgaard, Rainer Froese and Francisco Torres Jr. "Fishing down marine food webs," *Science*, Vol. 279, No. 5352, June 2, 1998.

312. **Another study of global catch data:** Myers, Ransom A. and Boris Worm. "Rapid worldwide depletion of predatory fish communities," *Nature*, Vol. 423, May 15, 2003, pp. 280–283.

312. **"From giant blue marlin":** Editorial. "Few other fish in the sea," *Montreal Gazette*, Montreal, Quebec: May 19, 2003, p. A.22.

313. **"Look out at the boundless ocean":** Milstein, Michael. "Ranching the open ocean," *The Oregonian*, Portland, December 23, 2003, p. 1.

313. **The fish are particularly susceptible:** Hites, Ronald A. *et al.* "Global Assessment of Organic Contaminants in Farmed Salmon," *Science*, January 9, 2004, Vol. 303, pp. 226–229.

313. **Of the 1,006 quota licences:** Statistics provided by the West Coast of Vancouver Island Aquatic Management Board, Port Alberni, B.C., 2003.

314. **"Men ate what they had not raised":** Steinbeck. *The Grapes of Wrath*, p. 30.

314. **"A true crime against nature":** Steinbeck. *The Log from the Sea of Cortez*, p. 207.

315. **"They're most definitely back":** DeSantis, John. "Ready for sardines' comeback," *Monterey County Herald*, Monterey, May 16, 1999, p. 1.

SELECTED BIBLIOGRAPHY

Abraham, Dorothy. *Lone Cone: A Journey of Life on the West Coast of Vancouver Island.* Victoria: Tiritea, 1945.

Abraham, Dorothy. *Romantic Vancouver Island: Victoria Yesterday and Today.* Victoria: Acme-Buckle Printing Co. Ltd., 1964.

Agassiz, Louis. *Methods of Study in Natural History.* (1863). New York: Arno Press, reprinted 1970.

Allee, Warder Clyde. *Animal Aggregations: A Study in General Sociology.* Chicago: University of Chicago Press, 1931.

Allee, Warder Clyde. *Animal Life and Social Growth.* Baltimore: The Williams and Wilkins Co., 1932.

Allee, Warder Clyde. *The Social Life of Animals.* Chicago: University of Chicago Press, 1938.

Allee, Warder Clyde, et al. *Principles of Animal Ecology.* Philadelphia: W. B. Saunders Co., 1950.

Ariss, Bruce. *Inside Cannery Row.* Pacific Grove: Lexikos, 1988.

Arnold, Martin. "Of Mice and Men and Novelists," *New York Times.* February 7, 2002. p. B3.

Astro, Richard. *John Steinbeck and Edward F. Ricketts: The Shaping of A Novelist.* Minneapolis: University of Minnesota Press, 1973.

Astro, Richard and Joel W. Hedgpeth (eds.) *Steinbeck and the Sea: Proceedings of a Conference held at the Marine Science Center Auditorium, Newport, Oregon, May 4, 1974.* Newport: Oregon State University, 1975.

Bawlf, Samuel. *The Secret Voyage of Sir Francis Drake 1577–1580.* New York: Walker & Company, 2003.

Beegel, Susan F., Susan Shillinglaw and Wesley N. Tiffney, Jr. (eds.) *Steinbeck and the Environment.* Tuscaloosa: University of Alabama Press, 1997.

Benson, Jackson J. *The True Adventures of John Steinbeck, Writer.* New York, Penguin Books, 1990 (first edition, New York: Viking Press, 1984).

Bloom, Harold. *Bloom's Notes: John Steinbeck's* The Grapes of Wrath. Broomall, PA: Chelsea House Publishers, 1996.

Boelscher, Marianne. *The Curtain Within: Haida Social and Mythical Discourse.* Vancouver: UBC Press, 1988.

Bossin, Bob. *Settling Clayoquot.* Sound Heritage Series Number 31. Victoria: Province of British Columbia, 1981.

Brabant, Rev. A. J. "Reminiscences of the West Coast of Vancouver Island," in *Mission to Nootka, 1874–1900* (ed.) Charles Lillard. Sidney, BC: Gray's Publishing Ltd., 1977.

Bringhurst, Robert and Bill Reid. *The Raven Steals The Light.* Vancouver: Douglas & McIntyre, 1984.

Bringhurst, Robert. *A Story as Sharp as a Knife.* Vancouver: Douglas & McIntyre, 1999.

Calvin, Jack. " 'Nakwasina' Goes North," *National Geographic,* July 1933, Vol LXIV, No. 1.

Cameron, Tom. "The Grapes of Wrath Author Guards Self from Threats at Moody Gulch," *Los Angeles Times,* July 9, 1939, pp. 1–2.

Campbell, Joseph. "Bios and Mythos," in *Psychoanalysis and Culture* (1951). Essay reprinted by the Joseph Campbell Foundation, 2001.

Campbell, Joseph. *The Hero with a Thousand Faces.* Princeton: Bollingen Foundation/Princeton University Press, 1949.

Campbell, Joseph. *Myths to Live By.* New York: Viking Press, 1972.

Campbell, Joseph. *Transformations of Myth Through Time.* New York: Harper & Row Publishers, 1990.

Campbell, Joseph, and Bill Moyers. *The Power of Myth.* New York: Doubleday, 1988.

Canada. Royal Commission on Aboriginal Peoples. "Chapter 10: Residential Schools," *People to People, Nation to Nation: The report of the Royal Commission on Aboriginal Peoples.* Ottawa: Government of Canada, 1996.

Costello, Jimmy. "Steinbeck, Ricketts Embark on Cruise," *Monterey Peninsula Herald.* Monterey, March 11, 1940, pp. 1–2.

Cousineau, Phil. (ed.) *The Hero's Journey: Joseph Campbell on His Life and Work.* San Francisco: Harper & Row Publishers, 1990.

Cowles, H. C. "The ecological relations of the vegetation on the sand dunes of Lake Michigan," *Botanical Gazette,* 27: 95–117, 167–202, 281–308, 361–391, 1899.

Croker, Robert A. *Pioneer Ecologist: The Life and Work of Victor Ernest Shelford, 1877–1968.* Washington: Smithsonian Institution Press, 1991.

Darwin, Charles. *The Descent of Man.* London: John Murray, Albemarie Street, 1871, (Princeton: Princeton University Press, 1981).

Darwin, Charles. *The Origin of Species.* New York: Avenel Books (1979 edition), 1859.

Darwin, Charles. *The Voyage of the Beagle*. Ware, Hertfordshire: Wordsworth Classics, 1997 edition.

Dalzell, Kathleen E. *The Queen Charlotte Islands*. Vol. I. 1774–1966. Queen Charlotte City: Bill Ellis Publisher, 1968.

Dalzell, Kathleen E. *The Queen Charlotte Islands: Volume 2 Places and Names*. Queen Charlotte City: Bill Ellis Publisher, 1973.

Desmond, Adrian and James Moore. *Darwin*. London: Michael Joseph, 1991.

Ellis, David W. and Luke Swan. *Teachings of the Tides*. Nanaimo: Theytus Books, 1981.

Enea, Sparky and Audry Lynch. *With Steinbeck in the Sea of Cortez*. Los Osos: Sand River Press, 1991, p. 9.

Gardner, Gary. *Invoking the Spirit: Religion and Spirituality in the Quest for a Sustainable World*. Washington, D.C.: Worldwatch Paper No. 164, December 2002.

Goethe, Johann Wolfgang von. *Faust*. Translated by Philip Wayne. New York: Penguin, 1949.

Gore, Rick. "Between Monterey Tides," *National Geographic,* Vol. 177, No. 2, February 1990, p. 2–43.

Graham, Donald. *Keepers of the Light*. Madeira Park, B.C.: Harbour Publishing, 1985.

Guppy, Walter. *Clayoquot Soundings: A History of Clayoquot Sound, 1880s–1980s*. Tofino, B.C.: Grassroots Publication, 1997.

Hayes, Derek. *Historical Atlas of the North Pacific Ocean*. Vancouver: Douglas & McIntyre, 2001.

Hayashi, Tetsumaro. *Steinbeck's* The Grapes of Wrath: *Essays in Criticism*; Muncie, Indiana: Ball State University, Steinbeck Essay Series, No. 3, 1990.

Hedgpeth, Joel W. (ed.) *The Outer Shores*. Eureka: Mad River Press, 1978.

Hedgpeth, Joel W. (ed.) *Treatise on Marine Ecology and Paleoecology*. Washington, D.C.: Geological Society of America, 1957.

Hemp, Michael Kenneth. *Cannery Row: The History of Old Ocean View Avenue*. Pacific Grove, CA: The History Company, 1986.

Homer. *The Odyssey*. (E.V. Rieu, translator) Baltimore: Penguin Books, 1946.

Hunt, Tim (ed.). *The Collected Poetry of Robinson Jeffers: Volume I 1920–28*. Stanford: Stanford University Press, 1988.

Hyman, Stanley Edgar. "Of Invertebrates and Men," *The New Republic,* February 16, 1942.

Jackson, Toni ("tj"). "Forgotten Nootka: Two Silver Spoons in Power Politics," *What's Doing*. Monterey, August 1946, Vol. 1 (5), p. 30.

Johnstone, Kenneth. *The Aquatic Explorers: A History of the Fisheries Research Board of Canada*. Toronto: University of Toronto Press, 1977.

Jungk, Robert. *Brighter than a Thousand Suns*. Translated by James Cleugh. New York: Harcourt Brace Jovanovich, 1958.

Keen, Sam. "Man & Myth: A Conversation with Joseph Campbell," *Psychology Today*. July 1971, p. 35.

Knox, Maxine and Mary Rodriguez. *Steinbeck's Street: Cannery Row*. San Rafael, CA: Presidio Press, 1980.

Larsen, Stephen and Robin. *A Fire in the Mind: The Life of Joseph Campbell*. New York: Doubleday, 1991.

Lisca, Peter. *John Steinbeck: Nature and Myth*. New York: Thomas Y. Cromwell Co., 1978.

Lisca, Peter. *The Wide World of John Steinbeck*. New York: Gordian Press (new edition), 1981

Lovelock, J. E. *Gaia: A New Look at Life on Earth*. New York: Oxford University Press, 1979

MacDonald, George F. *Chiefs of the Sea and Sky*. Vancouver, UBC Press, 1989.

Mangelsdorf, Tom. *A History of Steinbeck's Cannery Row*. Santa Cruz: Western Tanager Press, 1986.

McCosker, John E. "Ed Ricketts: A Role Model for Marine Biologists," *The Steinbeck Newsletter*. San Jose: San José State University, Fall 1995, pp. 12–14.

McCosker, John E. "The View From The Great Tidepool," *Pacific Discovery*, October–December 1987, pp. 34–41.

Morris, Rod. *Coasters*. Victoria: Horsda & Schubart Publishers Ltd., 1993.

Moyers, Bill and George Lucas. "Of Myth and Men" *Time*. April 26, 1999 (Vol. 153, No. 16).

Myers, Ransom A. and Boris Worm. "Rapid worldwide depletion of predatory fish communities," *Nature*. Vol. 423, May 15, 2003, pp. 280–283.

Nicholson, George. *Vancouver Island's West Coast 1762–1962*. Victoria: Morriss Printing Company, 1962, p.286.

Osbon, Diane K. (ed.) *A Joseph Campbell Companion*. New York: HarperPerennial, 1991.

Owens, Louis. *The Grapes of Wrath: Trouble in the Promised Land*. Boston: Twayne Publishers, 1989.

Parini, Jay. *John Steinbeck: A Biography*. London: Random House, 1997.

Pauly, Daniel, Villy Christensen, Rainer Froese and Maria Lourdes Palomares. "Fishing down aquatic food webs," *American Scientist*. Vol. 88, No. 1, January 2000, p. 46.

Pauly, Daniel, Villy Christensen, Johanne Dalsgaard, Rainer Froese and Francisco Torres Jr. "Fishing down marine food webs," *Science*. Vol. 279, No. 5352, June 2, 1998.

Pauly, Daniel, Villy Christensen, Sylvie Guénette, Tony J. Pitcher, U. Rashid Sumalia, Carl J. Walters, R. Watson and Dirk Zeller. "Towards sustainability in world fisheries," *Nature*. Vol. 418, August 8, 2002, pp. 689–695.

Railsback, Brian E. *Parallel Expeditions: Charles Darwin and the Art of John Steinbeck.* Moscow, Idaho: University of Idaho Press, 1995.

Ricketts, Edward F. "Ed Ricketts covers the waterfront for 20 years," *Monterey Peninsula Herald,* February 27, 1942, pp. 1–2.

Ricketts, Edward F. "Scientists report on sardine supply," *Monterey Peninsula Herald,* April 2, 1948, p. 1.

Ricketts, Edward F. "Science studies the Sardine," *Monterey Peninsula Herald,* March 7, 1947, pp. 1–3.

Ricketts, Edward F. and Jack Calvin. *Between Pacific Tides* (Third Edition), Stanford: Stanford University Press, 1962

Rodger, Katharine A. *Renaissance Man of Cannery Row.* Tuscaloosa: University of Alabama Press, 2002.

Romano-Lax, Andromeda. *Searching for Steinbeck's Sea of Cortez.* Seattle: Sasquatch Books, 2002.

Scott, R. Bruce. *"Breakers Ahead!" on The Graveyard of the Pacific.* Sidney, B.C.: Review Publishing House, 1970.

Scott, R. Bruce. *People of the Southwest Coast of Vancouver Island.* Victoria: Morriss Printing Co. 1974.

Scudder, Geoffrey G. E. and Nicholas Gessler. *The Outer Shores.* Proceedings of the Queen Charlotte Islands First International Scientific Symposium, University of British Columbia, August 1984. Queen Charlotte Islands Museum Press, 1989.

Shillinglaw, Susan. Introduction to *Cannery Row.* New York: Penguin, 1994.

Sloan, N. A. et al. *Living Marine Legacy of Gwaii Haanas: Marine Invertebrate Baseline to 2000 and invertebrate related management issues.* Ottawa: Parks Canada, Report 35, 2002.

Spearman, A. D. "Steinbeck's Grapes of Wrath Branded as Red Propaganda," *San Francisco Examiner,* June 4, 1939, p. 12.

Spengler, Oswald. *The Decline of the West.* Oxford: Oxford University Press, 1991.

Steinbeck, Elaine and Robert Wallsten (eds). *Steinbeck: A Life in Letters.* New York: Penguin, 1989.

Steinbeck, John. *Burning Bright.* New York: Penguin, 1994.

Steinbeck, John. *Cannery Row.* New York: Penguin, 1995.

Steinbeck, John. *East of Eden.* New York: Penguin, 2003.

Steinbeck, John. *The Forgotten Village: With 136 Photographs from the Film of the Same Name.* New York: Viking Press, 1941.

Steinbeck, John. *The Grapes of Wrath.* New York: Penguin, 1992.

Steinbeck, John. *In Dubious Battle.* New York: Penguin, 1992.

Steinbeck, John. *The Log of the Sea of Cortez.* New York: Penguin, 1995.

Steinbeck, John. *The Long Valley.* New York: Penguin, 1995.

Steinbeck, John. *The Moon Is Down.* New York: Penguin, 1995.

Steinbeck, John. *Of Mice and Men.* New York: Penguin, 1993.

Steinbeck, John. *The Pearl.* New York: Penguin, 2000.

Steinbeck, John. *Sweet Thursday.* New York: Penguin, 1995.

Steinbeck, John. *To a God Unknown,* New York: Penguin, 1995.

Steinbeck, John. *Tortilla Flat.* New York: Penguin, 1997.

Steinbeck, John. *Travels with Charley: In Search of America.* New York: Penguin, 1980.

Steinbeck, John and Edward F. Ricketts. *Sea of Cortez.* Mount Vernon, NY: Paul P. Appel, (2nd reprinting 1982), 1941.

Stephenson, T. A. and Anne Stephenson. *Life Between Tidemarks on Rocky Shores.* San Francisco: W. H. Freeman and Company, 1972.

Suzuki, Daisetz Teitaro. *Essays in Zen Buddhism.* London: Luzac and Company, 1933.

Shwartz, Mark. "Credit where credit is due: The controversial decision to remove Ed Ricketts as co-author of *The Log of the Sea of Cortez*," *Stanford Report.* December 3, 2003.

Tedlock, E. W. Jr. and C. V. Wicker (eds). *Steinbeck and His Critics.* Albuquerque: University of New Mexico Press, 1969.

Thurman, Harold V. *Introductory Oceanography.* (8th Edition). Upper Saddle River, NJ: Prentice Hall, 1997.

Turner, Robert D. *Those Beautiful Coastal Liners.* Victoria: Sono Nis Press, 2001.

Twigg, A. M. *Union Steamships Remembered 1920–1958.* Campbell River, B.C.: A.M. Twigg, 1997.

Tzu, Lao. Translated by Arthur Waley. *Tao-te-Ching.* Ware, UK: Wordsworth, 1997.

United Nations. *Global Biodiversity Outlook.* Montreal: Secretariat of the Convention on Biological Diversity, 2001, pp. 70–71.

United Nations. *State of the World Fisheries 2002.* Rome: Food and Agriculture Organization, p. 8.

Walbran, John T. *British Columbia Coast Names, 1592–1906.* Vancouver: Douglas & McIntyre, 1971 edition.

Wilson, Edmund. "The Californians: Storm and Steinbeck," *The New Republic.* December 9, 1940, pp. 785–787.

Worster, Donald. *Nature's Economy: The Roots of Ecology.* San Francisco: Sierra Club Books, 1977.

ACKNOWLEDGMENTS

THIS book was researched and written largely with the assistance and kindness of strangers. In the spring of 1999, I set off from my hometown of Ucluelet, British Columbia, to California with nothing more than a copy of Ricketts' "outer shores" typescript in hand. Over the past five years, no matter where I traveled on the Pacific Coast, from San Diego to Sitka, from university archives to an offshore archipelago, the phrase "Ed Ricketts" seemed like a password to generosity. Everyone I met agreed that history hadn't given Ricketts his due. People gave so freely of their knowledge, energy and hospitality to facilitate my research that the only word to truly describe their behavior is *Rickettsian*. The list of those who contributed to the writing of this book is long. I shall begin at the beginning.

First and foremost, special thanks must go to Ed Ricketts Jr. and Nancy Ricketts. They have supported this project in so many ways. They provided me with unhindered and unconditional access to their father's personal correspondence and records and openly shared details of his life that may have made others feel uncomfortable. I spent hours interviewing them both, even prying into their personal lives. Ed's extensive transcription and indexing of his father's correspondence was a researcher's dream come true. And from the moment I stepped off the Alaska Marine Highway ferry in Sitka, Nancy took me under her wing, housing me, feeding me and giving me the most splendid tour of Sitka. Ed Jr. and Nancy also reviewed the manuscript, correcting and commenting extensively on the text. I am greatly indebted to them for their kindness and trust.

I have subtitled this book the "untold odyssey," but of course this odyssey isn't entirely untold. Indeed, Dr. Joel W. Hedgpeth has done more to tell the story of Ed Ricketts and keep his scholarship alive than anyone. In 1988, Dr. Hedgpeth provided a copy of Ricketts' outer shores typescript to the Royal British Columbia Museum in Victoria. If I had not stumbled upon this document in November of 1998, this book would not exist. My heartfelt thanks also goes out to Dr. Hedgpeth's son Warren, who provided me access to his father's personal collection of letters, notes, drawings and papers.

There were many others who were a constant source of inspiration, advice and knowledge, or provided me with their personal collections of letters and documents. Thanks to Tanis Bestland Malminen for frankly commenting on my original book proposal and to Kate Jacobs for encouraging me to "think big." Thanks to Mary Purvis, the granddaughter of Jack and Sasha Calvin, who gave me a copy of the logbook of the *Grampus* and for lending me (a complete stranger!) her car while I was in Sitka. Thanks to Ruth White, Mary McLeod, Ken Gibson and Walter Guppy, all from Tofino, for their knowledge of local Clayoquot history and photographs; Sharon Whalen for providing me with a splendid tour of Stubbs Island; Toni Volcani (Jackson) for sharing her stories of Ed Ricketts with me; Neil Robertson, a former crewman on the *Princess Maquinna*, for his recollections; Robert D. Turner for a rare photograph of the *Maquinna* in 1945; Steve Webster at the Monterey Bay Aquarium for his thoughts on Ricketts' contribution to science; Katie Rodger, author of *Renaissance Man of Cannery Row*, for her painstaking work of publishing Ricketts' letters and for being a sounding board for my ideas; Keith R. Benson at the University of Washington for providing me with an unpublished paper on pioneer ecologist Victor Shelford; Michael Hemp of the History Company for arranging a tour of Ricketts' lab in Monterey; Frank Wright for his reminiscences about the lab and Cannery Row; Pat Hathaway for allowing me to view his extensive historical photo collection; and Peter Ramos for the use of his spectacular photographs on the cover of the book.

Special thanks to the following individuals and institutions for granting me access to and assistance in their archives and special collections: Polly Armstrong and the friendly staff in the Department of Special Collections, Stanford University Libraries; Richard Buchen, special collections librarian at the Joseph Campbell & Marija Gimbutas Library in Santa Barbara; Dennis Copeland, special collections librarian in the California History Room of the Monterey Public Library; Neddra Shutts in the archives of the National Steinbeck Center in Salinas; Susan Shillinglaw, director of the Center for Steinbeck Studies at San José State University; Joe Wible, head librarian at Hopkins Marine Station in Monterey; Estelle Taylor for tracking down Sir Robert Bruce Lockhart's diaries in the Records Office of the British House of Lords in London; the Department of Special Collections at the University of British Columbia in Vancouver; National Archives of Canada in Ottawa; B.C. Archives in Victoria; Special Collections at the Vancouver Public Library; Canadian Pacific Archives in Montreal; Museum at Campbell River; Courtenay Museum; and the Indian Residential School Survivors Society in West Vancouver.

Many scientists across North America and beyond must be thanked for tracking down specimens Ricketts collected: Bob van Syoc in the Department of Invertebrate Zoology at the California Academy of Sciences in San Francisco; Mark E. Siddall, associate curator (Division of Invertebrate Zoology) at the American Museum of Natural History in New York; Lennart Cederholm in the Museum of Zoology at Lund University in Sweden; Karsten E. Hartel and Ardis Baker Johnston, curatorial associates, at the Museum of Comparative Zoology at Harvard University; Jochen Gerber, collections manager (Division of Invertebrates), and Barry Chernoff, curator (Division of Fishes), at the Field Museum of Natural History in Chicago; and Cheryl Bright and Diane Pitassy at the Smithsonian Institution in Washington, D.C. Also, thanks to Thomas M. Niesen, professor of marine biology at San Francisco State University, for providing the common names of many *rickettsi* species.

One of the great difficulties of writing a book on Ed Ricketts is that, as Steinbeck said, "His mind had no horizons. He was interested in everything." It would take a lifetime to become expert on the various interests of Ed Ricketts and so I am indebted to several scholars in science, mythology and literature for their insights. Thanks to Jim Kelley, former dean of the College of Science and Engineering at San Francisco State University who taught a course on Ricketts and Steinbeck for more than twenty years; Stephen and Robin Larsen, authors of *A Fire in the Mind*, a biography of Joseph Campbell; and Ed Ricketts Jr. and Nancy Ricketts for reviewing the manuscript. Thanks also to Michael Nicoll Yahgulanaas for his thoughtful comments on chapter 11. Their input greatly strengthened the manuscript. All remaining errors, of course, are mine and mine alone.

I am also indebted to the literary scholarship of Susan Shillinglaw, one of the top Steinbeck scholars at San José State University; Jackson J. Benson, Steinbeck's biographer; and Richard Astro, author of *John Steinbeck and Edward F. Ricketts: The Shaping of a Novelist.* Their writing significantly informed my understanding of the Ricketts-Steinbeck relationship.

My literary agent, Amy Rennert, who signed me on as an unknown writer and who immediately understood the significance of this "untold odyssey," cannot be praised highly enough. Amy has been a great source of both editorial and publishing advice. Her enthusiasm and passion have helped me to bring this tale to life.

A heartfelt thanks to Jofie Ferrari-Adler, my editor at Four Walls Eight Windows, for his honesty, insight and keen editorial judgment. For a first-time author, the production of a book can be a daunting task. I will always be beholden to Jofie for directing me through this process with great tact and skill and indeed friendship.

I'm also greatly appreciative of friends who while not contributing editorially to the book were essential nonetheless. Thanks to Sunny, Tim and Malia Jefferson in Mountain View, California, for welcoming me into their home while I conducted research at Stanford University. And thanks also to my friends Brett Schneider in Los Angeles, Eric Akines in Portland and Noella Edwards in Prince Rupert, B.C., for their hospitality during my extensive trips along the Pacific Coast.

Finally, it must be mentioned that the research and writing of this book was privately financed. At one point I applied for a writer's grant, absolutely convinced that I would receive it, and, like Ricketts in his attempts to finance *The Outer Shores*, was astonished when my application was declined. The book was a time-consuming and costly endeavor nonetheless—and well beyond my meager means. Against his better judgment as a prudent businessman, my brother Victor personally financed much of the research costs of this project. Without his generous and unconditional support, the book simply couldn't have been written.

Eric Enno Tamm
December 27, 2003
Ucluelet, British Columbia
Canada

INDEX

Colletto, Ratzi "Tiny," 43, *44*
Conger, Gwyn. *See* Steinbeck, Gwyn Conger
Cook, James, 58, 61, 66, 68, 116, 117, 202
Covici, Pascal, 48–49, 53, 295
Cowles, Henry C., 8

Darwin, Charles
 on evolution, 216, 220–21
 in Galapagos, 211, 220, 221–22, 244
 influence on Ricketts and Steinbeck, 43,
  203, 220, 221–22
 places named for, 202
 on religion, 241
 survival of fittest, 9, 100
Dawson, George, 202
Ditidaht people, 63–64
Dixon, George, 202
"Doc" characters in Steinbeck's work
 Cannery Row, 127–29, 133, 173, 258–59,
  292–93, 294
 In Dubious Battle, 23
 idealization, 304
 The Moon Is Down, 50
 "The Snake," 129
 studies of, 298
 Sweet Thursday, 302–5
Donne, John, 137
Dust Bowl, 33, 39–40, 93–94, 283

ecology
 classifications of organisms based on,
  91–93
 cooperation among animals, 9, 97, 196
 deep, 239
 definitions, 8
 Dust Bowl crisis, 33, 39–40, 93–94, 283
 history of field, 8–9, 67, 93–94, 100–101
 of human relations, 138, 245
 marine, 67, 222
 Ricketts' approach, 254–55, 256–57,
  281–84, 315
 as science of relationships, 254, 255
 of seashore, 27–29
 See also environmental movement
ecosystems, 255–56, 281–84
Edenshaw, Chief Albert Edward, 207–8
endangered species, 97–98, 311
Enea, Horace "Sparky," 43, *44*
enlightenment, 109
 See also breaking through
environmental movement, 66, 137, 183, 297

 See also ecology
Erdman, Jean, 190, 237
evolution, 94–96, 220–21

Fadiman, Clifton, 35
Farmer, Betty, 74, 75, 77–78, 79, 126, 136, 161,
  164, 232, 271
FBI (Federal Bureau of Investigation), 34
Fisher, W. K., 28–29, 92, 137, 244, 273
fisheries
 aquaculture, 313
 cannery towns, 116–17, 118, 226, 227
 industry in British Columbia, 66–67, 81,
  118, 307–8, 309–10, 313
 overexploitation, 312–14
 Pacific Ocean, 66–67
 salmon, 118, 307–8, 309–10, 313
 See also Cannery Row; sardine fisheries
Flanders, Howard and Emma, 275
Fleming, Ian, 18
Forbes, Edward, 67
Ford, John, 35
The Forgotten Village, 112–14
Fraser, C. McLean, 202, 244

Galigher, Albert E., 9
Garcia, Johnny, 299–300
Gislén, Torsten, 27–28, 244
Goethe, Johann Wolfgang von, *Faust*, 13, 31,
  134, 250
Gosse, Philip Henry, 67
Graham Island, 202, 206–14, 217–19, 225
Grampus, 16–17, 180–89, *182*
Grapes of Wrath (Steinbeck)
 Casy character, 173–76
 controversy surrounding, 34, 35, 46
 ecological theme, 34–35, 40, 50, 296
 film, 35–36
 Pulitzer Prize awarded to, 46
 reviews, 35, 39, 175, 296
 success, 35
 writing of, 35
Gratiot, John, 268–69, 270, 272
Great Plains Committee, 94
Great Tide Pool, 85–86, 98, 133, 275
Greenpeace, 137
Guggenheim Fellowship, 242–45, 246, 281
Gulf of California expedition, 41–46, 112, 135,
  311–12, 314
 See also Sea of Cortez

PHOTO BY KATHARINE A. RODGER

ERIC ENNO TAMM was raised in the village of Ucluelet on the "outer shores" of British Columbia, where his family has worked as commercial fishermen for four generations. Besides salmon trolling himself, he has worked as the executive director of the Coastal Community Network in B.C. and as a freelance journalist in Europe. His writing has appeared in *Wallpaper**, the *Globe and Mail*, *Los Angeles Times Magazine*, *Canadian Geographic* and the *Georgia Straight*. He holds a master's degree in journalism from University of Southern California and a master's degree in European affairs from Lund University in Sweden. Tamm lives in Vancouver; this is his first book.